# LIBRARY LIT. 9-
# The Best of 1978

edited by

## BILL KATZ

The Scarecrow Press, Inc.
Metuchen, N.J. & London
1979

ISBN 0-8108-1213-4
Library of Congress Catalog Card No. 78-154842

# CONTENTS

# INTRODUCTION

This is the ninth collection of the year's 30 best articles
about librarians and libraries. The year as understood by
the judges is from November 1977 to November 1978.

In the generally receptive reviews of this series, the
reviewer often puzzles over criteria used to evaluate "best"
and "better." There is no totally objective, quantitative
method of evaluation.

Anyone who has disagreed about the merits of a book,
film, television show or any form of communication with otherwise intelligent rational, even cool and objective opponents
will understand the difficulty of ticking off points which decide the argument one way or the other. You and your opponent, due to societal and philosophical biases, may come
from the same general background, even share 20/20 vision
and birthdays, but radically disagree about, say, last year's
winners of the National Book Awards or even the admittedly
commercial Oscars. This is not to deny the benefits of education or the benefits of carefully worked-out evaluative criteria, only to recognize few of us judge matters quite the
same.

The infuriating lack of consistency is apparent at any
of the judge's meetings over the past nine years. Otherwise
thoughtful, courteous and generous people turn into combat-
tants of no mean resolution. The stamping ground of decision ends with the 30 articles you now have in this collection.

Still, one must offer critics a better explanation than
pure subjectivity and lack of resolve about criteria. I suppose, to repeat the outline from last year's introduction,
that the rules for selection may be listed as follows: 1) The
message is the major consideration, particularly if the writer
has something new to say about libraries, information and the

future of communications; 2) Next, and sometimes equally important, is the skill and style of the writer. Presentation even of the fact that the world is round must be done with more than statistics to convince anyone this side of Columbus and the statisticians. No, the judges do not expect everyone to write like Henry James or Flannery O'Connor, but they do look for respect for grammar; 3) Originality of thought, based on research, observation, and opinion is certainly a factor; 4) Intelligent, imaginative and appreciative understanding of the library and its place in the world is counted, too.

Beyond that, judges seek to: 1) Strike some type of balance between the major interests of readers; 2) Look for new issues which are likely to be of concern to librarians in the future; 3) Finally, to avoid total dependence upon articles from the well known journals.

After nine years it becomes increasingly apparent that librarians, taken individually or as a mass, can think, write and function as well, if usually not better, than those from other professions, other walks of life. The time is long past when a librarian need apologize for the quality of writing in professional literature. To attack it all for failure of some, is a tremendous error of masochistic proportions. Actually, a surprising amount of library literature is excellent, quite up to anything found in other professional journals, and, as indicated, a notch or two above most such writings.

If this collection is a fair example, librarians may be proud of being members of a profession that places so much importance upon the written word.

Bill Katz
School of Library and
   Information Sciences
State University of New
   York at Albany

## ACKNOWLEDGMENTS

The 1978 Jury

The jurors this year were: Ms. Pat Rom, Ellen Clarke Bertrand Library, Bucknell University; Ms. Pat Schuman, President, Neal-Schuman Publishers; Professor Maurice

J. Freedman, School of Library Service, Columbia University; Eric Moon, President, Scarecrow Press; and Bill Katz.

Again thanks to Ms. Elizabeth Horvath, my graduate assistant who for the second year did so much to make this book possible.

Part I

LIBRARIES AND LIBRARIANS

LET MY PEOPLE KNOW--

ACCESS TO INFORMATION IN A POSTINDUSTRIAL SOCIETY*

Fay M. Blake

Let me quote to you from a fairy tale, a very modern fairy
tale. It was written by a captain of industry (or of "post-
industry"?), Howard J. Hilton of Hilmark United Corp., and
he calls it "An Ideal Information Access System. "

> The technical requirements [of this ideal informa-
> tion access system] include both the hardware and
> the software necessary to meet the varied needs of
> both the users and the producers of knowledge and
> information. The users require hardware that is
> capable of providing access through all available
> media. It should cover the full range of cost and
> benefit, from the simplest and least expensive to
> the most sophisticated, providing a central store
> and backup for the individual systems supporting
> local users throughout the world.
> With present hardware, the sophisticated system
> would have time-shared terminals linked by broad-
> band satellite communications to major computer
> centers throughout the world; optical readers for
> high-reduction microforms; cathode ray tubes (CRT)
> with high resolution capability; buffered storage for
> static alphanumeric and graphic material; switching
> capability for audio, video, and television reception
> at distant stations; an optical computer for conduct-
> ing Boolean searches and reading binary data into
> the main computer at nanosecond rates; and micro-

---

*Reprinted by permission of the author and publisher from
the January 1978 issue of the Wilson Library Bulletin, pp.
392-99. Copyright © 1978 by The H. W. Wilson Co.

fiche and hard copy print capability from both the
optical reader and the CRT.

For the near future, the most sophisticated system may be a combination of the laser and holo-
graphic technology. And beyond that, who can guess
what the future holds?[1]


## Time out for fairy tales

Once upon a time, when I was more vitally interested in
fairy tales than I am now, it was all a lot simpler. A girl
kissed a frog, and presto, he turned into a prince, and everyone lived happily ever after. Now, if this monstrous dream
of Hilton's is the ideal information-access system, for whom
is it ideal?

Let me tell you part of another story. In 1965 the
Cleveland Public Library began an experimental project for
"limited readers. " That's a euphemism for illiterate adults,
and there are 50,000 of them in Cleveland and about 11 million in the United States. And the number is rising, not
diminishing. The Cleveland PL asked the people who parti-
cipated why they were in the literacy classes, and among the
reasons they gave were:

> Fill out application forms and get better jobs; read
> the papers one signs; use a telephone directory;
> ... read street signs; ... read letters brought
> home from school by children; read bedtime stories
> to small children; read labels and directions on
> medicines, cosmetics, food packages, detergents,
> etc. ; ... understand Social Security, Medicare,
> welfare ... instructions. [2]

I can find nothing in Hilton's ideal system that would
help Cleveland's illiterates very much, and I rather suspect
that financing Hilton's project would torpedo Cleveland's.
That's our dilemma in thinking about the first step into ALA's
second century. Unless we have a pretty solid idea of what
kind of society we're providing with information, we may end
up running rapidly backwards.

Now I'm very reluctant to play seeress and look into
crystal balls to describe the future. Not out of any false
modesty, you understand, but because I believe that the future
is the future and that what we do or fail to do creates that

future.   But I have heard some arrant nonsense about this
postindustrial society we're evolving into.

Pooh-Bah-in-Chief of the futurologists is Daniel Bell,
whose Coming of Post-Industrial Society (1973) signaled a
new fad.   Bell sees some immense societal changes as a result of advances in technology.

> By producing more goods at less cost, technology
> has been the chief engine of raising the living
> standards of the world.   The achievement of tech-
> nology, the late Joseph Schumpeter was fond of say-
> ing, was that it brought the price of silk stockings
> within the reach of every shopgirl, as well as of
> a queen.   But technology has not only been the
> means of raising levels of living, it has been the
> chief mechanism of reducing inequality within West-
> ern society. [3]

Well, I just saw the Queen of England attend a gala in her
honor at Covent Garden on TV.   I work with a couple of
dozen library clerks (the equivalent of Schumpeter's shopgirls),
and I can assure you the clerks don't dress like the Queen,
don't eat like the Queen, don't spend their days or their
nights like the Queen, certainly don't have her job security,
and even if they can afford silk (silk?) stockings, are no
more equal to the Queen--or to her nontitled counterparts in
this country--than they ever were.

Schumpeter, Bell, and Company are peddling the same
nonsense about equality that Anatole France exploded almost
a century ago when he wrote:   "The law, in its majestic
equality, forbids the rich as well as the poor to sleep under
bridges, to beg in the streets, and to steal bread" (Le lys
rouge, 1894).

In "areas of the world which have become highly industrialized, " a recent paper tells me, "society is increasingly characterized by having its labor force concentrated in
the sphere of services, professional and technical, rather
than ... extractive industries ... or manufacturing and dis-
tributive industries. "   One result of this change will be that

> our primary institutions are expected to be the uni-
> versity, the academic institute, the research cor-
> poration, the industrial laboratory, the library; our
> economic ground, science-based industries; our

primary resource, human capital; our political
problem, science policy and education policy; our
structural problem, the balancing of the interests
of the public and private sectors.  Upward access
through the social-economic strata of this society
is assumed to depend upon advanced education even
more than at present. [4]

This analysis, based on a number of recent publications by assorted pundits, reminds me of the administration
courses I took in library school.  It was assumed that every
one of the students was destined to become the director of
the Library of Congress and that we were all panting to discover how to get more work out of all those lazy bums we
were going to administer.  Nobody even whispered naughty
words like "money" or "unions"; even "job" was a no-no.
We were going to get "positions. "

Well, it's true that our society has fewer farmers
and miners and assembly-line workers in the labor force than
we used to have, but outside of that, the analysis sounds
like still another fairy tale.  It certainly doesn't describe
the society I see about me.  Our postindustrial society is a
world of work and not very exciting or interesting work.
Economist Robert Heilbroner warns against glib assumptions
about his postindustrial society.  He says:

Let me warn against the misconception of ... a
massive emigration from industrial work.  Nothing
of that kind is visible....  The industrial 'core'
remains roughly constant ... the industrial factory
worker ... continues to account for approximately
the same proportion of the total work experience of
the community ... the blue collar group constituted
25. 5 percent of the labor force in 1900 and 34. 9
percent in 1968. [5]

Sure, we've got more service workers, but for the
most part, they're not professionals and technicians.  Service
workers are janitors, bartenders, dishwashers, midwives,
baggage porters, hairdressers, police, and firefighters, more
than 19 million of them according to the 1970 census and
more than 23 million in 1975.  And in most of these jobs,
upward access doesn't depend on advanced education.  There
isn't any upward access--and these days, more and more
often, not even a job.

Recently I visited University Microfilms in Ann Arbor,

Mich., and I shall never again look at a piece of microfilm
without remembering the workers I saw there--mostly women, mainly black, sitting or standing at technologically advanced machines (high-speed cameras, copiers, calculators,
and readers) and endlessly feeding bits of paper or film into
one end, endlessly inspecting bits of film at the other end.
Would you like to go tell these women about the postindustrial society and how "equal" it has made them?

## Repetitive, mindless routine

We've got more clerical workers.  It used to be that clerks
were differentiated from blue collar workers by somewhat
higher wages, somewhat higher prestige, and somewhat
higher chances of making decisions within their jobs.  No
more.  Rationalization, mechanization, technology, and science
have all been enlisted to reduce clerical work to the same
kind of repetitive, mindless routine the factory worker has
always known.  What characterizes a large part of the labor
force, then, is, in the words of Harry Braverman,

> the growth at one pole of an immense mass of
> wage-workers.  The apparent trend to a large non-
> proletarian "middle class" has resolved itself into
> the creation of a large proletariat in a new form.
> In its conditions of employment, this working popu-
> lation has lost all former superiorities over work-
> ers in industry, and in its scales of pay has sunk
> almost to the very bottom. [6]

The professionals--the engineers and doctors and
librarians who constitute about 20 percent of the labor force--
work, many of them, under no better conditions.  More and
more of them are employees in large enterprises, deciding
very little about their jobs and performing routine and repetitive tasks.

So for whom is the university, the research corporation, and the library the primary institution?  Whose economic ground is science-based industry?  Whose political problem is science policy and education policy?  Only that small,
select minority in our society who make the decisions that
determine how the rest of us live and work--if we can find
work.  The institution that most governs our lives is not the
university or the library, but the corporation.

## The corporate power

John Kenneth Galbraith says: "The institution that most
changes our lives ... is the modern corporation. Week by
week, month by month, year by year, it exercises a greater
influence on the way we live than unions, universities, poli-
ticians, the government."[7] The economic ground most of us
will be most deeply engaged in is sheer survival, as we're
buffeted between inflation, fear of losing our jobs, and increasing taxes. And our political problem?--neither science
policy nor education policy, except peripherally, but latching
on to some political power, enough to pass legislation serving the majority.

Well, given that kind of society, what kinds of information do most people need? I don't know. That doesn't
seem to be the question our profession has been addressing.

● The library schools seem to be involved in teaching young
white males how to succeed older white males in the information world.
● The National Commission on Libraries and Information
Science seems to be concerned with guaranteeing the establishment of a profitable information network.
● The information industry seems to be engaged in lobbying
for the private sector's right to design and profit from an
international automated information pipeline.
● The academic libraries seem to be engaged in serving rich
faculty who can afford fees for services.
● The public libraries seem to be deeply concerned with the
quickest way to slap user fees on their services.
● Maybe school libraries are still interested in finding out
what information most kids need and giving it to them--but
funding for school libraries seems to be going out of style.

So before we can even approach the subject of access, maybe we need to devote our collective minds to the problem of
what kind of information most people need access to.

What most people don't need most of the time is a
bibliography. And to most librarians and information scientists, that particular non-need translates itself into a generalized, "Well, then, they don't need information."

Let me give you examples of a very simple thesis:
All people need information, but the kinds of information
most people need is different in form and content from that

required and made available by the educated elite for its own
use.

## The vital need for information

During a recent international conference on the "Origins of
Human Cancer" sponsored by the Cold Springs Harbor (N.Y.)
Laboratory, the Harvard School of Public Health, and the
National Cancer Institute, it was reported that studies show
a huge increase in the risk of breast cancer and cancer of
the lining of the uterus for the millions of women who have
been given estrogens during the menopause. [8]   Other studies
show an increase in breast and womb cancer among populations whose diet is heavy in animal fat, especially when live-
stock are fattened on synthetic estrogens, as they are in this
country.

Now the information that most women in this country
need is the information that estrogens taken into their own
bodies or those of the animals they'll consume are dangerous
to their health, but our information networks are not designed
to give us access to such information.   Scientists have access to it, and the pharmaceutical industry has access to it,
and agri-business has access to it; but they're not about to
make it generally available.   Neither will the designs of the
leaders in librarianship and information science.

If you walked into any library in the country today and
asked a layperson's question:   Will taking estrogens during
menopause increase the risk of cancer?, you would not get a
straight "yes" no matter how sophisticated a data base the
librarians manipulated for you--at a fee.

My second example is a report of a survey carried
out in Finland:

> In 1972 the workers on a building site near Helsinki,
> who were living in prefabricated huts on the site
> because their home towns were too far away, were
> interviewed as to their working conditions, the
> recreational opportunities available to them, hygien-
> ic conditions, etc.   The interview situation was
> based on a questionnaire which had been filled out
> previously.
>     In the interviews, 60 percent of the respondents
> stated that they were entirely satisfied with the

conditions prevailing on the site. When, however,
the questionnaire papers were put aside and the
respondents were (deliberately) engaged by the
interviewer in free conversation, the same individuals brought out numerous and serious complaints
about conditions which obviously had bothered them
considerably. [9]

Elina Suominen, the author of the article, is a researcher at the Finnish Ministry of Justice and secretary of
that country's National Committee on Data Systems. In a
most perceptive analysis she goes on to say:

> The media use primarily the language and the
> terminology familiar to the highly educated section
> of the population, the terminology which those with
> less education have not completely mastered. They
> talk about issues so abstract that they do not reach
> the audience, and in a manner shunned by the
> working class. Furthermore, messages with a
> 'serious' subject, such as history, politics, or
> economics, are carried out primarily by those
> media (newspapers, books, etc.) which are favored
> by the educated classes, whereas television, week-
> ly magazines, and the like tend to stress entertain-
> ment and sensational material.
>
> With the constant increase in the share of
> 'light communication' produced outside Finland,
> chiefly with American capital, the share of national
> material is declining. Anxieties, fears, and a
> shortened span of interest are becoming more and
> more common. Parents, struggling with money and
> housing difficulties, do not have either the ability
> or the time to guide their children in the best use
> of media. In other words, those who have the
> greatest objective need of information often feel
> the least subjective need.
>
> This conclusion has far-reaching consequences.
> A society based on material inequality is built in
> part precisely on this disproportion between objec-
> tive and subjective information need. For example,
> when Elizabeth Taylor spent a night in a Helsinki
> hotel on her way to Leningrad, dozens of papers
> described her 300 pounds of luggage, her male
> companion, and her clothes. If a survey had been
> done at this point, it would have shown Finns to
> be considerably better informed about Miss Taylor's

baggage than about the difficult and complex labor
negotiations going on in the country at the same
time. In objective terms, the contract concerning
wage and price increases had a considerably more
far-reaching effect on the everyday life of a vast
majority of the population than the number of Miss
Taylor's suitcases. [10]

## Drop the "prime market" approach

So the central problem in the public access to information is
what kinds of information we're giving the public access to.
And the providers of information, we librarians, need to
dedicate ourselves to discovering the information needs of
most people, not of an elite already fairly well served, and
to providing that information rapidly, intelligibly, and respon-
sibly. The reasons we have not done so are subtle and complex, and we need to struggle to understand them better.

Most of us are not consciously the tools of rapacious
agri-business, deliberately keeping information from people.
Even agri-business isn't consciously doing that. But agri-
business is out to increase its profits and will not disseminate information that endangers those profits. And librarians
have lent themselves to that restrictive aspect of information-
gathering and dissemination. Out of a combination of timidi-
ty, irresponsibility, snobbery, ignorance, and miseducation
we have never spoken for the right of everyone to information.

As a matter of fact, some pretty high-level library
leaders have gone on record urging us to stop worrying about
the information needs of some lost souls. Our own Robert
Wedgeworth suggests, "Young people who come from poor,
broken homes, belong to street gangs, and are flunking out
of school are not our prime market." What is it exactly
that we are "marketing"? To whom? I would suggest, in
contradiction to Wedgeworth's analysis, that unless we find
the ways to provide necessary information, as well as food,
jobs, housing, and clothing, to those same young people from
poor, broken homes, they will people our prisons and hospitals and welfare centers--and that Wedgeworth's more lucra-
tive "markets" will be devoting lots of energy to paying huge
societal costs.

Even if we were to recognize, collect, and dissemi-

nate the kind and the form of information a majority of our
population needs, we have allowed so much of the business
mentality to seep in that our ability to function as professional information-providers has already been deeply eroded--
and not just by modeling library organization on business organization. That's bad enough because it often results in
libraries that simply have not conceived that real needs
aren't always best served by "efficient" organizations. Profits maybe, but not necessarily user needs.

What's worse is an indecent rush to make use of new
technology without considering the most socially effective
ways to pay for that technology. User fees are often the
only approach ever considered, with no concern for possible
alternatives and with no concern for the social inequities that
user fees in a public service impose. I must sound a warning here that the indiscriminate imposition of fees for library
services may be the library profession's contribution to the
breakdown of public access to information. Public access
must not be taken to mean the "rich public's" access.

## We, too, shall overcome

We have been too timid to demand money and resources at
least equal to those distributed to the private sector. We
have been frightened of taking responsibility for the accuracy
of the information we do dispense. We have secretly relished
the "importance" of our calling, the provision of information
to the "decision-makers," complacently accepting a hierarchy
of information needs and users. We have been content to
define intellectual freedom as an abstract concept (and I hear
ominous rumblings that taking action for educational programs
against racism and sexism is somehow to be equated with
censorship). And we have [until last summer's ALA confer-
ence] refused to take a stand for the principle of free services without direct user charges, provided by our society
as a whole to guarantee equality in access.

Not that I believe librarians to be incapable of
courage and responsibility and generosity and just plain good
sense. On the contrary! I believe that most of us, most
of the time, want so much to provide the widest kind of access to the most accurate kind of information that we shall
collectively find ways to overcome tremendous pressures--
but only when we understand that inequality in public access
to information can determine whether our society continues to
survive.

## References

1.  Howard J. Hilton. "An Ideal Information Access System: Some Economic Implications," in Information for Action: From Knowledge to Wisdom, ed. by Manfred Kochen. New York, Academic Press, 1975, p. 206-07.
2.  Eleanor Frances Brown. Library Service to the Disadvantaged. Metuchen, N.J., Scarecrow Press, 1971, p. 450.
3.  Daniel Bell. The Coming of Post-Industrial Society. New York, Basic Books, 1973, p. 188-89.
4.  Rollin P. Marquis. "Post-Industrial Society and the Growth of Information: The Impact on Libraries," unpublished review paper, Jan. 13, 1977.
5.  Robert Heilbroner. "Economic Problems of a 'Post-Industrial' Society," Dissent (Spring 1973), p. 163-76.
6.  Harry Braverman. Labor and Monopoly Capital; the Degradation of Work in the Twentieth Century. New York, Monthly Review Press, 1974, p. 355.
7.  John Kenneth Galbraith. "UGE: The Inside Story," Horizon, 19 (March 1977), p. 5.
8.  Judith Randal. "The Social Origins of Cancer," Change, 8 (November 1976), p. 54-55.
9.  Elina Suominen. "Who Needs Information and Why," Journal of Communication, 26 (Autumn 1976), p. 116.
10. Ibid., p. 117-18.

# THE PROFESSION'S RESPONSE

# TO A CRISIS-BASED SOCIETY*

Thomas J. Galvin

My assignment is to try to provide a link between Chancellor Mitchell's discussion of the character of the "crisis-based" society, in both its general dimensions and in its specific implications for education at all levels, and the discussions that will occur later in the smaller groups that are scheduled to look at some specific alternative strategies for library and information science education such as accreditation, packaging, new specialties, and new clienteles. I would like to try to identify and examine a few of the, probably more obvious, specific implications of the crisis-based society for library and information professionals, and the agencies and organizations for which we are responsible.

Let me suggest that a useful way to begin might be to focus on a single question. What are the conditions for the effective practice of the library and information professions in a society characterized by crisis as a normal operational mode? Having raised a question that I judge is not easy for us to answer in any wholly satisfactory way, let me offer a partial response simply for the sake of discussion. I would like to suggest that one criterion for judging the effectiveness of the performance of library and information professionals is that it achieves maximum social utility. That is simply to remind all of us that libraries and information centers exist in order to serve social needs, and that their justification for continued existence and support resides chiefly in the extent to which they are effective in meeting social needs as society collectively defines those needs.

*Reprinted by permission of the author and publisher from the Spring 1978 issue of the Journal of Education for Librarianship, pp. 269-77.

14

Now, how do we recognize a crisis-based society
when we are in the middle of one? Clearly, it is one
characterized by rapid change. The poet Richard Shelton
recognizes that all change is painful to some degree, and
that rapid change can be singularly and acutely painful. He
writes, "Tomorrow has already happened, how fortunate we
are that we can't remember it."[1] So, one aspect of the
crisis-based society is that change occurs at what may seem
an intolerably fast pace. Perhaps more precisely, the consequences of social change rush in upon us so quickly, that
just as we have begun to deal with one, another is upon us.
Yet the painful experience of living has taught us that we can
learn to be aware of the distant-early-warning signals that
alert us to change. These sometimes show up far enough
in advance that if we can learn to recognize and respond to
them, we can buy time to identify and evaluate alternatives
before these are simply forced upon us. Two examples
come readily to mind. The end of the teacher shortage was
predictable at least a decade before it happened, by a simple reading and recognition of the consequences of readily
available hard demographic data. Either we did not notice
these data, or, more likely, we were simply incapable of
persuading ourselves collectively to recognize and deal intellectually with their implications. A second illustration
can be found in our own field of librarianship. For at least
a decade, it has been apparent that the rapid growth in the
number of new titles published annually by the world's
presses, when combined with inflationary increases in the
price of books and journals that were substantially higher
than the general rate of inflation, would compel a series of
basic changes in the character of library purchasing. That
we did not, in general, respond in a timely fashion by creating resource sharing mechanisms that would provide viable,
operational alternatives to local ownership of materials again
suggests that we either did not recognize the signals, or that
we were unwilling to identify and seriously contemplate radical alternatives to traditional ways of operating libraries and
building collections.

These examples also suggest that a second indicator
of social crisis is that it necessitates a reconsideration of
basic assumptions which we have not previously imagined
might ever need to be subject to critical examination. For
example, many of the academics of my generation, who came
to their maturity in the fifties and early sixties, simply assumed that the students would never stop coming in greater
and greater numbers each year, inevitably followed, although

never quickly enough to suit us, by incremental budget increases to support a constantly expanding academic enterprise.   When developments of the last decade shook these
fundamental operating assumptions, the result was often
chaos and demoralization in the professorial ranks.   The
authors of Priorities for Action, the summary report of the
Carnegie Commission on Higher Education, describe the results in poignant terms:

> A traumatic loss of a sense of assured progress,
> of the inevitability of a better future, has occurred.
> Instead, there has developed more of a nostalgia
> for a Paradise Lost.   The tone of so much aca-
> demic thought now is more an attitude of how to
> hold on to as much of the past as possible--or
> even to retrieve lost aspects of it--rather than of
> how to confront the future directly; of how to
> avoid change, since most possible changes are
> thought to be unfavorable or even disastrous, rath-
> er than of how to plan and support constructive
> new developments.   The prevalent attitude is more
> to look back with longing than to look ahead with
> hope--the situation may be bad, but it cannot be
> improved; the Golden Age of the past is more at-
> tractive than any conceivable prospects for the
> future. [2]

May I respectfully suggest to my colleagues in this audience
that neither librarians nor library educators are immune
from this particular form of pernicious nostalgitis, which,
if untreated, is invariably institutionally fatal.   May I also
note here briefly a third characteristic of change in the
crisis-based society; that it has a high impact and is broadly
pervasive, rather than being limited or local or short term
in its significance.

Having looked at some of the symptomology of the
crisis-based society, I think it might be useful at this point
to identify very briefly some of the major social changes
that are currently in progress, or that can be anticipated in
the near future, that seem likely to have particular significance for library and information services.   In preparing
this portion of my talk, I had the good fortune to have the
benefit of Dean Martha Boaz's report of the results of the
Delphi Study, recently sponsored by AALS. [3]   This study
sought to identify and anticipate "future conditions and trends
which will affect the services of libraries and the programs

of library schools." If you have seen Boaz's report, you
will recognize how heavily and how selectively I have drawn
on it.

At least four critical and profound social changes that
I think must inevitably have a significant impact on libraries
are: the limits of economic growth, the transition to a post-
industrial society, the communications revolution, and the
revolution in adult learning. Let us look briefly at a few of
the likely implications for library and information services
of each of these.

The first stages of a future society characterized by
limited growth, slow growth, or no growth in the world and
national economies, and one accompanied by a major redis-
tribution of control of financial resources, in favor of the
developing nations, and at the expense of the industrialized
countries, has already shaken the American faith in education as a sure road to individual economic success, and
social and occupational status. We are witnessing the kind
of decline in those job markets traditionally considered appropriate for the college-educated that has been a major disruptive force in Indian society since independence. We must
be prepared for the likely consequence that this will occasion
a still further loss of confidence in education and its value
throughout American society. Hopefully, this will give way,
in the long term, to a more sophisticated understanding of
the purposes and objectives of education in relation to the
development of the total adult personality. This, in turn,
could result in the widespread adoption of new and non-
traditional individual patterns in the sequencing of the various
stages of education in relation to periods of employment.

No-growth probably means declining tax support for
public services of all types. We can also expect increased
competition for a diminishing supply of public dollars, which,
in turn, will have reduced buying power as a consequence of
inflation. At federal, state, and local levels, as governmental services are scaled down and begin to approach a survival
threshold, pressures will grow to close down entire agencies,
in order to assure the survival of the remainder of the
governmental enterprise. Social welfare, police, health care,
and sanitary sewers will inevitably rank higher on the priority
scale than education and libraries. The advent of sunset
laws and zero-based budgeting are harbingers of a time when
we may be required to contemplate the unthinkable, and to
seriously consider radical alternatives such as simply not

performing traditional library functions.  Perhaps this was
the scenario that Richard Brautigan anticipated in his library
novel, titled The Abortion:  An Historical Romance, when he
wrote:  "We were travelling so fast that it only took a few
moments before we were gone. "[4]

A second major change is the transition, seemingly
already in progress in Europe and North America, and which
the sociologist Daniel Bell has described as the evolution
from an industrial to a post-industrial society.  Bell's characterization of the post-industrial society is, no doubt, familiar to many of you.  He writes:  "Broadly speaking, if
industrial society is based on machine technology, post-industrial society is shaped by an intellectual technology.  And
if capital and labor are the major structural features of industrial society, information and knowledge are those of the
post-industrial society. "[5]

We need to ponder very seriously the implications of
information as a non-consumable resource.  In a future post-
industrial society, where information is the chief product,
and a majority of the population is no longer engaged in
manufacturing, but in service activities centering on the
production, organization, repackaging, dissemination, and
consumption of recorded knowledge, we can readily envision
the increased centrality and enhanced importance of existing
library and information services in society.  This may indeed
occur, but I think we also need to contemplate the potential
effects of the third major change that I mentioned, the communications revolution.  This could result in the creation of
entirely new social structures for the storage and dissemination of information that would wholly replace those existing
institutions and mechanisms that we represent--libraries and
information centers.

Elements of the communications revolution, such as
the home video recorder, are already commonplace.  We
can easily anticipate two-way video and computer communications in the home, with the CRT replacing or augmenting
the kitchen telephone.  What we need to recognize is the
significance of the widespread availability of these technologies in a period of continued rapid expansion of the base of
recorded knowledge, and the ultimate end of the primacy of
print as the highest ranking medium for information storage
and dissemination.  Should we have any doubt about the last
point, we need only consider the recent report of the U. S.
Bureau of the Census titled Social Indicators:  1976.  It in-

forms us that while "three out of every 10 persons said
television is their favorite pastime," at the same time, one
out of every five American adults is a functional illiterate and
"less than half could meet minimal standards of adequacy for
every day life, including filling out income tax and insurance
forms."[6] One potential characteristic of future society is
that enhanced access via on-line computers and telecommunications to enormous bodies of recorded data could serve
merely to exacerbate the problem of individuals who are already data rich, but information poor.

All three of the social phenomena I have just characterized are related to a fourth likely basic change which
might be termed the educational revolution.  There is a
growing body of evidence that America is becoming a life-
long adult learning society, with learning activities increasingly concentrated in non-traditional modes and media.  My
Pittsburgh colleague, Patrick Penland, has just completed a
study titled Self-Planned Learning in America.[7] It reports
the results of the first national survey of the prevalence of
adult self-directed learning.  Penland's data reveal that an
astonishing four out of every five adult Americans engage in
one or more systematic, self-directed learning projects each
year.  Four out of five adult learners, however, reject traditional courses as a means of pursuing these interests, and
only a handful consider the library a significant informational
resource.

My enumeration of critical social changes has admittedly been incomplete, selective, and brief.  Let me risk
being equally incomplete, selective, and brief in identifying
a few major potential implications for library and information services.

First, a recognition by government at all levels, but
especially by Congress and the Executive Branch, of the central importance and economic value of information in the
post-industrial society could lead to the formulation and adoption of a true, broad-based national information policy.
Major elements in a national information policy would include
a priority of governmental support from public funds for the
production, organization, management, and dissemination of
information, a recognition of the obligation of government to
assure timely and effective access to recorded information
for all citizens, and examination of such issues as copyright
and privacy in the larger context of questions of public policy.
I suggest that the forthcoming White House Conference on

Library and Information Services, scheduled for the fall of
1979, offers an unprecedented and extraordinary opportunity
for library and information professionals to lay the legislative
foundations for a national information policy.

To take maximum advantage of the opportunity that
the White House Conference and the 58 state, territorial,
and special conferences that are scheduled to precede it offer will, in my view, require a nationwide organized effort
among library and information professionals, as well as those
in the information, publishing, and communications industries.
I hope that AALS, along with other professional groups, will
give the highest priority to contributing to the coordinated
collective effort that I believe will be required to assist the
National Commission on Libraries and Information Science to
meet its statutory responsibility to prepare for, conduct, and
follow-up on the White House Conference.

A second implication for libraries and information
centers is, I believe, an urgent need to recognize that we do
not exist in isolation, but that increasingly we must see ourselves and our agencies as elements in a broad-band multi-
media spectrum of information-related industries and organizations which collectively serve a growing social need.
Specifically, librarians and information scientists need to
link themselves and their organizations more closely to the
information and communications industries on the one hand,
and to the formal educational structure on the other.   We
need to develop a clearer understanding of the multiple channels and mechanisms that now exist and are being created in
response to the total information needs of society.   Our present bibliocentric view of ourselves in relation to society's
informational needs will, in my judgment, if it is not corrected, ultimately prove as limiting as was the unwillingness
of the anthropocentrists to contemplate the Copernican model
of the solar system.

It is surely coals to Newcastle to observe to this
audience that libraries will continue and accelerate the pace
of rapid adoption of computer and new telecommunications
technologies for organizing, storing, and accessing knowledge
records.   To fail to embrace and utilize these new technologies would be to consign ourselves and our institutions to
social oblivion.   There are clearly significant problems that
must be resolved, however.   The most urgent, at the moment, would seem to be the distribution of the costs of in-
stalling and operating these systems, sometimes simplistically

expressed as a choice between "fee vs. free." Beyond this, there are serious emerging issues relating to management decisions in terms of the form and timing of the implementation of technological change in relation to existing manual systems. There are also critical questions of governance in relation to the control of the computer systems and data bases that are central to the emerging networks.

In my view, however, the most significant questions of all center on the uses to which we will put these new technologies in terms of a redefinition of institutional norms for the delivery of documents and information to our clienteles. Specifically, the new technology offers us the opportunity, if we choose to respond to it, to achieve not only a massive upgrading in the quality of existing document and information delivery services in libraries, but also the real prospect of achieving a fundamental alteration in the character of library services, by moving from a materials-centered library to a truly client-centered mode of operation. The materials-centered library measures its accomplishment in terms of collection size, rate of current acquisitions, and collection use as reflected in the number of items borrowed by clients. In the radically altered social, economic, and governmental environments that are increasingly upon us, such measures of institutional accomplishment will not, I suggest, be adequate to assure continued public support.

By contrast, the client-centered library evaluates individual and institutional performance, at the most elementary level, by its capacity to place needed information in the desired form in the hands of its clientele in a timely fashion. The basic measure of library performance, then, becomes client-satisfaction. To the extent that it succeeds in achieving client satisfaction, the library can be said to have maximized its social utility. A more sophisticated view, however, requires that we look beyond mere document delivery, and examine instead the success achieved by the library in making information accessible to its clientele, that is to say, in facilitating the information transfer process.

At the level of information transfer, we must recognize that the notion of access incorporates at least three levels: bibliographic access, physical access, and intellectual access. Traditional library service has emphasized the first of these. Consequently, we have devoted a large share of our collective professional energies to improving the scope and quality of the bibliographic record and, more recently,

with the advent of computer-centered telecommunications networks and on-line bibliographic systems, to augmenting the
local bibliographic data base through access to remote records.

Clearly, the existence of a comprehensive, accurate,
accessible bibliographic record is fundamental to the provision of more sophisticated library and information services.
But we have come to recognize lately that, from the user's
point of view, there is a significant difference between making an item accessible bibliographically and the capability to
place a desired document promptly in the hands of a client
who needs it.  It is clear that in many instances, at present,
we can move a bibliographic citation across the country more
quickly and easily than we can move a needed book or journal across the street, from one library to another.  The
growth of the body of recorded information, along with our
technologically enhanced capability to generate a plethora of
citations in response to an informational request, suggest
strongly that we must increasingly direct our attention to the
extent to which language, format, level of presentation and
similar characteristics of knowledge records become barriers
to intellectual access to information for individual clients.
If our objective, and the ultimate measure of institutional
and individual professional performance, is the facilitation of
the information transfer process, then it becomes obligatory
that library and information professionals develop both the
ability and the will to respond to individual client needs and
capacities through the abstracting, analysis, evaluation, re-
formating, and repackaging of the intellectual content of
knowledge records.  It is these kinds of activities that, in
my view, will characterize the client-centered library or
information service.

In the few remaining minutes that I have, I would
like to attempt one final, brief enumeration.  Let me simply
try to list, for your consideration, and without elaboration,
some of the implications of all of this for the future of library and information science education:

First, a broader based education that will enable library and information professionals to function effectively in
a wide variety of information-related agencies, organizations,
and environments.  The changing character of the job market for beginning librarians alone will necessitate this for
schools that have, up to now, been essentially single-product
industries.  May I simply suggest that if the sword is de-

signed from the outset to double as a plowshare, then little
or no beating is required at the point of conversion.

Second, a kind of education that emphasizes the development of broad, conceptual understandings of the nature
and use of information, rather than one that focuses on the
acquisition of narrow vocational skills. Such education is
less subject to obsolescence in environments characterized
by rapid, broad technological change.

Third, an education that develops the capacity of the
student to identify general principles that are relevant to
specific problems of professional practice, to exercise sound
judgment in modifying and adapting these to the needs of a
particular environment and/or an individual client, and to
accept responsibility for the consequences of exercising independent professional judgment. What I am describing here
is a learning environment that rewards problem-solvers, not
answer-producers; one that is responsive to Jerome Bruner's
suggestion "that perhaps a student would be given a considerable advantage in his thinking, generally, if he learned
that there were alternatives that could be chosen that lay
somewhere between truth and complete silence."[8]

Fourth, an education that prepares the individual to
function effectively as a professional in an environment where
basic assumptions may be subject to searching review,
sweeping modification, or even discarded completely in light
of changing environmental conditions. In passing, I cannot
resist the temptation to point out that much of current professional education in our fields is based on the usually un-
stated and often perhaps not recognized assumption that
future institutional, technological, and social structures will
essentially resemble those of the present.

Fifth, an education grounded in a much expanded,
empirically derived, body of general knowledge about the
nature of information, and the character of the information
transfer process. The need here is twofold, I think--both
to broaden the theoretical base on which the library and information professions rest, and to translate these newly
developed understandings into their operational terms.

Sixth, an education that prepared library and information professionals to assume higher level responsibilities,
with minimal supervision, early in their careers, to compete
effectively in competitive employment markets, and to func-

tion effectively as trainers and supervisors of nonprofession-
als and paraprofessionals.

Seventh, a pre-service education that lays the foundation for lifelong, self-directed, independent learning.  This,
in turn, demands an educational establishment that is prepared to share responsibility with the community of practice
for the development of alternate learning packages and delivery systems.  It also demands schools and faculties that are
credible as a continuing education resource for the community of practice.

In closing, I would like to propose one more agenda
item for library and information science educators.  That is
the assumption of increased responsibility to monitor the
quality of prospective new entrants to our professions.
Vigorous recruitment, in which practitioners must play the
key role, combined with the development and validation of
alternatives to subjective judgment and instinct in the identification of professional aptitudes, are central elements in
our collective response to this more urgent mandate.  The
times, by their nature and as a consequence of the pace of
change in the larger society, present us with a mandate for
excellence to which, I believe, we as educators, are obliged
to respond.

## References

1.  Shelton, Richard:  "The Future," You Can't Have Every-
      thing.  Pittsburgh, University of Pittsburgh Press,
      1975.
2.  Priorities for Action:  Final Report of the Carnegie
      Commission on Higher Education.  New York, McGraw-
      Hill Book Co. , 1973, p. 6.
3.  Association of American Library Schools.  "Study of the
      Future of Library and Information Science."  1977.
4.  Brautigan, Richard:  The Abortion:  An Historical Ro-
      mance, 1966.  New York, Simon and Schuster, 1970,
      p. 137.
5.  Bell, Daniel:  The Coming of Post-Industrial Society.
      New York, Basic Books, 1973, p. xiii.
6.  The Boston Globe, Dec. 26, 1977.
7.  Penland, P. R.:  Self-Planned Learning in America.
      Pittsburgh, University of Pittsburgh, 1977.
8.  Bruner, J. S.:  The Process of Education.  New York,
      Vintage Books, 1960, p. 65.

# THE LANGUAGE OF OUR TRIBE*

David Gerard

Those of us who saw Tom Stoppard's television play
Professional Foul recall that one of its main themes
was the significance of language--professional, political,
personal. A theme of direct relevance to librarians
who are agents in the daily transmission of a verbal culture and who need to assimilate the message
that the use of language, particularly professional
language, matters deeply not only to our own but to
future generations of professionals. The language of
the tribe is an important clue to its vitality; that
is why there is cause for concern about the present
condition of our library dialects.

A recent (February 1978) issue of the Record illustrated this graphically though quite unconsciously when it
printed between the same covers a piece of 18th-century
prose applied to a most utilitarian purpose, the advertising
of a catalogue, and alongside it some characteristic 20th-
century prose chiefly relating to that current obsession, research. In a sense the subject of both was the same--yet
how different, how revealingly different--was the implicit attitude. Here were two widely contrasting models of language
with different, somehow incompatible criteria. Quite simply,
what differentiates the contemporary from the 18th-century
prose is the lack of a human referent, its lifelessness.
When a typical piece by one of our busy professionals forces
a protesting cry of pain from its readers it is not only be-

*Reprinted by permission of the publisher from the May 1978
issue of the Library Association Record, pp. 229, 231.

25

cause of the automated syntax, the inert substantives and
supine passives, the rhythmless sentences without a heartbeat, but the essential vacuity, the absence of an individual
pulse.   This is not just a stylistic objection; it is evidence
of dissociation.   The men and women who write, the subjects
they write about, and the readers for whom they write seem
to have no connection with each other; there is no person at
either end, only a signal.   Could anything be more desolate
than these random examples from that issue of the Record:

> Process or problem-solving models of research
> are eclectic in their use of theories on which to
> base hypotheses; they tend to be interdisciplinary
> and demand boundary-crossing by researchers.

Apart from the high crop of vogue words in one sentence
nothing else is memorable.

And again:

> What they should be doing is looking for an ongoing
> manpower system.

--that is a fair sample of the vernacular.

Another:

> Programme Planing Evaluation is the chief feature
> of the ILP ... data collection ... and the utiliza-
> tion of that data in decision-making.

There is the busy tone of urgent activity that bangs
to and fro down a corridor of echoes, generating resonance
but actually banal.   From the British Library Research and
Development Newsletter many such examples could be drawn
but the pervasive note is plainly detectable from the random
scatter of words in most common use: "Evaluate" (usually
"packages"); "Develop"; "User requirements"; "Criteria by
which ... "; "Performance measurement"; "Data" (a sovereign favourite).   The aggregate of all this material activity
is always awaiting "analysis" in terms of perhaps "staff cost
per book selected" or "level and cost of staff used for selection of books. "   And the recycling process continues with a
resolve to "identify" (another favourite word) "a number of
application areas on which research might be undertaken. "

The idiom is now universal and must be adopted as a

guarantee of valid work--it is self-authenticating (and I
apologize for that word).   In a recent document, A Spatial
Interaction Model of Library Usage, by P. J. Whitehead, we
hear of "an outline of the application of an attraction con-
strained spatial interaction model to the study of library
usage."   And that "collective provision means that conceptu-
ally individual demand curves are difficult to define."   Yet
the conclusions seem obvious enough (though that is a too
easy gibe and not part of the real objection) when the same
report submits at the end that "there are inequalities in use
of the library service in Leeds."

Another feature of this waste landscape is the number
of synthetic creatures which inhabit it.   Some are mere con-
tainers like Workshops, Review Panels, Research Secretariat,
Colloquia, all manufactured and programmed to utter the
Newspeak that is the standard form of address.   Somehow
they all seem to be omnivorous as well, consuming raw
material from which more material is processed, and like
one such construction called Centre for the Study of Primary
Communications they declare their aim is "the collection of
relevant statistics to provide data for further research."
We live not only in a corridor of echoes but a hall of mirrors.   It is not that facts and discovery are not important--
of course they are, but that the kind of experience transmitted does not relate to the kind of knowing and receiving
which each of us experiences every day.   It is as if there
is no palpable interest in a commonplace encounter--me
speaking to you--a human being seeking a response, but instead a barrage of non-human counterfeit noise.   The language in which our professional discourse is carried on so
often sounds like one huge promotional exercise, the diligent
production of words in print about disembodied hypotheses
far from the separate, subjective life we actually live as
individuals.   The projectors of this swarm of words must
feel they are distancing, dissociating, themselves from what
they record.   So its value diminishes.   Presumably the oppressive quantities of reports and data are required by pro-
liferating agencies, the productivity approved in itself.   The
ultimate human need in terms of information is intrinsically
the same as ever, but there is now a vast amount of activity
around it, directing attention away from the subject paradoxically to the blank concept--we wrap everything up in
envelopes with labels like "Userfile."

At the moment (it seems inescapable) the movement
of thought within the library profession is a linear progres-

sion--measurement in one dimension only.  Graphs, grids,
and "guidelines" map the Promised Land, plotting our course
unerringly in one way, though in another telling us nothing.
The aim is praiseworthy:  we are frequently told that the
purpose of this or that inquiry is to "link librarians' knowledge with users' knowledge," but somehow the verbal outcrop
thickens and the columns of our periodicals darken with the
jargon.   In place of enlightenment there is a sense of numb-
ness.   In the context of the language of robotry there is no
room or relationship between this researcher, this view of
his (XB/13/doc. H. 17) and the people (where, in what shape
or capacity?) for whom he undertook the work.   To illustrate this, compare the above samples of current prose with
this, from the proposal to print the Harleian Catalogue, published in the Gentleman's Magazine, December 1742.  Quaint
and diverting it may seem to be but the enterprise has a
clear aim that must now embarrass us:

> That our catalogue will excite any other Man to
> emulate the Collectors of this Library to prefer
> Books and Manuscripts to Equipage and Luxury and
> to forsake Noise and Diversion for the Conversa-
> tion of the Learned and the Satisfaction of extensive
> Knowledge, we are very far from presuming to hope,
> but we shall make no scruple to assert, that if any
> Man should happen to be seized with such laudable
> Ambition, he may find in the Catalogue Hints and
> Information which are not easily to be met with ...

Of course the world has grown complex in the intervening 200 years.   In place of the Harleian Catalogue we
have, for example, the Bath University programme of catalogue research, which is proportionately more complex, but
doesn't the former by its very sound, the nature of its appeal, alter our feeling for what is being undertaken when
compared with the latter's expressed aims (cf. British Library R&D Newsletter, No. 11, p. 1)?   The first is a man
talking to men (and women), and the comparison quite fair
because the reader of the Gentleman's Magazine would be
the kind of professional person who would peruse the Record
today.

There is a moralizing tone which we find faintly irri-
tating, but this is part of the piece's integrity (in all senses)
where the whole intention betokens a real human interest and
a genuine engagement with the matter in hand--even if it is
only soliciting subscriptions there is a larger purpose and

yet it is precise.   By confining himself to humanly recogniz-
able conditions the writer is evaluating both readers and
catalogue in terms we can understand, not in terms of
"quantitative projections" or "first-stage assessments" or an
instigated questionnaire.   The drab catalogue is at once il-
luminated by this:

> Nor is the Use of Catalogues of less Importance
> to those whom Curiosity has engaged in the Study
> of Literary History, and who think the intellectual
> Revolutions of the World more worthy of their At-
> tention than ... the Rout of Armies and the Fall
> of Empires.   Those who are pleased with observ-
> ing the first Birth of new Opinions, their struggles
> against Opposition, their silent Progress under
> Persecution or sudden Extinction ... how Learning
> has languished for want of Patronage and Regard
> or overborne by the Prevalence of fashionable
> Ignorance ... may find in Catalogues like this at
> least such an Account as is given by Analists ...

Too theatrical?   Superfluous?   If we think that then
we must think that cataloguing itself, whether in four hand-
some volumes or in machine readable form, is superfluous.
For this kind of approach is an appeal to the whole man,
the assumptions implicit, the rewards plain, the purpose
irrefutable, and the prose matches the nobility of the design.
Today we have lost the touch.   The intimate relationship between reader and printed matter has been translated into
something neutral called Information Transfer, something
that effectively alienates us.   For a recovery of professional
touch we will have to restore the personal touch, reject
automated language and express our shared human concerns,
professionally speaking, in language of an individual tone.
There might then be a dialogue of real content.

# WOMEN WHO "SPOKE FOR THEMSELVES"*

Laurel A. Grotzinger

The role of women in librarianship, and especially in academic and research libraries, has been characterized as
one that dominated in physical numbers but did little to provide the leadership essential to a profession struggling to
define and justify its own existence. Unfortunately, such a
quick assessment does not point out the special significance
of those unique women who did provide that leadership while
overcoming long-standing and oppressive social traditions,
which not only circumscribed their opportunities but also
buried their contributions.

Even in 1976, analyses of those who rose to "prominent posts" note a Windsor, but not a Katharine Sharp, a
Williamson, but not an Isadore Mudge; cite as notable con-
tributors to the library literature a Billings, but not an
Adelaide Hasse, a Bishop but not a Margaret Mann; or find
reason to mention a Charles Smith, but not a Flora Belle
Ludington or a Genevieve Walton. [1]

Yet the women were there and, as Holley notes,
while there were "stories of women having asked 'Papa'
Poole, Lloyd Smith or some other male librarian to speak
for them in the deliberations at early conferences, they
quickly learned to speak for themselves. "[2] In that speaking
and in their doing lie many biographical studies; the following paragraphs address only six of those "library ladies"
and their impact on the academic and research libraries of
the twentieth century.

---

The major period of expansion of academic and research libraries in the United States dates from the 1870s
and 1880s.  By that time, the foundations of the system of
postsecondary education were well established, and the basic
variations--the colonial college, technical institutes, coeduca-
tional institutions, land-grant and other state universities--
were easily distinguished.  Not so clear, however, was the
office of the librarian and the responsibilities of that office
in terms of building an educational resource.  As McElderry
succinctly states, academic libraries, regardless of institutional "type," were often "a miscellaneous assortment of
books, primarily gifts, few in number, poorly housed, and
scarcely used. "[3]

At the same time, major public research collections,
such as the ones in Los Angeles, Pittsburgh, and New York,
were growing rapidly but had yet to be adequately housed,
organized, and opened to the public with the full range of
services that are commonplace to today's user.  Although a
number of women were involved in or closely identified with
the development of academic and research libraries and/or
the provision of special services, one of the first was
Katharine Lucinda Sharp.

## Katharine Sharp (1865-1914)

Katharine Sharp was associated with two key aspects of library history in the U. S. :   education for librarianship and
the promotion of a strong, accessible collection.  Her direction of the first library school in the Midwest, at the Armour
Institute of Technology in Chicago, from 1893 to 1897, and
the continuation of that program at the University of Illinois,
from 1897 to 1907, gave impetus to the acceptance of formal
library education as a basic component of preparation for
professional work.  Graduates of the Illinois program found
positions in libraries and library schools throughout the
country.  As Dewey did before her, Sharp and her faculty
colleagues imbued the majority of their students with a sense
of the dramatic future of librarianship; those graduates, in
turn, became influential advocates of the role of libraries
and library service, which Sharp, herself, exemplified.

Katharine Sharp probably would be notable if she had
done nothing but build a strong library school, but, in addition, she was instrumental in collecting and organizing the
nucleus of the vast research library that currently exists at

the University of Illinois.  Illinois, one of the first of the
land-grant universities, had a library when Sharp arrived in
1897.  However, no previous librarian had the foresight or
knowledge to take the odds and ends of materials that had
been acquired until that time and make them accessible
while encouraging the expansion of the collection.  Yenawine,
in his study on "The Influence of Scholars on Research Library Development at the University of Illinois," documents
her ambitious undertaking.

> Guided by library statutes and assisted by a
> Faculty Library Committee, Miss Sharp [by 1900]
> had consolidated the Library's resources in the Li-
> brary Building, had departmentalized the work and
> trained a staff, had systematized procedures for
> book selection and acquisition, organized reference
> services, and had recataloged a large part of the
> collection. 4

Such an accomplishment was not due to chance.  All
of her preparation had emphasized principles of "library
economy" and a logical approach to collection development.
In fact, that preparation and her own unique personality made
her one of the widely recognized leaders of that period.

Sharp, in contrast to a number of other pioneers of
that age, was a completely midwestern product.  Born, on
May 21, 1865, in Elgin, Illinois, she was fortunate in her
attendance at the Elgin Academy, a progressively liberal
school.  She completed her studies at the age of fifteen and
a year later was enrolled in Northwestern University.  In
1885 she received the degree of Bachelor of Philosophy with
Honors in General, Latin, and Special Scholarship.  Ultimately, she also earned a B. L. S. in the New York State Library
School, a master's degree from both Northwestern and the
New York State Library School, and, after her retirement,
was given an honorary degree by the University of Illinois.
There was little doubt that she was a brilliant student and,
more important, was able to apply what she learned in a
variety of situations.

Her first position involved teaching at the Elgin
Academy, but this proved unsatisfactory, and she became an
assistant librarian in the public library of Oak Park, Illinois,
in 1888.  Shortly after she began her second year of library
work, she applied for admission to the infant library school
that had just been transferred to Albany, New York, after

Dewey's lost battle with the trustees of Columbia. Sharp's decision to apply to that school was a gamble, since she had to resign her position, move to the east, and study for two years under a man who was an extraordinary leader but also one of the most controversial individuals in the country. It was, at least with respect to her future, a fortuitous choice, since Dewey was the professional contact who provided access to the "old boy network" of that period.

During her years of study at Albany, Sharp gained further experience cataloging and organizing small collections in Illinois and Ohio. Her record at the library school was excellent, and she was, as Dewey noted, "easily first"[5] in a class that also included Edwin Hatfield Anderson, Mary Esther Robbins, and William Reed Eastman. Dewey's identification of her as "the best man in America"[6] to direct the library and library school at the new vocational institute in Chicago was the only recommendation necessary to place her in a position from which she could build a reputable educational program and, four years later, begin her consolidation and creation of the foundations of the research library at the University of Illinois.

The years of Katharine Sharp's career were relatively brief in number. She opened the Armour school in the fall of 1893 and some fourteen years later, in 1907, resigned from her position as head librarian, director of the library school, and professor of library economy at the University of Illinois. Although it was anticipated that she would eventually return to her library career, her delight in her position as vice-president of the Lake Placid Club and her tragically early death in 1914 at the age of forty-nine left no opportunity for that future involvement. Regardless, less than two decades of service to the profession produced accomplishments that are neither insignificant nor transitory. Her outstanding work in establishing the Illinois library school and formalizing the curriculum leading to a degree in library science was probably the factor most important in assuring the continuation of university-associated education for librarianship in the Midwest.

Her lifelong dedication to the future of library services in the state of Illinois led to the formation of the state library association and brought an extension of library service into many communities--through her founding and direction of a bureau of information and through the library courses she and her staff taught outside the Chicago and Champaign/

Urbana communities.  Although Sharp was unable to bring
about the creation of a state library commission, she left a
strong association, interested citizens, and numerous well-
prepared librarians who were dedicated to the same ideals
of service and library expansion to which she had devoted
her professional life.  She was an active and contributing
member of other professional associations including ALA,
where she served ten years on the council and two terms as
vice-president.

        Katharine Sharp's life, however, may not be best as-
sessed in terms of the events just chronicled.  In many respects, her most significant role came in the influence she
had on others of that period--especially on the young women
with whom she came in contact in those formative years of
library work, who, in turn, brought their forces to bear on
the library community.  One such individual, a member of
Sharp's staff at the University of Illinois, was Isadore Gilbert Mudge.

## Isadore Gilbert Mudge (1875-1957)

In McElderry's analysis of the evolution of the academic library, five categories are identified, which, he suggests,
represent chronological trends in service to readers.  His
first and second periods are described as ones concerned,
as was Katharine Sharp at the University of Illinois, with
the "accumulation of materials" and the "organization of resources."[7]  The third facet of library growth, the "personal
assistance to readers," was also of singular interest to
Sharp, who brought to Illinois, in 1900, a woman who was
to earn a special place in the history of library reference
services.

        Isadore Gilbert Mudge, as her biographer, John Wad-
dell, notes,

                was born March 14, 1875, the oldest child of
                Alfred and Mary Ten Brook Mudge.  Both her
                parents had been raised to respect the importance
                of higher education and to appreciate the satisfac-
                tions of professional achievement.  Her maternal
                grandfather, Andrew Ten Brook, was a minister,
                a professor, and for many years the librarian of
                the University of Michigan; her paternal step-
                grandfather, Charles K. Adams, was the president

of Cornell and later of the University of Wisconsin
and was instrumental in the building of fine new
libraries at both places.... It was a family of
achievers. [8]

Mudge, just ten years younger than Katharine Sharp,
also reached college age at a time when she was able to attend an institution of higher education other than those that
catered solely to females; she could think seriously about a
career other than marriage. Given her background and fine
educational preparation at the Adelphi Academy in Brooklyn,
she found little difficulty in matriculating at Cornell University in 1893.

She was an excellent student who was one of three
elected to Phi Beta Kappa in the junior year but, more important, was given the opportunity to study under a number
of superlative professors and to make use of an excellent
library: "Probably nowhere else in the world could a young
woman of her age have had access to such a strong collection, and it is obvious from the nature of the courses she
took and the high grades she made that she must have spent
countless hours using its resources. "[9]

Mudge enrolled in the New York State Library School
in 1898 and graduated in 1900 having earned the B. L. S. de-
gree--again with an outstanding record including a "100" in
reference. Not surprisingly, she was recommended to the
"demanding" Miss Sharp of Illinois, who wanted only the best
for her library staff and her school.

Katharine Sharp had recognized the need for specialized reference personnel early in her career. When the library school was transferred to the university, Sharp fought
to employ highly qualified individuals to carry the responsibility of both giving and teaching reference service. As she
wrote in 1901, "without a reference librarian to devote her
entire time to the work, a university library must be restricted in one of the most important phases of its work. "[10]

When Mudge arrived in the summer of 1900, she had
a tremendous task to handle, with what was then a paltry
collection compared to those resources available at Cornell
or some of the other universities of the East. However,
even in these early years, she had a certain sense of the
role of an effective reference librarian. Her statement of
the function of the reference department, in 1902, noted that

"an all-round, well-balanced collection of the best reference
books in English" should be built; that it should be located
"where it can be most easily and conveniently consulted";
and that the librarian should "give personal help in the use
of the library whenever possible and in giving such help to
endeavor always to help the student to independent and intelligent use of the library resource."[11]

During the same years that Mudge gained valuable
first experiences at the reference desk, she also taught in
the library school. Although her teaching methods were not
comparable to those of later years, given the nature of the
Illinois collection and the relatively elementary nature of its
curriculum, the involvement and her contact with Sharp,
Margaret Mann, Minnie Sears, and others provided the basis
for future friendships as well as for professional development. Sears became a special friend and collaborated closely with Mudge in both her library and literary work of the
next several decades.

By 1903 Mudge was ready to return to her beloved
east coast. An opportunity for advancement came in the acceptance of the position of head librarian at Bryn Mawr. It
is likely that Dewey was again involved, since graduates of
the Albany school had been earlier librarians at that college;
Sharp also recommended her and wished her success.

Sears went with Mudge to Bryn Mawr as her cataloger, and both left the college in 1907 to spend a year travel-
ing in Europe. After the year there, during which she and
Sears compiled A Thackeray Dictionary,[12] she spent the
next three years in a variety of activities. From 1909 to
1911 she worked with William Dawson Johnston, librarian at
Columbia, in compiling a directory of special collections in
American libraries.[13] In 1910 she was employed at Simmons College library school where she was recognized for
her teaching ability.

In the same period she contributed the first of numerous reviews to Library Journal, and, possibly most important, Mudge took over Alice Bertha Kroeger's Guide to the
Study and Use of Reference Books[14] and published supple-
ments in the Library Journal. In 1917 Mudge edited her
own first full edition, the third of the Guide; it became the
undisputed leader among reference tools of that type. Mudge
eventually edited four editions--1917, 1923, 1929, and 1936--
before her successor, Constance Winchell, took on the job.
As Winchell later wrote

> Miss Mudge became the outstanding authority on
> reference books, and her Guide has been known
> and consulted in libraries throughout the world....
> Her thorough familiarity with reference books and
> reference techniques, her clear thinking, her wide
> knowledge and remarkable memory, and her deep
> interest in the subject and in the student or research
> worker, all combined to impress her influence on
> succeeding generations of students, colleagues--all
> who used her book. [15]

Closely tied to her ability to earn this reputation and
produce the Guide was Mudge's career at Columbia University. Although Simmons College desired to keep her as an
instructor, Mudge claimed that she had "for some reason
set my mind on wanting Columbia from the days that I was
at Cornell."[16] Her interest in the institution eventually led
her to accept a position in gifts and exchanges, which began
February 6, 1911. A few months later, on June 15, she
was appointed reference librarian, a position she held until
her retirement thirty years later, in 1941.

In 1927 she added the second element to her distinguished career when she was made an associate professor of
bibliography of the recently opened School of Library Service,
which had grown out of a merger of the New York State Library School at Albany and the library school that operated
within the structure of the New York Public Library. The
combination of Mudge's dual role as reference librarian and
instructor plus the superb facilities of the university library
provided the environment that shaped the future of much of
reference work in America. During the years of her tenure
she focused on the centralization and expansion of the collection, the selection and education of staff, and, key to it all,
the definition of professional service to the scholar.

> Word of mouth reputation of Mudge's services
> spread, so that in a relatively short time she was
> able to demonstrate factually to the library admin-
> istration something of the achievements and the
> growth of her department.... Staff and collection
> were important in furthering the development of the
> reference department, but the real key to success
> was, of course, Mudge's almost superhuman skill
> in answering questions of great variety in subject
> and in level, and in training her carefully chosen
> assistants to learn to do almost as well. In later

years she phrased a glib prescription for success
in reference work, which she called the three M's--
material, mind, and method. [17]

A glib prescription or not, Mudge's three "M's" became the basis for her resourceful and influential classes in
the library school--classes that in turn produced future instructors who based their methods on her work.   As Winchell
later wrote, "probably no other one person has contributed so
much to raising the standards of reference collections and
reference service in the libraries of this and other countries. "[18]

That rare spirit was eventually recognized by the
American Library Association, which established in 1958 the
Isadore Gilbert Mudge Citation to be given to others who had,
in the image of Mudge, made a "distinguished contribution to
reference librarianship. "

## Margaret Mann (1873-1960)

"Her chief service to librarianship, " wrote Bishop in 1938
when Margaret Mann was preparing for retirement after a
career that had spanned four decades, "... is the training
she has given her students in earlier and in later years.
She has shown them that cataloging is work of absorbing
interest and never-ending variety; that classification of books
calls for a happy combination of scholarship and practical
sense; that both are fundamental processes in the conduct of
any library. "[19] William Warner Bishop, perhaps, overem-
phasized the final years of Mann's professional life, when
she was the best known instructor in cataloging and classification in America.

Mann had spent at least as many years in cataloging
materials as she spent in teaching, and her contributions in
this area, if not unmatched in her time, surely identified
her as an expert in the field.   At the same time, her cli-
mactic years in the library school at the University of Michigan did focus her ideas about the organization of resources
in such a way as to produce her classic text, Introduction to
Cataloging and the Classification of Books, [20] a work described by Lehnus, in his analysis of "milestones in cataloging" as "not only the most cited manual, but also one cited
as much as others which have had more recent revised editions. ...   Even though there are more recent texts than that

of Mann, hers has proven its superiority through its quality. "21

Margaret Mann's entrance to librarianship did not
build on the educational and cultural strengths seen in the
background of both Sharp and Mudge.  She was born on
April 9, 1873, in Cedar Rapids, Iowa, and her early years
were circumscribed by the rural community in which she
was raised and in which her father worked as a dry goods
merchant.  After Amasa Mann moved his family to a suburb
of Chicago in 1890, Margaret was able in 1893 to obtain her
secondary diploma from Englewood High School.  She was
then twenty years old.

As with many young women of that period, her options for employment were limited, but she was able to
benefit from the circumstances that brought, in the year of
her graduation, the opening of the Armour Institute library
school.  She passed the application test for the Armour Institute library course with ease and was one of twelve young
women who began study on September 14, 1893, in the first
class of the Department of Library Science.  From that day
on, Margaret Mann's future in the profession was assured--
both by her own abilities and her contacts with Katharine
Sharp and, through her, Dewey.

Records indicate that she was an all "A" student who
was so expert that Katharine Sharp hired her, in 1894, after
only a year of study under limited conditions, to catalog in
the Armour library and, also, while taking a second year of
work, in 1895-96, to serve as an instructor in the beginning
classes.

Mann was especially attracted to the area of cataloging and classification; it not only appealed to her own well-
organized habits and intellectual interests, but it was, at
the time, the only area of librarianship that was codified in
any systematic way--there was something upon which to base
decisions.  Moreover, she was an advocate of the basic assumption that the catalog was the key to effective library use
and that its value was based on the skill of the cataloger.
She not only practiced this belief, as is evident in her innovative and user-oriented catalog modifications found at the
Carnegie Library in Pittsburgh and the Engineering Societies
Library in New York, but she made it the emphasis of her
courses in which she stressed the discipline of the subject.

> [The study of cataloging] develops an exact way of
> thinking and doing, and the student comes to real-
> ize through such a course the importance of sys-
> tem, accuracy and order.  He comes to accept
> the fact that, no matter how much knowledge one
> acquired in handling books, unless this knowledge
> can be satisfactorily passed on to others, the li-
> brary is not fulfilling its purpose. [22]

When the Armour Institute library school was transferred to the University of Illinois in 1897, there was never
any doubt that Mann would make the move with Sharp.  A
close and special friendship had developed between the instructor and student.  During the period at Illinois, Mann
did much to support the massive changes that Sharp had to
bring about in order to get the library and library school
operating in an efficient manner.

Prior to Sharp's arrival, there had never been a consistent policy of cataloging and classification so that many of
the resources needed, at the very least, to be accessioned,
shelflisted, and prepared for the shelf; other material needed
major reorganization.  The only help came from the library
school students who had to be closely supervised, but, by the
end of the first year, the annual report could state that the
library had its material "arranged for easy reference, with
its records all systematized. "[23]

By 1899 Mann was serving both as assistant librarian
and senior instructor as well as personally handling all
government documents, college catalogs, and other miscellaneous resources.  When Edwin H. Anderson, then librarian
of the Carnegie Library at Pittsburgh, offered her the position as head of the Cataloging Department in 1902, she could
not refuse and, from 1903 to 1919, was instrumental in directing the development of the catalog at that institution.

> The Carnegie Library of Pittsburgh enjoys a
> peculiar distinction among American libraries--a
> distinction which it owes directly to Margaret
> Mann.  It is the sole American library of size and
> importance which has published a classified and
> annotated catalog on a large scale.... The execu-
> tion of this huge and formidable task was carried
> out under Miss Mann's close and continuous super-
> vision. [24]

Although her long years of work at Pittsburgh began

to suggest that she might eventually retire in that community, Mann readily accepted a totally new challenge in 1919 when Harrison Craver asked her to bring order to the assorted libraries of the United Engineering Societies in New York City. This work in a special library not only added to her cataloging experience but brought to a forefront her ideas about adapting a collection to the needs of the user and producing a usable catalog. As she wrote several years later,

> ... libraries are formidable places at best. ...
> People who use the library are immediately aware
> of their shortcomings and very few like to expose
> the fact that they do not know the answer to the
> question they want to look up. ... With this situa-
> tion it is much better for the shy reader (and
> there are many of them) to be able to go to the
> catalog and look up his own information. He will
> be more likely to come again if he can help him-
> self. [25]

In addition, she was quick to utilize the idea that a classed catalog worked more effectively than a dictionary catalog, when used with certain subjects--so the Societies' library had a special classed catalog that gave, she noted, "a logical arrangement of titles to supplement the illogical dictionary arrangement." [26]

After five years, the collection of the Engineering Societies was largely recataloged and well-organized. It was then that Mann turned her attention to a different and even greater challenge--teaching cataloging and classification in Paris at the Ecole des Bibliothécaires. She taught there for only two years, 1924-26, and although she might have stayed longer, family concerns, several teaching offers, and an agreement to write the ALA textbook on cataloging enticed her to return.

Bishop persuaded her to come to his newly formed library school at the University of Michigan; it was Margaret Mann's last professional home. The final twelve years of her active career, 1926-38, were a fitting capstone as she was internationally recognized as an exceptional, talented teacher whose textbook became a classic almost as soon as it was published.

Adelaide R. Hasse (1868-1953)

In 1897, an issue of the San Francisco Call ran a two-
column illustration of Adelaide R. Hasse and headed it with
the phrase, "Famed for her Library Knowledge." As the
information under the picture noted, Hasse had formerly
been employed by the Los Angeles Public Library and had
later "distinguished herself" in the Bureau of Public Documents in Washington. Furthermore, the notice went on, "no
woman in the country has a more thorough knowledge of the
public documents of the United States than has Miss Hasse.
So complete is her information in that line that the head of
the bureau has often referred to her as the 'living index.'"[27]

The occasion that had caused this glowing commentary
to be published was Hasse's appointment as head of the documents department in the Astor Library, which had just been
consolidated with the Lenox Library and the Tilden trust to
form the New York Public Library. Within a few years,
the documents collection "became, the Library Journal observed, 'so completely equipped and so well organized as to
form a model of its kind....' Miss Hasse and her staff
produced valuable bibliographies and checklists [and] in 1911
... they provide[d] service directly to the public."[28]

Adelaide Hasse, as was true of Sharp, Mudge, and
Mann, brought her own unique personality and background
into focus when she became a librarian. Born September
13, 1868, in Milwaukee, Wisconsin, Hasse grew up in a
family in which her father, a successful surgeon and renowned botanical researcher, gave his children many opportunities to study with private tutors and to share in his own
literary interests. Dr. Hasse moved his practice on several occasions, and Adelaide also came to enjoy different environments and to delight in travel.

Adelaide's penchant for what she called "collecting,"
which originally referred to her enthusiasm for reading and
discovering information of all kinds, quite logically brought
her to a place where collecting was keen--the Los Angeles
Public Library. There, in 1889, Hasse became the library
assistant to Tessa L. Kelso and took the first steps on her
remarkable career path. Years later Hasse noted:

> ... collecting is great fun. Every employer I
> have had has been a collector. My first employer
> was a woman, and it was she who gave point and

> direction to my natural bent towards collecting.
> She herself was a remarkable collector of experi-
> ence.  Having had but little library experience her-
> self, she was able, by her ability as a collector
> of the experience of others, to avail herself there-
> of and, on the strength of it, to build up one of
> the livest, most progressive libraries I have known
> ... [She] aroused my interest in the possibilities
> of specializing in government documents.  She was
> so sympathetic in her efforts that, almost without
> being aware of having done so, somehow I had
> organized the collection of documents, not incon-
> siderable, in the Los Angeles Public Library, de-
> vised a classification for them, and had begun a
> checklist of them. 29

From that checklist came the first of nearly two
dozen bibliographies that were published during the sixty
years of Hasse's career--publications that were instrumental
in identifying and organizing state, federal, and foreign
documents on a variety of topics including, among others,
public archives of the thirteen original states, demolition-
blighted areas, the trade paper press, finance, Department
of Agriculture publications, foreign affairs, and her invaluable Index of Economic Material in Documents of the States
of the United States, 30 a monumental reference resource,
which was "in itself a life work for any less industrious and
persistent person."31  Moreover, from 1894 to 1939, there
are more than fifty articles by Hasse, published in a variety
of library and nonlibrary sources, that perceptively define
an active and competent library institution as well as chas-
tise an often inactive and incompetent library staff.

Hasse's work in the Los Angeles library was singular
enough to bring her to the attention of individuals who had
major difficulties in document organization--the U. S. government.  The first section of her checklist of public documents,
which dealt with agriculture, brought a request from that
department for its publication. 32  Shortly thereafter, knowledge of Hasse's skill in this area was such that, in 1895,
she was offered the position of librarian of the office of the
Superintendent of Documents.  This position and the office
were created by the passing of the Printing Act of 1895,
which centralized the distribution and sale of government
publications as well as the preparation of bibliographies that
would index them.  Her duties in Washington

were to care for the current documents after they
had been recorded by the cataloguers and to collect all other documents.   The Richardson Bill
gave to the Superintendent of Documents the authority to remove to his custody from all the departments all the accumulations of documents not
in use for the business of the departments.   The
removal of these accumulations fell to me. [33]

Two years after she arrived in Washington, John
Shaw Billings, then director of the New York Public Library,
visited the documents office, observed her efforts, and offered her a position in the Astor Library.   She accepted the
position and, in 1897, moved to New York.   Hasse had tremendous respect for Billings, who had, in her estimation,
an international perspective on the functions of a research
library and the scope of its resources.   She was given the
opportunity to travel and acquire materials and was responsible, in 1902, for locating a copy of the supposedly lost 1695
Bradford Journal, which she later edited. [34]

After Billings' death in 1913, Hasse lost much of the
momentum that had, with his support and interest, helped
her to build an excellent documents collection and develop
user-oriented services for businessmen.   He had supported
her in the compilation and publication of several significant
bibliographies; her work in ALA also led to her preparation
of a catalog handbook for documents. [35]

The new administrator of the library, E. H. Anderson, was not judged by Hasse to be a worthy successor to
Billings.   A disruptive and destructive personality conflict
between Anderson and Hasse developed.   She was not one to
bear her troubles silently, and Anderson would not, could
not allow her criticism to go unanswered.   With the outbreak of World War I, matters grew even worse and rumors
circulated throughout the staff about Hasse's pro-German
sympathies.   She perceived what she considered to be inferior work all around her; a catalog she had spent years developing was given to another department to manage; and,
ultimately, she believed that she was purposely "ostracised
from any activities of the library"[36] including, in 1917,
omission in the annual report of the librarian of reference
to the work of her Economics Division, whose effective
and resourceful services had become famous in the New York
business community.   By 1918, the entire matter had gone
beyond reasonable reconciliation, and Hasse's resignation was

requested.  Never one to retreat, Hasse refused to leave
quietly and requested a hearing before the executive committee.  Her request was refused, and in October her employment was "terminated."

For anyone other than a personality of the strength
and determination of Adelaide Hasse, the affair would have
ended a professional life.  Hasse, however, in addition to
her own drive, had many colleagues who supported her regardless of their interpretation of the incident.  She returned
to Washington, by request, and during the years from
1919 through the early 1940s continued to organize records,
prepare bibliographies, serve as a research consultant, and
teach in the local universities.  She officially stopped working in 1952 at the age of 83, with her last major effort
directed to the editing of state records for microfilm publication. [37]

### Flora Belle Ludington (1898-1967)

Although all the women profiled to this point had active
careers in regional, state, and national associations, only
Flora Ludington was able to scale the political ramparts that
produce American Library Association presidencies.  She
was still a novice librarian when Sharp was dead, Mann an
internationally known cataloger, Mudge an increasingly recognized authority on reference works, and Hasse a thirty-year
veteran of special library services for the economics and
business world.

Ludington came to the profession of librarianship
when it was in the throes of serious criticism about its educational system, had yet to establish and clarify many of
its standards, and had far more unanswered questions about
users than it had answers or even the right questions.  During her distinguished career, which was involved with two
colleges--Mills and Mount Holyoke--and international library
development, Ludington never lost

> sight of the first responsibility of the librarian--
> to bring together books and people, and she would
> add, "books that will inspire the mind, that will
> throw fresh lights on current problems ... books
> on a variety of subjects, not necessarily new books
> ... good books."  Her reading as well as her
> writings, encompass[ed] many diverse fields, and

are worldwide in their extent.  She [was] librarian,
bookman, collector, and, perhaps, of greater importance, an informed and active citizen of the
world. [38]

Flora Belle Ludington was born November 12, 1898,
in Harbor Beach, Michigan, but while still a child, she
moved with her family first to Idaho and later to Wenatchee,
Washington.  Her earliest association with library work came
at the age of fourteen when she served as a volunteer in the
local Carnegie public library.  That experience and her life-
long enchantment with the delights of reading and the joy of
learning also involved her in work in the library of the University of Washington, Seattle, where she took her B. A.
degree in librarianship, in 1920.

In her work in the library classes at Washington, she
came under the strong guidance of William E. Henry.  He
was extremely supportive of the educational precept that "no
one can teach efficiently who lacks enthusiasm for the subject
taught, or who is deficient in human interests as distinguished
from mere subject interest."[39]  The instructors at the library school were selected because Henry believed that their
interest was the "welfare of the student."  In addition, he
espoused the then basic philosophy that the instructors should
be practicing librarians.  When this emphasis on the personal touch was combined with small classes and field work in
the library, the stage for the Ludington career was well established.  As one graduate and later professor of the school
wrote,

> ... every student went out with a call to service....
> As future librarians we became aware that we
> would have in our charge the recorded history of
> mankind ... we were responsible to see that books
> and information were diffused as widely as possible.
> There was nothing passive about librarianship and if
> we were to measure up to the demands of the pro-
> fession, we must be up and doing. [40]

"Up and doing" was soon to be a life-style for Flora
Ludington.  Upon completion of her bachelor's degree, she
was employed to work as an assistant in the circulation department of the university but left to gain additional knowledge by studying for a year at the New York State Library
School.  That year, 1922, ended with her first significant
appointment as reference librarian at Mills College, California.

Ludington remained at Mills for the next fourteen years. She was promoted first to assistant librarian, then added the role of assistant professor of bibliography, and, from 1935 to 1936, was associate librarian. (In addition, she took the opportunity to earn a M. A. in history from the college; it was awarded in 1925, and, in that same year, she was granted the B. L. S. from the New York State Library School. )

The institutional memory at Mills College of her devotion, as well as her competence, was keen enough to bring the award of an honorary Doctor of Laws degree in 1953. The citation read: "Alumna of this college, and held in its affections; librarian who is a lover of learning as well as a custodian of books; leader in her profession at home and its honored representative abroad. "[41]

In 1936 Ludington was appointed librarian at Mount Holyoke, and she held this position until she retired in 1964. Although her primary responsibility remained in her work at Holyoke, she also carried on three other professional involvements: teaching, international library work, and association activities. From 1930 to 1943 she taught in the library schools, on one occasion or another, at the University of Texas, San Jose State, and Columbia University. Ludington's international library concerns were linked with her ALA work on the International Relations Board. During World War II, she was chairman of the Special Committee on International Cultural Relations and took a war leave from Mount Holyoke so that she could direct the U. S. information library in Bombay, India, from 1944 to 1946.

Miss Ludington served for several months in 1948 as visiting expert on information libraries in Japan for the Supreme Command for Allied Powers and was awarded the Certificate of Achievement of the Civil Information and Education Section. She [was] a member of the USIA's Advisory Committee on International Cultural Relations [from 1957 to 1964. ] As Chairman of a committee working with the ALA and the Ford Foundation to establish a library school at the University of Ankara in Turkey, she visited libraries there and in Lebanon in 1957. In 1959 she studied library development in Africa under a Rockefeller Foundation grant. [42]

Ludington was chosen as vice-president and president-

elect of the American Library Association in 1952; she was
president in 1953-54.   Her election to that post came after
years of service to a number of committees and boards.   In
her inaugural address she noted that

> with the growth of libraries and consequent civiliza-
> tion, the bond which has kept the profession to-
> gether is a firm conviction that books and the read-
> ing of them are important in a free society.... In
> an age of mass communication by means of the
> motion picture, radio and television the book may
> well offer a unique opportunity for one mind to
> meet another mind....   The freer the society, the
> greater is the responsibility of the individual to be
> informed on the issues of the day. [43]

Her words were lucid reflections on a contemporary issue of
monumental concern:  it was the era of McCarthyism and
intellectual freedom was under concerted attack.   The Los
Angeles conference during which she spoke endorsed the
declaration "On Freedom to Read," which then and now
enunciates the principle that the library "offers the opportunity to gain the information needed to understand diverging
points of view on local, national and international affairs....
It imposes no thought control. "[44]

Not separate, but certainly distinctive in its own
significance, is the administrative role Ludington played at
Mount Holyoke.   In the 1930s Mount Holyoke was in the
midst of a major educational revision; it was apparent that
the collection needed to be evaluated, and Ludington was
quick to recognize that a small college needed to cooperate
with other institutions.   Her emphasis on library cooperation
was a major thrust of her life, and, when the Hampshire
Inter-Library Center, Inc., was formalized in 1951, she
would declare

> no institution is an island sufficient unto itself,
> especially a library.   It is rather a reservoir,
> continuously fed from many streams, but differing
> from other reservoirs in that the substance of
> which it is composed is not expended. [45]

Ludington's life, as well, was a "reservoir, continu-
ously fed from many streams."   She constantly sought to fill
that reservoir for herself and for others through the libraries
she fought to build and to save.   At the height of the 1950s
controversy, she wrote

> ... if libraries indoctrinate for anything it is for
> civilization, for liberty, for free press, for free
> religion, for free schools, for self government and
> democracy.  Help the users of your libraries to
> preserve the inquiring mind whether it be how to
> make a better slip cover for a chair, or to over-
> come the sense of futility or belief that just one
> vote doesn't count, or to help those who are
> frightened or resistant to new ideas.  Knowledge
> can be our greatest resource. [46]

Flora Belle Ludington retired as librarian of Mount
Holyoke in 1964 after more than forty professional years of
expert and influential contributions to twentieth-century libraries and librarianship.

## Genevieve Walton (1857-1932)

In 1976 Cynthia Cummings, at the University of Wisconsin
Library School, compiled and published "A Biographical-
Bibliographical Directory of Women Librarians." Five lines
constitute the paragraph on Genevieve Walton; it is the brief-
est entry of the eighty-one women who are included.

> Very little information could be found on Genevieve
> Walton.  She appeared to be the librarian of Michi-
> gan State Normal College Library from 1892, and
> until at least 1930.  She also helped found the
> Michigan Library Association, and served as its
> first woman president. [47]

In concluding a biographical series on six women who "spoke
for themselves" with a sketch of Genevieve Walton, the beginning as well as the end of an unusual period of library
development is reflected.  Unique women, as stated in the
introductory paragraphs, have often been misplaced in the
history of academic and research libraries.  Despite their
speaking and their doing, the result has been reduced to a
minimum of record and a lost recognition.

So it was with Genevieve Walton, who spent forty
years as "a distinguished librarian and book lover"[48] in a
single position, librarian of Michigan's first "normal"
school, now Eastern Michigan University, in Ypsilanti.  Appointed as librarian in 1891, she continued to work in the
library until a few months before her death in April 1932.

The culmination of her dedication to that institution occurred
in January 1930 when she was able to attend the formal
opening of the new library building.  Charles McKenny,
president of the institution, wrote of her contribution, both
to the institution and the library:

> It has been the good fortune of the Michigan State
> Normal College to have as chief of staff in the
> library department a woman of unusual gifts as
> librarian.  With personality, technical training, a
> grasp of the far reaches of her office and at the
> same time a gift for detail, Miss Genevieve M.
> Walton ... has been the directing spirit of the
> college library, has made a notable contribution
> to the life of the campus.... Miss Walton's
> hundreds of friends, on the faculty, among the
> citizens of Ypsilanti and among the alumni of the
> college, congratulate her on her years of unusual
> successful administration. [49]

It seems difficult to perceive that an individual, who
was as knowledgeable and who had as much influence on library development in the state of Michigan as did Genevieve
Walton, should have so little record outside of that state.
As William Warner Bishop commented, "Her work, year
after year, for the Michigan Library Association in planning
and carrying through library institutes, has had results far
beyond those which lie on the surface."[50]  Since Michigan
was noted early for its emphasis on libraries and often
pioneered in areas of library innovation that have become
standards for other states, Walton's commanding role at a
turning point in its library history should not be overlooked.

Genevieve Walton was born June 25, 1857, in the
city, Ypsilanti, in which she lived her entire life and died;
her family is recognized as "one of the pioneer families of
that city."[51]  She attended St. Mary's Academy in South
Bend, Indiana.  Her major interest during those years was
in the study of art, especially painting.

Walton's transition from a young girl interested in
painting and the world of art to that of a dedicated "career"
librarian is not recorded in great detail.  As did Hasse,
Mudge, and Sharp, she rejected the teaching profession per
se and became involved in the emerging field of library work.
Prior to Walton's appointment to the position of librarian at
the normal school, there is no indication that she attended

any special courses or worked in a library, although the
role of "bookman" was clearly hers before the 1890s.  However, in April 1891 William I. Fletcher, then librarian at
Amherst College, offered

> a brief course calculated to give beginners in li-
> brary work or the librarians of small libraries
> who have not been brought in contact with modern
> improved methods, enough instruction in such
> methods to answer their immediate demands. [52]

This "brief course" became a five weeks' program
taught by Fletcher himself; Genevieve Walton attended the
Fletcher program and supplemented that background "through
the meetings and journals of library associations and personal contacts with other librarians.  Problems of book selection, classification and cataloging she met with what
limited tools were available, adapting them to her own
special situation. "[53]

This constituted her preparation; the dramatic results obviously built heavily on personal ability.  Walton was
thirty-four years old at the time of her appointment as librarian; she is judged to have initiated the "modern era" of
the Michigan State Normal College library.  Michigan State
Normal College, founded in 1852, had grown considerably in
the intervening years between its establishment and the Walton appointment.  However, in 1892, the faculty still numbered only 31, with a student enrollment of 1, 002; there were
11, 000 volumes in the library and Walton had one assistant
who worked three hours a day.  When the "new" library
building was opened in 1930, it was a model facility, largely
designed or influenced in its design by Walton.

The college had, in the thirty-eight years of Walton's
tenure, expanded in many ways.  By 1930, the enrollment
had gone above 2, 100, the faculty numbered 200, and there
were 70, 000 volumes in the library.  Walton's staff had enlarged from one part-time helper to eleven staff members
and fifty-eight student assistants.  The library plan reflected
that growth and Genevieve Walton's personal involvement.

As efficient as Walton was in the basic administration
and development of the collection and the facilities, it is
even more important to note her leadership in selecting a
staff that would reflect her own ideas of service.  President
McKenny noted that skill when he commented that "it would

be difficult to suggest in which way the staff could be improved.  Alert, courteous and devoted are terms which
could properly be applied to this group of workers which
Miss Walton has brought together and inspired by her own
sense of obligation. "[54]  That "obligation" was, in the final
assessment, the truly outstanding factor that capsulizes her
impact on the normal library and state library concerns.

   Although Walton was not the prolific contributor to the
library literature that can be seen in the writings of Hasse
and Mudge, she did present a number of papers at both state
and national conferences on topics related to the joy of reading and the "friendly book. "  She was invariably described,
one colleague noted, as "a woman who can discuss books so
that you can hardly wait to read the ones she talks about. "[55]
Her many friends claimed, as did Anne Carroll Moore, that
their friendship was "rooted in love and admiration of good
comradeship in books and good fellowship in human relations. "[56]

   In the end, it is difficult to conclude.  Prophetically,
in 1925, Genevieve Walton gave a commencement address at
the Pratt Library School; it was entitled "The Lost Librarian. "[57]  Although the speech dealt with book lovers and book
loves, its title has a special knell when associated with an
individual of whom it was said, "no one who has met Miss
Walton ever forgot her. "[58]

   The richness of her contributions to the library world
once resounded in the phrases of those who knew of her work
and those who knew her.  "Her professional zeal, breadth of
interest, concern for the training of teachers, positive character and personal charm"[59] were common knowledge.  Her
"fidelity to high ideals, amid discouragements and delays, "[60]
the "intellect [that] demanded and deserved attention, "[61] made
her the woman who stood "head and shoulders above us. "[62]
That Genevieve Walton should become the "lost librarian" of
the 1970s reflects, once again, how little the profession
knows and values its heritage.


Conclusion

There is no real conclusion to a series of biographical pro-
files of influential women librarians.  Each one, in her own
individuality, made special contributions to the field while
all, together, represent only a small sample of those who

might as logically have been included. Yet, Sharp's contribution to education for librarianship in the Midwest and her
concern with collection, organization, and development at the
University of Illinois can only be regarded as significant library factors at the turn of the century. In the case of
Isadore Mudge, there are few who would challenge her place
in the history of reference work, which suggests that what
she did became a model for academic and research libraries
and library schools. Margaret Mann justifiably emerges as
one of the first practitioners of classification and cataloging,
who made the teaching of that difficult field a matter of logic
and method while preserving the creatively challenging role
of the cataloger.

Controversial, dynamic, and innovative, Adelaide
Hasse explored resources and advocated services that went
beyond most contemporary perceptions, while Flora Ludington defended with magnificent strength and clarity the most
valued ideal of the library world, the freedom to read.

Finally, a librarian who has been forgotten or never
known, Genevieve Walton, could reach what the entire profession ultimately strives to achieve: "few that ever had
any contact with her failed to benefit in some way by it."[63]
These were six who "spoke for themselves."

## References

1. Robert B. Downs, "The Role of the Academic Librarian, 1876-1976." College & Research Libraries
   37:491-502 (Nov. 1976).
2. Edward G. Holley, "Librarians, 1876-1976," Library
   Trends 25:183 (July 1976).
3. Stanley McElderry, "Readers and Resources: Public
   Services in Academic and Research Libraries, 1876-
   1976," College & Research Libraries 25:408 (Sept.
   1976).
4. Wayne Stewart Yenawine, "The Influence of Scholars on
   Research Library Development at the University of
   Illinois" (Doctoral dissertation, Univ. of Illinois,
   1955), p. 36.
5. Letter of Melvil Dewey to Francis Simpson, March 21,
   1922 (Sharp Memorial Correspondence, Univ. of
   Illinois Archives).
6. Ibid.
7. McElderry, "Readers and Resources," p. 409.

8.  John Neal Waddell, "Mudge, Isadore Gilbert," in
    Encyclopedia of Library and Information Science (New
    York:   Marcel Dekker, 1976), 18:287.
9.  John Neal Waddell, "The Career of Isadore G. Mudge:
    A Chapter in the History of Reference Librarianship"
    (Doctoral dissertaion, Columbia Univ. , 1973), p. 46.
10. Letter of Katharine Sharp to Lodilla Ambrose, April
    17, 1901 (Sharp Papers, Letterbook 7, p. 113, Univ.
    of Illinois Archives).
11. Univ. of Illinois, Library, Reference Department, An-
    nual Report, 1902-03, p. 16.
12. Isadore Mudge and Minnie E. Sears, A Thackeray Dic-
    tionary:   The Characters and Scenes of the Novels
    and Short Stories Alphabetically Arranged (London:
    Routledge; New York:   Dutton, 1910).
13. W. Dawson Johnston and Isadore G. Mudge, Special
    Collections in Libraries in the United States.   U.S.
    Bureau of Education Bulletin, #23 (Washington, D.C.:
    Govt. Print. Off. , 1912).
14. Alice Bertha Kroeger, Guide to the Study and Use of
    Reference Books:   A Manual for Librarians, Teachers
    and Students (Boston:   American Library Assn. ,
    © 1902).
15. Constance M. Winchell, "Preface," in Guide to Refer-
    ence Books (7th ed.; Chicago:   American Library
    Assn. , 1951), p. v.
16. Isadore G. Mudge, "Reminiscences of Nicholas Murray
    Butler," in Columbia University, Oral History Collec-
    tion, October 15, 1955, quoted in John Neal Waddell,
    "The Career of Isadore G. Mudge," p. 126.
17. Waddell, "Mudge, Isadore Gilbert," p. 288-89.
18. Winchell, "Preface," p. v.
19. William Warner Bishop, "Margaret Mann," Catalogers'
    and Classifiers' Yearbook (Chicago:   American Li-
    brary Assn. , 1938), 7:14.
20. Margaret Mann, Introduction to Cataloging and the
    Classification of Books (Chicago:   American Library
    Assn. , 1930).
21. Donald James Lehnus, "Milestones in Cataloging, 1835-
    1969; An Attempt at an Objective Approach to the
    Growth of a Subject Literature" (Doctoral dissertation,
    Case Western Reserve Univ. , 1973), p. 168.
22. Margaret Mann, "Specialized Cataloging in a One-Year
    Library School," Libraries 34:307 (July 1929).
23. Univ. of Illinois Library, Report of the Head Librarian,
    1897/98, p. 13.
24. Bishop, "Margaret Mann," p. 11-12.

25. Margaret Mann, "What it Means to Catalog," Library
    Notes and News 8:288 (1927).
26. Margaret Mann, "Selective Cataloging in a Public Li-
    brary," quoted in Dorothy R. Shaw, "The Life and
    Work of Margaret Mann" (Master's thesis, Drexel
    Institute of Technology, 1950), p. 10.
27. "Famed for Her Library Knowledge," The San Fran-
    cisco Call, July 9, 1897.
28. Phyllis Dain, The New York Public Library: A History
    of Its Founding and Early Years (New York: The
    New York Public Library, 1972), p. 115.
29. Adelaide Rosalie Hasse, The Compensations of Librar-
    ianship (Privately printed, 1919), p. 3.
30. Adelaide Rosalie Hasse, Index of Economic Material in
    Documents of the States of the United States, Pre-
    pared for the Department of Economics and Sociology
    of the Carnegie Institute of Washington (Washington,
    D. C.: Carnegie Institution of Washington, 1907-22),
    22v.
31. R. R. Bowker, "Women in the Library Profession,"
    Library Journal 45:640 (Aug. 1920).
32. Adelaide Rosalie Hasse, List of Publications of the U. S.
    Department of Agriculture from 1841-1895, U. S. Dept.
    of Agriculture Library Bulletin No. 9 (Washington,
    D. C.: Govt. Print. Off., 1896).
33. Hasse, The Compensations of Librarianship, p. 5.
34. New York (Colony), General Assembly, 1695, House of
    Representatives, A Journal of the House of Represen-
    tatives for His Majestie's Province of New York in
    America. Reproduced in facsimile from the first
    edition printed by William Bradford, 1695, with an
    introductory note by Adelaide R. Hasse (New York:
    Dodd, 1903).
35. Adelaide Rosalie Hasse, United States Government Pub-
    lications, A Handbook for the Cataloger (Boston: Li-
    brary Bureau, 1902-03).
36. Hasse, The Compensations of Librarianship, p. 14.
37. William S. Jenkins, Collecting and Using the Records
    of the States of the United States; Twenty-five Years
    in Retrospection (Chapel Hill, N. C.: Bureau of Pub-
    lic Records, Univ. of North Carolina, 1961).
38. Margaret L. Johnson, "Flora Belle Ludington: A Biog-
    raphy and Bibliography," College & Research Libraries
    25:376 (Sept. 1964).
39. William E. Henry, quoted in John S. Richards, "Uni-
    versity of Washington School of Librarianship: The
    First Fifty Years," Library News Bulletin 28:12 (July-
    Aug. -Sept. 1961).

40.  Richards, "University of Washington School of Librar-
     ianship," p. 12.
41.  Anne C. Edmonds, "Ludington, Flora Belle (1898-
     1967)," in Dictionary of American Library Biography
     (Littleton, Colo.:  Libraries Unlimited, 1978), p. 322.
42.  Johnson, "Flora Belle Ludington," p. 375.
43.  Flora B. Ludington, "Taproot, Trunk and Branches,"
     A. L. A. Bulletin 47:371-72 (Sept. 1953).
44.  Ibid.
45.  Flora B. Ludington, "Hampshire Inter-Library Center,"
     A. L. A. Bulletin 46:10 (Jan. 1952).
46.  Flora B. Ludington, "Our Common Interests and Pur-
     poses," PNLA Quarterly 18:80 (Oct. 1953).
47.  Cynthia S. Cummings, comp., "A Biographical-
     Bibliographical Directory of Women Librarians"
     (Madison:  Library School Women's Group, Univ. of
     Wisconsin, 1976).
48.  Anne Carroll Moore, "From Miss Moore," Michigan
     Library Bulletin 21:75 (March 1930).
49.  Charles McKenny, "The Contribution of the Library to
     the Michigan State Normal College," Michigan Library
     Bulletin 21:66 (March 1930).
50.  William Warner Bishop, "From Mr. Bishop," Michigan
     Library Bulletin 21:73 (March 1930).
51.  "Miss Walton," Michigan Library Bulletin 23:98 (July
     1932).
52.  American Library Association, "Proceedings, 1891,"
     Library Journal 16:88 (Dec. 1891).
53.  Egbert R. Isbell, A History of Eastern Michigan Uni-
     versity:  1849-1965 (Ypsilanti:  Eastern Michigan
     Univ. Press, 1971), p. 298.
54.  McKenny, "The Contribution of the Library," p. 66-67.
55.  Elisabeth Knapp, "From Miss Knapp," Michigan Library
     Bulletin 21:77 (March 1930).
56.  Moore, "From Miss Moore," p. 75.
57.  Genevieve Walton, The Lost Librarian (New York:
     1925).   Also published in the NYPL Bulletin 29:529-39
     (1926).
58.  Katharyne Sleneau, "From Miss Sleneau," Michigan Li-
     brary Bulletin 21:82 (March 1930).
59.  Isbell, A History of Eastern Michigan University,
     p. 297-98.
60.  Bishop, "From Mr. Bishop," p. 73.
61.  Knapp, "From Miss Knapp," p. 77.
62.  Agnes Jewell, "From Miss Jewell," Michigan Library
     Bulletin 21:81 (March 1930).
63.  "Miss Walton," p. 97.

# PUT A PRUSSIAN SPY IN YOUR LIBRARY*

Jack King

Reference librarians like their jobs. Lots of people to talk
to. Lots of action most of the day. A feeling of real service to people.

The only problem is that the reference desk is not a
very effective way of dealing with user information needs.
An example: An undergraduate asked me how to find a 1966
U. S. Supreme Court case as part of a course he was taking.
I sprang into action, found the case, and we discovered the
Supreme Court had sent it back to a lower court. The undergraduate said he just wanted to read the briefs of both sides
in the lower court. Away we went to the Law Library
across the street. We found the case. My client was happy,
thanking me profusely for my brilliance. I was happy.

Twenty-four hours later a student staff member who
was taking the same course told me that the professor had
said it was a 1967 case in the U. S. Supreme Court, and
copies of it were outside the office of the Professor. The
students were to pay particular attention to one justice's
opinion. My reference interview had been splendid. My
search strategy reasonably adequate. My client ecstatic.
The effectiveness of help--worthless!!

There is a widely held opinion in the profession that
half the reference questions asked are answered incorrectly,
an opinion backed by research, such as that conducted at
Hamline University in 1968.

*Reprinted by permission of the author and the American Li-
brary Association from the Fall 1977 issue of RQ, pp. 30-37;
copyright © 1977 by the American Library Association.

If a pocket calculator gave you the answer correctly half the time and incorrectly the other half, you would junk it or demand your money back. Why does an honorable profession like librarianship tolerate such sloppy work?

There are two professional rationales for inadequate reference work.

● There is no better way to operate.

● Maybe your reference service is ineffective half the time; our reference service is a lot better than that. Maybe you should become a cataloger or a library administrator.

But, there is a better way, developed over the past two centuries and in common government use throughout the world.

The methods were originally developed by the Prussian General Staff, refined by the German General Staff in the late nineteenth century, and then used in the United States from around the beginning of the twentieth century as part of a reorganization of the U. S. Army General Staff.

Like the modern Israelis, the Prussians were surrounded by powerful military forces. The necessity for a well-managed army was obvious, and one area the Prussians realized must be improved was their planning of military strategies. The system they developed provided their military decision makers with the information they needed to make the best possible plans and implement them most effectively. As the Americans adapted the system for providing information to decision makers, there are four steps.

1. Develop the essential elements of information.
2. Collect the information.
3. Record, sort, evaluate, and interpret the information.
4. Disseminate the processed information to the user.

The entire process is cyclical. The essential elements of information are continually being modified as the objectives and tasks of the user are modified. The complete process is frequently diagrammed as a circle (figure 1).

The essential elements of information are determined by an interview with the user. In the interview the objec-

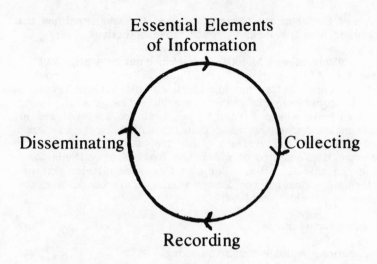

Fig. 1. Process of Providing Information

TABLE 1
Tasks and Essential Elements of Information

| Task | Essential Elements of Information |
| --- | --- |
| 1. Determine price range. | 1. Amount of funds available for purchase. |
| 2. Determine what models of AM-FM receivers are available. | 2. Visited hi-fi dealers to see models of different manufacturers and obtain brochures. |
| 3. Obtain evaluation of each model of receiver. | 3(a). Citation, for each evaluative article about each model receiver. |
| | 3(b). Obtain a copy of each evaluative article. |
| 4. Determine the best receiver in the price range. | 4. Read and compare the evaluatory articles and prices. |
| 5. Purchase the desired receiver. | 5. Know the address of the local dealer. |

tives of the user are determined, and the tasks outlined that the user must perform to reach those objectives.

General von Moltke, Prussian chief of staff, could have the objective of capturing Paris.  To do so he would need to know the terrain his armies would have to cross, so that he could plan his route of march.  The general would want to know where French troops could be deployed and in what strengths, so he could both lay out his route of march and schedule the movement of his troops.  He would have to be sure that supplies of water and food were available for men and animals alike.  Some of the essential elements of information General von Moltke would expect his intelligence office to provide would be:

● Topographic maps.

● Locations suitable for bivouacking.

● Location of French troops.

● Defense plans of the French.

● The speed with which the various military forces could be expected to move.

The intelligence officer on the staff of the general would turn to the "reference librarians," the Second Bureau (also known as "IIIb") of the Prussian General Staff.  The Second Bureau would study maps and atlases, biographies of French military leaders, and French military theory; calculate the speed with which different military units could move; locate the French garrisons; perhaps send spies to steal French defense plans.

An overall information collection plan would be designed by the Second Bureau to provide the essential elements of information.  As the information began to come in, the Second Bureau would evaluate it for the reliability of the source and the accuracy of the information.  When evaluated, the information would be compiled into maps and reports. These "reference tools" would be developed for each task General von Moltke and his staff planned to perform in order to reach the objective, the conquest of Paris.  This information would be arranged as an appendix to each task, so that the military decision makers could easily locate the information they needed to successfully complete each task.

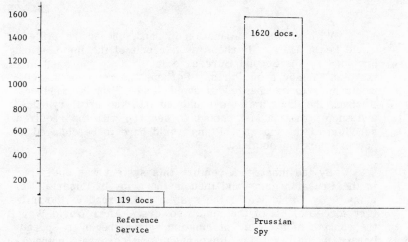

Fig. 2. Documents Identified
in the Hamline Library

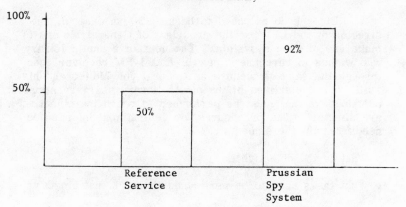

Fig. 3. Percent of Documents Found Useful or
Very Useful by Students

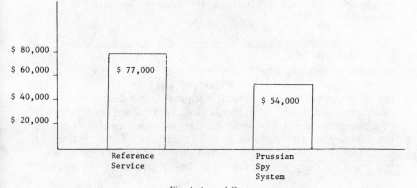

Fig. 4. Annual Cost

With all this information in hand, the entire cycle would begin again. Perhaps as a result of the information provided by the Second Bureau, a major flaw appeared in the plan to march on Paris. Perhaps the route of march would have to be changed to avoid strong French garrisons. Perhaps the draft animals could not pull the artillery guns and supply wagons fast enough to keep up with the required schedule of the march. Plans would have to be changed and new information obtained.

By the nineteenth century this system was operating in the Prussian army and then in the army of Imperial Germany. By World War I the system had spread to the military forces of all of the major powers. After World War II the concept of such an information system began to spread beyond the military into government and corporate management.

But you do not need to be a Prussian general, the director of the CIA, or the president of General Motors to make use of such a system. The user of a public library who wishes to purchase a new hi-fi AM-FM receiver goes through the same procedure as General von Moltke and his staff. The objectives of the public library user are simpler, so the tasks that must be performed to reach the objective are simpler. The procedures for determining information needs remain the same.

● What is the objective?

● What tasks need to be performed to reach that objective?

The hi-fi owner has a clear enough objective: purchase a hi-fi AM-FM receiver. The tasks and the essential elements of information are then determined as outlined in table 1.

With the essential elements of information determined, the collection of information can begin. The user will have to determine what funds are available. While the library could provide information about the various models available, the user wants to see actual equipment and learn what the discounts are from local dealers. With observations of the equipment in mind, as well as prices, the user then visits the library to find independent evaluations of the equipment. Consumers Index is used to find the needed citations, and the local library collection or network provides the needed

articles for the user to read.  The user can then make a
selection, based on the information that has been gathered
from dealers and the library.

The experienced reference librarian may well conclude
that such analysis happens in every reference question.  There
is one fundamental difference.  The system devised by the
Prussian Second Bureau puts the burden of knowing what the
objectives and tasks of the user are on the information system, rather than assuming the user has clearly defined the
objectives and tasks.  The Prussian Second Bureau then de-
vises the essential elements of information the user will
need to complete the tasks and reach the objective.

The reference librarian assumes that the user has
clearly set forth, at least in his or her mind, the objective
he or she is trying to reach and the tasks that must be performed to reach that objective.  The reference librarian also
assumes that the user has determined the essential elements
of information necessary to complete those tasks and reach
the objective.  For the reference librarian, there is only the
job of eliciting the questions from the user that can be answered in the library.  It is up to the user to fit the answers
to the questions into the essential elements of information.
For example:

> User:  Do you have Audio?
> Reference Librarian:   Audio?
> User:   Audio, you know the hi-fi magazine.
> Reference Librarian:  Let me check.  Yes, we have

it.  It's right over there (pointing) on the shelves labelled
"A. "

Now, if the telephone rings, the reference librarian is especially busy, or the reference librarian is lazy, the reference interview is over.  The user is sent off to Audio magazine with an unknown objective and an unknown information
need.

A better reference librarian, or a less busy one,
might be able to extend the reference interview, perhaps by
offering to take the user to the stack area where Audio is
shelved.

> Reference Librarian:  Do you want the latest issue?
> User:  Oh, I don't know.  I just want to browse

through them to see if they have any evaluation of equipment.

Reference Librarian:  Do you know what kind of equipment you're looking for tests on?
User:  Sure.
Reference Librarian:  These magazines usually have an index of some kind, and you can see what equipment they have evaluated.

Better, but not as good as the Prussian Second Bureau would do for its clientele.  The reference librarian knows that the user is looking for equipment evaluations but has no idea what the objective of the user is and why the information is relevant.  Hence the reference librarian only offers assistance on the use of a single magazine, Audio. A more aggressive reference librarian, with available time, might extend the reference interview.

Reference Librarian:  Sometimes one magazine won't evaluate what you're interested in.  If Audio doesn't have it, High Fidelity or Stereo Review might have done an evaluation.
User:  Do you have those?
Reference Librarian:  Sure.  We even have Consumer Index, which indexes all of those magazines.  If you know what equipment you want to see evaluations on, you could look it up there.
User:  I've got a list right here of the equipment I want to read about.
Reference Librarian:  You must be in the market for a hi-fi set.
User:  Just the receiver.  I want to buy a receiver. I've been around to the dealers and looked at what they had. Now I want to see the evaluations.

The reference librarian is now at the same point the Second Bureau would be.  The objective of the user is finally known.

Even the best of reference librarians cannot compete with the efficiency of the Second Bureau of the Prussian General Staff when a bad reference situation arises.  Telephone interruptions, too many users to be handled at the same time, the inability to establish priorities among the users, shy users--all are situations that contribute to the 50 percent failure rate of the reference desk.  To provide more effective information service, the solution for the reference librarian is to apply the techniques of the Second Bureau of the Prussian General Staff to reference service.

● Identify the specific clientele.

- Identify the objectives of that clientele and the tasks they must perform.

- Analyze those tasks to determine the essential elements of information.

- Collect the information.

- Disseminate the information to the user.

What amounts to a prototype for such a method of operation in public or academic libraries is the undergraduate information system of Hamline University. Developed over a period of years with grants from the National Science Foundation, the system now operates as a normal part of the information service for undergraduates. Although the system was designed with the most modern of research and development techniques, it bears a remarkable resemblance to the methods of the Second Bureau of the Prussian General Staff.

The Hamline model serves the undergraduate students and undergraduate faculty. It is based on the theory that the information needs of both faculty and students are centered on the undergraduate courses. The faculty need information to develop and teach the courses. The undergraduate information needs result from taking the courses the professors teach.

Essential elements of information are determined by librarian/information specialists. The information specialist interviews the teacher to learn the objectives of each course. The tasks both teacher and students must perform are determined during this interview. Once that is done, the essential elements of information can be listed for each task.

The needed information comes from a variety of traditional and nontraditional sources. The library collection provides most of the information. The next most important source of information is the library network, again providing books and articles. Some of the information must be processed. This can be simple processing, such as putting the materials needed for intensive classroom use on reserve. More complex processing might be special reports prepared by the information specialists in which they include information gathered from many sources.

The essential elements of information are constantly

being revised as completed tasks are reviewed with the
teacher.    In addition there are a variety of written evaluation forms completed by teachers and students about the information service they have received.    All these activities
provide feedback to the information specialists about the
value of the service being provided.    More detailed and fully
documented descriptions of the system may be found in the
items listed at the end of this article.

This is a modular system, which is capable of supporting all or selected parts of the curriculum.    While the
system is fully implemented at Hamline, it is possible to
provide this service, for example, only to the science
courses.    The rest of the curriculum could be left to traditional reference services.    It is also possible for the library to work only with one or two departments at first,
adapting the basic methods of the "Prussian Spy" to a limited service area.    It would even be possible to serve only
a limited clientele within a department--faculty, undergraduates, or graduate students.    A public library could establish a similar strategy.    Clientele could be selected from
the variety of people served by the public library.    These
could be organizations, like the League of Women Voters,
or they could be school-teachers, senior citizens, those in
small business, or other identifiable groups of clientele.

In addition to being modular, this is also an effective
and economical system.    The following figures give some
indication of the superiority of the Prussian spy system over
the traditional reference service.

Figure 2 (p. 61) shows the number of library documents--
books and periodicals--identified by the reference service
and the Prussian spy for the library users.    The traditional
reference service identified 119 documents in the Hamline
Library for students seeking materials needed to perform
course work during a sample term.    The "Prussian Spy System" identified 1,620 documents in the Hamline Library for
students seeking materials needed to perform course work
during a sample term.    A dramatic, 1,400 percent increase
in the quantity of service provided to the student body.

Evaluation of the service also showed another dramatic increase, after the implementation of the "Prussian Spy
System," in the usefulness of the service.

While 50 percent of the users found documents pro-

vided by the traditional reference service were useful, 92
percent of the users found documents provided by the Prussian spy were useful (figure 3, p. 61).

Not only is the Prussian spy system effective in
serving users, it is less expensive than traditional reference
service. This system costs only 70 percent of the annual
cost of the traditional reference service (fig. 4, p. 61). The
significant decline in cost is due simply to the more effective
employment of the librarians, which the Prussian spy system
makes possible. Fewer librarians can do more and do it
more effectively.

Despite the effectiveness of the Prussian spy system,
librarians are reluctant to adopt it. One problem is that
reference librarians like being reference librarians. They
like the endless variety of reference questions presented at
the reference desk. They like the busy reference desk
world of jangling telephones and impatient clients. They like
the superficiality of the relationship with the client. The
client expects little and is frequently amazed and gratified
when some information is provided, even though the information is frequently irrelevant or incomplete. There is also
the infinite variety of the human race appearing at the reference desk, who never cease to intrigue the reference librarian.

The Prussian spy system limits the variety of clientele coming to any single librarian. Its systematic approach
is less exciting than the anarchy of the reference desk.
Still, there are rewards for the Prussian spy. There is the
reward of seeing a user achieve an objective, with all of the
required information received, at the right time and in a
useful format. There is the reward of working with a
clientele more effectively, as the working habits and methods
of the clientele are better understood.

Library administrators fear that such a system will
be more expensive than the traditional methods of operation.
There are several reasons why this should not be the case.

First, the diversity of clientele information needs may
prove to be considerably less than expected. As a result, a
significantly larger number of clients can be served by a
single professional than originally estimated. At Hamline
University the number of clients who could actually be served
by the system was tripled from the original estimates without an increase in cost.

Second, the training of the personnel required at the
reference desk may be less as the system is developed.
Professional staff members may be increasingly diverted to
the system, replaced at the reference desk by paraprofessionals.   Clients will tend to seek out their information
specialists, rather than going to whoever is at the reference
desk, and gradually the need for professional librarians at
the reference desk will diminish.   At Hamline the reference
desk has completely vanished.

Third, as the system is established, the professional
staff will be able to schedule their time better during the
normal working day, since they can control to a considerable
extent the hours that their clientele will seek them out.
More normal hours permit the professional staff to take on
additional administrative or technical service duties in addition to their service to a specific clientele.

The Hamline experience has seen this more efficient
use of former reference personnel gradually eliminate the
distinction between reference/information specialists, technical service professionals, and library administrators.   The
entire professional staff serves as information specialists
with an assigned clientele, as well as handling the chores of
library administration and technical services.   The transition
was not planned but evolved as the most reasonable way to
operate.   The result is a much better understanding of total
library problems by the entire professional staff, as well as
more professional time devoted to the clientele.

The effectiveness and costs of the system can be
measured relatively easily.   In the Hamline situation, for
example, costs can be measured in the same fashion as in
any library.   In addition to determining the costs of the
program offered by a library, the effectiveness of the programs at Hamline are measured more easily than the conventional reference service can be.   This is because the
Hamline situation assigns a specific clientele to each information specialist.   Feedback from this clientele permits the
information specialists to determine which parts of the information support program are working and which are not.

Two basic programs were used at Hamline.   The first
was a measure based on the effectiveness of the documents
that were delivered to the clientele.   The program measured
the document delivery system in two basic ways:

1.  Time elapsed from the time the document was requested by the user until it was delivered to the user.

2.  Usefulness of the document to the user.

Each document delivered from the networks to which the Hamline Library belongs, a private library network and a state network, was evaluated.

Since turnaround time, the time elapsed from user request for a document until user receipt of a document, is critical to the learning process, this measurement monitored a potential source of system trouble.

The usefulness of the documents delivered was determined by questionnaires attached to each document.  Two basic questionnaires were used.  One was for faculty, and one was for undergraduates.  When the system was first established, each document had a questionnaire attached to it.  Approximately 90 percent of the questionnaires were returned.  This high rate of return was due partially to telephone calls reminding delinquent recipients to return their questionnaires.

Unfortunately the data gathered by the system was to be processed by the computer center of the college.  The computer center was unable to handle the data for more than a few months, and the program to measure effectiveness was suspended.  Only recently have efforts been resumed to revive the program.

The new program of effectiveness measures will be considerably simpler.  The measurement of time elapsed will be confined to measuring the period between the date a document request is received by the library to the date when the document is available to the user from the network. Samples will be used to reduce the amount of data to more manageable proportions.  Questionnaires to measure the usefulness of the document will be issued during sample time periods.  It is further planned to include questionnaires with materials circulated from the library collection as well as material received through the network.

The second basic evaluation of the system is based on the faculty evaluation program.  Modifications of student evaluation forms for teachers have been developed for the

librarian/information specialists. Essentially these forms
attempt to determine the value of professional service to the
students. In addition the librarian/information specialists are
evaluated by their faculty clientele with modified faculty
"peer" evaluation forms. The data from these forms is
compiled in the office of the Liberal Arts College dean and
then considered by the Faculty Personnel Committee. This
committee is responsible for determining the promotion and
tenure of all faculty, including the library faculty. Individual faculty members can also examine their evaluations.

The members of the Second Bureau of the Prussian
General Staff would hardly be surprised at the efficiency of
their system. They designed the system to be efficient and
enable them to survive in the midst of their enemies. They
might be surprised at the wide range of applications their
systematic procedures have had--including libraries. They
might also be surprised at the side benefits of their procedures: The enhancement of professional jobs, because of
the in-depth support for a specific clientele, which enables
the professional to apply a wide range of information support techniques. They might not be surprised to discover
that the clientele of the information specialists liked the system. After all, the Second Bureau was founded to be more
efficient in supplying the information needs of its clientele.

Much as librarians may admire Melvil Dewey and his
organization of library materials, they should consider that
an older and--possibly--more relevant system of information
support sprang from a most unlikely source, the Second Bureau of the Prussian General Staff.


Bibliography

Johnson, Herbert F. , and King, Jack B. "Information Sys-
    tems Management in the Small Liberal Arts College."
    College and Research Libraries 30:483-90 (Nov. 1969).
Johnson, Herbert F.; King, Jack B.; and Mavor, Anne S.
    A Feasibility Study for Establishing an Information
    Switching Center at Hamline University. Submitted
    as annual report under NSF grant GN-786. St. Paul:
    Hamline Univ. , 1970.
King, Jack. "Communication Trends in Modern Library
    Practice." Adult Services 9:4-6 (Fall/Winter 1971).
King, Jack B.; Johnson, Herbert F.; and Mavor, Anne S.
    "What Future, Reference Librarian?" RQ 10:243-7
    (Spring 1971).

Mavor, A. S. , and Vaughan, W. S. , Jr.  Development and
    Implementation of a Curriculum-Based Information
    Support System for Hamline University.  Landover,
    Md. :  Whittenburg, Vaughan Associates, Inc. , 1974.
Schumacher, Anne W.  A Small College Information System:
    An Analysis and Recommendations.  St. Paul:  Ham-
    line Univ. 1968.

# LET'S TALK TURKEY:

## A Librarian Cries Fowl to Libraryese*

David Isaacson

With how many patrons did you interface today? Do you answer reference queries? Are your media instructional? Are your colleagues information personnel? Do you negotiate information transactions? (And when you negotiate them, do you receive inputs and produce outputs?) Is the relationship between you and your patrons an interactive and nonjudgmental learning experience?

When I read expressions like these I often get rather warm under the collar. When I actually hear them spoken, I want to mutter something about "professional duties" calling me elsewhere and beat a hasty retreat from what might be an embarrassing scene. Expressions like these cause this ordinarily temperate fellow to draw--for his dictionary.

My label for such language is libraryese. Libraryese is a hybrid, a bastardized jargon loosely compounded from some very questionable, though by no means casual, liaisons. Its parents are social science-ese and officialese. Libraryese has at least one rather dismal sibling, educationese, and one fairly new kissing cousin, computerese. These are the members of the immediate family. The clan to which the family belongs is gobbledygook. Other members of the clan include special "dialects" that have less excuse for unintelligibility, such as the jargon of literary and art criticism. Librarians are by no means the only people who confuse simplicity and simplemindedness.

*Reprinted by permission of the author and publisher from the September 1978 issue of Wilson Library Bulletin, pp. 64-70. Copyright © 1978 by The H. W. Wilson Co.

I object to libraryese not merely because it grates
on my ears.   That would be to raise an aesthetic, and perhaps only a subjective, issue.   My objection is not merely
a matter of personal taste or opinion.   It is a matter of
judgment.   Habitual users of libraryese defeat the primary
purpose of language:   They may express themselves, but
they do not communicate clearly with others.   A number of
writers have exhorted librarians not to use jargon,[1] but just
what this jargon is has yet to be determined.   In this article
I will speculate on the causes of gobbledygook in general and
libraryese in particular.   I hope this discussion will help
distinguish between useless libraryese and useful library
jargon, as well as help us to communicate more clearly
among ourselves and with our patrons.

## Talking turkeys

The term gobbledygook was coined by Maury Maverick, the
late Representative from Texas, in an article published over
30 years ago.[2]   Maverick was true to his name.   Although
a government official, he mocked officialese.   He defined
gobbledygook as

> talk or writing which is long, pompous, vague,
> involved, usually with Latinized words.   It is also
> talk or writing which is merely long, even though
> the words are fairly simple, with repetition over
> and over again, all of which could have been said
> in a few words.[3]

Maverick cried "fowl" to bureaucratese by likening it
to the sounds made by turkeys.   He said the word gobbledygook had an uncertain origin:

> People asked me how I got the word.   I do not
> know.   It must have come in a vision.   Perhaps
> I was thinking of the old bearded turkey gobbler
> back in Texas who was always gobbledygobbling and
> strutting with ridiculous pomposity.   At the end of
> the gobble there was a sort of gook.[4]

(I don't think Maverick meant any disrespect to turkeys.   It might be objected that the phrase "let's talk turkey"
means just the opposite of gobbledygook.   Yet the vagaries of
American slang are such that saying "he's a turkey" seems
to be in keeping with Maverick's definition.   At any rate
gobbledygook is one kind of turkey talk we can do without. )

Another early, and more famous, critic of bureaucratic prose was George Orwell. In his essay "Politics and the English Language," Orwell discusses a number of examples, each of which is characterized by one or more of the faults he identifies as stale imagery, verbal false limbs, pretentious diction, and meaningless words.[5] Orwell's indictment is broader than Maverick's; he does not describe these offenses as an aberration from standard English--he simply calls such language "modern English."

Later, in his novel 1984, Orwell created Newspeak, a particularly inflexible language that, by eliminating intellectual and moral nuances, makes it easier for the state to control the minds of the populace. The entire category of bad or evil things has vanished: Actions or thoughts are simply good or "ungood." Newspeak is not far removed from the language of Watergate, which made it convenient for the culprits to abrogate moral responsibility by calling their previous false statements "inoperative."

Orwell proposes a translation of a famous passage from Ecclesiastes as an example of modern English. The original is:

> I returned and saw under the sun, that the race is
> not to the swift, nor the battle to the strong,
> neither yet bread to the wise, nor yet riches to
> men of understanding, nor yet favour to men of
> skill; but time and chance happeneth to them all.

And the translation:

> Objective consideration of contemporary phenomena
> compels the conclusion that success or failure in
> competitive activities exhibits no tendency to be
> commensurate with innate capacity, but that a con-
> siderable element of the unpredictable must be
> taken into account.[6]

As Orwell points out, this parody robs the original of all of its concrete words, replacing them with vague and abstract ones. The original is shorter, uses simpler words, and is also immediate and personal, but the translation hides behind the passive voice and a seemingly objective but really objectionable and unnecessarily impersonal tone. In short, the original has life, while the translation is moribund, if not already dead.

Crying Fowler

A more recent critic of these and other language abuses is
Edwin Newman, who has satirized various forms of gobbledygook in two popular books, Strictly Speaking and A Civil
Tongue. [7] With these books and numerous television com-
mentaries, Newman has done much to publicize the problem,
but he does not always distinguish clearly among grammatical
errors, current language fads, inelegancies of style, and
various forms of intentional and unintentional distortion.

I do not mean to suggest that libraryese is always as
inflexible as Newspeak, as unintelligible as gobbledygook or
"modern English," or as reprehensible as Watergate-ese.
But it is related to these metalanguages.  In my attempt to
define libraryese, I have found H. W. Fowler's A Dictionary
of Modern English Usage to be as helpful as Maverick, Orwell, or Newman.  Fowler does not have an entry on gobbledygook, but he makes a cross-reference from it to jargon.  He
defines jargon as "talk that is considered both ugly-sounding
and hard to understand" and then distinguishes three senses
of the term:  1) "the sectional vocabulary of a science, art,
class, sect, trade, or profession"; 2) "hybrid speech of different languages"; and 3) "the use of long words, circumlocution, and other clumsiness."[8]  I agree with Fowler that it
is a pity that the meaning of jargon has not been confined to
the nonpejorative first sense of the word.  Frequently, because the term is used only pejoratively, the neutral first
sense of the term is lost. [9]

Libraryese is a form of unnecessary jargon.  It is
crucial that we distinguish between our quite legitimate special vocabulary and the illegitimate, or at least questionable,
locutions we have borrowed from other sources or coined for
ourselves.  It is these unnecessary terms--and more importantly the mentality often associated with their use--that I
call libraryese.  I propose the following definition:  Any language used by a librarian or information scientist that is
characterized by one or more of the following faults:  inappropriate or unnecessary use of abstraction, euphemism, redundancy, circumlocution, or the passive voice, and unnecessarily complicated or pretentious diction and syntax.  In its
most innocuous forms, libraryese causes temporary confusion;
in its more harmful varieties, it distorts meaning.  It is
annoying in speech, but often distressing in writing.

I object to libraryese because I prefer clarity to cant.

I do not propose a snobbish, or even an elitist, code of language etiquette to replace libraryese. A library language academy might do more harm than good. I <u>might</u> feel inclined to bristle, as Edwin Newman and other language purists do, when people misuse a word like "hopefully," forget to cross their <u>T</u>'s, or otherwise mind their language <u>P</u>'s and Q's. But solecisms are minor errors compared to the harm done by libraryese. (I am not talking about the lovably ignorant or careless language abusers like Mrs. Malaprop or Mr. Micawber, whether they appear in a novel, in a library, or in library literature. It is not necessary to take a narrowly prescriptive view of language to be opposed to libraryese.)

## Scientism is the mother of libraryese

Libraryese is usually grammatically correct. Grammar is not the issue. Good sense is. I do not object to "interface" or "input" when the context is appropriate. Taken by themselves, no one of the characteristics of libraryese is particularly offensive. But the habitual use of this sort of language is disturbing because it requires unnecessary effort to understand it.

The major cause of libraryese is scientism: the misunderstanding or misapplication of the goals and methods of genuine science. Libraryese frequently occurs as a result of confusion about the precise meanings of words we have borrowed from one of the social sciences. And the confusion is compounded when the originators of these terms use them too loosely in the first place.

Every profession needs a special vocabulary to say things for which ordinary language is insufficiently precise. "Catalog," "index," "bibliography," and other words we use every day are legitimate and necessary jargon. If we disagree about their meanings, it is because these words are important enough to have more than one meaning or complex enough to make precision difficult to achieve. We would not agree any more than anthropologists would agree that a culture is simply or only a set of characteristics shared by a group of people in society.

## Ask a stupid query ...

Libraryese often is born of the confusion between the complex

meanings of legitimate jargon and the pseudocomplex meanings of illegitimate jargon. For instance, it may be acceptable for an information scientist (or information specialist?)
to "query" a retrieval system. It may be true that "query,"
in the language of information storage and retrieval, has a
specific meaning for which "question" is an inadequate synonym. But I am talking libraryese if I insist on calling a
question about the use of the card catalog "a reference
query." This word may dress up the "transaction," but it
calls unnecessary attention to itself.

Nor do I think it increases my status if I say I have
"positively responded to patrons' information needs" instead
of answered their questions. And while it may make some
sense to refer to a person concerned with the analysis of
how information is transmitted between source and a user as
an "information specialist,"[10] this term does not accurately
convey the variety of responsibilities of a reference librarian.

I am not arguing against the use of new words when
they identify new things or ideas. Calling a computer an
electronic data processor is not usually libraryese, since
that is sometimes a more correct description of what this
machine does than to say it computes. But I do prefer to
exchange ideas with people rather than to receive "input"
from them. Is it unreasonable to assume that input gets
put into data bases but that people do not "input" one
another?

## Who appropriates my jargon, appropriates trash

Librarians have learned many useful things from the fields
of education and psychology, but we have also appropriated
some of their unnecessary jargon or misappropriated some
of their necessary jargon. Some librarians, as well as
teachers and "educationists," no longer give assignments:
They create "learning experiences." But unless we are unconscious, everything we do counts as experience, and almost any experience, if we attend to it, can teach us something. Perhaps this phrase originated about the same time
teachers (and some librarians) became known as "facilitators."
It might be regarded as repressively old-fashioned, I assume, for a teacher to give assignments; presumably, a
facilitator "facilitates" a "nonthreatening learning experience."

It might sound even more impressive if the student
had a "supportive" or an "interactive" learning experience.
With the addition of words like these and similar ones borrowed from psychology--such as "authentic encounters" and
"self-actualizing"--"psychobabble" becomes mixed with
educationese. [12]  The intention behind these terms is usually
laudable, but the effect is often verbal mush.


## The discriminating palate

In an effort to avoid the presumed illiberal taint of the word
"judgment," some psychologists, educators, and librarians
have adopted the unfortunate term "nonjudgmental." Apparently, the word "judgmental" might be associated with a
word like "discrimination." "Discrimination" has been so
often used as a synonym for "prejudice" that it is beginning
to lose its original meaning--the capacity to distinguish or
differentiate.  Hardly anyone today uses "disinterested" in
the sense of impartial; are we also to lose "discriminating"
and "judgmental"?  Perhaps they will simply become "ungood."  If we begin to be afraid of using a word like "judgment," we may begin to lose faith in the quality for which
the word stands.  Very ironically and sadly, the erosion of
our language--of which the use of "nonjudgmental" is a symp-
tom--seems to be taking place just when there is a pervasive
social acceptance of the need not to be discriminatory.

The following paragraph was part of a statement prepared two years ago by the Standards Committee of the Reference and Adult Services Division of the American Library
Association:

> The librarian/information specialist must be the
> intermediary or the negotiator for unlocking these
> multifarious information resources.  This responsi-
> bility places the concept of good service on the
> ability of the librarian/information specialist to be
> an effective facilitator in this transaction.  In all
> transactions the librarian/information specialist
> must be impartial and nonjudgmental. [13]

In this paragraph "intermediary," "negotiator," "multifarious,"
"facilitator," and "transaction" might be regarded as at best
over-formal; "places the concept of good service on the
ability," as syntactically awkward; and "nonjudgmental" as
redundant with "impartial." But if the term "judgmental" is

taken to mean exactly what it says, the committee is assert-
ing that reference librarians should relinquish one of their
fundamental professional responsibilities:   the making of
judgments.   Of course, they do not mean that; they mean
that a librarian ought not to make arbitrary or partial judgments.   However unintentionally, the effect of such a term
to one not familiar with libraryese is the direct opposite of
what is meant.

I do not mean to slight the hard work or good intentions of this committee.   I do not mean to find special fault
with any particular group or librarian.   None of us is innocent of libraryese.   Such language is endemic not only in
"learning resource centers," but throughout our society.   It
may be too late to do much to correct or alleviate it.   But
as Ruth Warncke said nearly ten years ago, librarians may
have a special responsibility to put up a fight:

> Librarianship is supposedly a career for people
> who care about ideas and information and the forms
> in which they are expressed.   Its practitioners can
> convey this concept of their identity best by the
> care and respect with which they use words--in
> spite of everything, the principal currency of com-
> munication still. [14]

## Subprofessional who?

Sometimes legitimate jargon can be confusing.   But this is
an unavoidable, typical semantic problem, not a problem of
libraryese.   We do not have to change the name of the circulation desk to "checkout counter" just because we can expect some patrons not to understand the conventional name.
However, we ought to avoid saying to a patron, "You have
an incorrect citation there; it requires bibliographic verification."   Many people would not understand such a mouthful.
In this case the error is not libraryese; it is fussy overcor-
rectness.   The librarian would have been speaking libraryese
(and adding insult to injury) had she or he gone on to say,
"Effect that verification process, and the matter will be processed by one of our subprofessional personnel."

Libraryese exists whenever we use words to confer a
false importance to something that would, ironically, have
more dignity and clarity if expressed more simply.   "Interface" is a useful term for describing a common boundary be-

tween adjacent regions or as a metaphor for the overlapping
of concepts or functions, but it is a pompous substitute for
the "relationship" between a librarian and a patron.   We
may use interface in this context in the mistaken belief that
it is a more "scientific" term, but the misuse of the word
only creates a pseudoscientific effect.

## Towering Babel

We have come to trust--we have to trust--the expertise of
many specialists.   It is natural for each profession to create
its own jargon.   Crossbreeding of jargon between professions
may also be natural.   It is sometimes difficult to distinguish
hocus-pocus from reliable knowledge, or pseudoscience from
genuine science.   But we can try.   I am not arguing that
our writing, let alone our speech, ought always to be polished
or studied--just clear.

Of course, because librarians work in so many different types of institutions and in so many different jobs, it
is sometimes difficult for us to understand one another.    But
we don't have to build another Tower of Babel.   Librarians
have to learn computer jargon, but we should not be required to "disambiguate" rather than "clear up" our search
strategies.   Unless experiments are actually conducted in
the room, there is no reason to call libraries "learning
laboratories."   I will continue to use a telephone rather than
a "remote interactive device."   Classrooms may serve their
purpose as well as, if not better than, "learning modules."
I will continue to use books and other forms of information
and knowledge, not "knowledge objects," or "knowledge-
bearing artifacts."   "Media" are plural.

Advice to readers may be just as effective as "assistance in independent learning."   A conversation with a colleague from another discipline does not have to be called a
"crosscampus consultantship."   I refuse to provide "career
awareness" until I discover what career wants to be aware
of itself.   I do not have--and may never have--a "shelving
rationale."   Given a choice, I would rather admit to a prejudice than an "attitudinal barrier."   I would rather be friendly
than "receptive to a patron-initiated request."   And until it
is established that the latest fashion in psychotherapy is the
New Dispensation, I will not have "authentic encounters" with
patrons, but I will try to put them at their ease.   I will not
encourage patrons to have "library experiences" if I simply

want them to visit the library. I would rather see libraries
work together effectively than "explore the viability of compatible networking. "

I would much rather talk and write English than libraryese, or any other form of gobbledygook.


References

1.  Among the most useful of these commentators are: D.
    Philip Baker. "The Name of the Game," Wilson Li-
    brary Bulletin, 51 (December 1977), p. 308-09; Ronn
    Fink. "Who's Circulating 'Round the Reference Desk's
    Vertical File?," Wilson Library Bulletin, 45 (Novem-
    ber 1970), p. 308-09; Haynes McMullen. "Winning
    Words for Library Writers," Journal of Academic Li-
    brarianship, 4 (March 1978), p. 12-13; Ruth Warncke.
    "War on Words," Library Journal, 94 (July 1969),
    p. 2575; Raymund F. Wood. "Do We Need a New
    Terminology for Librarianship?," California Librari-
    an, 29 (October 1968), p. 274-78.
2.  Maury Maverick. "The Case Against 'Gobbledygook,'"
    New York Times Magazine, May 21, 1944, p. 11.
3.  Ibid.
4.  Ibid.
5.  George Orwell. "Politics and the English Language,"
    in A Collection of Essays, New York, Doubleday,
    1954, p. 162-77.
6.  Ibid. , p. 169.
7.  Edwin Newman. Strictly Speaking: Will America Be
    the Death of English? Indianapolis, Bobbs-Merrill,
    1974; and A Civil Tongue, Indianapolis, Bobbs-Merrill,
    1976.
8.  Henry Watson Fowler. A Dictionary of Modern English
    Usage. New York, Oxford University Press, 1965,
    p. 315.
9.  Ibid. , p. 315-16.
10. B. L. Kenney. "In the Land of Jargonese: A Key to
    Understanding," Reference Quarterly, 5 (Summer
    1966), p. 11. This article, unlike those cited in my
    first reference, does not exhort librarians against
    jargon; Kenney defines some key terms in information
    science that traditional reference librarians may have
    trouble understanding.
11. Fink, op. cit. , p. 309.

12. Richard Dean Rosen.   Psychobabble.   New York,
      Atheneum,  1977.
13. Standards Committee, Reference and Adult Services
      Division,  ALA.   "A Commitment to Information
      Services," Library Journal,  101 (April 15,  1976),
      p.  973.
14. Warncke, op. cit. , p.  2575.

# RATIONED LIKE RICE--

## Information Service in the People's Republic of China*

Karl Lo

January 12, 1977--it was our first day in China. The sun
was bright. The air was cold. The street was icy. Thirty
minutes after we checked into the Peking Hotel, Professor
Robert Kapp, Professor Matsuo Tsukada and I walked across
the Wang-fu-ching Street into the Hsin Hua Bookstore. The
bookstore was very cold. We were reading the floor plan
in the lobby when I heard some rustling behind us. I turned
around and found we were surrounded by some 20 youngsters,
all in blue jackets and hats. As we turned around they
closed in on us to read our bilingual name tags, and then
they said to each other, "From the University of Washington
of the United States." I said, "hello" in Chinese, and asked
them who they were. Two or three of them said they were
high school students. The others silently examined us from
head to toe. I asked them what they were doing in the bookstore and they replied they had come in to look at the books.
One of them asked me what city I was from and if I was an
overseas Chinese returning to Peking. I told them I was
born in China but had never been to Peking before. Professor Kapp joined in the small talk. We paused often to think
of new topics, only to have each topic concluded with brief
answers. After a brief exchange, the group dispersed. As
we walked through the store two or three of them followed
at a distance. Many followed us with their eyes. To people
not accustomed to Chinese manners these youngsters could
be considered cold. To me they acted very properly, in a
Chinese manner I used to know. They were curious, yet
hesitant to intrude; they were friendly and sincere, yet quiet.

---

*Reprinted by permission of the author and publisher from
the Fall 1977 issue of PNLA Quarterly, pp. 4-8, 20.

At that moment the youngsters were curious about our purpose in visiting the bookstore; we were equally puzzled about
their purposes.   In reflection I think they were coming to
the best library that was available to them.   To make my
point let me now describe the store and then compare it
with other libraries that I saw.

The bookstore was a three-story brick building of
spartan design.   The lower two floors were the retail departments.   Each floor was a huge rectangle with counters
along the walls and two islands of counters in the middle.
Most of the books were displayed in glass-topped counters,
or behind them with relaxed but attentive clerks stationed
liberally in each section.   The store was lighted by fluores-
cent lamps hanging down from the ceiling.   The intensity
was dim, probably about fifteen candlefeet.   Reading in the
store was a straining experience, partly because of the contrasting bright winter light outside coming through the windows above the shelving.

There was a variety of subjects in the store, but the
choice of titles within each subject was few.   I walked by
all the counters and purchased several items, two or three
of which are very difficult but possible to obtain outside of
China.   The rest of the books I saw, however, were mostly
elementary books on various subjects, and many editions of
Chairman Mao's works.

The most interesting features of the bookstore were
on the second floor.   There was one counter marked "rental
department" from which books were rented for about half a
U. S. cent per day per volume.   A deposit was also required.
The rental stock was comprised of a good and varied selection of titles published in the last few years, and included
Chinese classical studies, fiction, writings of Chairman Mao,
and a sampling of other subjects.   After scrutinizing the
rental books I found the selection far better than books
available for over-the-counter sales.   Out of curiosity I
asked a clerk why there were so many books available for
rental but not for sale in the same bookstore.   The young
woman told me that most of the books go out of stock soon
after they are published, thus leaving only the rental stock
available.

Another interesting feature was the reading department, across from the rental department.   It was a small
alcove with books on shelves and some wooden benches in

front of the shelves.  Under the dim lights two or three
dozen young people crowded together on the benches, reading
intensely.  I did not look over their shoulders to identify the
books they were reading, but judging from the books I could
see on the shelves, the selections seemed more or less the
same as the rental department.  We stood and watched the
routine checking in and out of books with curiosity while we
were ourselves objects of curious observation by the customers and clerks of the store.

     During my eighteen-day stay in China I visited five
more Hsin Hua Bookstore branches in Peking, Shanghai,
Wuhan, and Sian.  I also visited a number of the Foreign
Language Bookstores and Chung Kuo Bookstores.  These are
the only three chains of bookstores in China, and they sell
the same type of merchandise in each chain.  The Hsin Hua
Bookstore on Wang-fu-ching Street was the biggest store of
all.  All the Hsin Hua Bookstores I visited were quite crowded, and without exception every time I walked into one of
them I was surrounded by curious onlookers.  People were
generally friendly, showing a great degree of curiosity, but
they were not very talkative and rarely would start a conversation.

     The Foreign Language Bookstore, in spite of the
name, does not sell books from foreign countries.  It sells
books published by the Foreign Language Press, which includes many foreign language editions of the works of Chairman Mao, and some translations of currently available
Chinese novels.  There were far fewer patrons in the Foreign Language Bookstore than in the Hsin Hua Bookstores.

     The third chain, Chung Kuo Bookstore, sells old and
used publications.  Most of the books I found were printed
in the early 20th century and were of much earlier writings.
A few translations of Russian and English technical books
were found in some of the stores and at least in Peking there
was quite a good selection of works by Confucians.  They
were sold under a sign saying that they were for reference
use to criticize Lin Piao and Confucians.  There were only
a few patrons in the Chung Kuo Bookstores I visited in
Peking and Shanghai.

     Book prices in China are very reasonable compared
to other countries.  An average price of a new issue of a
magazine is about 8¢ per copy.  The People's Daily was
selling for 75¢ per month.  Chairman Mao's poems, pub-

lished in 107 pages, can be obtained for 20¢.  An eight-
volume paperback set of the Chin dynastic history was selling for $4.40 per set.  As I was told by the guides, the
price of books is somewhat high for the young, inexperienced
workers whose monthly salary is about US $30.00 but it is
still within reach of the working class to buy a few books.

        During this trip I did not have an opportunity to see
any small public or school libraries.  Although I asked at
every commune, street committee and school that I visited
to see their libraries, my request was always rejected by
the host.  At one place I was told that the library was dam-
aged by the earthquake and was under repair; and at another
I was told that it was so far away that it was not worth the
walk because of the tight schedule.  At other places I was
told that the library was so small the time might be better
spent visiting other facilities.  I can fully understand some
of the circumstances that made it inconvenient to visit their
libraries, but I couldn't help but feel that people were reluctant to show foreign visitors their libraries, mainly because the libraries were small.

        We visited four of the largest libraries in China.
The biggest is the National Peking Library, which has some
nine million volumes.  The Shanghai Library has 6.5 million
volumes, the Peking University Library has 3 million volumes serving 6,000 students, and the Wuhan University Library has 1.2 million volumes serving 2,000 students.  By
any standard these are good sized libraries for their purposes.  Not only are their Chinese language collections good,
but also they reportedly have very good foreign language collections.  For example, the University of Peking Library has
800,000 volumes of foreign language materials in the stacks.
During my brief visits to their reading rooms and stacks I
was impressed by the quality of the books I saw.  There
were current publications from all areas of the world, and
many were not ideologically agreeable to the Chinese political ideal.  The collections of rare books in the Chinese language in all these libraries are overwhelming in quality.

        We might not have visited these libraries at their
peak service hour.  None of them were very crowded and
the traffic at the doors was very light.  At the Shanghai Library a librarian told me that 3,000 patrons attend their
weekly study sessions on Marxism and Mao thought but at
the time we were visiting there weren't very many people in
the Marxism and Mao Thought Reading Room.  It had about
104 chairs, and there were only 12 people in the room.

After the visit to our first library, the Peking University Library, Professor Kapp asked me what my impression was about the Library. With no hesitation, I replied they have an excellent library and the users of this library are lucky users indeed. Professor Kapp challenged me by saying how could I make such a conclusion after only a casual, hour-long tour walking quickly through the library building and seeing only a few of their reading rooms and reference rooms. I said that I make my conclusions based on two observations, and a number of deductions. My first observation is that in the reading room they have a broad current selection of journals from foreign countries including that of the United States and Japan. My second observation was based on the traffic in front of the reference and circulation desks. The traffic was generally light in all areas and there was no waiting line evident to me. One of the reference circulations files I saw was very small with a student identification card attached to each loan slip. My deductions were that the broad selections indicated a generous book budget and the up-to-date publications indicated an efficient acquisitions plan. The light traffic in front of the desk and the relatively small circulation file that I saw indicated each user can have generous attention from the librarian. When the library has a large book budget, an efficient acquisitions plan, and generous librarian assistance to give to the users it is a very good library for their purpose indeed. I have no question in my mind that users of those four libraries that we visited were among the most fortunate library users in the world. However, I was most curious as to what kind of library service was available to the youngsters, the youngsters like those we met in the Peking Hsin Hua Bookstore, who may not make use of these excellent libraries.

How much does a Chinese high school student read outside of his class assignments? It is an interesting question for which I do not have a definitive answer. When we visited a high school in Wuhan we did not see the library, but we saw the dormitories. Inside the brick-wooden buildings there were bedrooms with six beds per room. There were two desks in front of a window, but there were no books in sight in any of the rooms we visited. For that matter, there was not much clothing in the barely furnished rooms either. What we saw was neatly arranged beddings, wash basins, toothbrushes, towels; but no books. The teacher who showed us the dormitory told us that the students were doing their work in the classrooms and therefore there was

no need to bring back books to the dormitory.  This was indeed a rather shocking experience for an American to see no
books in a dormitory.  But taking the suggestion of the
guides to compare today's China with the China of the past,
rather than with highly industrialized capitalistic countries,
I remember that in my high school days in Macao (a Portu-
guese colony at the mouth of the Pearl River near Canton)
we had few books displayed in our dormitory room, and that
was the best high school in Macao.  I also remember that
much of my reading was rented from the book stalls or borrowed from the library, one at a time.  The dormitory I
saw in Wuhan was not a shocking comparison; there were
many similarities.  But then, I can't say that my Macao experience was ideal.

Besides the crowded Hsin Hua Bookstores and the
sparingly used libraries there were other reading facilities
for the Chinese.  There were the big character posters on
the streets, the People's Daily and other newspapers displayed in windows and glass cupboards on the street, and
some small book stalls at street corners.  People congre-
gated in these areas to read.  However, in my eighteen days
in China I encountered only three people actually holding
newspapers in their hands and reading in public.  Two were
taxi drivers waiting for their customers in Peking, and one
was reading a newspaper on a crowded Canton city bus.  One
of our guides responded to the question of why there were so
few Chinese reading newspapers.  His answer was that since
most of the news can be obtained through the radio and the
papers posted on the street, there is relatively little need
for people to have personal copies.  I agree with that explanation.  It is quite possible in China to get as much news
from the radio as from the newspaper.  Some families have
a radio which may make the cost of a newspaper subscription unattractive.  The monthly cost of U. S. $0. 75 is about
2. 5% of a young worker's salary, or 10% of his food, or 25%
of his rent.

The immediate reaction of most Americans would be
that the media in China is controlled for ideological purposes; thus there is little to read or listen to.  This argument may have some validity but I would not say the Chinese
government wants to suppress all information in order to
present only that which is desirable to their viewpoint.  It
is true the quality of bookstores was uniform, and we did
not find any foreign publications outside of the four libraries
that we visited; and the newspapers did not contain, as a

rule, foreign news agency releases.  It may also be true
that there were few books available in public or school libraries which we did not see.  The radio repeats news all
day long and television has little to report.  But at least on
one occasion, in Wuhan, I heard radio broadcasts from Taiwan.  After a lunch we were relaxing in the sitting room of
the restaurant overlooking the East Lake.  There was a table
radio sitting in the corner.  I walked over to it, turned it
on to the shortwave band, and moved the dial from one end
to the other.  I heard a station identified as one from Taiwan at news broadcast time.  I motioned to one of the guides
to join me and listen to the news broadcast, which came in
loud and clear, as much as a shortwave broadcast can be.
After a minute or so I asked the guide if he could receive
radio broadcasts from Taiwan.  The guide looked at me with
a smile and said, "We can do it all the time but nobody does
it.  It is full of undesirable things."  I pushed a little further and asked him, "What do you think of this news broadcast?"  He listened and said, "People in Taiwan speak with
no feeling at all."  I couldn't help but break into laughter
for he commented on style rather than content.  My point is
that at least once I heard a radio broadcast from  sources
other than the New China News Agency.  By the clear quality
of the broadcast I assume that anyone with a shortwave radio
could listen to that broadcast.

     We rarely saw television sets except those sets that
were displayed in the department stores, with prices comparable to those in the United States, I saw no customers
around the display counters, but there were usually several
customers buying at the radio counters.  I spent one evening
in Peking watching television.  There were two channels in
Peking; one in color, the other black and white.  I shared
the television room on my hotel floor with ten teenagers,
most of them hotel workers.  A couple seemed to be there
as invited guests.  The movie, a color film titled "Red
Militia on the Hung Lake" concluded about 9:30 p. m. which
was followed by news.  There were only two items reported.
One was that an African delegation was visiting Peking; the
other that David Rockefeller was also visiting Peking.  There
were no pictures of the announcer; his voice was in the background.  The news was quickly concluded in a minute or so,
and then the color channel went off the air for the evening.
Somebody switched on the black and white channel; it was a
recital of poems to glorify the revolution.  At that time the
television was turned off and everyone stood up and left the
room.

In order to explain why there is such limited information available to the mass of Chinese people, I would speculate that economy is one of the reasons.  If censorship was
strictly applied, the Taiwan broadcast could have been easily
jammed and shortwave radios would not be displayed in department stores.  China is still a poor country; the government admits it, and the guides who accompanied us reiterated
the point several times.  Not only are books in short supply,
but almost all industrial and agricultural goods are in short
supply.  I believe that China cannot afford to publish and
circulate a newspaper comparable to the New York Times in
its diversity, size and circulation figures.  This is economically impractical in terms of the priorities of the country.
When the quantity of media is limited by the economy, they
obviously must decide what to disseminate.  Without any
doubt the political thoughts of Chairman Mao come high in
priority.

It is within the letter of the constitution of China that
the media is to serve the revolution.  One can go on and
argue whether the media in China is controlled by the government and whether any unfavorable information is suppressed
by the government, but I'd rather leave the argument for
another occasion.  I would now compare it to the rationing
of rice in China.  Rice is rationed to individuals according
to their age and occupation.  For example, the laborer is
rationed more rice than the office worker.  According to my
guides there is enough rice for everybody; in fact, the ra-
tions are generous and more than enough for people.  They
told me the reason for rationing is only to prevent hoarding.
True enough.  Rice has such a great psychological impact on
the Chinese mind that even in a free port like Hong Kong its
quantity in reserve and the price are tightly manipulated by
the British government.  At the time of our visit, and in the
cities that we visited, there was no rationing of meat.  Evi-
dently there was enough meat to go around at that time in
those places; however, the guide admitted that there were
times when meat was rationed.  Information, then, is also
rationed according to the need of individuals and the ability
of the country to provide.  Researchers who have access to
the big libraries that we visited enjoy excellent quality of information with the assumption that they need them.  But for
most people on the street their information needs are assumed to be very limited; thus the supply is limited.  Thus
my impression of the Chinese library service is that besides
the large research libraries, which were lightly used, there
are no libraries that the Chinese people are proud to show

off. The best, most convenient library is most likely the neighborhood Hsin Hua Bookstore where people can buy, rent or borrow books. This is supplemented by the radio. By and large an average Chinese has a very small amount of information available to him through the mass media.

Would China have more information available to her people when the country becomes economically wealthier? During our many rides on the touring buses I had occasion to sit with the guides and we had conversations on many topics. On one occasion we were talking about reading and the information available to the people. The guide asked me what my evaluation as a librarian was. I told him quite frankly that if I return someday to find an even more progressive China, evidence of this would be more information available to the people. When there is a larger quantity and a bigger variety of information made available, I will take it as a sign that China has grown stronger economically, and can afford to allocate more resources for information. In order to prepare the Chinese youth to accept the responsibility of the country in the future, I believe that they need more information to prepare them. Not only do they need essential information like that in the People's Daily, but they also need information from foreign countries. My guides agreed with me and said the situation worsened during the dominance of the Gang of Four. Now that the Gang of Four has been dealt with, the country, under the leadership of Chairman Hua, will advance in all directions and the people will be able to read more. In the meantime, I expect that information will continue to be rationed.

Because of the limited information available the average Chinese knows little about the United States. I feel sorry about that. I feel even sorrier though for the average American. How much does the average American know about China, even though we spend a good amount for a newspaper subscription, fees for book clubs, taxes for public libraries, costs for radio and television, and a lot more. Facing an abundant amount of information available to the Americans, have we become obese with information? Is there a basic diet of information? Is there an optimum amount of information for an individual? Is there an economy in information? How should we allocate our large but limited resources for the purpose of information? Is information a means or an end?

China provides such a contrasting picture that it is provocative to look at.

# THE STATE OF THE UNION, JACK. *

Eric Moon

This is, I think, the second most difficult speech I've had to deliver in a very long time. The hardest was last June, when I was inaugurated as ALA's President. I have always been more comfortable, like Michael Foot perhaps, in opposition and the warm minority of the back bench, and I do not adjust easily to august occasions, the polite nothings of diplomacy, or the aura of history.

I remember how I struggled to get started on that inaugural speech. A certain amount of reverence is conjured up by events like inaugurations, but I didn't want to start off sounding like a pompous ass. The pathway through the dilemma was cleared by my favourite American columnist, Russell Baker of the New York Times. He's my breakfast diet three mornings a week and he's good for the soul and stomach both. He serves up perspective and a sense of proportion about the horrors and inequities and foolishness recorded daily in other pages of the paper, and he roundly and regularly deflates pretentiousness.

I had saved a column he had written in the Autumn of 1976 entitled "Historic Occasion Fatigue." This is how it began:

> It is disappointing to hear that the Ford-Carter debates will be historic. One had hoped for more. Almost everything is historic these days, except for speeches, which all seem to be major.

*Reprinted by permission of the author and publisher from the November 1977 issue of the Assistant Librarian, pp. 166-72.

> It's been years since anybody has given a minor
> speech or taken part in an unhistoric occasion...

And so on.   And it got better from there.   Well, that
column was just the ticket for me.   We had packed all our
historic occasions into 1976; the nation's bicentennial, the
ALA's and Library Journal's 100th birthdays, and the inau-
guration of my friend and predecessor, Clara Jones, as
ALA's first black president.   I could feel secure, after all
that, in the knowledge that 1977 could only be anticlimactic--
certainly far from a historic occasion.

But here, Russell Baker is of little help.   This is
the LA's centenary; it is a historic occasion.   So I had to
grope for another handle to open the door to this speech.
Well, librarians are supposed to have some training in logic
(who can forget the library school hours spent poring over
Jevons and Mill and Hulme, and even Howard Phillips' collection of multi-coloured rags?), and it seemed logical to
me that one might find some kind of entree to a historic occasion in history itself.

## A Hundred Years Ago

At that Conference of Librarians a hundred years ago in
London, at which the Library Association burst upon the
scene (if that's not too explosive a term to describe such a
seemingly sedate occasion), the American Library Association, a strapping one-year-old, was present in impressive
force.   The numbers aren't quite certain.   LJ counted 21 or
22, though with Dewey doing the counting, I'm surprised he
didn't come up with 21.5.   Budd Gambee, ten years ago in
the Journal of Library History, records a definite sixteen.
Whatever, it was a creditable proportion of ALA's then mem-
bership--and certainly of its establishment.   Included were
such giants as Cutter and Dewey, Poole and Justin Winsor,
and even Dewey's future bride, Miss Annie Godfrey of
Wellesley.

Most of ALA's Executive Board being on that "junket,"
as Gambee calls it, it seems they tried to put things in a
better light by having a couple of Board meetings on ship-
board, one on the way over, another on the way back.   The
return fare for the "best accommodations," Gambee informs
us heartrendingly, was $90.   I can assure you that our Ex-
ecutive Director came up with nothing so appealing as a long

leisurely ocean voyage or a fare that even puts Jim Laker
in the shade.

Like Dewey, I don't seem to count very well and I'm
not sure how many Yanks are here, but Bob Wedgeworth and
I were most insistent that ALA recognize this occasion prop-
erly--as you did ours a year ago, with no fewer than eight
British librarians present in Chicago, and many more from
the Commonwealth.  I know we have with us four of ALA's
five top officers--all save the Treasurer, who is back home
grimly holding on to the association's vulnerable purse
strings.   And I know we have a fair number of other American librarians here to do you honour and share this great
week with you.

It's interesting to speculate about some of the differences between these two conferences, one hundred years
apart.   One thing's for sure:  they had a lot more staying
power (for meetings, at least, if not for swinging boat trips).
The first session of that 1877 Conference lasted four and a
quarter hours, including announcements, the inaugural address and subsequent discussion, and two other major papers,
discussion on the last of which had to be "deferred till the
evening."   Since the session started at 10 a. m. they had already gone right through lunch!

The interests of the American visitors have undoubtedly changed somewhat in the past century, too.   Those
doughty 19th century American librarians were concerned
over the fact that Englishmen wore their hats in the reading room; that few English women were employed as librarians (there are still some of us who like a lot of women
around!); and that the bookcases in British libraries were so
high that ladders were required (which brings back 30-year-
old memories for me of the Birmingham Reference Library).

The fascinating papers at that founding conference included one of "An Evitandum in Index-Making, Principally
Met with in French and German Periodical Scientific Literature."   If that doesn't grab you, there was a scintillating
thriller "On the Alphabetical Arrangement of the Titles of
Anonymous Books."

A Good Press

But the most remarkable aspect of that conference,  seen

from today's perspective, was the press coverage. LJ, then
the only library periodical around, was having its difficulties.
The October 1877 issue began with an apology: "We had
hoped to give in this number a letter from Mr. Dewey sum-
marizing the results of the gathering in London, but have
been disappointed in its arrival." It wouldn't be the last
time that old Melvil proved to be something less than a hot-
shot reporter. Waiting for Melvil, LJ meanwhile picked up
snippets of news from the London papers and a source described as "elsewhere." The Times was a goldmine. Gambee says it "reported every sitting with a stenographic
thoroughness second only to the official transactions." Would
that librarianship--on either side of the Atlantic--could attract such national press attention today!

But there were, then as now, cynics among the press
corps. One rather jaded journalist, writing for the Globe,
declared that he was "not young and hopeful enough to imagine that much good will result from the conference." He
saw the "meeting as a pleasant social incident ... likely to
produce a certain esprit de corps and sentiment of brotherly
acquaintance" (he apparently also noticed the paucity of women!).

"The Conference," said the opinionated Globe reporter,
"will doubtless be attended with some conflict of opinions and
a good deal of useless talk; and when the discussions have
closed with the usual interchanges of compliments and cour-
tesies, the orators will return to their homes little wiser
than they left them.... But it may safely be predicted that
the conference will have no revolutionary consequences."

Here, it occurred to me, was the clue I had been
searching for in the historical record. Though I have shared
that Globe reporter's sentiments through some pretty deadly
meetings and conferences, it seemed to me that a conference
on an occasion like this is particularly vulnerable to sinking
into the quicksand of platitudes and pleasantries, and that it
ought to have some revolutionary consequences. And if the
AAL is still remotely like the AAL I used to know, this
is the place to explore the possibilities, because the AAL,
if anyone, ought to be a prominent instigator in ensuring that
revolutionary consequences result. This, perhaps, was the
hook I could hang this talk on.

## British Librarianship

Before I reached that point I had toyed with the idea of
venturing some comparisons of libraryland, British and
American subterritories, and to prepare for the exercise
had launched into a fast survey of some of the British library literature I hadn't read these past twenty years.   It
was a dispiriting exercise.   The more I read, the more apparent it became that I knew so little about British librarianship as it now is that it would be a gross arrogance for me
to attempt to comment on it at other than surface depth.
The landscape has been transformed so dramatically by the
panorama of revolutionary developments that have taken place
these last two decades that my view from the Finchley,
Brentford & Chiswick, Kensington, and the Chaucer House
of the fifties is comparable to what one sees through the
wrong end of the telescope.

Two massive local government reorganizations--which
have even created place-names I don't recognize (Tower
Hamlets, indeed!)--the total reorganization of your national
libraries, and endless parade of reports (Parry, Plowden,
Maud, Mallaby, Dainton, the Library Advisory Councils,
etc.), the wonder of your Open University, new national library legislation, library education transfigured with an academic facelift, libraries nestled under the wing of the Department of Education and Science, my old colleagues Sewell
and Jones as some kind of Gogol-like government inspectors
of libraries--all this was a world created in my absence, a
library world I didn't understand at all.

## A Strong Organization

Clearly, the home wicket was likely to be a little less sticky
and it would be wiser to dig in there.   In the U.S., presidents always talk about the State of the Union, which was
one reason for the title of this talk.   Another was that when
I was asked for a label I hadn't even envisioned the jacket
to which it would be attached.   But I could not resist that
confluence of Union and Jack, and that little comma in the
middle was there to represent my still mid-Atlantic leanings.
At any rate, ALA is the union whose state I have to care for
this year (though it surely wouldn't much like the word), and
some of the revolutionary changes I've seen in it since I
crossed the water are what I want to discuss today.   I may
yet risk a few comparative points along the way, impression-

istic as they must be--and if my impressions of this side of
the Atlantic are, as say, "way off base," as they may well
be, let me apologize in advance.

When I went to the States, as editor of LJ, on Guy
Fawkes' Day, 1959, two of the first things I noticed were
the avoidance of controversy and the absence of anything like
the AAL. I even thought there might be a connection somewhere between those facts. In one of my earliest LJ editorials I compared ALA's Junior Members' Round Table (the
only and nearest equivalent we then had) with the AAL. The
concluding paragraph of that editorial read:

> The weakness of the Junior Members' Round Table
> is that it does not have the AAL's potential for
> power. It does not have a strong local or region-
> al organization; it is not represented in the inner
> conclaves where it can have influence upon the im-
> portant activities of the association. There must
> be angry, or at least dissatisfied, young men (and
> women) in the library profession. A vital junior
> organization should provide avenues for the con-
> structive energy generated by that anger or dis-
> satisfaction. It will not happen while younger li-
> brarians are herded into a 'dolly' organization
> where they may play, but where guns are forbidden.

Later, I came to understand that there was even more
to our lack of an AAL than that. A little over a year ago,
my wife and I were at a Canadian Library Association conference. We watched and listened as a comparatively young
man (of course, today that means anyone under fifty, to me)
handled a very thorny and potentially explosive meeting with
complete aplomb, quiet skill and total authority. He clearly
knew parliamentary procedure, and just as clearly had solid
experience on the platform. His accent was unmistakable,
even to an American, and my wife said: "How come all you
British librarians are so good at this stuff?" I knew that
British librarian, and knew where he had learned that "stuff."
I said, simply, "He's an old AAL type."

I don't know how many hundred conferences, meetings,
committees I've sat in on during my years in America, but
I can tell you that I've seen dozens of meetings mangled,
mired in confusion, suffused with boredom, flooded with
anger, when that kind of competence in the chair, or even
at the floor microphones, might have prevented any of these

reactions. In general--and of course there are a good number of shining exceptions--American librarians do not handle
such matters as well as you do, and I think the early training in the heat of the kitchen that younger librarians get
through involvement in the AAL may really account for some
of the difference.

The JMRT has improved somewhat, I think, but it
still lacks clout and, though it does some useful things, it
still in my view is more social than activist.

However, we did have something of a library revolution in the Sixties in America, and many other units and
sub-units have emerged in ALA, some of which certainly
cannot be described as tame or inactive. One is our Social
Responsibilities Round Table, which for a time I hoped might
emerge as our equivalent of the AAL. There is no doubt
that, over the past six or seven years, it has been our
"ginger group," as the AAL has so often been called. But
it, too, lacks the AAL's organizational talent and established
place in the power structure, and it has never developed into
the cogent force some of us hoped it might become.

Revolution in Librarianship

This is not to say that it has not had impact. SRRT came
out of the cauldron of controversy and rebellion that was the
United States in the Sixties--a cauldron kept boiling with in-
gredients like the Vietnam War, assassinations, Kent State,
Martin Luther King, student activism, riots in our major
cities, the Black Panthers, the CIA and FBI, and many other
elements. Many saw this as a terrible period in our history;
others of us saw it as hopeful, as a reawakening of consciousness. In any case, it had its impact on libraryland, and
what there was of a revolution in librarianship reached its
high point at the most incredible and exciting conference I've
attended in nearly four decades in the profession: the 1969
ALA Conference in Atlantic City.

Leading the activism there was a new group called the
Congress for Change, its membership heavily, though not
exclusively, library school students. They kept the establishment (or some of them) on the brink of nervous hysteria and
our membership meeting began to resemble one of those
Congressional filibuster scenes they used to like to make
movies about. I seemed to be one of the relatively few

people both sides knew and felt they could talk to, and I
remember both those on the platform and those jamming the
front seats and the floor microphones, each asking me about
the other, "What do they want?" That simple question
seemed to me to say everything about our problem: the
tremendous gulf of understanding that existed between the
top and the bottom of the profession.

## Social Issues

Let me backtrack for a moment to the early Sixties to record my own awakening to the fact that libraries had two
choices: to be a significant thread in the social fabric, an
active participant in social change, or to face a dodo-like
slow passage toward extinction or existence as a historical
relic. I did not have to be in the States very long to see
that, in some library circles at least, there was a much
greater awareness of social issues as they affected librarian-
ship--of civil rights matters, of the need constantly to man
the free speech barricades, of where libraries fitted into
such governmental dreams as Johnson's War on Poverty--
than I had ever known in nearly twenty years in British librarianship.

The consciousness was in some ways an old one. In
the fifties, when much of America cowered before the indiscriminate fire of Tailgunner Joe McCarthy, the ALA, one of
the few organizations not to remain silent, issued its ringing
Freedom to Read Statement: it's still a document and a
moment to make one proud to be a librarian. And back in
the thirties, poet Stanley Kunitz, then editor of the Wilson
Library Bulletin, wrote an editorial called The Spectre at
Richmond which was years ahead of the profession generally
in social consciousness and exposed the shameful treatment
and indignities black librarians could expect at their own
professional association meetings.

## Segregated Libraries

This is not to suggest that ALA was a model of social consciousness in the early sixties (or that it is now, as we
shall see). Indeed, some of us battled right through that
decade trying to prove to some of our colleagues that social
issues were library issues. On the other side were those
who wanted not to let us talk about Vietnam or poverty or

whatever unless we could demonstrate a "library" connection.
Apart from the morality, where did they think the money
was coming from to kill all those people so many thousands
of miles away?   Right out of the hides of our library services and of other social services, that's where.

Nevertheless, the U. S. Supreme Court's historic
Brown decision calling for integration of schools throughout
the United States was almost a decade old in the early sixties, and racial awareness and activism were growing fast.
Both John Wakeman, my former assistant at Finchley, who
was then editing the Wilson Library Bulletin, and I, over at
LJ, quickly became embroiled in the raging debate over civil
rights issues--and particularly over segregated libraries and
segregated library associations in the South.   Nothing either
of us had ever experienced in British librarianship was preparation for such involvement; we had to learn the hard way.
Meanwhile, the ALA acted, often reluctantly, usually under
great pressure, sometimes too slowly and unconvincingly,
but act it did, and some of the wrongs in our associations
and our library services began to be alleviated, if by no
means removed altogether.

We are still far from home or on safe ground on
racial issues.   If people, whatever their heritage or colour,
may now use most libraries without distinction or barriers;
if any librarian may now join and attend the meetings of his
or her association, we have still not achieved equal treatment in recruitment, training, hiring and promotion of librarians.   White, middle class people still run most libraries, and they naturally tend to gear their services to the
needs they know.   We don't have to be naive enough to believe that prejudice can be eradicated to insist that such visible and unjust results of prejudice be eliminated.

Worse, perhaps, after all these years of grappling
with racial problems, is the degree to which otherwise intelligent people remain grossly insensitive in this area.   We
faced the results of such insensitivity again this year at our
annual conference in Detroit, where a film called The Speaker, made we must assume with good intentions, and with
the sponsorship of ALA's Intellectual Freedom Committee,
managed to split our association wide open on racial lines,
to a degree we have not experienced in more than a decade. [1]

## The Voice of Enoch

I am sure that some of you are feeling at this point that all
of this is far removed in time and spirit from anything that
has impact on you or on British librarianship, but, like
Andrew Young, our U.N. ambassador, I don't believe racism
is a national characteristic.   It blooms, like weeds, in any
overcrowded garden where the soil is not carefully tended.
You have growing and already substantial racial minorities
in this country, and even from across the Atlantic we see
and hear familiar omens.   The voice of Enoch Powell, accent apart, does not sound so terribly different from  that of
George Wallace.

    With the appearance of Bob Usherwood in the columns
of the Assistant Librarian some years ago there seemed to
be signs of a budding social consciousness.   I remember,
for example, an article by Peter Jordan on "Social Class,
Race Relations and the Public Library"[2] and thinking, "here's
a breakthrough."   I remember reading elsewhere of a speaker at a one-day conference of the Library Association a couple of years ago who was concerned that British libraries
were offering a very conservative and racist service.   And I
remember a comment in a recent chapter by Arnold and
Usherwood, that "the harsh reality remains that few librarians or library authorities are really prepared for the chal-
lenges and opportunities which are provided by a multi-racial
and multi-cultural society."[3]

    I hasten to add that I do not know from experience
how accurate such comments are, but these rumblings in the
British library literature seem to suggest that you are really
just beginning to discern the potential dimensions of an issue
under whose shadow the United States has lived throughout
its history.   Two things I can tell you.   One is that inaction
and delay--that abused Supreme Court phrase, "all deliberate
speed"--will not make things easier, but much worse.   And
secondly, if you haven't done it already, you ought early to
get some black and brown advice; whites alone cannot find
the answers to problems of racism.

    Now maybe you are already going out and actively
recruiting Pakistani and Indian and West Indian and African
librarians and getting them into library school so that you
will have people in your libraries who understand the needs
and problems of many readers (and probably many non-users
of libraries) in this society who were not reared on Trollope

or Agatha Christie.  If you are doing these things, fine; if
you are not, it may be growing awfully late to make a serious start.


## Ginger Group

I offer such advice humbly, not in the often arrogant manner
of Americans abroad, who can be over-generous with their
expertise.  Their message is, "Look how we've progressed,
you can learn from us."  It is not mine.  But, please, there
is a lesson in the agony of our experience.  If you take note
of that, and of the record of it in our literature, you may
avoid duplicating the turmoil, the anger, the indignities that
we had to go through on the road to whatever understanding
we've yet achieved.

    I hope the AAL, in its rôle as ginger group, will
give high priority to convincing the LA and the profession
that books and other media, the needs of the research community, the customary services to the white middle class,
are not the whole library story.  If libraries have a serious
rôle in society, they must be aware of society's needs and
problems, and must take an active rôle in attempting to
solve them.

    In a way, while I've said I'd like to see our SRRT
take on some of the characteristics of the AAL, the AAL
seems the natural body over here to undertake some parts
of SRRT's rôle in ALA.  Its charge, in the ALA Handbook
of Organization, includes:

          To provide a forum for discussion of the responsi-
          bilities of libraries in relation to the important
          problems of social change which face institutions
          and librarians ... to act as a stimulus to the as-
          sociation and its various units in making libraries
          more responsive to current social needs....

    The best job SRRT has done during its existence is to
heighten awareness, increase the association's consciousness
of needs and issues.  It has done it in a variety of ways,
but the usual first step has been to form what it calls a Task
Force.  One of these created an Alternative Books in Print
to give recorded life to the publications of small and underground presses that didn't get into established bibliographic
sources like Books in Print.  Others deal with library service

to minorities or to other groups which have been ill-served, such as migrant farm workers. Some task forces respond to the cause of those in our profession who lack influence or have suffered discrimination or lack of representation--two very different examples are Chicanos and gay people. But if SRRT (and other groups, like the Black Caucus in ALA) heightened our awareness of the needs and problems of minorities, SRRT also put up front and centre another long-standing problem in our profession and in society: discrimination against the majority. That is, women.

## Equal Rights Battle

You may remember that those American librarians who came to the 1877 Conference were concerned about the lack of women in British librarianship. That certainly is not the case today. On our side, the library profession is about 80% female. I don't know what it is here, but I'd guess no less than 70 to 75%. But where are the women in the leadership positions?

The sexual revolution lagged behind the racial one by a few years, but it is really with us now and a nationwide battle is going on to pass an Equal Rights Amendment to the United States Constitution. At this year's Detroit conference ALA joined in that battle, passing a resolution that after 1981, it would no longer hold any of its conferences or meetings in states that had not ratified the ERA. One of those states is Illinois, where our headquarters are located!

One new symbol of ALA's rising consciousness in this area is that we now have a new, major Council committee on the Status of Women in Librarianship, part of whose charge is "to ensure that the Association considers the rights of the majority (women) in the library field."

Now this time I'm not just venturing an impression; there's no doubt in my mind that the LA and the AAL need some such mechanism. I could scarcely believe it when, a few months ago, my friend Norman Horrocks, another expatriate Englishman who serves on ALA's Executive Board, said to me: "Do you know the LA's only had one woman president in 100 years?" and asked, "Are you going to say anything about that?" "You're damn right, I am," I said.

Well, the AAL, I thought, with misplaced loyalty, will

have done better than that. So I looked. My count may not
be totally accurate, but it seems you have done better. Not
much, however. I count less than half a dozen women presidents of the AAL in its history, which doesn't exactly reek
with justice or equity either. And the Miss Book World
beauty contests and the Assistant Librarian's parade of pin-
ups don't quite speak to any advanced level of consciousness
of women as anything other than sex symbols. It's not that
I have anything against sex symbols. In fact, I'd rather like
to be one; but, like many women, I'd want someone, sometime, to notice that I might have something else, too.

I spoke of all this with a couple of visiting British
librarians in the States recently, and while the male member
of the duo admitted that one woman president of the LA in
100 years seemed "a bit off," he added, "but we wouldn't
appoint someone President just because she's a woman."

The implications of that remark are devastating, if
you think about it. If, given the mathematical proportions
of membership, there has not been discrimination against
women, it means that women are, generally, inferior to men
and thus have only a very small chance of making it to the
top of the heap. It's an attitude and a situation that is awfully familiar to blacks, and in recent years, in the U.S. at
least, women have become increasingly aware of, and vocal
about, the fact that they have been similarly and just as consciously discriminated against.

Talking of presidents and representation takes me on
to another issue which was a major element of our internal
ALA revolution in the sixties and early seventies, one aspect
of which I saw raised a few years ago in an Assistant Librarian editorial on the "question of confidentiality and open
meetings."

When I was active in the AAL many of us were concerned then that the upper echelons of the Library Association seemed to operate like one of those old-fashioned gentlemen's clubs. If you grew to be accepted, finally, after
twenty or thirty years, you might be admitted to membership
in the club. In the meantime, they weren't about to tell you
what the hell was going on about anything. When Bill Smith
and I took on the initial editorship of Liaison (which was the
AAL's idea), we insisted on being able to attend any meeting
we wanted to, and to call the shots in print the way we saw
them. Sayers and Cashmore, I remember, were among the

elders who were horrified at the thought, but Frank Gardner, a former Assistant Librarian stalwart who by then had climbed the rungs of power, prevailed.

It wasn't too unlike that in ALA at the time of my arrival. As editor of LJ I wanted no strings on what I could report and I used to "crash" closed meetings regularly. I got very promptly marched out of quite a few. But the message got across and others began to understand the perils of privacy, and began to insist that the doors be opened. Today, it is a requirement that all ALA meetings be open to members, and to the press. You have to have a very solid reason for an executive (that is, a private) session--for example, a meeting at which individuals may be being considered for some appointment--and even then, the results must be reported in open session. Our Council meetings are major public events in the Association and are heavily attended by members, since they take place during our annual conference and our Midwinter meeting.

## The Dix Mix

With the doors open, the campaign to democratize the association took on a new head of steam. As a result of the revolutionary fervor of the late sixties we emerged with a succession of committees with exotic acronyms like ACONDA and ANACONDA, set up essentially with the purpose of bringing forward proposals for reorganization and democratization. I liked their unofficial name best. It derived from our then president, Bill Dix of Princeton, who appointed the original ACONDA (in short, the Committee on New Directions). The committee became known by a name that sounded like a Variety magazine headline, "the Dix Mix. "

It's hard to nail down exactly what came out of all this, but one thing that certainly did was a larger awareness among members that they could use the system, the by-laws and regulations, to their purposes. They didn't have to sit back and accept dictates from above, even as to what candidates they could have and vote for in elections of their officers and their Council.

One mechanism that began to be heavily used by members and by activist groups in the association was the petition process. The usual procedure was (and still is) that a Nominating Committee, appointed by the President, puts for-

ward a slate of candidates.   You can see how self-perpetuating
a process that can be.   Under this system you have some
choice, but not much, and the limits of the choice are determined by what the Nominating Committee thought.   What
changed was that members began putting forward their own
candidates.   Under our by-laws now, all you have to have
are twenty-five legitimate signatures on a petition to put a
candidate of your choice on the ballot.   Here was democracy
in action, and though some people have tried to put a brake
on it, it has prevailed.   Clara Jones and I are here this
week as living proof that it works:   two ALA presidents in a
row who were nominated by petition and beat the official
slate, indicating that, at least in those two years, the Nominating Committee was apparently not in tune with what the
membership wanted.

Here, I would have thought, is a reform that might
appeal to the AAL, indeed to spirited members generally.
I find it hard to believe that there is general acceptance and
equanimity about a procedure by which a small group of
senior citizens of the association retires to a small, closed
room, like some medieval Star Chamber, later to emerge
and tell you who your next president will be.   Not only do
you have no voice in the matter; you aren't even offered a
choice between two.   It doesn't sound like the democracy for
which Britain is famous.   Certainly, American librarians
would not sit still for anything so authoritarian.   Who knows,
with a more democratic system, you might even get another
woman president!

The big issue in ALA today, as I see it, the one that
will occupy center stage perhaps for the next several years,
is more obviously a library service problem than some of
the others I've discussed.   It was raised here, in an Assistant Librarian editorial as long ago as 1970, [4] and it has been
looming as an increasingly threatening spectre the past few
years on our side of the Atlantic.   I'm referring to the
troublesome question of fees which are more and more being
charged for library service.   This development, I believe,
poses the most serious threat to the philosophical foundations
of library service that we have yet seen.

Information is becoming (is!) big business.   What has
become known, loosely, as the information industry is, perhaps, if you consider its conglomerate whole, already the
largest industry in America.   My inaugural address, titled

"Data Bank Is Two Four-Letter Words," which may establish
my viewpoint, was largely concerned with the ramifications
of this development.  The combination of ever more costly
information storage, location and delivery devices, and the
probability of continued economic stringency makes the maintenance of what we have known as "free" library service
even more difficult because it becomes such a vulnerable
target.  But now, while the temptations are so enticing for
the commercial entrepreneurs, is no time for us to vacillate
or equivocate.  If this door is left ajar, commerce will in-
vade and destory principle as surely as Hitler's troops
waltzed around the Maginot Line.

My whole presidential program in ALA this year is
based on the belief that free access to information is the
very foundation, not only of our profession and its services,
but of individual liberty.  My one big effort this year, through
ALA, is to persuade President Carter that it is as important
for us to have a National Information Policy as it is to have
one concerned with energy problems.  And a basic ingredient
of any such policy has to be that simple, moral declaration
contained in the Unesco Public Library Manifesto, that a public library "should be maintained wholly from public funds,
and no direct charge should be made to anyone for its services. "

I mention this here not because I expect you to be
interested in the details of my presidential program, but because the problem, the threat, is undoubtedly a worldwide
one, or will be if it is not yet.  This problem is one that
calls for a united international effort by the library community, and I hope this is one terribly important, creative area
where we, and other library associations, can work together
in united purpose.  There have been too few such instances
where we have done so, and agreement on a Cataloging Code
will not save us.

I hope you are not disappointed that I chose mainly to
talk on this occasion of library associations rather than libraries.  I did so because I believe our associations are the
place where we can and should gather in force and unity.
They are our political potential for change and influence.  It
is there that we must clarify our communal thinking and
translate it into influence and action.  What we say and do
there has much to do with the kind and quality of our front-
line services in libraries.  If we do not, as organized bodies,
understand today's world turmoil, or the reasons for it, that

misunderstanding will be reflected in increasingly irrelevant services in our libraries. If we choose not to participate in the certain massive changes ahead in society--here, in the U. S. and elsewhere--not only we but our libraries will become relegated to the rôle of bystanders.

There was a nice poster going the rounds in the U. S. a few years ago, which picked up a line of Eldridge Cleaver's. It read: "If you are not part of the solution, you are part of the problem." That, it seems to me, is the clear choice for us all.

## References

1.  See "Head-on collision: ALA in motor city." Wilson Library Bulletin, (September, 1977) pp 30-42.
2.  Jordan, Peter. "Social class, race relations and the public library." Assistant Librarian, Vol. 65 No. 3, (March, 1972) pp 38-41.
3.  Arnold, Brian and Usherwood. "The Library in the Cultural Framework," in Harrison, K. C. (ed). Prospects for British Librarianship. The Library Association, 1976, pp 126-139.
4.  "Time for action" (Editorial) Assistant Librarian, Vol. 63 No. 9 (September 1970) pp. 133-134.

# HOW MY HOMETOWN LIBRARY FAILED ME*

Anne Nelson

The public library is in the middle of my hometown, right across the street from the county courthouse.  The first thing you see as you walk through the large oak doors is an enormous circular desk, the bastion of two librarians.  There is no mistaking them, because they look every inch the way you expect a librarian to look:  genteel and grey-haired, one dour and forbidding, the other mild and bird-like.  The dour one seems to resent the idea of anyone using her books, and in the ten-odd years I used the library, her visible pain at the check-out counter made me feel like a small-time thief. Eventually I felt compelled to justify her suspicions, and I became a bona fide library criminal around the age of 14, sneaking books out of and back into the library for the thrill. Getting them back in was the hard part.

She caught me once, reading a "missing" copy of Kenneth Clarke's Civilisation right under her nose in the reading room's big leather chair.  "Where did you get that?" she demanded sharply.  I stammered a lie, pretending that I picked the book up every day, read it, and innocently misplaced it in the same wrong shelf.  She didn't believe me, but she didn't say so.  Instead, she let me off with a short lecture on how she'd been searching for it.  It was more the rush of embarrassment than a sense of guilt that ended my life of library crime.  I would never have dreamed of stealing a book--a sin against the book as well as the public-- but this librarian gave me an irresistible desire to bollix up her system.

*Reprinted by permission of the author and publisher from the February 1, 1978 issue of Library Journal, pp. 317-319. Published by R. R. Bowker Co. (a Xerox company); copyright © 1978 by Xerox Corporation.

I felt differently about the building itself.  It is made
of yellow sandstone, right out of the local hills, and on a
late summer afternoon, when the temperature easily pushes
over a hundred, the library walls absorb and suffuse the
strong light until the library glows like a piece of rough
amber.  I liked the fact that it was a WPA project, built by
the people who had the most to gain from its resources.
The Carnegie libraries are too philanthropic by comparison,
with the Horatio Alger bootstrap built right into the masonry,
and the federal boxes that sprang up in the sixties have no
sense of place, as if they could be in Toledo, Honolulu, or
in Tulsa.  Our library was paid for by the government, but
it was built by local hands, and to me this was a metaphor
for the two ways a public library should serve the public:
first as a conduit to the rest of the nation and through it,
the world; second as a looking glass to the local community.

To understand this library's role as information-giver
you have to consider the alternatives.  There are about
40,000 people in my hometown, including the student population.  It has one newspaper, which prints little national news
and less international.  The handful of statewide papers do a
little better, but not much, and only a fraction of the town
subscribes to them.  Two student bookstores sell texts and
paperbacks and there is a single dusty bookstore on Main
Street that sells hardbacks, most of them used.  Television
and magazines are the library's only effective competition.

Everyone who leaves a Southwestern town speaks
knowingly of the "time warp," which means, in effect, an
information warp.  Those who remain are aware of an event
that makes the six o'clock news or a personality glossing the
cover of Time, but subtler ideas and styles take their time,
sifting in from the coasts.

This was brought home to me when I went from an
Oklahoma high school to an Eastern college.  In 1972, the
year I left, 400 Oklahoma students would hold their first
major demonstration, against ROTC.  High school girls were
finally allowed to wear their skirts more than two inches
above the knee and students with long hair still ran the risk
of getting beaten up by cowboys.  Meanwhile, my new class-
mates in the east buried themselves in what the newspapers
were calling "the new pre-professionalism" and began to re-
consider ROTC as a way to get a good job.  Skirts hung to
a length that would satisfy any Southern Baptist deacon, and
the Ivy League barbershops were back in business shearing
locks.

In a few ways the public library served as an antidote
to the time warp. There was a list of about 20 new books
a month published in the town newspaper, and a periodical
shelf fairly well stocked with "good" magazines. But in
many other respects the library was a product, or even a
cause, of the lapse in information. The newspaper list frequently disappointed me; I would scan it eagerly, and perhaps
among the gardening books and gothics, the auto repair manuals and movie star memoirs, might be an interesting piece
of serious fiction or a work of political analysis. Most of it
was safe--too safe. It wasn't that my standards were esoteric or academic; after all, my only sources were the book
review sections of Newsweek and Harper's. When those
magazines touted someone like Erik Erikson or John Fowles
I could be fairly certain that a trip to the card catalog would
leave me empty-handed. For the most part the book collection was to modern literature what AM radio is to modern
music, but in my hometown nothing could be found in that
library that might be dangerous or too hard to digest. My
only question was whether this lack was due to oversight or
the will to protect.

There are some ways in which the public library can
be compared to its natural enemy, the television network.
The two share the duty to inform and the need to entertain,
and there will always be a large and grateful audience for
soap operas and gothics. Doubtlessly the librarian, like the
programming executive, has ratings to consider, however
they are measured, and ratings usually show that it's more
fun to entertain.

The network executive falls back on the excuse that
informing the public may not turn a profit. The librarian
has anything but this excuse, since the same system that
stocks the shelves and feeds the librarians depends upon an
opinionated citizenry, and the only valid opinions are those
formed from the most complete information and the most
persuasive conflicting arguments possible.

Wandering through the library was not unlike browsing
in a half-price paperback stall, where you are sure to encounter something you'd like to read, but little or no chance
of finding what you're looking for. There was never a
shortage of worthwhile things to read; the Russian novels
lined the shelf, dressed in their laundered Garnett translations, and in another corner stood a massive series of
"Great Books." Thanks to some editor who bound them all

in color-coordinated leatherette, the librarians were obliged
to acquire Aquinas, Hobbes, and Rabelais because they wanted
a matching set.

But my disappointments at the card catalog were legion.  The moment of truth came when I looked up one name
in particular and found only these two entries: "Marx, Karl--
'Capital, Selections from'; and 'A Boy's Life of'."  This was
in 1970, and it struck me as criminal neglect.

A later trip to the catalog rewarded me with a collection of Lillian Hellman's plays.  On reading The Children's
Hour I was puzzled at its abrupt ending; then I realized that
the last 20 pages had been carefully excised by a razor.  I
still wonder who it was that wanted to protect me from any
intimation of homosexuality, a librarian or some self-appointed
censor.  That mystery will never be solved, but the incident
as a whole fit in with my feeling that the library wanted to
shield me from unsettling ideas, not challenge me.

Information is a two-way street; a message is useless
unless you know who's on the receiving end.  A library has
a duty to collect broad cultural information that applies to
the national community, but at the same time it must be
aware of the uniqueness of its locality.  There are questions
that people everywhere should be able to address, like
Marxism and homosexuality.  At the same time, any city,
even one as small as my hometown, has its own history,
character, and problems.  A public library has a special
role as shaman at this point in time.  The old story-tellers
on the courthouse bench die off, and America is running the
dangerous risk of becoming as standardized as its interstate
highways.  The public library made a good stab at collecting
local history, and for this I am grateful, even if the resources mainly consisted of "pioneer books," filled with
cloudy photos of people's ancestors and shots of familiar
streets and unfamiliar buggies.  You could also find Federal
Writers' Project guides to the states tucked away in corners,
wonderful in their recherché details.

But these were flukes of local history buffs and the
Depression.  The library had no organized response to the
community as it exists, and a response was badly needed.
My hometown has its problems:  steady industrialization, a
beaten-down black population, Indians who are invisible in
city politics but the mainstay of the welfare office.  Nobody
spoke of these things, especially the library, when it was

the library that should have been crying: "Look at this!
Here are some answers that others have found."

The underprivileged had no place in the library. I'm
sure they were ostensibly welcome, but there was no effort
to draw them in. The place had the air of a housewife's
retreat when she got bored with her bridge games. I've
heard of urban libraries that have taken on the role of om-
budsmen, guiding the confused through mazes of red tape to
find solutions to specific problems. What a boon this must
be! Better still, it is a way of overcoming the discomfort
the under-educated feel towards libraries in general. Once
a library proves itself to be the democratic institution it's
supposed to be, its aura of false gentility will fall away and
it can become a public servant in the true sense of the words.

I wonder about the children and the grandchildren of
the WPA laborers who built the library some 40 years ago,
whether they ever use it, whether they walk past it with any
sense of pride of identification. I doubt it; the library has
taken the easy way out too often. There are many ways of
limning social distinctions, but the distinctions the library
must make are between the seekers, the readers, and the
illiterates. The readers are the easy ones to service--
they'll chew on anything--but the seekers and the illiterates
are paying taxes too, and they are the public libraries'
most challenging and rewarding users.

The seekers call for an organized way of dealing with
contemporary thought, and they are usually articulate enough
to demand it. The illiterates are crippled in dealing with
society, and the public library is one of the few public institutions that could stand a chance to help. Of course it's a
complicated question. Of course it would call for lots of
imagination and even more funding. Librarians might have
to be trained in ways that would take them beyond the mere
acquiring, ordering, and repairing of books. They would
need to learn a little about sociology, politics, law, and
history and they would have to keep their eyes wide open as
to how they could apply their knowledge for people who don't
know how to ask for help. I would think that many librarians, perhaps even the dour nemesis in my hometown, would
find this exciting; I've seen librarians' eyes light up in rec-
ommending a book. Why not take that excitement farther?

A library is often defined as both a building and a
collection of books. I think of the times a church was defined as both a building and a collection of people, and what

I would like to see is the definitions combined in a new idea
of the public library: a building, books, people. I don't
think librarians have much idea of their own impact in shaping people's lives through the information they allow them to
have. They are more than curators; they are prime movers,
whether they acknowledge it or not.

I don't wish to imply that I blame the library for the
provincialism of a small Southwestern city. It is too much
to expect a Brecht production to follow Pirates of Penzance
at the local community theater, or a foreign film house competing with the Walt Disney movies downtown. On the other
hand, the library does not have to clear a profit, and there
is every reason why it should take advantage of that status.

I feel like something of a traitor in writing these
words, since I feel gratitude for the benefits I culled from
the library. It always performed its minimum purpose
nicely: a quiet place to read and roam the shelves; an ideal
after-school stopping-off place for perusing old volumes of
Life. There is much to be said for a place that permits you
to discover authors on your own time, perhaps because you
like a cover, perhaps because you respond to the sound of a
name. And there is also a reverberation that comes from
such an experience; you run across a book at random and
suddenly it echoes in your life, almost by accident, like a
word that you look up and then find jumping out of every
page. That is not a quality that a library can lose, however,
and the very sense of randomness can build to a burning
frustration in someone who is seeking a moral order.

In the end, my public library failed me. It had lost
touch. It could never have been a panacea for the problems
of my hometown, let alone the world, but it failed me in the
moment when I needed to learn what the problems were.

I left my hometown five years ago, but the library
card remains in my wallet. I use it a couple of weeks of
the year when I return to visit my family. I walk in through
the oak doors and greet the librarians, who still remember
me well (after all, they didn't revoke my card), and savor
the smell, and consider old spines of books I didn't get around to
reading ten years ago. I silently compare it, smiling, with the
New York Public Library in its grand chaos and I am glad that
my hometown and New York can co-exist, more or less peace-
fully. On a selfish, nostalgic level I suppose I don't want the
library to change, but when I think about the place I left and my
reasons for leaving, I wish to hell it would.

# THE UP-SIDE-DOWN LIBRARY*

Jesse H. Shera

John Keats in a moment that could be characterized as something less than poetic ecstasy, once wrote in a letter to a
friend, "The sun from Meridian Heights illumines the depths
of the sea and the fishes beginning to sweat, cried dammit
how hot we shall be." This in language not too metaphorical
but to be taken with a certain degree of realism, I think,
represents the plight of the librarian today. For the librarian, poor fish, confronted by this paradoxical time of inflation, deflation, of rising costs, declining revenues is certainly finding out what it is like to be in hot water. Let us
look for a moment briefly at history to see how we have gotten ourselves into this situation.

There are, of course, multiple causes, but let me
look at a few that I think are basic to this. I am not going
to get into economics, but libraries began from ancient
times, ancient Greece, Rome, so on through the Middle
Ages as instruments created for the preservation of the record. The records of the state, education of the youth, the
religious belief, faiths, the operations of day to day economy,
these were presided over by scholars, men who were really
scholar-librarians who not only collected this material, organized it, but worked on it, worked on the texts, interpreted
its meaning and in other ways made it useful to the community. As we move down through the centuries in a very substantial leap, we come to our own shores and we find out,
beginning with Benjamin Franklin (who really, I think, got the
idea from England)--about Franklin's junta and the whole
Philadelphia Library Company, developed by a little group of

---

*Reprinted by permission of the author and publisher from
the Spring 1978 issue of Utah Libraries, pp. 11-19.

men, young artisans in Franklin's period who developed what
we later called social libraries.

These were society libraries, founded by little bands
of people who needed books in their work--the teachers, the
ministers, the scholars, the lawyers, the doctors and so on.
They needed books so they entered into a contract to contribute money each year, dues to the associations, to buy these
books to which they could all have access.   These were contracts in the Lockean sense of a group entering into a contract with its members to secure things that they could not
secure individually; not in the Hobbesian sense of entering
into a contract with a higher power to get whatever it was
they wanted.   These little society libraries began in Philadelphia, as I said, spread up the coast through New England;
spread out into the Middle West and were even carried on to
California.   They were voluntary associations but it soon
became apparent that voluntary association would not accomplish what was wanted.   The membership either lost interest,
or they died, or moved away and after ten or fifteen years
or so the organization disappeared.   It was not long until
another organization started, so one had the first social library and the second social library and the third social library in some New England towns.

This began, then, in 1732, and we still have some of
those around today.   The Boston Athenaeum, I suppose, is
the primary example--also the Redwood Library in Newport,
Rhode Island; but we finally concluded that voluntary contributions and associations would not solve the need for books.
So first in Salisbury, Connecticut in 1805, and Peterborough,
New Hampshire in 1832, the citizens voted money from the
town treasury to start a library supported from public funds
and, of course, the crowning achievement of that period was
the establishment, in 1854, of the Boston Public Library,
and then the public library was on its way.   Along in due
course came Andrew Carnegie with his grants, and I have
often wondered--in one of those questions that cannot be an-
swered--what would have happened if Andrew had not given
it the push that it needed?   I presume we would still have
had it, but it might have been a somewhat different institution.

The point I wish to make from this gallop through
history, is that a private elitist institution turned itself into
a public institution that was supposed to serve the whole
citizenry.   It was born of this belief in the 1830's and 40's,

in the perfectibility of man; the boundless optimism of the
frontier; the belief in democracy; the belief that a country,
if it is to be a democracy, must have enlightened electorate.
A way to have an enlightened electorate was to make books
available to everyone.  Horance Mann talked of the public
library as the "crowning glory of the public schools."  John
Adams, showing the other side of it, said that "the public
library was a nest to hatch scholars."

So you see you have two really opposing points of
view.  You have what was basically an elitist institution, and
the debate that raged in the first board of trustees in the
Boston Public Library, this comes out very clearly, was the
Boston Public Library to be for scholars or was it to be for
the common man?  You have George Ticknor representing
one side and Edward Everett the other.  This paradox has
persisted down through the years in the philosophy, if you
want to call it that, of the public library.  The public library you see, is a part of the public sector, and the public sector is always unbounded so its point of view was not
only paradoxical, but in the case of the public support institution it had no, I won't say no raison d'etre, it had too
many raisons d'etre--too many opposing points of view, and
it still today reflects this image.

Then along came Melvil Dewey and all those founding
fathers of the later years of the 19th century and early years
in the history of the public library, and they too reflected
this internal conflict.  These men formed the American Library Association.  They tried first to form the Association
in 1853 but the coming of the Civil War and a number of
other social situations developed and the Association failed
after only one meeting, but if you go through the proceedings
of that early conference you will see that most of the things
they talked about were scholarly or at least quasi-scholarly
problems:  bibliographic organization of materials, how to
make materials available, the problems of cataloging, the
problems of preservation, all that kind of thing.

Then came, in 1876, the founding of the American
Library Association and it was not long until the Association
began to be primarily a publicity agent for the library profession.  The Association turned the corner where it began
to think less and less about the problems of what it was
supposed to do and began to promote itself, to proselytize
if you will.  They set up the Washington office of ALA to
work for library legislation and the library which originally

was centripetal, that is moving toward the center, pulling in
toward the center, on itself, became centrifugal and it
reached out.  We all know about outreach and all this sort
of thing.

Taking books to the masses, educating people in spite
of themselves, if you will, was a radical shift.  I do not
think any of us who lived through it (I have, partially, at
least), were quite aware of the change that was taking place.
Nobody really sat down and thought about what the library
should do.  The library tried to be all things to all people
and it was very like the chameleon who turned red when he
was put on a red cloth and green when he was put on a
green cloth and died of vexation when he was put on a scotch
plaid.  This became an internal conflict and the powers of
mass education, (and I am not opposed to mass education by
any means), but this developmental attitude became a very
serious problem.

There is a nice little passage by Finley Peter Dunne,
that Irish philosopher.  Mr. Dooley, and he and Mr. Hennesey
have long discussions.  One day, about 1902 I think the column appeared, Mr. Dooley was talking about the library and
Mr. Hennesey said, "What is a library?"  Mr. Dooley said,
"Don't you know what a library is?"  He said, "I tell you.
A Carnaygie libry is a large, brownstone, impenethrible
buildin' with th' name iv th' maker blown on th' dure.  Libry,
fr'm th' Greek wurruds, libus, a book, an' ary, sildom--
sildom a book.  A Carnaygie libry is archytechoor, not
lithrachoor."[1]

My old friend and former editor, Kathleen Molz, in a
very distinguished article that appeared in the American
Scholar about ten years ago, made a very pessimistic, but I
think also a true statement of the situation.  She says, "the
public library stands dead center in the midst of muddle....
The notion that the public should get what it pays for has so
chipped away at the foundations of the public library that today in most communities, the public library is a reference
arm for the burden of community homework; a solver of rid-
dles for the communities' contestants; a purveyor of cheap
best sellers for the titilation of the middle class."[2]  Those
are pretty severe words, but I think if we will look back at
the public libraries we have known, they are in many instances, all too true.  (Kathleen is an old friend of mine,
and a devout Catholic, so I have occasionally teased her by
accusing her of nailing her theses on the door of the Public

Library.) The library has lost its way in trying to be all
things to all people.

I can remember as a youngster, a brash youth I was
in those days, now I am somewhat older--still brash--that I
used to tell my colleagues in the depth of the depression,
that the trouble with the library was that it had never developed a philosophical frame of reference. It has never
thought seriously about what it is trying to do. It has bab-
bled about adult education, it has talked about being the
crowning glory of the public schools and on and on and on,
but it never has really reached any consensus. My elders
and my, I guess I'll be kind and say my intellectual superiors, said, "this is all very nice little boy, but run along
and play with your philosophy, we've got to meet a payroll."
I think we are paying today the penalty for that neglect of
what it is we are trying to do. We have become enamored
of things. Books are things you see, and we have devoted
all our time to how to manipulate these things, how we can
organize them; how we can shelve them; how we can build
more and more stately mansions for our professional souls.
We cannot go on doing this forever.

We have gotten the notion you know, that bigger is
better, the New York Public Library is better than the
Cleveland Public Library, because it is bigger, and the
Cleveland Public Library is better than the Columbus Public Library because it's bigger, without thinking of better
for what? A library, as my old friend, S. R. Ranganathan,
distinguished Indian library philosopher, said, is a growing
organism. Organisms all grow to a certain size and then
stop. A mouse does not become as big as an elephant, and
when it reaches a certain point, it grows not by celluar ad-
ditions but by replacement. The time's rapidly approaching
I think, when we are going to have to think of libraries as
not growing continually but growing by replacement. I'm
sure that for every situation there is an optimum size for
the library, we do not know what the optimum size is and
when I say this we all agree, but what are we doing about
it? We keep on buying more books; there is safety in numbers.

There is always the fear of the librarian that somebody is going to come to the library some day and not find
the book he wants and we're going to be embarrassed. This
is all very well and I applaud it for the spirit that is behind
it even though I criticize the mental processes by which it

is achieved.  I think the day is going to come when the
problem for the librarian will not be book acquisition but
book elimination.   This is a far more difficult job because it
is always easy once you get a book to keep it--oh it is there,
it's not doing any harm, let it stay, it's difficult to say this
stuff is no longer valid.   Let's get rid of it.   We have had
studies of one kind or another that have shown that the major
use of the library related to (particularly in the sciences,
less true of course, in history) what was published in the
last five or ten years and you get rid of everything else and
you will not bother the work of the physist or the chemist or
the biologist very much unless he happens to be a historian
of science.

Literature of course is patterned differently.   In all
of these disciplines, and we have not recognized this, we
solve the problem simply by getting more and more, and
now we have reached a point that libraries are supposed to
double, originally I think they said in 16 years and now they
have it down to ten years and the multiplication of books can
be a real embarrassment of riches.

I remember telling my friends when I was on the
staff of the Library of Congress and it had then only about
seven or eight million volumes (I think this was in the early
forties) that there I was surrounded by books, books on all
sides, in front of me, in back of me volleyed and thundered,
and I never felt so isolated by books in all my life.   The
thing was just so big.   You could not get your fingers around
it.   The card catalog didn't help you unless you were looking
for a specific title.   Then about ten years later I was doing
a history paper for a Chicago conference (by that time having
moved to the library school in Chicago) and I had to be in
my old home town of Oxford, Ohio, for the 25th anniversary
reunion of my class.   I decided that I would do some work
on the paper while I was there.   The library of my old alma
mater had then I would guess 150 to 200,000 volumes excel-
lently selected, and I found out how much easier it was to
use that library than even the library at the University of
Chicago which then had something over a million volumes.
Books do get in your way.

Someone, now unhappily forgotten, has said that he
was alarmed by the growth of two things in our society--li-
braries and cemeteries--and proposed cremation as the solution to both.   Certainly libraries and cemeteries are the two
phenomena in our culture that are predicated on a perpetually

rising inventory. We never thought about this problem. If
we thought about it we certainly never thought about it very
constructively, simply because we have not reached the point
of thinking seriously about what the purpose of the library is.
Is it to pile up books endlessly? Making of good books they
say there is no end. The same is true for the making of
bad books. The whole problem, you see, is what do you
keep? What do you eliminate? Librarians are so afraid of
being considered censors that they almost reach a point
where they have no selection policy, certainly no rejection
policy or elimination policy and this has hampered us.

We do not know what reading does to people; we do
not know how it affects activity or whether it affects activity
at all. We do not know what the impact is, the censors
know that! They know if you read "bad" books you will commit anti-social acts, on the other hand, we say that if you
read "good" books this will do you a lot of good. I cannot
see how we can have it both ways. Contrary to the censors,
we say that bad books will not hurt you but good books will
do you a lot of good, so we have painted ourselves into a
corner--we are so scared of being accused of censorship.
Whenever I have talked about censorship in my classes when
I was teaching, I always got a big argument started about
censorship and it always came out the same way which is
to say it does not come out at all. We keep churning the
argument around. We flounder when we try to talk about
libraries and think about them because we are tied not to
the idea, not to the concept, not to knowledge as knowledge,
but to the book as a physical embodiment of knowledge.

A book is only marks on paper or some other substance, it is a collection of symbols that have meaning to
us and we say traditionally that a book says so and so. A
book does not say anything. It is we who say it. There
are all sorts of definitions of a book of course, and all sorts
of metaphors and similes applied to it. Some say a book is
like a window it gives you a view of the outside world or it
can ventilate the mind or it can be something of pure physical beauty like the great Rose Window at Chartres. But the
definition that I have always liked best comes from an old
eighteenth century German Physicist and writer of aphorisms
Georg Christoph Lichtenberg who said "a book is a mirror;
(Ein Buch ist ein Spiegel) if a jackass looks into it he won't
see Saint Paul looking back. "[3]

The book reflects what the reader brings to it. This

is one reason, of course, why our problem has been so difficult. Here we are happily day after day dispensing books and thinking we are doing a good job and so we count statistics and say January was better than December, because we charged out 5,000 more books this month than we did last. It does not mean anything. It just means that a number of people actually picked up that number of books signed their names on the charge cards and went out with them. We do not know whether they read them. We have all taken books out of the library and not gotten to reading them, you have all had the same experience. Also it does not tell us that maybe some other people in the family read the books too, so in one way it over-estimates the "use" of the books, and in another way it under-estimates; it's just numbers that we push around. We have gotten too tied to the book without thinking of what the meaning of the book is--the idea content--the book on the intellectual plain.

We are all compulsive readers. People like you and me read constantly. It becomes habitual, we read because for some reason we just have to read. We sit down to breakfast in the morning and we read what is on the corn-flakes box not because we want to know what it says--we know what it says, we read it yesterday morning--but we have to read. So we take reading for granted without thinking what happens. Reading you know is an amazing thing physically as well as intellectually. What happens when reflection of light on a printed page is transmitted to the eye, from the eye to the brain? We have had all sorts of analogies between the computer and the brain which are valid analogies up to a point but only up to a point. Actually the brain, what little we know about it, and we know precious little about it, is really a whole series of computers. We know that it goes by minute electric currents which are the mechanics of the brain.

What about the intellectual processes of thinking about what goes on? Again my old friend Ranganathan calls this the idea sphere, he always had various spheres for everything including the conceptual sphere. This is something that we do not know anything about so we use kind of a shotgun attack and hit it at every point in the hope that some of the things will strike home and do some good.

What can we do about this? This is where I get into what I call my upside down library. I say it is upside down because we have directed all our attention to the physical

unit book instead of the intellectual content of the book and
we have done this I think because our libraries are improperly organized.  You go to a head librarian and ask how is
your library organized, you know what he does, he reaches
in the top right hand drawer of his desk, it's always in the
top right hand drawer and he brings out an organization
chart.  The organization chart has at the top the board of
trustees and under the board of trustees is the librarian and
under the librarian maybe there is an associate librarian,
then heads of departments--reference department, cataloging
department, acquisitions department, special collections department, reserve book room, circulation department--house-
keeping functions, maintenance, janitorial services and so on
down and at the bottom is the public and we say we are
working for the librarian and he working for the board of
trustees.

Well it is completely upside down; we are working for
the public not for the board of trustees.  I would put the
public at the top and I would put the board of trustees at the
bottom, just where they belong.  We talk glibly, of how the
board of trustees sets policy (whatever that is we do not
know) and the librarian and his staff are supposed to implement the policy.  The board of trustees of a library is very
much like the board of trustees of a college or university.
Henry Wriston that very famous president of Brown University for so many years, in his little book The Academic Pro-
cession, in which he is talking about the university but the
same is true of the library, says he has two rules for
trustees, work, wealth and wisdom, or on the other side,
give, get or get out.

I used to argue with my old teacher Carleton Joeckel
of Chicago who wrote at that time the definitive book on
government of the American public library, that the board of
trustees was adopted, and he was right, in this respect, from
the idea of lay control of public institutions and it was borrowed from business and industry.  But I used to say, "Jock,
the boards of trustees of business and industry are not laymen, they are board members of other corporations, they
are executives themselves.  I said when General Motors will
put a librarian on its board of trustees I will accept a General Motors executive on the board of trustees of a library."
We have gotten this curious notion that the general public
knows more about our business than we do ourselves.  This
is crazy.  Well, of course, he always drove me into the
corner and said what would you substitute for the board of

trustees? Would you have the librarian naked, so to speak, before the city council? I said, no I would not want that either, but there is something wrong with this setup.

Between the board at the top and the public at the bottom we are also improperly organized. In our present structure, the departments tend to become pockets, these become little principalities--powers. I think the thing is, instead of being vertical it should be horizontal. We should begin not with people doing operations, manipulating books, but with people with subject competence, with subject capability who can begin with the idea. I think we should train librarians who are not just book pushers pigeon-holing books in various marking and parking places, as my old friend Robert Fairthorne says, but beginning with the needs of the people, understanding what the people's needs are, the scholar, the child, the youth, and the university student and so on. Let these subject experts take charge of the whole operation. They would take charge of acquisitions, of the organization of the material, of the cataloging, of the classification and with the reference work.

Now we do this all the time in languages that are not written in Roman alphabet. When we set up an Oriental Library, Far East Library, and Middle East Library we obviously have to have people who can read the language. I'm sure you have all known bibliographers in these areas who are responsible for the whole operation. They go out on book buying trips, build collections in those fields; no one else can do it because no one else can read the language. They communicate directly with the appropriate faculty in the university community or the scholars in the community in the public library if there are such, and they organize this material, they catalog it, they have to do it. I was fascinated yesterday in going over to the Archives of the Mormon Church at the Chinese typewriter that they showed me. I do not know how on earth anybody ever works it but this little Chinese girl was making it work for fair. All right, they do the reference work in this field and it works supremely well. Where they can do these in the non-Roman alphabet languages why can't we do it in the Roman alphabet languages, English for example?

Why can't we staff our libraries with specialists who know the field, who know the ideas that are ebbing and flowing in the areas for which they are responsible. Substantive areas which really anticipate the needs of the person in their

fields and can speak their own language and know the kind
of materials they ought to have.  We have badly missed the
boat in this respect.  In part the library schools are very
much responsible for this because we have put all our attention on things, manipulating things--how you catalog, how
you do reference, how you acquire material, how you bind
it, repair it, etc., and we have neglected the fact that these
books contain ideas and they are used not as books but as
sources of knowledge and I hope wisdom.

        Well my friends maybe now, as they told me so many
times in the 1930's, this is not the time to think about it.
We have horrendous financial problems to face; and I submit
one of the reasons we have such horrendous problems to face
is that we have not done our job as we should.  We have not
understood that a librarian is librarian of something--he does
not get up or she does not get up someday and say I am going
to be a librarian and then starts running around all over the
landscape "librarianing."  You are a librarian of a high
school, a college, a public library, an industrial organization, etc., and it is this something of which you are librarian that is the important part.  The rest are just tools and
you see we have mistaken the tool for the substance, the
thing for the intellectual process.  I think we are going to
pay the penalty for this even more in the next few years.
I wish I could give you glad tidings of great joy but I can
not, I end as I began with Keats' fish in hot water and
Kathleen Molz's charge against the public library.

        The problem of the unrestrained growth of libraries
does, nonetheless confront us with new responsibilities.
Derek deSola Price in Science Since Babylon, foresees a time
when science cannot advance because it can no longer en-
compass the information that it has generated, and thus is
stymied by the proliferation of its own findings.  James
Thurber, in one of his last short stories, has one of his
characters say, "So much has been written about everything
that it is difficult to find out anything about it."  We have
all of us heard this statement about the growth of knowledge
repeated ad nauseam, but we do seem powerless to bring all
this data under control.  A headline writer in a recent issue
of the Christian Science Monitor, wrote, "Data data everywhere, and not a thought to think."  Tony Oettinger of Harvard's Program on Information Resources Policy, has said
that "there are more statistical abstracts, more numbers,
more data, more unread Books floating around, but what is
as scarce as ever before is sound, believable knowledge."

He estimates that half the labor force is engaged in what he
calls "information occupations," that is teaching, publishing,
news media, etc.  These he says, in a pejorative sense,
do not produce anything.  He goes on to say that 25 percent
of the gross national product is consumed in information
products, i. e., telephone calls, radio and television programs and similar messages.  The world is rapidly growing
out of parking space for its information, even earth's spectrum space, the territory through which radio frequencies
travel, is becoming congested with satellites and the flow of
information.  We are indeed threatened with an information
overload.

        The great danger that is inherent in this threatened
information overload, is that society might overreact and
turn to a new anti-intellectualism.  In our enthusiasm for
science, particularly, we may have oversold the graphic
record.  There is no proof that our so-called "scientific
age," will continue to make new discoveries, continue to
"enhance" our much-touted standard of living.  Our capacity
for construction may turn to destruction.  Wherever we look
we see danger threatening at the margins.  There are indeed
ominous clouds on the horizon.

        I know you who are school librarians certainly en-
countered that very fine series of books for the middle years
from between childhood and adulthood, novels dealing with
England after the departure of the Romans and the devasta-
tion and chaos and so on, beautifully done books, an adult
can get a great deal from them too.  At the end of one of
these books which is called The Lantern Bearers, the old
man and the young man, I never can remember their names--
they are very strange--are standing on a hill looking down
over this desolate landscape and the young man is terribly
distraught.  His father has been killed, his sister has been
taken away, he does not know to what, and the old man said
to him, "I sometimes think that we stand at sunset and it
may be that the darkness will close over us in the end, but
I believe the morning will come again.  The morning always
comes again after the darkness except, perhaps, for those
who saw the sun go down.  We are the lantern bearers my
friend,"--this is a phrase to which I would direct your attention particularly.  We are the lantern bearers my friends,
for us to keep something burning, to carry what light we can
forward into the darkness and the wind--that my friends is
the apotheosis of librarianship, and I am very much afraid
that the time will come when we librarians, like the medie-

val scholars of old, may be called upon to shield the flickering lamp of learning from winds of a new barbaric storm.

## Notes

1.  Finley Peter Dunne.  Mr. Dooley on Ivrything and Ivry-
    body.  New York:  Dover, 1963.  p. 226.
2.  Kathleen Molz.  "The Public Custody of the High Pornog-
    raphy."  American Scholar.  v. 36 (Winter 1966-1967)
    pp. 102-103.
3.  Georg Christoph Lichtenberg.  Aphorismen, Brief,
    Satiren.  Dusseldorf, Koln.  Eugen Diederichs Verlag.
    1962.  p. 48.  The German gives, monkey (Affe) and
    apostle, but I have taken the liberty of changing the
    monkey to a jackass, and identifying the apostle as
    St. Paul.

# TOWARD A CONCEPTUAL FOUNDATION FOR A NATIONAL INFORMATION POLICY*

David Kaser

## The problem

Thomas Jefferson once observed that there is probably no branch of knowledge that is not of potential use in governing a nation. In a democracy, where government is built upon the aggregate judgments of individual voters, all branches of knowledge must therefore be available to all people. For in a democracy everyone has both the responsibility to participate in the decisions of the nation and the accompanying right to expect access to such information as will enhance the quality of that participation.

People need to be adequately informed not only to exercise their franchise judiciously, but also to live productive lives in physical, mental, and moral strength and to pursue the intellectual and spiritual fulfillment of their myriad and diverse motivations. The full actualization of a democracy depends, perforce, upon the full actualization of each of its inhabitants.

For these reasons information cannot truly be viewed in the United States as a commodity to be bargained for in the marketplace; it is, rather, a vital life fluid coursing throughout the body politic, essential to its continuing renewal and growth. It is thus incumbent upon the nation to provide the requisite arterial system as well as the free and

equitable flow of all nonproprietary, nonconfidential information to each individual, regardless of location, level of comprehension, economic status, or other circumstance.

This right of free and equitable access to information
is not new in the American social ethic, but has, rather,
been the lodestar of the American public library movement
for almost a century and a half.  The nation's advancing
social requirements and technical capabilities during that
time, however, have resulted in vast changes in the nature
of libraries, so that today they embrace not only traditional
repositories of print materials but also computer-based data
stores, information and reference centers, film and tape collections and services, and other similarly diverse activities, many
of which are more costly to operate than were their less-complex
predecessors.  Whatever their cost should ultimately become,
however, the cost to the nation of not so providing information to
its inhabitants seems certain to be higher.

The nation must therefore reaffirm its mandate to its
publicly supported libraries to seek out and deliver to all
people the information they need or desire, as well in the
newer, more expensive modes as in the older, more traditional
ways.  For out of information comes knowledge, and out of
knowledge comes wisdom, and those nations that determine
their actions most wisely seem destined the longest to endure.

The proposition

The information needs and aspirations of this nation can be
fulfilled only through the attainment of five separate, but
related, "universals."  All information must be available to
all people in all formats purveyed through all communication
channels and delivered at all levels of comprehension.  If any
one of these five qualities is compromised, the whole is ener-
vated, and the national enterprise as a consequence suffers.

All information
The essential nature of total information to business and
industry, science and technology, education and the professions, is immediately apparent and, consequently, is seldom
if ever questioned.  Likewise, the information needs of public and private-sector institutions and establishments are
usually assumed.  Of equal moment, however, although sometimes overlooked, are the information requirements of indi-
viduals--information on such social concerns as laws, services, and public policy; on such life needs as health and

housing, food and transportation, employment and welfare
assistance; on such human problems as aging, the family,
sex, work, politics, love, and leisure; on such issues as
will permit the meshing of American society and culture
amicably and beneficially with others in the world.

All information means all information--that perceived
to be false as well as that thought to be true; that designed
to inspire or to appeal to the imagination and that of immediate practical application; that enjoying acceptance and that
thought to be repugnant; that viewed as meeting current
social standards and that above or below or outside of such
standards; that of obvious utility and that for which no use
is known--for the motivation in all of mankind to put knowledge to work is as boundless as the human psyche itself.
No impairment can be brooked in this flow of information.
It must neither be rendered inaccessible by the imposition
of fees upon the individual users, nor staunched by censorship official or unofficial, nor impeded by intimidation overt
or covert.

All people

Access to information must be equitably available to everyone.  Everyone means everyone:  children and adults, the
rich and the poor, the institutionalized and the migrant, the
bright and the dull, the place-bound and the mobile, the
leaders and the followers.  A universal populace can perhaps
most easily be visualized as a grid, with categories of individuals and groups ranged along one axis (e. g. , parents,
corporations, teenagers, aliens, workers, students, agencies, consumers, families, etc.), and specific characteristics ranged along the other (e. g. , race, sex, age, location,
state of mind, language preference, strength, ethnic heritage,
economic status, etc.).  Viewed thus, the possible variations
can be seen as limitless.  Flexibility of service programs,
moreover, is necessary, because there is constant movement
on the grid, as individuals need information in one capacity
at one particular time and in a very different capacity at
another.  The commonweal demands that the information
needs of everyone on the grid be equitably attended.

All formats

Universal accessibility to information can be achieved only
when all possible formats are available for its delivery.
Much information, of course, is normally found in printed
form in books, magazines, and newspapers.  Other kinds of
information, however, are often best purveyed pictorially,

orally, or digitally.    Each of these formats also has sub-
parts.    Pictorial presentation of some information, for example, can be effectively accomplished through still pictures,
whereas other kinds require moving pictures; some can be
purveyed in black-and-white, whereas others might require
color.    In still other cases the information to be transmitted has requirements which transcend the capability of flat
pictures to convey, so that models, realia, and other three-
dimensional formats sometimes become necessary.

      The nature of the information being transmitted is not
the only determinant of format.    The location of a person
needing information, for example, may dictate that it be delivered orally by telephone.    A group may be best informed
by audiotape or motion picture.    A blind person may require
a braille or talking book.    A person lacking the ability to
read will obviously require a format other than print.    For
all people to be equitably furnished with information, all
known delivery formats will at one time or another be called
into service, and the public must therefore have access to
libraries which stock them all.

                      <u>All communication channels</u>
Not only must publicly funded libraries stock information in
all formats, but they must also obviously possess the communication mechanisms and the requisite expertise to deliver
information in those formats.    For information transfer to
be effective, there must be a match between the channel of
delivery and the natural predilection of the receiver.    Perhaps the most common representation of information today,
for example, is the printed book, yet the recipient must be
able to read if full use is to be made of the information
transmitted through that medium.    It is a logical corollary
to the principle of universal access to information that a
variety of channels of communication be maintained so that
access is never foreshortened as a result of mismatch between one's personal or physical capabilities and the properties of the communication channel.    Care must be exerted to
ensure that attention is not devoted to one or two particular
channels of communication to the exclusion or detriment of
others which might be less used, more expensive, or perhaps less glamorous.

      It must be recognized in this connection that a li-
brarian can be, in a very literal sense, part of a communication channel, or indeed in some cases even the very channel itself, capable of affecting profoundly the behavior of so-

ciety.    This becomes true when the librarian brings in what
is in effect "disembodied" information to persons lacking the
requisite ability to receive information stored in any conventional format.    A comprehensive national information policy
must therefore make as much provision for the preparation
of competent librarians as for the development of sophisticated information hardware.

                                    All levels of comprehension
Information, by definition, must have the capability of effecting a change of state in the recipient.    This fact dictates
that libraries must be designed and stocked to deliver information that can be assimilated by people at several levels of
comprehension:  by those of limited intellect as well as by
those with substantial capacity for understanding; by the un-
learned as well as by those of greatest erudition; by those
who are fluent in English as well as by those whose heritage
is in a language other than English; by those who can communicate in the standard language of the nation and by those
who must have it translated into a local or colloquial idiom
before it becomes meaningful to them.

        Equitability of access to information requires that
every individual be within reach of information pitched specifically at his or her level of comprehension.    This fact
brings with it an attendant requirement that the information
needs of all people be equally understood.    Many documents
are written in ways that are not easily understood by the
people whom they affect most.    Libraries must be prepared
in such cases to modulate information to levels of compre-
hensibility capable of being assimilated by those to whom it
is significant, so that information losses or gaps do not
occur.

        Without fulfillment of these five universals--of infor-
mation, of users, of formats, of channels, and of levels--
some Americans are destined to become information-rich and
others are destined to become information-poor.    Information is power, and an information-elite is a power-elite,
neither of which has any place in a democracy.    The nation
must in its own interest strive sedulously to ensure that such
pockets of privilege do not come into being.    The nation's
publicly funded libraries are its primary line of defense
against such an eventuality.

## The need

Despite long and widespread recognition of the compelling and integral role of publicly funded libraries in the nation's information delivery capability, conditions are not now optimally conducive to the fulfillment of their responsibilities in this role. The United States has in recent years fallen behind such diverse nations as the United Kingdom, Jamaica, Denmark, and the Soviet Union in providing a statutory environment in which libraries can best accomplish the tasks assigned to them by society. Legislative changes are needed in the United States, some entailing funding and some not, to ensure that its overarching information policy, now being developed, will enable its libraries to serve its citizens most effectively. The ensuing paragraphs define the principal legislative modifications now needed.

1) An appropriate locus must be identified or established in the federal government for the implementation and administration of a national information program. Certain components of such a program are already charged to the Library of Congress and others to the National Commission on Libraries and Information Science. Neither, however, has full authorization to proceed, and early resolution of this impasse is essential. If a single agency cannot be developed, then a strong interagency library authority might be appropriate, but at this time that would appear to be a second-best solution. At any rate, this locus of authority should have the benefit of ad hoc and continuing counsel from two kinds of advisory bodies: one representing the entire user community to assure that its information needs are clearly understood, and another comprising representatives of library professional organizations to participate in the determination of appropriate systems and processes for meeting those needs.

2) Federal funding is necessary for adequate library and information service. In view of the competition for federal funds among essential national programs, the costs of these library services might best and most fairly be met by a tax transfer assessed against those components of the private sector that derive increased productivity from the utilization of information. Federal funds should be sufficient:

    a) to ensure that threshold levels of library service, with necessary collections and plant facilities, be available in the local communities;

    b) to develop and maintain an adequate number of

librarians, educated and continually up-dated in their
training, to provide requisite library service;
c) to provide centrally the core components for a
total information system required at the national level,
including the preparation of standard bibliographic
data, the rendering of library processing support, the
identification and administration of "last copies" of
all publications wherever located, and an appropriate
research and development capability;
d) to design, implement, and maintain a computer
and telecommunications network adequate to these
needs.

3) The provision of library service is a joint responsibility
of federal, state, and local government, yet the equitable
distribution among them of the responsibilities and costs of
library service is a matter of debate.  This issue needs to
be resolved.  State governments seem clearly to have an obligation to plan and coordinate statewide library and information services, to develop and maintain information networks
appropriate to their respective jurisdictions, and to participate in the funding of requisite library services at the local
level.  Legal authority for such involvement needs to be developed in those states where it does not now exist.

4) Just as information needs transcend jurisdictional bounds
within the United States, so also do they transcend international boundaries.  Thus, it is incumbent upon this country
to develop its total information system in such a manner that
it will articulate smoothly with those of other nations, a
responsibility that could easily lend itself to the imposition
centrally of rigid, monolithic constraints.  Yet diversity is
the hallmark of a democracy, and every effort should be
exerted to protect a "right to diversity" within the nation's
information policy.

5) It is an irony that the free flow of information also implies some constraints and protections that can best be provided under federal auspices.  It seems certain to be in the
national interest that some kinds of information be considered
"confidential," yet there is great unclarity surrounding that
term.  Likewise, the common good would seem to require
that some kinds of information be treated as "proprietary,"
although here again the issue is cloudy.  Some feel that a
confidential relationship must be preserved between a librarian and a patron, but under present law such status does
not appear to exist.  These three issues need study, resolu-

tion, and accommodation as warranted in the laws of the land.

6) And finally, it is important that a nation's information policy cover all information--that it be conceived in recognition that universal knowledge is greater than the sum of its parts, that there is an inviolable unity and coherence to the record of man's experiences and imaginings, his strivings and disappointments, that is imperiled when fragmented by special interests. No segment of knowledge is more or less deserving of the favor of public policy than is any other. Searchers after truth, or solace, or joy, or inspiration, or profit, or wisdom, or escape, have equal right to share the benefits of this nation's vast information resources, a right that must be protected in the symmetrical and balanced development of those resources under public stewardship.

Note

This statement was drafted by a special committee for the American Library Association's "President's Program" at its 1978 Midwinter Meeting. The ad hoc committee, chaired by David Kaser, was made up of Fay Blake, Mary K. Chelton, E. J. Josey, S. Michael Malinconico, Peggy Sullivan, and Roderick Swartz.

# Part II

# TECHNICAL SERVICES/READERS' SERVICES

SOME THOUGHTS ON PUBLIC LIBRARIES

AND THE NATIONAL BIBLIOGRAPHIC NETWORK*

Maurice J. Freedman

Introduction

A series of myths concerning public library cataloging needs
should be dispelled. These myths have too long held sway,
and without their destruction, any national bibliographic network including public libraries will do them a disservice.

The first myth is that there must be a single national
standard catalog record for all libraries. Prima facie, considering the number and diversity of libraries populating the
United States, this ought to make no sense at all. Indeed,
it does not make sense to the National Library of Medicine,
which chooses to enmesh itself in its own NLM subject headings, nor to the host of other medical libraries around the
country following NLM's lead.

The second myth is that a single catalog record with
a single articulated punctuation style should be placed in all
the catalogs in all the countries of the world. It's hard to
sustain this under the rubric "myth," since it's so recent in
origin. But its advocacy by the proponents of Universal
Bibliographic Control requires that it be disposed of, be it
labelled "myth" or merely "errant do-gooderism."

The first two myths can be attributed in large part to
over-zealous technical services administrators, abetted significantly by the Library of Congress. Nota bene, however,
that public librarians must take full credit for the third myth:

---

*Reprinted by permission of the author and publisher from
issue #28 of the HCL Cataloging Bulletin, pp. 4-14.

the notion that the catalog is something which has to be put
up with (or put down!), that a set of cards from the cheapest
source is sufficient for user needs, and that it makes no
difference what's on those cards or what preceded them into
the local catalog, so long as the cards purport to characterize the item purchased.   This myth is held by too many public library administrators.

Dispelling these fables is a prerequisite for an informed discussion of public library national bibliographical
network needs.   While the first part of this paper must perform that essentially negative enterprise, the second part
deals with the positive task of defining public library needs
and sketching a model for satisfying them.

## Cataloging myths

The prevalence and nurturing of myths is usually a function
of their value to the people who believe them.   Two integral-
ly related concepts underpin the perpetration and acceptance
of Bibliographic Myth #1.   First, the notion of standardization serves as a buttress that no iconoclasts, regardless of
their fearlessness, would challenge.   Second, and in several
obvious respects flowing from the first, is the reality of
cost.   A universally accepted standard catalog record which
can be popped into any catalog file, anywhere, at any time,
is cheaper and easier to process than a catalog record locally produced by highly paid professionals who tailor it to exclusively suit the local library's needs.   This, of course, is
unchallengeable.   So what's the gripe?   Why has there been
this raging cry for mythicide?   A close examination of the
three myths should provide the answers.

Let's begin by agreeing that public libraries cannot
afford to ignore standardization and economy in bibliographical control.   When an institution as great as The Branch Libraries of The New York Public Library is forced to its
knees because of budget cutbacks, attrition, and layoffs; and
when it is consequently forced to investigate acquiring its
materials commercially processed, then it's most difficult,
especially for me, to ignore the persuasiveness of the cost
savings obtained by accepting standardized bibliographical
products.

Rather than repeat the extensive arguments presented
elsewhere (e. g. , "Processing for the people," LJ, 1-1-76),

here is only a brief review of deficiencies in the present
standard bibliographic product and their basis in history and
practice.  Simply put, the LC catalog record is chiefly created to serve the needs of the Library of Congress, whose
primary responsibility is to the United States Congress.
Second, this bibliographical entity must be consistent with
and fit into the card catalog of the largest research library
in the world.  Two immediate inferences can be made from
the fact that LC's a research library.  One, LC's books and
other materials are collected on an archival basis.  Second,
and following from the first, is the fact that the card catalog
representing those collections is monstrous in size.  Thus,
any change in terminology, especially for extensively used
headings, will be hideously expensive and resisted for practical, if not theoretical, reasons.  Our colleagues at LC
really do know that "FIRST WORLD WAR" or "WORLD WAR
I" are phrases more commonly used to describe a particular
period of history than "EUROPEAN WAR, 1914-1918."  But
it would literally cost LC thousands of dollars to reprint all
the cards upon which this heading appears.  Further, the
University of California, Berkeley, as well as other research/
archival libraries with huge card catalogs, finds it more
practical to retain some of the less offensive and anachronistic LC terms than to incur all of the labor-intensive costs
associated with improving them.  (As an aside, it's gratify-
ing to note at this time that LC in many cases agrees with
criticisms of its name and subject forms.  Unfortunately, it
still refuses to change them, but for practical and economic
reasons.  On my more optimistic days I view this as progress.)

        Public libraries, with the exception of the very larg-
est ones like the privately-supported NYPL Research Libraries, are not archival, nor do they generally collect materials for the express purpose of supporting scholarly research.
What this means, especially for the urban branches and medium and small public libraries, is that the bulk of their materials will turn over in five to ten years.  Barring special
collections of local material, even titles of more enduring
value will be replaced by newer copies because the earlier
purchases have become worn or, as we all too frequently
say, "lost in circulation."  The implications of this are obvious.  For the thousands of public libraries a change of
entry is a temporary inconvenience that can be handled by
appropriate "see also" references.  After five or ten years,
the number of cards remaining with the old term or name
will be few at best.  They could be far more economically

changed at that time, or the library can choose to wait.
Remember that LC has approximately 17,000,000 volumes in
its collections.    At 3.2 cards per volume (a guess), that's
about 54,400,000 cards.    A public library with 100,000
volumes, and possibly a 10-20% duplication of titles, does
not face LC's catalog maintenance problems.

   Conclusion: It is unfair and unjust to saddle public
and other non-archival libraries with cataloging decisions
that derive from LC's internal catalog maintenance problems.
The first myth is that a single catalog record can be used
for all libraries.    As shown in a perhaps oversimplified
manner, this single catalog record is based primarily on the
practical and theoretical considerations of the Library of
Congress.    And LC usually accommodates the needs of other
libraries only when they do not conflict with LC's internal
requirements.

   The second myth, the notion of an international catalog record virginally dropping into catalogs of all countries,
is hard to discuss rationally.    As an outspoken critic of the
International Standard Bibliographic Description (ISBD), I
would nonetheless admit to its utility for the world's national
libraries from the standpoint of data conversion.    But just
recently the proponents of Universal Bibliographical Control
seem to have finally run amok.    They have proposed, in effect, an international thesaurus of subject terms.    Economiz-
ing has its limits.    It is patent madness to use a subject
term constructed in a foreign country when it conflicts with
the term used in one's own--simply for the sake of international standardization.    For example, why should the English
use MOTOR-TRUCKS (for that matter, why should Americans?) when their primary reference is to LORRIES?    Why
can't a whole country afford itself the luxury, nay the necessity, of a thesaurus of terms and names suiting its internal
needs:    the needs of the national population it's supposed to
serve?

   As to ISBD, its adoption by LC and ALA was a sad
day for public libraries.    ISBD had as an expressed goal the
easier communication of cataloging data across national bor-
ders and different languages, as well as decreasing the cost
of machine conversion of catalog records in a variety of languages.    Latin abbreviations, the truncation of "illus." to
"ill.," and the introduction of a variety of esoteric punctuation marks may serve the needs of LC's and Berkeley's
users, but the bafflement of non-research patrons definitely

has to be a consequence.   It requires no empirical study to
know that there is little likelihood that the library patron
will understand an abbreviation of a phrase in a language the
patron does not speak or read.

        The second myth, that a single catalog record with a
single articulated punctuation style should be placed in all of
the library catalogs of the world, is especially searing to the
soul of the user-oriented public librarian.   Conservatively,
it is estimated that only 15 to 20% of the population uses the
public library.   Assuming 200,000,000 people inhabit this
country, approximately 30,000,000 of them, at least, use the
public library.   Would it not be unreasonable to claim that
constructing a format for the primary purpose of facilitating
recognition of catalog data by 30,000,000 American library
users is a valid enterprise?   It is at least as reasonable as
the construction of a format for the comparatively few library
users who need to examine catalog records in languages they
do not understand or national libraries wanting to more effectively control conversion costs.   Surprisingly enough, at
least to someone who does not understand the power and influence of a small minority of technical services librarians,
the needs of the few became the myth for the many.

        So much for the second myth with which public li-
braries have been saddled.   But the third has been of their
own doing.   Altogether too many public library administrators have taken the position that all that's needed is processing, that is, a set of cards.   They believe that what's on the
received catalog records or how they cohere with the records
which preceded them is relatively unimportant.   The conceptual and economic basis for this myth cannot be easily gain-
said.   The argument used earlier--that the books represented
by these records will eventually be removed and hence the
catalog records for them also--seems to make it less important for the non-archival library to be absolutely consistent.   The argument for practicality or cost follows in part
from the above, but from another argument as well:   Since
catalog records are available from an outside source such
as a commercial or central processor, there is no need to
dedicate expensive personnel resources to cataloging.   They
could then be assigned to public service work.   This latter
service normally cannot be contracted for nor purchased.   So
it seems reasonable to allocate available staff to serving the
public face-to-face, rather than expending it on an ephemeral
service that can be purchased cheaply from an outside source.

        The fact that many catalogers have managed to make

cataloging an arcane or esoteric art form, combined with
some of LC's less successful practices, have turned public
library administrators off of the fundamental notion that the
catalog can be something more than a hard-to-use finding
tool.   The notion that the catalog organizes the collection
and plays a positive and productive public service role is
foreign to too many of them.

        Where's the myth?   So far the public library admin-
istrator seems to be a practical and reasonable person.
Arguing from the standpoint of networking, or from the more
limited view of cooperation and interlibrary loan within a
federated system, what problems are produced by this myth?
(By federated system or cooperative, what is intended is a
voluntary association of independent libraries for the purpose
of mutual benefit. )   If the members of a cooperative do not
get their catalog records from a single, self-consistent
source, the chances for conflicts are maximized, and can be
safely guaranteed.   It is easy to see how a single library
can find it difficult to consistently serve itself.   By extension, the maintenance of uniformity between several individual libraries, receiving records from a variety of sources,
has to be well nigh impossible.

        Two alternatives and their respective consequences
can now be analyzed.   First, if the different sources are in-
consistent with respect to each other, the individual library's
catalog will have conflicts, and the catalogs of the various
federated libraries will also conflict.   Put simply, interlibrary loan for unavailable materials at Library A will be
difficult to procure from Library B if the works are cited
differently in the respective catalogs.   The second alternative:   If cooperative members get all of their cataloging from
the same source, a commercial processor creating records
from LC's MARC tapes, the chances of there being consistency between library catalogs is obviously much greater.
But unfortunately this uniformity leaves the public library
administrator saddled with the problems created by the first
myth.

        Furthermore, two critical considerations must obtain
if the public library catalog is to bear a semblance of utility,
even if MARC is the sole source of catalog records.   First,
like it or not, catalog support is required even for these
MARC records.   Cross-references and some form of authority control must be maintained if patrons are to effectively
find their way around the catalog.   Second, many public li-

braries use title-page cataloging for fiction, preferring to
have Gothic, mystery, and other ephemeral fiction forms
shelved by the author's pseudonym rather than by a single
form, which most commonly is the real name.  Under the
current rules, a single form is required.  The public library has to do its own fiction cataloging, linking the vari-
ant names of a given author by see-also references, if the
library is to lead the reader, via the catalog, to where these
books are shelved.  If one wishes to stay with MARC and
LC's entry forms, the only common alternative is to rig up
a system wherein "dummy" books are placed on the shelf
and the browser, i. e., the non-catalog user, is directed to
the LC-form by which the book is shelved.

The final argument offered for the third myth is
actually the ultimate "anti-catalog" argument:  smaller public libraries don't really need a catalog.  In such libraries,
so the argument goes, one need only stand in front of the
broad Dewey section of one's interest and individually examine the spine of each book in the hope that the title sought
will be there.  Of course, trying to reserve a volume not
found on the shelf will be made more difficult by the absence
of a local catalog.  First of all, no determination can be
made as to whether the library owns the item; and second,
a correct citation for interlibrary loan purposes will be far
more difficult to verify.

Essentially, the public librarians are dammed no
matter what they do.  Following LC as currently constituted
leaves one open to all the problems of the first myth.  The
alternative, the modification route, increases costs and max-
imizes the chances for conflict in the library's own catalog
and between the catalogs of the various cooperating libraries.
In all cases, effective reader service will usually require
linking references, a job requiring some application of cataloging rules and practices.

So we see that the myth is okay if the following unhappy alternatives are acceptable to the public library administrator:  a) limited cooperation between his or her library and other libraries; b) limited catalog access, at best,
for the works of a writer using more than one name; or c)
LC cataloging faults in preference to locally adapting the LC
record.

In summary, public libraries are confronted with this
bad choice:  accept LC cataloging and get less than the qual-

ity of the cataloging their users deserve; or do their own cataloging, or get it from another non-standardized source, running the risk of being unable to functionally cooperate with other libraries. The third myth produces a Hobson's Choice, i.e., a choice between undesirable alternatives, a condition which should be sufficient to dispel it.

## Some considerations on a model for public library bibliographic networking

The whole point of destroying the three myths was to clear away the sophistic and self-serving rationalizations which, for too long, have made the catalog a bibliographic barrier to public library collections. How shall we rise from the rubble? Let's begin by examining what elements of the bibliographical record need change. After that, additional variables can be specified to serve as preconditions for a national bibliographic network which would truly satisfy public library bibliographical control needs.

## A. Bibliographic elements

Several elements must be ingredient in any nationally distributed record. First, there must be contemporaneous, relevant and sensitive headings applied. Certainly, the fact of catalog maintenance problems at LC and other archival libraries is no self-sufficient reason for non-research libraries continuing to use anachronistic or insensitive terminology. Second, in the area of entry, many public libraries, ranging from the smallest reading center with 3,000 volumes to city libraries with hundreds of thousands of titles, enter fiction under the author's title-page name so that browsers will find it on the shelf under the name they associate with the work, the name by which it is popularly known and advertised. No brief is being issued for abandoning authority control and name establishment. The public library catalog user should be informed through comprehensive "see-also" references of all of the names by which an Eleanor Hibbert chooses to write. In this way, the principle of bringing together all of the works of a given author is met in spirit, even if not met literally. In defense of this slight diversion from the Paris Principles, Charles Ammi Cutter 73 years ago wrote in the 4th edition of his Rules for a Dictionary Catalog, "This elastic practice [of entering both under the real and the false name] will give a little more trouble to the cataloger than a

rigid rule of entry under the real name, but it will save
trouble to those who use the catalog, which is more important" (p. 28).   Of course, for non-fiction the LC main entry
should be acceptable, although there might be some minor
caveats.   Since virtually all public libraries classify non-
fiction, access is by classmark, which means that a real-
name or pseudonymous entry does not have primary impact
on shelf location.

The third bibliographical element involves more generous assignment of subject headings and other added entries.
This suggestion has usually met with a negative LC response,
because its already over-crowded card drawers, thickened by
several feet of cards under headings like TRANSPORTATION,
could not stand any extra increase, nor could LC's user,
who is already overwhelmed by the number of cards to handle
under the current, relatively restrictive policy.   Public library catalogs, especially the non-card-based ones, could
most advantageously use these extra headings and entries to
improve service, especially where collections are limited.
As noted in relation to the first myth, public library collections turn over and their catalogs tend not to have to sustain
the weight of antiquity's and posterity's needs.   They only
need to serve their present public.   So it's suggested that
these extra entries would be helpful for public libraries, and
would not be the major problem they are for archival libraries and their users.   One particular area where additional
subject cataloging would be welcomed is fiction.

The fourth bibliographical element really pertains to
the whole bibliographic record.   The overall physical display
of the catalog record must be subjected to rigorous empirical study.   The nearly non-existent library literature on the
subject of catalog record format, and the behavioral science
literature, especially those aspects concerned with perception
and readability, should both be examined with the objective of
setting up controlled experiments to eventually yield an optimized catalog record display format.   The proponents of
ISBD, in their headlong rush to inflict it on us for our own
good, performed no empirical investigations that I'm aware
of.   Let the determination to seek an optimized format for
displaying cataloging records be a progressive precedent;
that is, let research be the basis for developing cataloging
rules and procedures.   This will be a most welcome change
from what's been going on in recent years.

## B.  Assumptions

A national network model which would satisfy the bibliographic control needs of the nation's public libraries is something to offer only tentatively and with reservations.   Toward that end, these are some working assumptions:

1.  Public libraries want, need, and deserve a standard bibliographic record oriented toward the service needs of their clientele.

2.  Until proven otherwise, LC will still be the central creator and distributor of these records, but will no longer originate and maintain these records exclusively.   (It will probably still be the national custodian of files comprehending these records. )

3.  A single, comprehensive, machine-readable record can probably include the elements required by the various library publics LC is trying to serve. It is assumed that the MARC record can be modified to accommodate these changes.   For example, juvenile and NLM headings are currently included in the MARC records.   In addition, a host of changes have already been made to the MARC format, with more on the way, to accommodate CONSER, a cooperative archival libraries' serials project.

4.  The last assumption is that everything in the MARC record will not necessarily be printed on the LC card.   In other words, LC might have a research-library-oriented and a non-research-library-oriented card.   In fact, there will have to be two different cards once the optimized display format is developed.   (There's a strong likelihood that it will conflict with the ISBD. )   Of course, differing main entries for the same work would also necessitate different cards, but this only occurs in the limited case of fiction for which the title page entry contradicts the LC main entry.

## C.  Requirements

We have now reviewed and disposed of three myths, and laid

out four bibliographical elements and four assumptions, but
still have not gotten to the network model.  Kindly bear with
me a little longer.  It's necessary to stipulate some minimum requirements and parameters for the functioning of this
network.

The first requirement is that there be an unequivocal
commitment to get the approximate 24-35,000 domestic titles
acquired by public libraries cataloged by LC in a timely and
expeditious manner.  CIP, with its abbreviated entries and
incomplete records, is useful, but not sufficient.  Some unpublished studies indicate that thousands of CIP records for
books that have been published and available for significant
periods of time remain on the MARC file as incomplete catalog records.

The number of persons LC employs to catalog its
German acquisitions, or at most its German and French acquisitions, should be more than enough professional staff to
meet the cataloging needs of all of America's public libraries in a timely and efficient manner.  Assuming the books
would be acquired in a reasonable time, the possibility of
complete catalog records by publication date or earlier is
not wholly unreasonable.  In any case, the timeliness requirement would be met if LC were to treat America's public libraries with the same concentration of effort and concern it so marvelously evinced when it went into the different NPAC countries--in effect, a bibliographical Marshall
Plan for America's public libraries.

The second requirement is that LC take a far more
aggressive approach to the needs of its constituency that
collects such materials as sound recordings.  Recently a
decision was made, blamed primarily on funding, to get the
balance of the Roman alphabet languages into MARC.  Simultaneously, another delay was announced for the implementation of MARC music.  One would guess that there are probably 500 to 1000 libraries in this country that collect sound
recordings for every one that collects materials in the Roman
languages still outside of MARC.  It is not suggested that
these remaining languages should not get into MARC.  It is
fervently urged, however, that the collection requirements of
America's public libraries receive a priority comparable to
that enjoyed by the nation's research libraries.  It is assumed that this requirement and anything else stated here
would not conflict with LC's primary responsibility to Congress.

The third requirement is that LC maintain a national
file of authorities, headings, and references, which in principle can be maintained, that is, expanded and changed, on
a controlled basis by specified public library cataloging centers.   It is unrealistic to assume that all the changes required of LC names and headings can necessarily be handled
by LC's cataloging staff.   Not being a public library staff
nor having contact with the people using public libraries, it
seems unfair to expect LC's employees to always be successful at meeting the needs of the public library's constituency.
It would also put to an end the constant bickering, seemingly
from time immemorial, between LC and its critics over
whether certain research-oriented terms have any applicabil-
ity for non-research library users.   Having made provision
for alternate terms, the small percentage of headings needing accommodation will be minimal.   (For example, Hennepin
County Library, noted for its efforts to make its catalog responsive to its clientele's needs, freely changes an LC heading it finds unsatisfactory and freely adds a new one when it
determines that LC has not yet provided an appropriate de-
scriptor.   Even with this "Liberty Hall" approach, only 15
to 20% of the Hennepin headings either conflict with or were
not included in the valid terms currently comprising LC's
subject list.   This means that at least 80% of the headings
used by LC are acceptable to a public library which has few
reservations about rejecting LC terms in favor of its users'
needs. )

Should anyone be concerned about LC managing a
national authority file of dual headings, the National Library
of Canada, with its bilingual or dual headings, has established
its feasibility.   For the record, the precedent for automated
control of dual entries was established with the implementation in 1971 of the dual entry function in The New York Public Library's automated bibliographical control system.   Another alternative suggested has been the University of Chicago's Data Base Management System (Library Quarterly,
Jan. 1977), with its quadroplanar data structure.   In the
January 1977 Library Trends I tried to describe how Chicago's approach, as implemented by the Washington Library
Network, would allow for alternative, yet rigorously controlled, authority files.   Again, the authority control component was based primarily on NYPL's bibliographic system.
Having had nothing to do with its conception or development,
it's not self-serving to state as an aside that the NYPL system may not have on-line sizzle, but it sure is good for con-
trolling catalog data.

Further, I've been assured by more sophisticated colleagues that the various proposals contained herein are technically feasible.

The fourth requirement is that LC in principle accept original cataloging records for distribution purposes and for the national network data base that have been authenticated by and submitted from specified public library cataloging centers.  LC may continue to find it difficult to acquire and catalog certain categories of material (such as small press titles from the West Coast, according to one California public librarian), or may just miss specific titles for one reason or another, hence the need for contributed records.


D.   The model

At this point the model can be fleshed out.  At the center of the national bibliographic network would be LC, which would fulfill the creation, maintenance, and distribution functions.  LC would be providing a duality of bibliographic services by meeting the needs of the nation's archival and non-archival libraries alike.   This explicit duality of service goes beyond present LC services because it fully recognizes and accepts differences in the needs of these two major constituencies.  To reiterate, specified public library cataloging centers will contribute to the national network bibliographic data base as the participatory element on the non-archival side of the dualism.

Beyond LC, there are at least two other major elements in the model.   Already alluded to are those public library catalog centers which would interact with both the national authority file and the national bibliographic data base.  These centers would add to and change national network authorities as appropriate, contribute catalog records to the national network catalog, and probably serve as authentication centers for catalog records created by other public libraries which in turn could be added to the national data base.   This latter intermediary and authentication role is critical if there is to be any control over the national network catalog.

It is assumed that there will be only a single catalog record for a given bibliographic work.   The national network catalog should consist of a file of these unique records which in principle may contain alternate entry or access points to them.

The third element in the model is the bibliographic service center. Such a center can be a commercial jobber, a state library, a local processing center, or any agency with the capability to take the redefined MARC record and use it to provide bibliographic products and services on demand.

Two unanswered questions or problems to this point are: Who does the local public library inform of its holdings, and who maintains a record of them for the purpose of cooperation, interlibrary loan, regional catalogs, etc. ? These questions are not easily resolved. In the case of a Washington Library Network or an Illinet (the Illinois Library Network), the state agency seems more than equal to the task of masterminding and coordinating these activities. Further, in the case of Washington, it also provides service center functions. But in other cases, commercial vendors may provide service center functions, as indeed book catalog contractors do at present. Again, they must remain unanswered pending further study as to the best fit, and the hierarchical and horizontal relationships between the individual public libraries and the national catalog function and center. One solution has been proposed by Michael Malinconico. He suggests that bibliographic utilities, i. e. public library cataloging centers, serve as the bibliographic link between the national network catalog and the local library. This bibliographic utility would insure network standards, provide a standard interface to the network between the local libraries and cooperatives and maintain local and regional holdings files. These bibliographic utilities would not necessarily be restricted to public library catalog centers, but the service centers referred to earlier would not conflict with them, and in some cases would undoubtedly be one and the same institution. The Washington Library Network would seem to be a most pertinent example of this dual functioning.

In review, the model would have four components. At the top of the hierarchy would be LC as the custodian of the national network catalog and the primary contributor to that catalog and distributor of its contents. At the next level would be bibliographic utilities, including at least some public library catalog centers, which would interact with the national catalog in a carefully controlled and prescribed fashion. These utilities would also maintain local and regional holdings data and be the interface or link with the national network. Library service centers would have access to the information held by the utility, and would provide

products and services on demand to local libraries, regional
cooperatives, etc. Again, the service center could be identical to the utility, a commercial vendor, or a non-profit
corporation set up for the express purpose of providing these
products and services. This model is preliminary and
sketchy. The critical element for the present is not the
mechanics, but the data that will be transmitted. Subsequently these horizontal and vertical relationships must be
worked out. Ultimately all of the pieces must fit together
properly if the whole thing is going to work. We no doubt
are all tired of trying to sleep in a procrustean bed. This
proposal for a duality of service will hopefully allow standardized cataloging data from our national library to fit
more comfortably in all library catalogs.


Conclusion

These thoughts on public libraries and the national bibliographic network may disappoint those who want a detailed,
laid-out plan. To these people, an apology: At best, what
I've attempted is a rationale and a conception of how the
public library's public will gain faster and better access to
library materials through a standardized bibliographic record.

Among the tasks and studies that must be done if the
preceding is to be accomplished:

1. Making the specific modifications to MARC.

2. Defining in detail the national authority file and
   how the conflicting authorities will be controlled
   and linked.

3. Defining in detail the protocols by which the public library cataloging centers will interact with
   the national network catalog.

4. Defining in detail how the thousands of public libraries will all neatly fit into the national network and how they will relate to the public library
   cataloging centers--in other words, the mechanics
   of the network.

5. Defining the necessary and continuing role the
   commercial and regional processors will play.

6.  Defining the necessary relations between public
    and other kinds of libraries. Such relations are
    essential and assumed, but they must be speci-
    fied.

7.  Doing the "heavy" empirical research so that an
    optimized domestic catalog display format can be
    established.

Caveat Emptor:

# THE OWNERSHIP OF PUBLIC DOCUMENTS*

By Henry Bartholomew Cox

## The Nature of Replevin

As I have pondered whether individual purchase of public
documents is analogous to the fabled selling of the Brooklyn
Bridge, I am led to wonder if there would not be a more
difficult problem for the innocent purchaser of official manuscripts. A bridge is hardly invisible. He who would purchase must certainly nominally be aware that it is a thorough-
fare ostensibly titled in the public, and in almost continuous,
open and notorious use. Such an awareness, however, may
not exist concerning fugitive official documents. A public
document, after it has served its administrative uses, is
more often than not ignored. And in certain cases too numerous to mention it has been mistreated, even in the day of
scientific archival technique. Because many official documents have been discarded, they are still bought and sold
both publicly and privately. They are held by private individuals, as well as public repositories. Their visibility,
unlike the bridge, is quite low unless notoriety in the form
of legal action raises the formerly insignificant to the pre-
eminent.

A "Brooklyn Bridge" for private custodians is probably as valid a term as any to describe the fact that today
such custodians buy official manuscripts at their own risk.
But if any recourse to mythology were in order, I prefer an

---

*Reprinted by permission of the author and publisher from
the Sept. 4, 1978 issue of AB Bookman's Weekly, pp. 1243-61.

analogy to "The Emperor's New Clothes." New archival practice demands the citizen admit public records never left official custody. Resplendent only in the mind of the beholder, the texture of the custodial garment is complete despite any impolite remark to the contrary. And the moral of it all is that there can really be no bona fide purchaser of a public record. An archives does not need to buy because it always owned the record in the first place. A private individual may never own it, so it would be foolish for him to purchase. Let the buyer beware, and the fugitive paper be left alone.

If this be interpreted as facetiousness, it shouldn't be. Certain manuscript custodians have leveled a twenty-inch gun at the non-official holder, and have discharged it in the name of preservation. The Manuscript Society's response to professional archivists in October 1977 in Salt Lake City has made the Society of American Archivists quite aware of the fact that not only private collectors but also other professionals are seriously interested in the problems raised by the B. C. West case. Archivists have apparently thought enough of the importance of the issue to appoint a committee to study replevin and to render a report to the S. A. A. Though as of April 1978 that committee had not met, it probably will do so at the S. A. A. annual meeting in Nashville; and its membership is comprised of several custodians alert to the private collector's plight in owning what governments say had no right to be abandoned.

Replevin is a common law action for the recovery of personal property alleged to be wrongfully in the possession of another. [1] In the case of documents it could apply to stolen, abandoned, or discarded papers. A cardinal element of the legal cause of action is the fact that proof of ownership may not be presumed on the weakness of the defendant's title: that is, the plaintiff has to prove the removal of the article by improper or irregular circumstances.

Assistant Director William Price of the North Carolina Department of Cultural Resources states, in the American Archivist for January 1978, that his department's effort to recover a Washington letter from Parke-Bernet in early 1974, and the fact that there occurred a theft of manuscripts from the state archives in June 1974, alerted his staff to read catalogs of sale carefully. In late 1974 and early 1975, when B. C. West's offerings of the now famous Hooper district court documents appeared, Price says that despite the fact

he knew of no district court materials missing since the June
1974 theft, "we did believe that the documents might have
been stolen at some earlier time." Finding that the cases
referred to in the Hooper manuscripts were docketed in the
records in Raleigh as having been tried, the state proceeded
to define the Hooper manuscripts as demonstrably public records not legitimately out of official custody. Pride then
found that James I recovered crown papers from individuals
who took them from office after they left the service of the
king, and from England copies of the writs of recovery per-
taining to them were forwarded to archives director Thornton
Mitchell. North Carolina officials also discovered that Thomas
Frohock, to whom the Hooper indictments were addressed for
process, had been jailed in the early years of the Revolution
for failing to surrender his records as crown clerk to the
new state court. These tidbits of information were then
churned into the legal mill, and the rest of the story, broadly speaking, is familiar.

The complete account behind the replevin of English
crown documents is not accurately fabricated from snippets
of information woven into the casuistry of a lawyer's brief.
Adroit references to Thomas Frohock's jailing, James I's
attempts to get back officials' papers, or the fact that North
Carolina is the proud possessor of several Hooper indictments from the same district as the manuscripts offered by
Dr. West, are proofs of exactly nothing regarding this issue
in the case.

Many of the same type of Hooper indictments are still
owned by private collectors and dealers, while North Carolina state papers continue to be auctioned. At the April 26,
1978 Parke-Bernet sale of manuscripts formerly owned by
the Philip Sang Foundation, lot 107, consisting in part of
Nathanael Greene letters to Governor Nash of North Carolina,
was sold to Carnegie Book Shop of New York City for
$21,000. Perhaps now the North Carolina Department of
Cultural Resources will discover that such official materials
are missing or were "stolen" at some mysterious point in
the past. Inventories produced at the West trial showed the
Hooper indictments were not in the custody of North Carolina
prior to the 1930s. But even if the most careful inventory-
ing of all court records in that state or in any other could
locate such records as having been in state possession at
some time prior to the enactment of statutes providing for
their orderly disposition, it would not mean that clerks were
not legally fulfilling the duties of their office if they had

culled and disposed of official records without specific statutory mandates.  The reductio ad absurdum of this manifestly
impossible position would condemn out of hand most of the
present judges sitting in courts of record today who, as
clerks in court houses, have admittedly supervised or partic-
ipated in the wholesale removal of old court documents which
have been deemed surplus property, including the trial judge
who heard the West case.

## Historical Antecedents

A history of the custody of official papers (such as court
records) in England could well be the subject of a semester
course and is not properly treated in a few minutes' discussion.   Certain highlights, however, indicate that prior to the
establishment of the Public Record Office in 1838, neither
the king nor Parliament forbade the destruction, discard, or
abandonment of official records that were not necessary to
the conduct of the public business.   Research has not so far
uncovered a king's court decision restoring to public authority
without compensation documents that a county clerk or other
custodian may have discarded as waste paper, even though
some former crown officials' papers were demanded to be
returned. [2]   Instead, a series of enactments in England since
the early 14th century shows an astounding permissiveness
concerning the public record that could have easily been rem-
edied had the sovereign been concerned enough to do so.   In
fact, because of this inattention to the state of the British
documentary heritage, testimony before a Parliamentary commission in 1836 concluded that without legislation authorizing
a general repository, there was no legal foundation for any
replevin action to be brought against the owners of estrayed
manuscript materials.

The background of history forms a solid challenge to
the claim of the majority of the North Carolina Supreme
Court in North Carolina v. West, [3] that the king would not
have knowingly permitted the abandonment of official records.
Justice Beverley Lake's entire rationale is based upon this
premise.   But King George III, his predecessors and even
his successors, knew a great deal more about the state of
the records in their kingdom than Justice Lake gave them
credit for knowing; the English kings merely permitted the
wholesale removal of official records, as well as their com-
mingling with unofficial papers, to continue virtually unabated.
By his conduct, a sovereign authorized this removal.   And
such authorization is the linchpin of abandonment.

No one defends the possessor of an official record obtained from its custodian by theft. A thief cannot pass title. However, no allegation or proof of theft was ever raised by the state of North Carolina on the trial record in the West case; the matter was only speculated upon by the North Carolina Supreme Court in mere dictum. So far, any impact on other possible state courts' decisions on this point would be negligible. *

The discussion of the appropriateness or the impropriety of replevin can only therefore be meaningfully focused upon the situation of the so-called abandoned or discarded record whose omission from custody cannot otherwise be explained by the claimant. For a resolution of the issue, let us go to the facts.

King Edward III in 1335 ordered justices of assize, jail-delivery, and oyer and terminer to "send all their Records and Processes determined and put into execution" to the Exchequer at Michelmas every year. [4] There was no mention of what should be done with any records of undetermined causes of action. No penalties whatever were prescribed for failure to retain or to maintain such records.

Penalties were provided by Richard II in 1384 if either a judge or a clerk made a false entry of a plea, erased a record, or changed a verdict entered on the record, but

---

*The kind of recovery of a manuscript which is defensible, and assuredly would receive the cooperation of an archivist, scholar, dealer, and collector, is that related in the SAA Newsletter (July 1978), p. 5. Josephine L. Harper of the State Historical Society of Wisconsin reports that a letter of George Mason, lost from the manuscript collections of the society for 31 years, was recovered after its exhibit made the text known to documentary historical scholarship; and a judicious course of action, in which proof of provenance was unquestioned, led to the manuscript's recovery in which there was "neither intention nor desire to impugn the action of the collector" in acquiring it. The facts as recorded indicate unmistakably that the letter was stolen, unlike the Hooper papers in the West case; yet, no blame attached to the collector or dealer involved. Moreover, the provenance of the Mason letter was established for the first 175 years of its existence, clearly not the case with the Hooper legal papers in the West case.

stated nothing requiring the retention of all records created
by the government or the courts. [5]  In 1409, Henry IV ordered that every other year justices of assize should deliver
into the treasury the records of assize determined before
them, and that no record should be amended or impaired
after judgment was given and recorded. [6]

      A 1429 rule of Henry VI, cited with approval in the
state's brief on appeal in North Carolina v. West, required
that no legal judgment be reversed if any words in a record
were found erased, stricken, interlined, added to, subtracted,
or diminished and that

> if any record ... be willingly stolen, taken away,
> withdrawn, or avoided by any clerk, or by other
> person, because whereof any judgment shall be
> reversed; that such stealer, taker away, with-
> drawer, or avoider ... shall be judged for felons,
> and shall incur the pain of felony ... [7]

The state of North Carolina placed heavy reliance upon the
quoted language as the legal basis for stating that all indictments were required to be retained.   The North Carolina
Court of Appeals in reversing the holding of the trial court
agreed that 8 Hen. VI cap. XII was the foundation of modern
state law on the subject. [8]   The Supreme Court opinion, however, is entirely silent on the point, as well it might be,
since both the plaintiff and the majority of the North Carolina Court of Appeals misread the cited statute.   It simply
means that any embezzlement by a clerk of a court record,
which stealing caused a reversal of judgment in a case,
should be a felony.   Embezzlement is larceny of property
which comes into the taker's possession by virtue of his
employment.   Again, as in all of the earlier statutes cited,
there was no demand placed upon the record keeper permanently to retain every document in his possession.   In the
age of Bracton and Lyttleton, not to mention the succeeding
generations of common law advocates Coke and Blackstone,
a surfeit of legal talent existed properly to frame a statute
so that if all records were intended to be retained by their
custodians on pain of punishment there would have been an
unmistakable statement of that fact.   Clearly, the purpose of
the above statutes was to preserve the purity of the written
record in an age when handwritten copying contributed more
than enough error without prejudiced or bribed clerks' intentional falsification. [9]   Records custodians habitually behaved
as though access was a privilege and not a right; and their

autonomy was a subject of frequent comment by later writers. [10]

During the reign of Elizabeth I there began a paradox
with respect to the retention of official papers, particularly
the working correspondence of the queen's ministers. That
paradox was the apparent official desire to preserve the record but also the evident unwillingness of the sovereign to
exercise her prerogative to require by statute that all records be retained. In the Tudor period the various secretaries
of state generally kept their papers when they left their min-
istries. In order to try to stem this practice the State Paper
Office was established in 1578 with Dr. Thomas Wilson as
"clerk of the papers."[11] Both Wilson and his nephew in the
reign of James I made some effort to recover lost documents.
But without the sanctions of law, they were powerless to stop
the wholesale practice of removal even though a few papers
were recovered. Noble efforts such as Rymer's Foedera
were undertaken in the 17th century to publish extant state
papers in an effort to make their existence more widely
known, but publication could not help to make officials relinquish their records. The law of persuasion and not of prince
or parliament was appealed to by Bishop White Kennett in a
1718 speech in the House of Lords:

> I cannot but wish that all private persons who have
> any deeds, or writings that properly belong to any
> public office, might be, I would not say obliged,
> but might be encouraged to some public place of
> receipt, from which they might be distributed into
> those several offices. [12]

Why, indeed, not "obliged," if such return of papers was
mandated by statute, or even a strong common law tradition?
Because there was no authority requiring clerks to retain and
officials to leave public records. The law was certainly
powerless to require them to do so, and Kennett accurately
summarized the view of concerned members of Parliament at
the time of an inquiry into the domestic records during the
reign of George I.

The private collector, however, was not inactive during the time under discussion. He recognized the danger to
history that an unrelieved succession of official indifference
had already caused. Sir Thomas Bodley turned his thoughts
to the reinstatement of the public library at Oxford and the
adornment of it not only with printed books but also with what-

ever manuscripts could be procured.   Upon leaving the court
of Elizabeth I for the purpose,  he dedicated the remainder of
his life to searching after and buying in England documents
of supreme importance to British domestic history,  while his
agents on the Continent did likewise.   No state agency
replevied with or without compensation the official records
Bodley purchased,  or questioned his or Oxford's title to them.

Bodley's great contemporary Sir Robert Cotton was
equally diligent in forming a virtually unparalleled private
manuscript collection.   The Cottonian library survived successive government closings in the 17th century as well as
efforts on the part of contending parties in the civil wars to
destroy all legal or constitutional documents.   What a permanent replevin indeed would have been the result of such destruction!

Here was supreme irony.   Cotton as a collector was
fulfilling the often expressed desire of the sovereign to have
the great monuments of law,  history,  science,  and philosophy
collected and saved from oblivion.   He did personal research
in his manuscripts and permitted others the same privilege.
Yet,  at various troubled periods,  the Privy Council feared
disclosures from collected public documents and ordered the
library closed.   Fortunately,  by the late 17th century,  the
Cottonian library received the overdue governmental support
it should have had much earlier.

No further action was taken to inquire into the state
of records until 1800.   In that year,  extensive questions
were propounded to records clerks throughout the kingdom;
and a massive compilation of sworn testimony was published
by Parliament that only confirmed the suspicion of wretched
preservation methods among the clerks of the various coun-
ties. [13]   The committee concluded its preface by urging the
careful destruction of public books or papers "whereof the
Contents are afterward entered of Record ... without any
detriment to the Public."   The clerk of assize in Midland
Circuit,  Richard Lowndes,  replied to the committee's queries
that Midland's indictments,  informations,  examinations,  and
confessions earlier than six years previous might without any
inconvenience be discarded.   He personally regarded any official record more than 60 years old as waste. [14]   Despite
present lack of sympathy with such views,  they must be given
weight as exemplary of what occurred to many late 18th-
century court records in England with the full knowledge of
the sovereign and without any known sanctions being taken
against their custodians.

Perhaps one of the most revealing insights into the extent of officially permitted sorting and arrangement at that time comes from the Clerk of the Peace for the Parts of Holland in the County of Lincoln, Francis Thirkill. Thirkill in 1800 stated his belief that the quantity of justices' warrants, summonses, and other proceedings had accumulated so extraordinarily for the 150 years prior to his appointment as clerk that their permanent storage was no longer practicable. Between 1784 and 1800, he applied to the justices of the General Quarter Session "for Instructions, in what Manner the Papers and Proceedings of the Court should be disposed of ... stating how amazingly they multiplied; and by being in no kind of Order, were to become in a manner useless, and almost impossible to be referred to." The justices gave the matter of permanent records disposition their consideration, and granted to Thirkill the permission to arrange and sort the documents in his best judgment. They also ordered from their own budget an annual expenditure of £8 to provide a room that he could make use of for the purpose of sorting, not believing that the legislature would endorse such an expenditure. [15]

A court itself, therefore, saw nothing improper or illegal in permitting a county clerk of 18th-century England to cull, sort, and arrange the very papers of that court. Had every paper bearing the indicia of having been created under the aegis of that court since time immemorial been legally unfit or unready for destruction after it had served its usefulness, not only would Francis Thirkill have been subject to the law's penalty, but also it would have fallen squarely upon the shoulders of the justices of the County of Lincoln. It did not, because there was no such law. [16]

At the same time as 90 percent of the custodians polled in 1800 reported that English county records were in private homes, basements, garrets, subject to water, filth, vermin, heaped in disarray and with in almost no case even a desire among their custodians to see them indexed or calendared, [17] they also used the phrase "safe keeping" to describe their public charge, and invariably referred to themselves or some assistant as being responsible for the "safe" return of the records "to their proper places" after use. Many if not most of the keepers decried the abysmal condition of these documents; but more often than one could care to see in these reports is a nonchalance which discovered in the lack of finding aids a deliberate excuse to prolong a search for a paper and thus enlarge a fee. Enough is apparent from contemporary use to indicate that "safe keeping" was at best a relative term in the 18th century. The majority in North Carolina v. West, convinced that an English colonial court in remote America demanded the absolute retention of all court records whatsoever, says that the king never gave his permission to abandon or discard them. One must question carefully whether reason, experience, law, or history in the light of these facts ever demanded any such absolute. The king obviously permitted acts of spoliation, discard, and destruction which were freely admitted by those accomplishing them, and even judicially endorsed. Such actions went on beneath the banner of George III both before and after the English colony of North Carolina became a state. The only duty every officially required of such record keepers was responsible custody under the circumstances.

Still the final scene in this chapter of replevin's history remains to be unfolded. Enter Charles Purton Cooper, secretary of the Second Parliamentary Record Commission (1834-36) and a distinguished barrister. Cooper, before he undertook the grueling task of principal investigator of this commission, had written extensively on the most significant documentary monuments of the British kingdom, of the Harleian and Cottonian collections, the Year Books, and of early English legal treatises. He was a firm advocate of more ready access to the records, for their physical preservation and for a school akin to the Ecole des Chartes for the training of young persons in the use of records. Like scores of others, Cooper believed every passage of the 1800 report exhibited evils to which the lapse of 30 years had only served to give a more luxuriant and a more vigorous growth.

He concluded in his report of the Second Commission in 1836 a chapter entitled "Miscellaneous Evidence" containing the following questions and answers elicited from an unnamed witness, probably a member of the Select Board of Inquiry:

> Q. Considering that there are, in the metropolis alone, upwards of eighty offices containing public records, is it (in your opinion) possible to prevent that loss of records which results from removals, when a building is under repair, and especially in cases where the records of different offices are suddenly transported for some temporary purpose to one locality? --A. No.

> Q.   Or that loss which results from the records
> being sometimes taken to private houses for more
> convenient use?   --A.   No.
>
> Q.   Records may still find their way to a house be-
> longing to a royal fishmonger ... ?   --A.   Yes.
>
> Q.   And if they do not come to the heirs of a
> Master of the Rolls, they may chance to come to
> the heirs of a keeper or a clerk?   --A.   Yes.
> The records of many offices may, and probably do.
> You cannot prevent the recurrence of evils like
> these, unless you erect a General Repository, and
> make strict regulations for the government of it.
>
> Q.   Has not the Board often called attention to the
> custom, in some offices, of the keepers and clerks
> carrying the records to their own home?   --A.
> Yes.
>
> Q.   Has the Board any power to prevent it?
> --A.   None. [18]

The commission judged that there was no legal means of
claiming lost records since there was no law requiring their
indefinite retention.   The idea of a retroactive statute or
judicial decision condemning as contraband any official record in private hands did not occur because of its impossibil-
ity of enforcement; and, on that account, lawmakers realized
that records "lost" were legally abandoned since their keepers had willingly parted with them under official sanction.

Even after the Public Record Office was founded in
1838, eight tons of Exchequer records were sold that year
by order of the government and went in fact to a London fish
merchant, from whom groups of treasury records were then
bought by consignors of the records at auction.

Many of these documents were bought by a London
book and autograph dealer named Thomas Rodd.   Although
Rodd's suspicions were aroused and he immediately called
the appearance of the documents on the market to the attention of the comptroller general, that office assured him in
effect they were so much waste paper, whereas every document "bearing the description of a record has been carefully
preserved. "   But then, to his complete surprise and chagrin,
Rodd was subsequently indicted by the crown for the return
of one of the legal documents, a "filacer's roll. "[19]

Upon proof of the facts of his acquisition as being in pursuance of a government order, the case against Thomas Rodd was dismissed, before, as he bitterly observed, he had had the opportunity to produce his defense, i. e. , "to establish the right of individuals to possess records, and to buy and sell them when such Records have been sold by the Public Offices, or cannot be shewn to have been feloniously abstracted. "[20]  It is indeed unfortunate that Rodd did not have the opportunity to test the state of the English law of public document replevin in 1843, especially with reference to the status of archival material whose absence from custody cannot be explained by any recourse to known facts.  But the circumstances of the Rodd indictment and its dismissal are reliable support for the argument of the defense in North Carolina v. West, that the sovereign has the authority to separate official records from custody and to transfer both custody and title to the public.

## After the West Case

The few replevin cases involving public documents since the Rodd indictment was quashed have been summarized in briefs for the defense as well as amicus curiae briefs in the case of North Carolina v. West.  Suffice it to say that no statutory law and very little common law precedent has been generated relevant to the important principle sought to be defended in West.  The West case stands as the most substantive recent American litigation on the subject of replevin of official public records.  The immediate activities of archivists in the wake of this case have not been of such draconian proportions as would lead this observer to the belief that any general pattern is underway to seize privately held official papers. Certain steps have been taken, however; and events that have occurred in the year 1977-78 include the following.

The 1790 letter of George Washington to the governor and council of the state of North Carolina, that alerted the staff of North Carolina's archives to examine possible grounds for its replevin and thus began the West controversy, was returned to North Carolina one month after the West decision was rendered.  The state and the New York law firm of Coudert Brothers, representing the owner of the letter, reached an out-of-court settlement involving the letter's return in exchange for secrecy concerning the name of the former private possessor.

A probable explanation for the relinquishment without

a fight is the peculiar legal situation in New York state regarding replevin.   A case entitled Mayor of the City of New
York v. Lent was decided in 1868 against a collector who
possessed a Washington letter addressed to the Board of
Aldermen. 21   No explanation of the letter's removal from
custody was given.   The court held that there could be no
bona fide purchaser of an official document without a showing that it had been legally disposed of by the repository to
which it was addressed.   The Lent case is N. Y. state common law.   It could be applied in either a N. Y. state court
or a federal court in New York, which North Carolina sought
to do without the West case.   It is arguable that this ancient
precedent alone could have governed an action on the part of
an archives to recover possession of an official manuscript,
though there are plausible distinctions between the facts in
Lent and the facts of the West case.

Suddenly, the bonanza of West fell into the lap of the
North Carolina state archives.   If attorneys for North Carolina had thereafter decided to bring an action in New York
state court for the Washington letter, they might have won
their case on the strength of West's recentness, even though
it is not New York law.   In other words, it could be used
in New York as persuasive but not compelling precedent,
since it was not a New York decision.   The relevant Lent
case, coupled with a recent decision squarely against the
private collector's position, meant that the owners of the
Washington letter recognized, at least in New York state,
that a collector would not fare well in a confrontation with
archivists over the return of official manuscripts.   Thus,
the owner capitulated out of court.

Three months later, in October 1977 at Salt Lake
City, two state archivists declared their views of replevin.
Dr. Edward Papenfuse of Maryland Hall of Records stated
he believes the action can be successful in Maryland, and
that Maryland's highest court, the Court of Appeals, would
follow the West decision.   But Dr. Papenfuse hastened to
add he would not use replevin except in the case of theft,
and forcefully commented that West was counterproductive,
with every likelihood of driving material away from Maryland if not completely off the market.

In past years, the Maryland Historical Society has so
vigorously resisted former Maryland archivist Morris Rad-
off's attempts to claim official records from that society that
Papenfuse felt it the better part of wisdom to work out a

truce with the society so that now any former administrative
records of the state in custody of the historical society which
are made available for research will not be touched by the
archives.    Maryland has made its peace with Maryland.

By contrast, Dr. Louis Manarin of the Virginia State
Library and Archives asserted that he will bring replevin
actions according to his best judgment of the facts of each
situation.   His institution has many times obtained fugitive
materials from the Virginia Historical Society upon request
to John Jennings, the director of the society.   Mr. Jennings[22]
says his institution has quietly but not at all reluctantly in
the past 20 years surrendered manuscripts as a matter of
course to the state archives, but asserts there has been only
"modest pressure" on him to do so.   He says he would be
righteously indignant, however, if the society had paid for
any of the materials so surrendered.

As an example, Jennings relates the fact that several
thousand petitions addressed to the Virginia General Assembly in the 1780s were documented as being discarded by their
custodians in 1905.   They were literally picked up off the
trash pile and put into gunny sacks, hauled off to the historical society, and were carefully arranged and catalogued.
In the mid-1950s, or in other words, over 50 years after
this event of discard, the state archives--then deemed by the
historical society to be a better custodian--was again awarded
custody of them, where they are to this day.

Emphatically underscoring his belief that people generally do not want to have anything to do with government
agencies, Jennings recounted the fact that his organization
has recovered county records taken during the Civil War by
soldiers as souvenirs, has gotten back deed books, and recovered will books over the years from private citizens who
would rather the historical society have them than the government.   He states, however, that he has willingly cooper-
ated with the archives when it discovers that records exist
in his custody which "should be in the hands of an archivist."

The private individual has not fared so gently in the
never ending discrimination leveled by some governmental
officials against private citizens, while at the same time the
same officials accommodate repositories with no better title
to official manuscripts.   A 1978 Virginia case was that of
Alexandria book dealer Samuel Yudkin, whose newspaper advertisement of a 19th-century tax ledger for sale at auction

in 1977 alerted city officials to the possible use of one ledger
entry as proof of city ownership of the Potomac River waterfront in a title dispute with the federal government.    Arthur
Mittell, a former Alexandria resident who possessed the manuscript ledger, had obtained Yudkin's services for the sale of
the document on consignment and had sent it to him.    After
vehement protest, Yudkin surrendered the ledger to city attorneys and then brought legal action to recover it.    The case
went to trial in early 1978[23] but was lost by Yudkin at the
trial level.

A change of thinking on the part of the City Attorney's
office in early 1978, though it did not bring about a reversal
of judgment, did result in reimbursement of the owner.    City
Attorney Cyril D. Calley sent the Alexandria City Council a
memorandum on February 9, 1978, arguing that if the council
was willing to establish an award program for any official
public records that might be returned to the city by private
citizens, it might also adopt a resolution providing for compensation.    In the Yudkin case, the council moved on February 14 to provide a specific reimbursement to Mittell of
$200, the estimated price of the volume.    Yudkin reports he
received a commission of 10 percent, but incurred legal ex-
penses in defense of the action approximating $1,000.

Calley, when contacted by telephone, stated that the
council had not really responded to all of his memorandum,
since he also urged them to require the City Manager of
Alexandria to find an appraiser so that the proper value of
any official materials so surrendered could be established.
He is spearheading a legal battle with the federal government
over the ownership of the city waterfront and wants to get
any manuscript evidence of city ownership out into the open.
Regarding the valuing of such manuscripts as only an induce-
ment to recover real evidence and not as compensation to
bona fide owners, attorneys for the city take the position
that the state can recover any and all official records without compensation regardless of the length of ownership or
the circumstances under which such materials appear.

Review of the West Case

The keystone principle of the West opinion is Justice Lake's
view of a great and unbroken succession of rights in the new
state government[24] to the colonial or crown papers created
in the years preceding North Carolina's statehood.    He shows

quite correctly that sovereignty prevails, and with it both the laws and the official property of a predecessor pass intact and inviolate to a successor. He is on solid ground when he says that, by the Paris Peace of 1783, all papers formerly the property of the crown in the colonies became state-owned. He provides an admirable summary of the history of district and state courts in the section of North Carolina under discussion. He then comes to extraordinary conclusions from these facts.

The opinion concisely summarizes a portion of a 1767 act of the colonial assembly that requires the preservation of causes of action by requiring entry of them into well bound books, concluding from this language that all bills of indictment supplying the information for the entries into those well bound books were intended to be preserved. Careful reading of the act, however, yields a different interpretation. It requires enrolling of proceedings either having gone to judgment or not fully determined, but says nothing about the retention of all of the papers passing through clerks' hands providing the background for such a record. As has been indicated by the citation of earlier records-preservation statutes, crown interest in court records was demonstrably not in their physical manifestation but rather in their true content. As the court states a few sentences later, a paper was the property of the king and "its subsequent retention or disposition was subject to his direction and control." How could this be the case if the sovereign did not have the right to part with official property? And if that property could not in fact be thrown away after its purposes were served?

The king possessed official records if they were retained, and he relinquished them if they were discarded and was no different from any other man in this respect. So, a paper filed by the king's clerk drafted by the king's counsellor became royal property. It would have been also subject to recall by the king if removed from the clerk without authority. It could be reinstated in its former place if embezzled or otherwise purloined. No matter how debilitated it may have become, its ragged or forlorn condition would not sever its title from its custodian or from the custodian's master, the king. One step, alone, might sever that claim; and that would be a definitive act coupled with an intent to relinquish use as evidence of intent to give up utterly and irrevocably all interest in the subject matter. 25 Although the passage of time is not an essential element, it may be considered in connection with acts manifesting such intention.

Such an act would be the legal abandonment of personal property.

    Abandonment is not a ritual.  It is a question of in-
tent. [26]  It is not presumed, and proof supporting it must be
direct and reasonably produce the inference of the throwing
away. [27]  Yet, the West court completely omitted consideration of one of the most significant elements of the law of
abandonment in its attempt to fashion a common law of perpetual ownership of official manuscripts.  This is the fact
that abandonment is more likely the summary of conduct than
a verbal or written communication of the intent to abandon.
For Justice Lake, an overt act trumpeting the intent to abandon was required.  On the contrary, operative intent may be
established by mere conduct.  Abandonment does not have to
occur by mechanical formulae--writing a decree, speaking a
word, or requiring a would-be possessor to tap the former
owner on the shoulder to ask if he really meant what he was
apparently doing.  Circumstances and conduct may adequately
show an intent to abandon the use of property and indicate
the full and complete divestiture of any rights, which it is
the function of the fact finder to decide. [28]  Even the most
incriminating papers may legally be used against the one
discarding them if circumstances reveal an intent to abandon
them. [29]

    No administrative regulation on the part of George III
or any other monarch would have been required to permit
the discard of court records or any type of other official
records that, it may be reasonably inferred, were allowed
to be thrown away by British custodians since before the
middle of the 14th century or were in fact sold by the government to private persons, and for whose abandonment
judicial endorsement was obtained.  But despite the fact that
no apparent act of Parliament before 1776 nor of the colonial
North Carolina government specifically required all official
documents created under any monarch's reign to remain in
perpetuity, the majority in West holds that any which have
survived are state property wherever located.  The West
majority looked for something not found in North Carolina's
1767 act, to specify a requirement of permanent retention
that the Attorney General and the Lord Chief Justice of England could not find in British law in 1843 when that magis-
trate verified that the sale of Exchequer records in 1838 had
occurred according to law.  Instead of intent plus conduct
tending toward defining the requisite legal elements for an
act of abandonment, the West court requires new terms.

There must be a specific grant of authority on the part of
the abandoning party to his agent or delegates for the limited
purpose of discarding property:

> Nothing in the record indicates a grant by King
> George III or by the State of North Carolina to the
> Clerk of the Superior Court of Justice of the Salis-
> bury District or his successor in office by that or
> any other title to throw away these documents com-
> mitted to his custody. [30]

The court insists that an undefined metaphysical
subtlety distinguishes official from private property, the
former not subject to abandonment but the latter so subject.
It then declares "official" property is subject to the sovereign's prerogative to keep or abandon so long as the abandonment is highly visible by some unequivocal act.   Finally,
toward the conclusion of his opinion, Justice Lake writes
that

> ... instances in which clerks of courts in North
> Carolina have removed from their offices and dis-
> carded old records, does not establish abandon-
> ment of such property by the sovereign so as to
> confer upon the first subsequent taker thereof a
> title good against the sovereign.   In this respect
> the sovereign is like any other owner of property.

If clerks of court removed and destroyed records, what more
would be required, if the king was truly like "any other
owner of property," than to show the act of discard itself,
plus the informed knowledge of the practice for hundreds of
years?   Neither colony nor crown made objection to the
destruction of official papers, and thus permitted the rest
of the world to believe in their custodians' apparent authority to do as they had done.   While ratification of an agent's
action is never presumed, like abandonment, it may be im-
plied by a course of conduct.   If keepers disposed of un-
wanted records, as has been shown to have been contemporaneous practice in England, it cannot seriously be asserted
that the sovereign was unaware of the conduct of his agents.
Thus, it may be concluded that he implicitly ratified their
conduct. [31]

The court's confident premise that one cannot form
an intent to abandon what one does not know exists is neither
accurate nor properly determinative of the problems raised

in this case. Any addition to the formal rules governing application of this concept only adds to the possibility of confusion and injustice when it is applied to diverse areas of personal property both tangible and intangible, each with its own problems and policy considerations.

Of course, one of the most damaging misstatements that undermines the validity of this opinion is Justice Lake's mere guess as to the probable date or circumstances under which the Hooper indictments left public custody. Disparaging the defense's claim that the papers disappeared either in the turmoil of Revolution or at a later date when deemed of no more value, he states:

> It would seem more likely that they were intentionally removed from the clerk's office in more recent times, when discovered by one who was aware of their intrinsic value by reason of the presence thereon of the signatures of William Hooper, a signer of the Declaration of Independence.

The reader here is treated to gratuitous wisdom assuming facts not proved at trial and interjected as a surmise as to their disappearance.

The facts are that these documents at trial were proved to have been a part of a much larger group of court records of Salisbury District once owned by the Greensboro Historical Museum and a private citizen of North Carolina. There is absolutely no evidence of any piecemeal taking of the two examples solely for the autographs of William Hooper. Because there are 11 virtually identical examples of these district court files now in the state's records is no more proof that the two documents owned by Dr. West were improperly removed than the fact that millions of federal archives exist in the National Archives is proof that any other U. S. records found outside the federal archives system were improperly alienated. More than North Carolina's 11 Hooper district court documents signed have been sold at auction over the past decade, some of which are now owned by both dealers and collectors. The cloud that the North Carolina Supreme Court raises over this issue by introducing the specter of theft without any proof of it at trial negates absolutely whatever effect the court's further statements might have had concerning the bona fide of further takers or the conversion of the documents. Thus, the assertion that in-

tentional spoliation of these early records may have aided
the ravages of time is merely speculation.

The West case is not fully declarative of the rights
of every person who finds himself in the uncomfortable position of owning official documents.   Historical facts unknown
to the Supreme Court of North Carolina at the time West
was argued will now be brought to the attention of other jurisdictions.   Any further defense will show (1) the fundamental unfairness of discriminating in favor of title to the same
document for institutions over individuals, a state deprivation
of equal protection of the laws in violation of the Fourteenth
Amendment to the U. S. Constitution; (2) the fact that a state
or public authority indeed has the authority to abandon or
discard public documents just as it would have over any
other public property, and has legitimately exercised it[32]
both before and after the advent of archival or records management systems; (3) the fact that not merely a few but literally hundreds of public documents of every state lie outside
its custody and are being annually dispersed every year;
(4) the fact that the market in official manuscripts will continue despite the ill-advised attempts of some archivists to
stop it, the effect of which will be a highly developed underground market deleterious to scholarship; (5) the fact that in
forthcoming legislation, the federal government will not recommend the retroactive taking of noncurrent federal official
documents from any public or private custodian; (6) the elements of a common law action of replevin include the requirement on the plaintiff's part (the state) to prove that any
manuscripts claimed were irregularly removed from custody
and not merely the obvious conclusion that they have disappeared from custody; and (7) that there is manifest error in
comparing the duty of a 20th-century records custodian bound
by statutory requirements with a 17th- or 18th-century keeper of manuscripts unhindered by any but the most irrelevant
statutory mandate and guided by a practice that was untidy at
best, if not scandalous at worst.   All of these points and
more may be gleaned from the historical background of cases
preceding West, even as they are unsatisfactorily, if at all,
dealt with in the opinion itself.

## Applying "Caveat Emptor"

Caveat emptor may soon apply as never before to a significant market with far more dollar value than autographs, but
with much the same principles involved as the issues con-

cerned with the replevin of public documents.  The international art market is faced with a bill to put into effect a Unesco convention relating to the importation of art that would bar future imports of most ancient and primitive art under the slanted moral imperative of stopping "pillage and illicit trade in antiquities. "[33]

On the theory that archaeological sites should be preserved for the careful scientific analysis of an archaeologist, the proponents of this act are just as correct as trained archivists who argue that all official records should be in public repositories.  In theory both views are valid, but in practice things have just not worked out that way.  Population explosions will inexorably doom the absolute preservation of every known exploration site for artifacts, just as official needs for space and lack of utility for noncurrent records will continue to create archival estrays.  André Emmerich, a past president of the Art Dealers' Association of America and director of his own gallery in New York, has forcefully argued that without private acts of reclamation, many art treasures not recognized as such at the time they are abandoned would be irretrievably lost. [34]  He feels that trade in many kinds of antiquities is a valuable ingredient in their ultimate survival, since without their being recognized as personal property they will not be endowed with "sufficient monetary value to insure their preservation. " Recalling that American museums and collectors have purchased a part of the international cultural heritage, he asserts that American scholarship has more than repaid any "moral" debt connected with such acquisitions.

Cessation of such an ongoing trade is, of course, technically distinct from any mandate that materials already out of custody be returned, such as the Elgin Marbles of the British Museum; yet, the Supreme Court of North Carolina deemed it to be relevant when Chief Justice Sharp asked Special Deputy Attorney General Buie Costen, in oral argument on the West case, what would happen if the Egyptian government laid claim to all of the mummies in American museums, and Costen could give no meaningful answer. [35] Yet, if the state cannot find reason to oppose private retention of important artistic monuments by organizations or individuals outside their place of origin, it becomes difficult to see by what authority state officials automatically suspect that documents bearing indicia of origin in North Carolina were stolen if they appear anywhere else.

It is axiomatic that archives should maintain the noncurrent records coming to them by normal retirement from public agencies. But materials which agencies have legally abandoned either by implication or overt conduct over the years should not be forbidden to be preserved by anyone other than government officials. Banning the importation of art objects on the theory that their ownership outside their country of origin is illicit trade strikingly tracks the present thinking of many archivists regarding the chance paper that has escaped their grasp.

The Bavarian state government claims that World War II diaries of Hermann Goering are its property and has sought to enjoin their sale by Parke-Bernet despite the fact that several world governments and hundreds of private individuals possess official records of the Nazi government. [36] Mr. Emmerich's thesis relative to artistic monuments is thus startlingly relevant commentary on the so-called moralities of latter-day governmental concern throughout the world for all kinds of historic properties in which it can at least be said that private individuals seem never to have ceased to have an interest.

Although unlikely to be adopted by any jurisdiction with sensitivity toward the rights of private organizations and individuals who have contributed to the preservation of history's records, the following draft statute on archives commissioned by Unesco illustrates the ultimate in the "socialization" of private manuscript holdings:

> Any person or private body, not being a dealer, who has in his possession documents more than 40 years old must notify the director of the national or local archives. Within 60 days these must be examined by an archivist and may be declared to be of major historical interest. Once so declared, the state has the power of surveillance and the records automatically become open for research purposes. The owner must preserve the records in a suitable manner, catalogue and repair them, notify the national archives before transferring ownership or custody, and apply for permission to export. Deposit is to be encouraged by the award of a diploma of merit to the owner, the award of scholarships bearing his name, and the promotion of research on his documents.

Dealers must notify the national archives of all documents in their possession, give 30 days notice of intention to sell, and register the results of all sales, the register to be inspected by the archives service. The final provision of the draft allows for the expropriation of any documents in the hands of anyone who breaks the requirements of the articles relating to private archives. [37]

## Voluntarism vs. Confiscation

In sharp contrast to this ill-advised model statute, it is the principle of voluntarism that has caused the creation of the greatest public manuscript collections in America today. Documents making up the backbone of the Manuscript Division of the Library of Congress, the collections of the New York Public Library, the Historical Society of Pennsylvania, the Clements Library, the Boston Public Library, most college and university libraries, and hundreds of independent manuscript repositories were formed by the generosity of those such as Peter Force, Pierre du Simitière, and Thomas Addis Emmett. These names are only representative of thousands like them who have given their collections, which included both former public papers and private correspondences, to the public. The greatest irony is that the modern state archival movement also owes some of its foremost impetus to 19th-century historian-collectors of manuscripts who deplored the fact that earlier records custodians had perfidiously served history in discarding public records. Now, the spiritual descendants of some of the early collectors have found themselves subject to attack from some of the entities that they had a major hand in creating. [38]

Proponents of federal legislation today, on the other hand, after extensive hearings on two bills that would make the Presidents' official papers the property of the nation, have expressed absolutely no interest in any retroactive taking of official documents in private custody. One of the bills as drafted (H. R. 11001) could have a retroactive effect, but the other, authored by Representative L. Richardson Preyer (H. R. 10998) will apply clearly only to records of any President taking office after January 20, 1981. [39] If Mr. Preyer's version of the public ownership question becomes law, it will behoove state legislatures to adopt similar language as applicable to their own records management programs not only in terms of executive documents but also with respect to estrayed legislative and judicial materials. No state or federal agency should be permitted to seize without compensation any official records that were out of its custody before a systematic program for their proper maintenance was developed. It would thus be possible for state legislatures to follow the lead of the federal government in declaring only prospectively created papers to be official property, and thus seriously to restrict, if not in effect overrule, the West case with its retroactive application.

The alternative that is certain to result from an ill-advised and historically senseless attempt to seize papers alleged to have been alienated, who knows when and under what circumstances, will face vigorous resistance in the courts at least from those who can afford to defend their rights as bona fide purchasers and whose materials represent an investment worth fighting for.   Many individuals or institutions who possess challenged documents cannot afford to make such a defense and will either forbid research to be done from the manuscripts or will simply lock them up permanently.   In some cases, frustration and fear of prosecution will cause the records to be destroyed.   The basic aim of those seeking replevin of the records will thus be thwarted, and their preservation could be in extreme jeopardy.

None of this has to be.   Expressing his customary wisdom in matters of this kind, Julian P. Boyd, the great documentary editor of The Papers of Thomas Jefferson, once stated:

> Collectors and dealers have played a tremendously important part in the preservation of much of the record of our history, and the light thrown on that history would be the dimmer if it had not been for the materials they protected. . . .  One of the chief answers to our questions, then, is a mutual understanding of the community of interest that is shared. . . .  With such a mutuality of respect and interest, we can also see that collectors and dealers have their interests protected in the matter of archival estrays that they have acquired in good faith and protected with admirable zeal. [40]

Respect for the special contributions that each of many suppliers of sources brings to the study and appreciation of history is the only valid way in which the society may make the most effective use of its documentary heritage.   Suspicion, mistrust, and the possible loss or drying up of the sources

of history is an unacceptable alternative.  It is the genuine
collector's hope that history itself will not suffer from the
turmoil that will be caused by the precedent of granting a
state the custody of papers whose removal from public authority cannot be explained by the claimant, and whose legal
reliance is founded on irrelevant authority. 41

## Resolving the Stalemate

As the doctrine of access to public documents of all kinds
comes of age against a background of indecision as to precisely what should have been saved, the custodian reaches
out now to claim a heritage dispersed by the stupidity of a
former time.  Under the impetus of the Freedom of Information Act, data must now be supplied to the researcher both
as to what government possesses but will not reveal, and to
what government had but let slip away.

The bicentennial of the Olive Branch petition has
passed, to continue the Anglo-American metaphor; but it is
not too late to seek a higher ground to avoid the inevitable
head-on collision and resolve the present stalemate.  Dog-
matic approaches on either side will not achieve any resolution of the issue.  As an historical administrator and a collector, it is my fervent desire that from the painful background of the West decision and its aftermath there may
emerge at least a start to find a solution to the problem
which we all--king, Parliament, state, custodian, and col-
lector--have ignored entirely too long.

## Notes

1.    According to Black's Law Dictionary, replevin is the re-
      delivery of a thing taken from a plaintiff by removing
      it from the possession of the wrongdoer and replacing
      it in the plaintiff's custody.  It stems from the French
      "plevir" (to pledge) and relates to a plaintiff's giving
      of security to prosecute the action after he has seized
      the property in question, in order to test the legal
      validity of the seizure.
2.    The obligation to pay just compensation to an owner is
      one which has been uniquely developed by special
      amendment to the United States Constitution.  Early
      state constitutions, e. g. , Virginia, North Carolina,
      New Hampshire, did not contain or describe any ob-

ligation for payment of compensation.  Those who maintain that the power of eminent domain arises from governmental necessity, while the obligation to compensate inheres in the natural right of the individual, thus argue from a strong foundation.

3.  293 N. C. 18, 235 A2d 150(1977).
4.  9 Edw. III cap. V.
5.  8 Rich. II cap. IV.
6.  11 Hen. IV cap. III.
7.  8 Hen. VI cap. XII.
8.  31 N. C. App. 431, 229 S. E. 2d 826(1976).
9.  The real possibility of alteration or falsification of public records once they have left public custody was one early reason for the development of the requirements found in the "ancient documents" exception to the common law hearsay rule.  This rule of evidence requires that circumstances of custody be unaltered and that there be no suspected forgery of documents over 30 years old if such documents alone, without any other supporting testimony, are desired to be entered upon a trial record as evidence.  Most practitioners of archives administration still subscribe to the principle of provenance fully described by Theodore R. Schellenberg in The Management of Archives (N. Y. : Columbia, 1956), p. 90 ff. , and do not believe it is the mission of the archivist to piece together from strayed public records fragments of historical evidence in the fashion of an historian.  Public records are brought together originally in relation to activities that resulted in their production.  If torn apart, as by discard, much of the evidence of their working role in the office of which they were a part is lost or obscured.  "Archive quality survives unimpaired so long as their natural form and relationship are maintained. " Hilary Jenkinson, The English Archivist: A New Profession (London: 1948), p. 4.
10. William Searle Holdsworth, A History of English Common Law (London:  Methuen and Co. , 1909), II, passim.
11. Ibid. , 509.
12. Charles Purton Cooper, esq. , An Account of the Most Important Public Records of Great Britain and the Publications of the Record Commissioners:  Together With Other Miscellaneous, Historical, and Antiquarian Information.  Compiled From Various Printed Books and Manuscripts (London:  Baldwin and Cradock, 1832), I, xvi.  The emphasis in the quoted passage is Bishop Kennett's own.

13.  Reports From the Select Committee, Appointed to In-
     quire Into the State of the Public Records of the King-
     dom, &c. Ordered by the House of Commons to be
     printed 4th July 1800.  This was the first of two such
     massive reports which were to be published eventually.
14.  Ibid. ,  238-39.
15.  Ibid. ,  281.
16.  It could be objected that Francis Thirkill felt it neces-
     sary to request permission of the court because he
     thought there was a legal requirement to obtain it
     from someone.  If so, he cites no rationale for the
     request except for the extreme inconvenience in re-
     taining useless documents.  Most custodians reporting
     on the problem of antiquated papers cluttering their
     offices certainly were not so squeamish.  No one ap-
     parently looked over their shoulders, upbraided them
     for their conduct, or held subsequent purchasers re-
     sponsible for any error involved in their practices.
17.  Although the committee asked every custodian if his
     records should be calendared and indexed, no keeper
     of such records was ever sure that such an additional
     chore would be paid for by a supplemental budget al-
     lowance.  If the keeper had to do it himself without
     additional compensation, his natural inclination was to
     report that it was not necessary.
18.  Charles Purton Cooper, The Report of the Second Par-
     liamentary Commission (London: 1837), p. 246.
19.  Filacers were officers of the superior court at West-
     minster whose duty it was to file the writs on which
     they made process.  The office of "filacer" was
     abolished in 1837, just before the Public Record Of-
     fice was founded.
20.  Emphasis supplied.  Narrative of the Proceedings
     Instituted In the Court of Common Pleas Against Mr.
     Thomas Rodd, For the Purpose of Wresting From
     Him a Certain Manuscript Roll, ... (1845), p. 56.
     This privately printed document is part of a larger
     compilation of essays recently discovered in London
     by Jacob L. Chernofsky, Editor and Publisher of
     AB Bookman's Weekly, to whom I am indebted for a
     complete copy of the virtually unobtainable text.  The
     entire Rodd pamphlet is being edited by Mr. Chernof-
     sky for future publication.
21.  51 Barbour 19.
22.  Telephone interview, John Jennings with the author,
     May 8, 1978.
23.  In Holton v. Yudkin, the constitutionality of the Virginia

Public Records Act was upheld.  The court stated
that the book "... was created as a public record and
as such was the property of the city, and that having
been created as a public record it is and remains a
public record and the property of the aforesaid city,
unless or until it is or has been abandoned or otherwise disposed of by authorization of the City Council
of the City of Alexandria, Virginia. "

24.   State v. West, 293 N.C. 18, 235 S.E. 2d 150(1977).
25.   Merryman v. Bremmer, 250 Md. 1, 241 A 2d 558,
      565(1968).
26.   INS v. AP, 248 U.S. 215, 240, 39 S. Ct. 68, 63 L.
      Ed. 211(1918).
27.   Foulke v. N.Y. Consolidated R.R. Co., 228 N.Y. 269,
      273, 127 N.E. 237, 238, 9 A.L.R. 1384(1920); U.S.
      v. Cowan, 396 F. 2d 83 (1968).
28.   Morris' Appeal, 68 Pa. Rep. 16 (1871); Lawlor v.
      Town of Salem, 116 N.H. 61, 352 A 2d 721, 722
      (1976); Gilberton Contracting Co. v. Hook, 255 F.
      Suppl. 687 (1966).
29.   Defendants who discarded papers outside a building
      prior to their being seized by federal officials aban-
      doned them.  U.S. v. Minker, 312 F. 2d 632, cert.
      den. 83 S. Ct. 952, 372 U.S. 953, 9 L. Ed. 2d 978
      (1963).   Two trash bags containing papers and offset
      plates were ruled abandoned in U.S. v. Mustone, 469
      F. 2d 970 (1972).  In each of these federal cases,
      important 4th Amendment rights of defendants were
      concerned; and still the courts ruled that the facts
      clearly bespoke of instances of abandonment.
30.   293 N.C. 18, 30(1977).
31.   Ratification as it relates to the law of agency means
      the express or implied adoption and confirmation by
      one person of an act or contract performed or entered
      into in its behalf by another who at the time assumed
      to act as his agent; and whether or not there has been
      a ratification of an unauthorized act is usually a ques-
      tion of fact.  Fuller v. Eastern Fire & Cas. Ins. Co.,
      124 S.E. 2d 602, 608, 240 S.C. 75(1962).  It is not
      generally a question of law for the court.  Barber v.
      Carolina Auto Sales, 236 S.C. 594 115 S.E. 2d 291
      (1960).  What else is to be concluded from the early
      public records administration of a state that in 1817
      provided for an archives building to house its public
      records, yet in 1826 allowed historian Jared Sparks
      to carry away unknown numbers of official documents?
      Is not the knowledge of North Carolina's then Secretary

of State sufficient awareness on the part of the sovereign to be considered permission to abandon or discard such materials?  See John H. Moore, "Jared
Sparks in North Carolina," North Carolina Historical
Review XL (July 1963), 262.

32.  It is today possible for there to be an order of court
for the expunction of criminal indictments, to the extent provided in North Carolina General Statutes
90-113. 14, the section relating to first violaters of
certain drug-related offenses.  And whether or not
such indictments are brought, it was the sense of the
legislature in enacting this and other records management provisions of the statutes in the state of North
Carolina that certain records outlive their usefulness
and do not have lasting value to the state.  Today,
there is a legal means to dispose of any official
records of any county in North Carolina, including
any and all legal records.  See NCGS 121-5.

33.  The bill, H. R. 5642, was under consideration by the
U. S. Senate in February 1978 after having passed the
House with little fanfare in December 1977.

34.  André Emmerich, "Importing Antiquities: A Moral
Issue?," The Washington Post, February 6, 1978.

35.  Author's memorandum of oral argument for files,
March 9, 1977.

36.  The German War Art Collection, commissioned as
propaganda by the Nazi government and produced
throughout World War II, will probably be ordered
returned by the U. S. Army to West Germany pur-
suant to a recent request by the West German government.  Its seizure in June 1945 assured that such
propaganda materials related to the war would be
taken into Allied custody.  See Bess Hormatz,
"Captured German War Art," The Washington Post,
February 12, 1978, C-3.

37.  Kenneth Duckett, Modern Manuscripts (Nashville:
American Association of State and Local History,
1975), p. 82.

38.  See Mary A. Benjamin, Autographs: A Key to Collecting (N. Y.: R. R. Bowker Co. , 1946), Ch. XII,
"The Importance of the Collector."

39.  Senator Mark O. Hatfield to Mary A. Benjamin, May
8, 1978: "I concur with Dr. [Bart] Cox's perspective
that Congressman Preyer's bill is the best of the
pieces of legislation pending on this matter.  I think
it is most important that the retroactive impact of
such legislation be eliminated.  The Brademas ver-

sion is too open-ended in that regard, and necessary
steps must be taken to avoid its becoming law."
40.  Benjamin, op. cit., p. xvii.
41.  See Randolph G. Adams, "The Character and Extent of
     Fugitive Archive Material," The American Archivist
     (1939), pp. 85-96, for an early treatment of the is-
     sues involved in replevin of official manuscript ma-
     terials and the seasoned conclusion of a veteran his-
     torian that archivists should feel grateful toward in-
     dividual collectors and institutional libraries for seek-
     ing out, acquiring, and preserving archival records
     that would have probably perished without this atten-
     tion, as well as the assertion that the amount of
     archival material which has disappeared or is un-
     available would bulk much larger than it does without
     this help.

# BESTERMAN AND BIBLIOGRAPHY:

## AN ASSESSMENT*

Roderick Cave

"This attempt to prick Colossus demands an apology
and an explanation. "

With these words Theodore Besterman started his article on
"The Library of Congress and the future of its catalogue"
in 1946. [1]

It is a particularly appropriate opening for the present paper which attempts to assess Besterman's own colos-
sal role in bibliographical work in the past half century.
For explanation no more is needed than the fact of his death
in November 1976, without any plans for the continuation of
his bibliographical work in the way that his no less valuable
contribution to the study of the Enlightenment will be continued at the Taylor Institution. A critical survey of his
bibliographical work and methods is necessary as a preliminary step to any plans for continuing it.

Apology is due since such a survey must concentrate
less on the very obvious merits of Besterman's work than
on its defects and failings if it is to have value. "Only a
waster would spend the time to find the few mistakes in
interpretation and statements which inevitably must have
crept into so large an undertaking [as WBB 3]" wrote Rudolf
Hirsch. [2]  Perhaps so, and certainly only a polymath could
attempt a comprehensive review of Besterman's work.  There
is an element of effrontery in passing any judgement on this

*Reprinted by permission of the author and publisher from
the July 1978 issue of the Journal of Librarianship, pp. 149-
61.  Copyright © 1978 by The Library Association.

"one man bibliographical centre" which is in itself an instance of the difficulties there will be in effecting a continuation of Besterman's undertakings.  Nevertheless, since the
greatest value of his bibliographical work is to the reference
librarian rather than to the expert on a given subject, discussion of his work at a much lower level than that of the
polymath is worthwhile.

Though cast in an individual mould, and in many
facets of his life and work reminiscent more of Victorian or
earlier dilettante scholarship than of the present century,
Besterman was a child of his times, and influenced in his
views on bibliography by the contemporary climate of academic and professional thought.  As a young man (and it is
worth remembering that his first bibliographical compilation
was published when he was twenty), his approach was that
of the enumerative bibliographer. [3]  Other early endeavours
were by no means purely bibliographical--for example, his
Dictionary of theosophy published in 1927--nor when they
were, was the approach necessarily limited to authors, as
witness his work on The divining rod (1926) which he completed after the death of Sir William Barrett, adding to it a
substantial alphabetically arranged bibliography.

Not until relatively late in his development as an
enumerative bibliographer, however, does he appear to have
moved towards other areas of bibliographical work.  For a
life-long book collector, he seems to have come relatively
late into the non-enumerative aspects of the subject--descrip-
tive bibliography, historical bibliography--which normally
tend to dominate the bibliophile's thinking.  (Not until 1937
did he subscribe to the Bibliographical Society. )  Although
the history of the book trade and the aesthetic aspects of
book production were of very real interest to him, he published relatively little that can be categorized as "historical
bibliography. "  His splendid survey of The publishing firm
of Cadell & Davies; select correspondence and accounts 1793-
1836, which he edited for the "Oxford Books on Bibliography"
series in 1938, was his most substantial venture in this
field, and it remains an important source for studies of early
nineteenth-century publishing history.  In this work, Besterman was in the forefront of a development in historical
studies of the book, as Michael Sadleir noted in his enthusiastic review[4] in 1938:

    ... the term "bibliography" must henceforward be
      understood to include publishing and distributing

history, as well as that of printing, paper-making, and binding.

The credit for this re-definition of (historical) bibliography is not due to Besterman, to be sure (since Sadleir's own pioneering studies had been appearing for many years before this), but he was an early and highly competent husbandman in a field which has since been ploughed and cropped assiduously by others.

How far Besterman could have continued to play a significant role in the non-enumerative aspects of bibliographical endeavour is not worth much speculation: first the discontinuation of the "Oxford Books on Bibliography" (of which he was one of the series editors) on the outbreak of the Second World War, and then the destruction of his blitzed house in Hampstead compelled him to abandon his plans for a history of the text of Robert Burns. Thereafter his energies were wholeheartedly devoted to those other aspects of bibliographical work for which his individualistic approach and peculiar talents were better suited. His only other major endeavour at this time which attempted to span the gap between enumerative and other bibliographic studies was not a success. Early printed books to the end of the sixteenth century: a bibliography of bibliographies, published by Bernard Quaritch in 1940 as a contribution to the 500th anniversary of the invention of printing, was (like most other commemorative endeavours in that inauspicious year) considerably pared down from the original ambitious plan for "a fully annotated critical bibliography, accompanied by a lengthy introduction on the development of typographical bibliography." It received an appallingly unfavourable review from Sir Frank Francis in The Library[5]--enough to make a lesser man cut his throat, and even a Besterman to concentrate his efforts in areas less chillingly unfavourable than that of the McKerrow/Greg school of bibliographical thought. Since some of the criticisms levelled against his Early printed books have relevance to general consideration of Besterman's arrangement of bibliographies, this review in The Library will be considered further, below.

From the general librarian's point of view, no doubt the most important of Besterman's books before the appearance of the first edition of the World bibliography of bibliographies in 1940 was his study of The beginnings of systematic bibliography, which had its origins in a conference paper Besterman gave at University College London in November

1932. Published in an expanded form as the first of the "Oxford books on bibliography," it achieved a second edition the following year. As a plain, well-marshalled and succinct account of its subject it could scarcely be bettered, though the present writer must confess a preference for the more discursive treatment afforded these old bibliographers and their compilations by Archer Taylor in several of his books. In his History of bibliographies of bibliographies (New Brunswick, N.J., 1955), Book catalogues: their variety and uses (Chicago, 1957) and other works, Taylor has a more sympathetic approach; he judges the bibliographers more appropriately according to the standards of scholarship prevailing in their times, and the reader gains a better insight into the ways in which today he can still profit from consulting them. But such extra detailed mapping was easier with Besterman's preliminary survey to hand. Though a third, much revised edition of Besterman's pioneering essay was published in Paris in 1950 as Les debuts de la bibliographie méthodique, most Anglophone readers are too idle to use it, and a new English edition is a desideratum.

By the mid-1930s, Besterman's study of enumerative bibliography had progressed to the stage at which he was able to submit to Oxford University Press his proposals for what was to become the World bibliography of bibliographies. As one of the editors of the Oxford bibliographical series, he was in a much stronger position to gain sympathetic consideration than an outsider. Nevertheless, the heads of the London and Oxford branches of the Press told him "after prolonged study and reflection that the book was not worth doing, and that, even if it were, it was impossible for one man to bring it off." So Besterman described the incident in his charming 1973 Arundell Esdaile Lecture, Fifty years a bookman.

Humphrey Milford and R. W. Chapman were, as time has shown, wrong on both counts, though in the context of academic publishing in the mid-1930s their caution was understandable. One may dream of what might have been; an Oxford imprint would certainly have secured the future of WBB, and OUP publishing discipline could have moderated some of the less satisfactory features of the work. But it was not to be; a terrible blow which would have halted a lesser or poorer man than Besterman. But being Besterman, the setback re-determined him to go ahead and publish himself. In this he was no doubt encouraged to some extent by the attitude of the library profession, preparing a paper on "A new bibliog-

raphy of bibliographies"--in essentials, the same text that
he was later to use as the introduction to WBB--for the 1936
Library Association conference.  Though the discussion which
followed the paper was very brief, professional opinion was
by no means in agreement with the OUP decision.  Whether
Besterman hoped to persuade OUP as the work grew is possible:  there were other excellent reasons for Besterman to
employ the University Press to print WBB, but even if he
was not hopeful that the Press's controllers would change
their minds, he may have wished them to see what an opportunity they had rejected.  Nevertheless, the first edition of
WBB appeared (with a cancel title) with Besterman's own
name as publisher as well as compiler.  The policy of self-
publication remained the same for the second, "third and
final," and fourth editions, though Besterman's persona was
concealed behind the Geneva imprint Societas bibliographica
for the later editions.

Although the size of WBB more than tripled between
the first and last editions compiled by Besterman, there is
a very close resemblance between all the editions.  Once
the compiler's ideas had become set in a particular mould,
it proved almost impossible for other scholars to persuade
him to a more fluid approach, as indeed the gestation period of WBB showed.  At once Besterman's source of strength
and a weakness which was to flaw much of his work, its effect was to render the later editions of WBB less useful than
they might otherwise have been.  WBB is given further consideration in more detail below.

Most men would find it necessary to spend some time
recharging their batteries after the rigours of compiling and
seeing through the press such a work as WBB.  While at
work on WBB he relaxed with his private press, the Guyon
House Press, at which with assistance from Vivian Ridler--
who had previously worked with David Bland at the Perpetua
Press in Bristol, and was subsequently to become University
Printer at Oxford--he produced an edition of Magna Carta before the plant was destroyed by enemy action in 1940.  Instead of trying to resume practical work in fine book production, he turned back to bibliographical enterprises.

In his article on "The librarian's tools" which he contributed to the Autumn 1941 issue of Library Review, [6] he
anticipated the post-war development of the public library as
an information centre, referred to the new edition of WBB
he had in preparation for after the war, and made the first

call for what were later to become the British union catalogue of periodicals and the Aslib index to theses.   He followed this up in 1942 with further "Desiderata bibliographica"[7] in which he elaborated on the need for BUCOP, and
about the same time contributed a paper to Aslib's seventeenth conference in 1942 on the same topic.   Through his
work in persuading appropriate bodies to take an interest,
and his success in persuading the Rockefeller Foundation to
provide a grant for the purpose, the Council for BUCOP
came into existence formally in 1944 with himself as Editor
and Executive Officer.

Besterman's own vital role in the inception and execution of the project was little emphasized in BUCOP when
the first volume was eventually published, and it hurt him.
Nevertheless, the initial planning of the work on the lines
laid down by Besterman ultimately proved an economic im-
possibility, as were his later proposals for the revamping
of the Library of Congress catalogues.   A regard for the
normal economics of life was lacking from Besterman's
equipment; his were always grand plans.

In 1947 Besterman resigned his editorship of BUCOP,
having for some time already been occupied with attempts to
put into practice through Unesco some of his proposals for
post-war reconstruction in librarianship.   As Edward Carter
indicated in his shrewd assessment of Besterman's career,[8]
there was much in Besterman's earlier work and in his
ideals which was admirably suited to the plans being hatched
for Unesco's development in 1946.   His ideas, originally
noted in "Proposals for an international Library Clearing
House" at Aslib's eighteenth conference in 1943, and elaborated in a paper on "International library rehabilitation and
planning" at the 1946 Paris FID Conference, saw clearly the
problems which would face the profession, and in fact looked
forward to the international co-operative endeavours of the
1970s.

Another post Besterman felt compelled to resign in
1947 with his move to Unesco, was the editorship of the
Journal of Documentation.   As founding editor, Besterman
had created in J. Doc.   what was far and away the most
interesting as well as the most scholarly of British journals
in the field, and in a typographic dress of higher quality
than had been seen in the professional press.   Though increasing specialization has eliminated much of the interest
of J. Doc. for this reader, after thirty years clad in Best-

erman's splendid application of classical typography of the
Morison school, it still remains the best-looking journal of
librarianship produced.

Besterman's role in Unesco was neither successful
nor of long duration.   Though many of his ideas were in
themselves acceptable and accepted, Besterman's approach
was not.   In the special atmosphere of the international
agencies, so deliciously described by Shirley Hazzard in her
People in glass houses, [9] a man of Besterman's type could
not flourish.   Faced with criticism from Oxford for his WBB
plans, he could go it alone and demonstrate how far his
ideas had validity.   In the context of Unesco, his refusal to
compromise--to recognize that compromise was necessary--
could lead only to his resignation being demanded, and the
failure of his plans.

The abandonment of his European Union Catalogue
project was one aspect of his failure which he particularly
regretted, returning to the theme in 1958[10] and again in the
course of his Arundell Esdaile lecture in 1973.   To scholars
who find the American National Union Catalog ... pre-1956
imprints an invaluable tool, it seems almost inexplicable that
Besterman's powerful case for a European Union Catalogue
should have been ignored.   Once more, it was Besterman's
virtue that he could identify a problem and suggest a solution; his vice that his methods of doing so aggravated (instead of conciliated) the opposition.

Though Besterman's resignation did not mean that he
severed all connections with Unesco, as his compilation of
the third edition of Index bibliographicus (1952) showed, he
had relatively little thereafter to do with librarianship or
bibliography on a co-operative basis.   His major area of
activity in the next period of his life was in his Voltairean
studies.   To librarianship and bibliography his energies were
largely restricted (not altogether an appropriate word) to revisions of WBB, as if in recognition that it was only in this
specialized area that his very real contribution to librarianship was acceptable.

If Besterman's name is to live in professional circles
as more than that of a prickly individual who had some excellent ideas, and foresaw the need for greater international
co-operation, it will be because his bibliography of bibliographies continues to be used in libraries.   It is, however, a
wasting asset:   with Besterman's death the mechanics for its

marketing, as well as its revision, have disappeared.  Is
WBB such a useful tool in the international market that it is
worth setting up the machinery to produce further revisions
and expansions?  Or should the library profession, while
noting the advances in bibliographical technique employed by
Besterman, instead attempt to secure the publication of bibliographical works which will not have the defects and disadvantages of WBB?  The other course of (in) action--to go
on using WBB 4 without any attempt to secure a continuing
tool--will, if pursued, show pretty clearly that the sense
of professionalism in librarianship is in a bad state, and that
Besterman's contribution to bibliographical control has been
far less than we have been saying for a generation.

     The virtues of WBB are immediately obvious.  Any
listing of books ought to be based on personal examination,
but few have done so as thoroughly as Besterman, with the
result that his work contains few ghosts.  The standards
adopted for the entries are well thought-out and well applied,
so that in almost all cases one feels quite at ease with the
entries as printed. [11]  His practice of recording the number
of items in the bibliographies he lists is altogether admirable.  The typographical design and standards of physical
production can seldom be faulted, although the fact that the
running headlines are of heading only--and not of subheads--
slows searching.  The fact that the references in the excellent index are only to the columns in which entries appear
would not be a disadvantage if the spines or title pages of
the individual volumes of WBB included the numbers of the
columns they contain, but the fact that they do not, wastes
the time of the reader and must be counted a demerit.

     Several of those who reviewed the first editions of
WBB on their publication quibbled that Besterman had included such things as abridgements of patent specifications, [12]
or complained at the compiler's logic-chopping which allowed
in guides to manuscripts and excluded guides to prints and
other works of art--and one must admit that Besterman's
reasoning in admitting posters as a heading while omitting
(for example) book plates is hard to follow.

     Some commented unfavourably on Besterman's deliber-
ate omission of bibliographies which were not separately published, a rule to which he stated that he had adhered "rather
strictly. "

     Besterman attempted to disarm criticism by stating

frankly in the introduction to WBB that it was "somewhat illogical" to limit himself in this way, but followed this immediately with the extraordinary admission that "valuable
bibliographies are occasionally published in periodicals and
appended to general works." This phrase (which I have ital-
icized) was not just a hastily written and clumsily worded
justification for his policy of omission: since it recurs in
each edition of WBB, one can assume that Besterman genuinely believed that lists of value were only occasionally in
serials and other works. The confidence one feels in his
judgement, sustained or even created by the easy mastery
of the earlier part of his introduction, is immediately dis-
sipated. As Marc Jaryc in his review of WBB 1,[12] or A.
D. Roberts in his shrewd notice of WBB 2,[13] both pointed
out, and anyone who is well-read in any field of endeavour
knows very well, many of the most useful bibliographies appear as parts of other works or in journals, and are excluded by Besterman's rule based on an accident of publication.

Besterman revised and expanded his introduction in
later editions of WBB to note that a good many bibliographies
(of French learned and scientific work, was his example)
were reissued as separates after formal first publication in
a serial, and these he included. Rudolf Hirsch suggested[2]
that he believed many of the entries originated as magazine
articles. But lax application--or worse still, haphazard
application--of a bad rule is little justification.

Besterman's other reasons for the rule are no more
satisfactory. The number of bibliographies is such that not
an individual, not even a committee, could list all. Even if
they could, the vast majority of entries would be valueless.
To attempt to select the more valuable is vain, as selection
is possible only from "full resources." This is the gist of
his argument, which he concluded with the common-sense observation that, with his rule, we know where we are.

This is reminiscent of some of those childhood puzzles in logic--like that proving we can never arrive at a
point since we are perpetually halving the remaining distance
we have to go to reach it. Obviously, in theoretical terms,
a sound selection of bibliographies can be made only from
all bibliographies; in practice, the subject expert with bibliographical competence is perfectly capable of making a useful list of bibliographies in his own field. In quoting his
favourite Voltaire's phrase "Le mieux est l'ennemi du bien,"

Besterman was apparently unaware that his policy could be seen as the deliberate choice of the mieux of theoretical completeness in a limited field in place of the bien of an extended scope including some bibliographies in other works, with the imperfections that selection would imply.

Later on in his introduction, where he was discussing the degree of completeness of WBB, Besterman again referred to the need for "full resources"--this time in the context of a general bibliography of best bibliographies--using this to justify postponement of such selective work. One would like to know his reasoning in this, since it is in such phrases that an odd feature of his work in WBB is concealed.

In the early 1930s, the membership of the Bibliographical Society had been exercised about the aims of bibliography, [14] and the proper limits of the bibliographer's work. Their arguments were inconclusive and rather of the "where is the science in library science" kind, but probably A. W. Pollard's statement that "bibliographers have ... taken it as their function to enumerate everything, leaving to specialists the task of picking out what each of them wants" met general agreement. Besterman does not use this perfectly respectable argument for avoiding any selection of entries for WBB, though it was obviously germane. Did he believe himself, as a generalist, to be incapable of making sound selection? Or did he wish to give the impression that he could do it, if it were worth doing?

Besterman also eschews a critical approach in his policy on annotation of entries, though correctly praising Petzholdt's work in this respect. The reason he advanced (lack of space) does not ring true, and his thinking in what he described as a compromise--that is, his practice of indicating the number of entries contained in the works he listed--shows an odd conception of the use of bibliographies. In "a normal bibliography of a special subject," is it true that "we look, above all, for completeness" as Besterman claimed? In my own experience, and that of various people working in different fields with whom I have discussed this assertion of Besterman's, it is not true. At certain times, and for certain types of enquiry, the comprehensive bibliography may be just what we need. But for a large proportion of enquiry work, short well-chosen and suitably annotated reading lists will be of far more practical usefulness. Besterman appeared to despise these, to judge by his slighting references to "small lists issued by public libraries" ... "a great many absolutely trivial ones have been omitted."

Undoubtedly Besterman chose to omit certain categories of material from a mixture of motives, and the very clarity of his statement of method which he prepared for his Library Association lecture in 1936 (and which he used as the basis for the introduction to WBB) conceals some of the reasons, while distorting others. That a single individual should, in order to reduce his self-imposed task to a more manageable level, decide to include only "separately published bibliographies" is understandable. That he should feel incompetent to annotate we can understand. All this was all right for Besterman in his first edition of WBB (perhaps even for all editions prepared by his own hand alone) but should be remembered in planning for the future.

At times, one feels that Besterman's beliefs about the need for "full resources" caused him to create some rather inhospitable rules for plentiful classes of publication. His famous definition of a bibliography as a "list of books arranged according to some permanent principle" could be, and was, used to exclude a lot of material that any bibliographer working on a selective principle would also exclude.

To exclude booksellers' and auction catalogues as a general rule was, perhaps, equally desirable as a means of excluding much valueless material. Yet though many of these catalogues are useless, others are very highly valued for their scholarship--and the inclusion of such catalogues on a selective basis is one of the reasons that Petzholdt is still of value a century after his bibliography of bibliographies was published. Besterman preferred logic to convenience; to exclude (for example) the Gumuchian Livres de l'enfance catalogue, or the Birrell and Garnett Catalogue of typefounders' specimens--both so highly regarded by experts in their fields that offset litho reprints at a high price have been published--on the grounds that they were not bibliographies was the worst kind of pedantry.

In short, any plans for a continuation built on WBB, and which will presumably have to be undertaken by a team of workers rather than a single polymath, must come to terms with the need for selective critical inclusion of much material at present excluded by Besterman's terms of reference.

The alphabetical arrangement of WBB under a very large number of specific subject headings is not, of course, one which lends itself to easy continuation. Besterman

recognized that this method of arrangement, which he described as "the best and most practical method not only
theoretically but also pragmatically," would be controversial,
although it was, of course, the same basic plan as that used
by Peignot in his Répertoire of 1812, and by W. P. Courtney
in his Register of national bibliography (1905-1912). He
justified it on two grounds: the first that all classified arrangements become obsolete very rapidly, and that even the
decimal system's value is destroyed by the fact that nearly
all users have been obliged to modify it for their own needs.
His overriding reason for adopting the alphabetical arrangement, however, was the economy in the cost of production
that would come with the saving of perhaps 20 per cent of
the bulk.

For a man financing the work out of his own pocket,
this was perhaps adequate, even ignoring the fact that there
is apparently greater ease for the compiler to assign subject
headings than to slot his entries into a classified arrangement. No lover of classification myself, I have every
sympathy for Besterman's attempt to produce a tool on the
dictionary principle.

Unfortunately, Besterman's predilection for the dictionary form, and the warm admiration he felt for the British Museum's methods of subject cataloguing, blinded him to
the fact that obsolescence overtakes an alphabetical system
no less rapidly than a classified arrangement and that, unless there is a very generous policy of cross-referencing
(eating away the economic advantage he claimed), users of
the tool would often fail to find pertinent material which had
been hidden from them under an unconsulted heading.

No attempt has been made for this paper to gauge the
amount of revision to the system of headings between WBB 1
and WBB 4. A few instances will indicate the difficulties
that the user has with WBB at present, not only in locating
material but in understanding precisely what Besterman meant
by some headings.

WBB 1 includes the heading "The Caribbees": in itself a name which was quaint in its obsolescence in 1940.
In later editions it was changed to "Caribbean Region." However, in the usage of most of those interested in West Indian
affairs, "Caribbees" means the island chain of the Lesser
Antilles and only doubtfully those of the Greater Antilles.
"Caribbean Region," on the other hand, subsumes all the

islands, and parts of the Main as well--the Central American states, Colombia, Venezuela, and possibly Florida and the Guianas as well.

A matter of minor detail, perhaps, but other relevant material appears under the heading "West Indies" from and to which there are no references. "West Indies" does not mean the area of the defunct West Indian federation; it includes the Spanish, French, Dutch and American islands also. Some very important material relating to the British islands appears only under "Caribbean Region"; under the heading "Dominica, Dominican literature" are muddled together entries for the Dominican republic and for the separate British island; "Virgin Islands" does not distinguish the British and American Virgins, and so forth.

Elsewhere, material on the Netherlands Antilles is sometimes included under the heading "East Indies" (admittedly with a gloss explaining that bibliographies of the Dutch East Indies often covered the Dutch West Indies as well) or, of course, under the name of the individual islands. Some material on Belize/British Honduras appears under Honduras, some under Belize, without references. The heading "Guiana" covers French Guiana/Cayenne and British Guiana/Guyana, but not Dutch Guiana/Surinam, for which Surinam appears as a heading.

Other flaws, picked out almost at random, include Henry Wagner's Bibliography ... of possessions of the U. S. formerly Mexican (1917) only listed under "Mexico"; his The Spanish South-West only under "America. Latin America. History" although quite clearly these works on the bibliography of Arizona &c. are usually going to be required by those who will expect to find them listed under the heading "United States." There is a RAE List of references on box-beams under the heading "Shells," in which most entries are to the sort for which the reference "see also Conchology" is more appropriate.

"Only a waster ..." wrote Hirsch of such fault-finding, and it is a rather futile exercise to search for such minor flaws which are almost inevitable in any large work. But these flaws are there because of the system Besterman adopted, as often as through carelessness on his part.

Though Besterman's system is largely of specific subject headings, many of the larger subjects are extensively subdivided under the general heading--for example, "Printing," which indeed Rowman & Littlefield have published for Besterman as a separate subject bibliography.   Although Besterman's theory in arriving at these subdivisions is often faultless, his practice is not.

The scarifying attack on Early printed books to the end of the sixteenth century,  already referred to above, showed Sir Frank Francis's impatience with Besterman's system of arrangement very well. [5]   Francis pointed out very clearly the difficulties (for the compiler as well as the user) of the basic division between subject and country approach, and the arbitrary way in which Besterman had assigned entries to one or the other.   He noted the false economies that slight cross-referencing produced, and the barriers placed in the way of users by the omission of some categories of entry from the index.   After categorizing the many faults of omission and commission he believed the work contained, Francis concluded that

> Mr Besterman has not given us any reason to suppose that he has the equipment necessary to produce a book of this kind.   The mechanical searching of a limited number of periodicals and of the bibliographical shelves of, say, the British Museum is utterly useless to the specialist and misleading to the amateur.   To compile an adequate list of bibliographies of this period requires many years of intimate association with the period and the literature concerning it, to say nothing of continual watchfulness and diligence in the accumulation of material.

These harsh words may have helped reinforce Besterman's belief that his WBB should not attempt any critical or selective listing of material, since he had failed so signally in an area he could be expected to know relatively well.   The criticism of his arrangement he seems to have shrugged off: the second edition of Early printed books ... "revised and much enlarged," which he issued under the Societas Bibliographica imprint in 1961, followed exactly the same arrangement.   I have not compared the two editions to determine whether Besterman corrected the mistakes Francis had pointed out, but from the friendly but rather unenthusiastic notice of the work by James B. Childs, [16] it is clear that the bibliography was still far from comprehensive.

Francis was a specialist reviewing a specialist work.

Specialist reviews of WBB were always few.    A. D. Roberts
and Marc Jaryc were the most critical reviewers, as they
were the most detailed in their examination of the contents.
Many of the other notices that I have read belong simply to
the enthusiastic school, [17] for which, of course, there was a
place.   It was amazing that a single man should be able to
compile so extensive a work so accurate in the body of the
entries.

Neither awe nor enthusiasm ought to blind us to the
faults of WBB, however.   Specialists never use it for their
own area of specialization, but using it for subjects we know
little about is difficult, and we will not then notice the absence of many of the best bibliographies, either because they
are under a different heading or because their physical form
has secured their exclusion.   When the system of subject
headings is so complicated for the native English speaker to
follow, what hope have those for whom English is a foreign
tongue of discovering in WBB all those entries which are
relevant, for any but the most straightforward enquiry?   The
scholar has little use for WBB; the general reader cannot
use it.   Who does use it, apart from the hard-pressed librarian?   If WBB did not exist, would it be necessary to
invent it?

That librarianship has a need for the general bibliography of bibliographies was, of course, demonstrated by the
appearance of four editions of WBB in thirty years, each
one of which presumably paying its way rather more satis-
factorily than most bibliographical work.   Rowman & Littlefield's production of subject sectional parts shows just as
clearly that there is a considerable potential market for some
sectional lists in addition to the main work.   One can well
see that in a revision of the WBB planned in a classified arrangement, and with the addition of significant serially published bibliographies selected by subject authorities, there
will be a very substantial market for special sections as
bibliographies in their own right.   There will be the advantage that revised editions of the "growth areas" can be produced, while for static subject fields a slower rate of revision will be acceptable.   The classified arrangement will be
easier for the non-Anglophone user; a system of annotation
using symbols (indicating level, and so forth) on the guide-
book principle will be more useful than one with extensive
wordage.

In nautical usage, however extensively and however

many times a vessel is repaired and rebuilt, she remains the same vessel. The Mary Jane is the Mary Jane, though she has been so hacked about that not a single timber of her original building remains. Though a work of the kind visualized above will be very different indeed from WBB as we know it, will it not still be Besterman? Any other name for a bibliography of bibliographies seems unthinkable, which is, in a single phrase, a measure of Besterman's contribution to bibliography.

## References

1. J. Docum., I (4) March 1946, 194-205.
2. Coll. Res. Libr., 16, 1955, 424.
3. With his Bibliography of Annie Besant (1924).
4. The Library, 4th series, 19, 1938-1939, 364-368.
5. The Library, 4th series, 22, 1941-1942, 91-97.
6. Libr. Rev., 59, Autumn 1941, 82-87.
7. Libr. Rev., 62, Summer 1942, 190-193.
8. Theodore Besterman: a personal memoir. J. Docum., 33 (1) March 1977, 79-87.
9. Hazzard, Shirley. People in glass houses. Macmillan, 1967; Penguin 1970.
10. The European Union Catalogue Project. J. Docum., 14 (2) June 1958, 56-64.
11. One of the relatively rare exceptions is to be found under the heading "Jamaican literature" in WBB 4.
12. e.g. Marc Jaryc in PBSA 36, 1942, 321-324.
13. J. Docum., 6 (3) September 1950, 168-170.
14. Gaselee, Sir Stephen. The aims of bibliography [with a reply by Sir Walter Greg and a note by A. W. Pollard]. The Library, 4th series, 13 (3) December 1932, 225-258.
15. A New Bibliography of Bibliographies. Libr. Ass. Rec., 38 (6), June 1936, 297-303.
16. Papers of the Bibliographical Society of America, 56, 1962, 121-123.
17. e.g. R. R. Shaw, Libr. J., 80, 15 June 1955, 1474-1475.

# THE MISCHIEF IN MEASUREMENT*

Daniel Gore

The first rule in using any measuring instrument is to be
wary of its accuracy. A pilot relying upon a faulty altimeter
is in greater peril than a pilot flying by the seat of his pants,
for the latter's head is always wary of what his seat is telling him. Where much is at stake, redundancy in measuring
instruments is indispensable, for conflicting results will alert
you to the fact that at least one instrument is wrong, and
possibly all of them. That is why airliner navigation systems commonly exhibit multiple redundancy, to reduce the
probability of disaster.

The second rule of measurement is that the more
complex the phenomenon being measured, the more difficult
it will be to obtain precise, accurate, and reliable measurements. That is why the instruments of medical diagnosis
are so intricate, elaborate, and redundant. The probability
of error increases with the increasing complexity of the thing
being measured.

Librarians do not need to be convinced of the complexity of libraries, nor of the great difficulties inherent in
attempts to measure their performance. Experience daily
confirms those facts to us and makes us properly skeptical
of all techniques of measurement--to the extreme degree
that, until recent years, we have largely forsaken any efforts to measure library performance, except for gross

*Reprinted by permission of the author and publisher from
the May 1, 1978 issue of Library Journal, pp. 933-37.
Published by R. R. Bowker Co. (a Xerox company); copy-
right © 1978 by Xerox Corporation. Reprinted from To
Know a Library (Greenwood Press), copyright © 1978 by
Daniel Gore.

measurements of volumes circulated, volumes acquired,
dollars spent, and the like.

While a seriously faulty measuring device for libraries is worse than none at all, an approximately accurate one,
capable of calibration and cross-checking against other evidence, would clearly be much better than none at all.  Lately we have witnessed a variety of efforts to measure library
performance, none of them perfect, but all of them valuable
in that even the worst of them have awakened us to the possibility that useful measures of library performance can be
obtained, and presumably improved upon, through the stringent test of experience.  Richard Trueswell,[1] Michael Buckland,[2] Philip Morse,[3] Ben-Ami Lipitz,[4] and Ernest R. De
Prospo[5] are names that immediately come to mind in respect
to serious efforts to obtain usable measures of library performance.  I have made some modest efforts in this field
myself[6, 7, 8] and will report briefly here on subsequent efforts at performance measurements, drawing attention both
to their benefits and, especially, to their shortcomings.

While libraries rightly concern themselves with a
variety of services, it is fair to say that their cardinal mission is to provide recorded materials (books, journals,
phonorecords, etc.) to library users, and that among this
variety of materials the provision of books is in most libraries the paramount concern.  The efforts at measurement
reported here are exclusively concerned with the provision
of books to readers.  At Macalester Library I have attempted
to measure the following phenomena:

Holding Rate:  The percent of all books your patrons
want to read that are held by your library.

Availability Rate:  The percent of wanted books held
by the library that are available on your shelves when your
patrons want them.

Performance Rate:  The product of Holdings Rate
Times Availability Rate, or the percentage of all books (both
those you own and those you don't), immediately accessible
to patrons when they want them.

The results of my first effort to measure Availability
Rate are cited in "Let Them Eat Cake While Reading Catalog
Cards"[7] but the technique of measurement was not described.

## The reader survey

For a period of three weeks in 1974 (March/April, when
demand peaks) we placed stacks of "Reader Satisfaction Survey" slips at all catalog consulting tables, asking readers to
complete and return them (see figure I).   Over the three-
week period we obtained reports on about a thousand searches
for books we owned, of which only 58 percent were success-

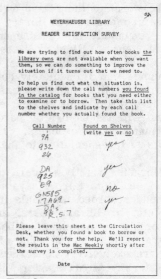

**Figure I**

ful.   The measuring technique is simple and virtually cost-
free; it is also a good deal less than perfect.   The following
shortcomings are immediately apparent:

● Apparently only one-third of actual catalog-based
book searches made during the survey period were reported
on by patrons.   There is no certainty that the one-third who
did report represent a random sample.   Self-selection of respondents obviously occurred, some (or much) of it by persons who had frequently been frustrated by the nonavailability
of owned and wanted books.

● The survey gives no clue as to how much of the
failure to find books on the shelves is assignable to patron
error.

Both of these shortcomings would tend to indicate a
lower Availability Rate than the true potential maximum.
The extent of error is not measurable.  Nonetheless, the
survey findings did confirm what we already believed to be
the case from the frequent, and sometimes bitter, complaints
registered at the Circulation Desk by frustrated patrons.

From these two pieces of evidence, we concluded that
systematic duplication of high-demand titles was urgently
needed to lower the frustration rate, and such a program was
accordingly inaugurated.

One year after the first availability survey was conducted, we made a second survey (April 1975) in all respects
identical to the first.  By that time we had added about a
thousand high-demand multiple copies to the collections.  We
had also reduced the general loan period from about five
weeks to about three.  The second survey indicated that over
a 12-month period the Availability Rate had risen from 58
percent to 70 percent--a very satisfying result, even though
the second survey suffered the same shortcomings as the
first, and furthermore could not be used to prove a causal
connection between the remedial actions we had taken and
the subsequent improvement in Availability Rates.  We infer
that such a connection did exist, but we cannot prove it.

Patron complaints about unavailable books dropped
sharply over the same period, confirming the second survey's
indication that Availability Rates had improved substantially.

The program of systematic duplication was continued,
and in April 1976 we conducted a third availability survey,
identical to the first two.  This survey yielded only about a
tenth of the returns received from each of the first two and
showed an Availability Rate of about 75 percent.  Although
satisfying in itself, we regard that result as totally unreliable
because of the very small response.  The meagerness of
response is significant, however, for it implies a sharp reduction in general patron concern about the availability problem.  That supposition is also confirmed by the fact that
complaints of nonavailability made to circulation attendants
had virtually ceased.

The availability surveys obviously told us nothing
about the library's Holdings Rate:  the percentage of wanted
books the library actually owned.  One way to determine
precisely the Holdings Rate is to follow the elaborate meth-

odology employed by Ben-Ami Lipitz[4] in his conclusive study
of catalog use at the Yale Library.   The difficulty with that
method is that it costs a great deal of money to carry out
properly, and the money was not available to us.

## The diary project

Still it seemed vital to get some approximate reading of our
Holdings Rate, in order to arrive at some judgment about
the adequacy of our holdings to our patrons' needs.   We seldom heard complaints on that score, but desired some better
confirmation (if it could be inexpensively obtained) that our
holdings were indeed satisfactory.   Several years' speculation
on the matter led me to the conclusion that there was probably no method for measuring Holdings Rates that was both
cheap and scientifically valid.   I therefore decided to seek a
cheap instrument of measurement, something akin to a thermometer, which in the event of a fever will signify something definitely is wrong (although it will not tell you what),
or in the absence of fever allows at least a reasonable supposition (absent other symptoms) that all is well.

The thermometer-like device I finally hit upon is a
student-kept diary, recording the results of all book searches in the Macalester Library over an entire academic semester.   A sample page of the diary, and of instructions for
keeping it, are reproduced in Figure II.

To insure faithful student work on the diary, some
quid pro quo seemed necessary, and we offered a payment of
$10 to each student who completed the work.   On that basis
we were not prepared to involve all 1600 students in the
project, nor even a statistically valid random sample, given
our then uncertainty about the magnitude of the problem, or
even of its existence.

The group actually invited to participate were all
those members of the junior class who were eligible for
membership in Phi Beta Kappa--presumably active users of
the library.   Of the 46 students thus eligible, 25 agreed to
participate, and 19 actually completed their duties, at a cost
of $190 to the library.   The project ran February-May 1977.

The only data tabulated thus far are those related to
Holdings Rates, Availability Rates, and interlibrary loans.

## Diary of Library Book Searches

It has but one purpose: to help library staff measure and improve their success in providing for you the books you want when you want them. When the project is over we'll give you a written summary of the group's results.

Reading, like thinking, is a personal matter, so your name shouldn't appear on the diary. The master cross-list of names and diary numbers will be seen only by me, and I will consult it only if a question of interpretation arises and I need help from an individual diarist.

So you'll be sure to have your diary with you whenever you use the library, please place it (in numerical order) in the Diary Box at the Circulation Desk when you leave the library—and of course pick it up there too when you come back.

If you run into problems or have any questions about the project, just drop in to see me at your convenience. Thanks very much for your participation.

Daniel Gore
Library Director
Macalester College
14 February 1977

## Notes on Diary Entries

Record only book searches made at the Mac Library.

A brief title will ordinarily suffice. Occasionally an author's name will be needed, as with "The Plays" of Shakespeare, where the name makes the title specific.

Course related: Are you seeking the book for a course you are presently taking? Answer yes or no.

In catalog: Write A, T, or S if you locate an entry in the Author, Title, or Subject catalog. Write "no" if you find no entry in a catalog search. Write B if you locate a book through shelf-browsing rather than a catalog search.

Call #: leave blank if you find no catalog entry or book. For a Reserve book, write "Res." after call #.

On shelf & interloan squares: Write yes or no or leave blank, as appropriate.

Use footnotes to explain special situations: e.g. a book turns out to be in the Olin branch, and you decide against making the trip to fetch it.

Fill in here the date you began the diary: _____

and the date you concluded it: _____

On the concluding date (or soon afterwards), deliver your diary to Mrs. Dorothy Barnes, Library Secretary, and she will present to you the honorarium of ten dollars for your contribution to our joint effort to measure and improve library performance.

..............

If you find diary keeping a nuisance and want to give it up, be quick to say so! No harm is done by simply dropping out. But haphazard participation will blur the group results.

**Figure II**

The methodology employed has no scientific validity whatever. One might, for example, expect to derive from it an artificially high Availability Rate, on the assumption that these bright juniors are more likely than the average student to seek relatively low-demand, abstruse materials for research papers, etc. One might also expect the indicated Holdings Rate to be lower than it is for duller students, and much higher than it would be for faculty engaged in rarefied research, and so on. We were only using a simple thermometer, which might at least be counted upon to tell us whether a fever was, or was not, present.

The results were about what I anticipated as regards Holdings Rate, and a good bit higher as regards Availability Rate.

Of a total of 422 books sought for by these students, we owned 378, for a Holdings Rate of 90 percent--which coincidentally matches the Holdings Rate determined by Ben-Ami Lipitz for the whole population of users of the enormous Yale Library. That strong showing also suggests why we so rarely hear complaints that the library does not own the books our students want to read.

Of the 378 books we owned, 331 of them were on the shelf when wanted, for an Availability Rate of 88 percent. As noted, this figure is probably higher than one would obtain from a truly random sample, but it nonetheless adds some confirmation to what we have previously learned from the three availability surveys already described: Availability Rates show strong improvement since the time when the duplication program was inaugurated and the general loan period shortened. A further explanation for the continuing improvement in the Availability Rate is that in February 1977 we installed electronic exit controls. That was done because data collected over the previous year showed that 15 percent of our general loans were not charged out--and were presumably kept out much longer than the three-week general loan period. Preventing the occurrence of so many long-term loans would predictably bring strong improvements in the Availability Rate.

The net Performance Rate is expressed as a percentage of books obtained against the totality of books wanted (331/422), or the product of Holdings Rate times Availability Rate (90 percent x 88 percent). Either way you figure it, of course the same result is obtained: a Performance Rate of 79 percent. That is to say, these students actually found about four out of five of the books they went after--a result that leads me to the judgment that at any rate no fever exists, and the library apparently is in healthy condition.

The Macalester Library owns about 200, 000 book titles. That works out to about four-tenths of one percent of all titles thought to have been published since Gutenberg. If our acquisitions program throughout the years had been conducted on a strictly random basis, one might then expect our actual Holdings Rate would also work out to a figure of four-tenths of one percent. The reason it comes out instead (provisionally) at 90 percent is that the collection was developed not randomly, but on the basis of the perceived needs of our own clientele.

In the same diary project, the data show that of the 91 books that were not available (for whatever reason) when wanted by the students, 23 (or 25 percent) were requested on interloan. Expressed as a percentage of the books they actually borrowed, the figure is seven percent. For the total population of users, that figure runs instead around four percent--a result that suggests that bright students are much more likely than others to take the trouble to pursue unowned (or unavailable) books through interloan.

These students also turned out to be far more unlucky than our general user population in receiving delivery of requested interloan books. Of the 23 books they requested, only 13 were delivered, for a decidedly poor showing of 55 percent. On an annual volume of about 1800 books requested on interloan by all Macalester patrons, our success rate runs an average of around 80 percent. The data obtained from the diary project furnish no clue as to the cause of these 19 juniors' extraordinary bad luck with interloan service. The very small number of requests involved might well be expected to yield statistical discrepancies--a deficiency that might also be imagined (in a lesser degree) as regards the indicated Holdings and Availability Rates, except that the latter two are approximately corroborated by independent evidence, while the diaries' interloan results are definitely undermined by our wholesale data on total interloan activity.

## Corrective action

Although these methods plainly lack scientific validity, they

nonetheless proved to have considerable managerial usefulness:  they enable us to confirm approximately a rather
serious deficiency in Availability Rates, and to correct the
problem at relatively low cost (about $24,000 over a four-
year period, or about two percent of our total library budget over the same period).  They also confirmed that no
serious problem exists with our Holdings Rate, despite the
fact that over the last seven years our volume of annual ad-
ditions to the collections has dropped by about 50 percent.

In the absence of these admittedly crude performance
measures, we might well have leapt to the conclusion that
what caused great problems for our patrons was a deficiency
in the Holdings Rate rather than the Availability Rate.  Had
we in fact reached such a mistaken conclusion, we would
have argued for maintaining the acquisitions volume at the
high level of seven years back.  Had we carried the argument successfully with the administration, we would have
spent about $500,000 more on adding even more new titles,
instead of the $24,000 actually spent on duplicates, and the
patrons' problem would still not have been resolved, for the
problem was with availability rather than Holdings Rates.

The DeProspo method

Other methods have indeed been proposed, and I turn now to
those lately developed by Ernest DeProspo et al. and published in Performance Measures for Public Libraries. 5  I
examine these methods in detail because they promise to be
widely used among public and perhaps other types of libraries, and the methods specifically proposed for measuring
Holdings and Availability Rates manifest gross defects--which,
if not clearly recognized by library managers employing these
methods, are likely to lead to courses of action exactly the
opposite of those warranted by a library's actual situation.

As a by-product of the original DeProspo work, Ellen
Altman et al. have recently published A Data Gathering and
Instructional Manual for Performance Measures in Public Libraries. 9  Workshops in the practical use of these measures
will be conducted around the country, to promote their utilization.

A further strong impetus to the widespread use of the
DeProspo methodology is its recent corporation (in condensed
form) in a chapter in Measuring the Effectiveness of Basic

Municipal Services, [10] which is the bible for city managers
interested in gauging the performance of various municipal
institutions--public libraries of course among them.  I believe that city managers who regard the DeProspo methods
as canonical--as they are likely to do--may impose courses
of action on public libraries that will lead to their becoming
less effective institutions than they are at present.

Of the variety of measurements proposed by the De
Prospo group, I will confine myself to those designed for
ascertaining a library's Holdings, Availability, and Performance Rates, because they are the only ones that fall within
my areas of experience, and the only ones I feel qualified to
discuss with any confidence.

To determine Holdings Rates, the DeProspo group
advocate drawing a random sample of 500 book titles from
the five most recent years of the American Book Publishing
Record and checking those titles against one's own catalog to
determine the percentage held. [5]   Thus if one discovers 200
of the 500 BPR sample titles in the local catalog, the Holdings Rate is alleged to be 40 percent.

To determine Availability Rates, the DeProspo group
takes the titles actually held among the 500 titles BPR sample and makes a shelf check to determine what percentage of
actual holdings are then available on the shelves.

In a Library Quarterly review[11] of DeProspo's Performance Measures for Public Libraries, Michael Bommer
briefly, but convincingly, analyzes gross defects inherent in
DeProspo's methods for measuring Holdings and Availability
Rates.   I quote the relevant passages in full:

> Another indicator purports to measure 'the
> chances that a user has in obtaining recently pub-
> lished books' (p. 34).  This indicator is derived
> by determining the proportion of books a library
> has available from a list of 500 randomly selected
> titles drawn from American Book Publishing Rec-
> ord (ABPR) for the years 1966-70.  Obviously, in
> general, libraries with the greater expenditures for
> books will have a greater proportion of these sam-
> ple titles available.  In addition, this measure in
> no way reflects the quality of a library's collec-
> tion.   A library that randomly selects books from
> ABPR will receive a rating comparable to that of
> a library of similar size that may make great ef-

forts to select books that are of most interest to
its users.  This same criticism applies to the
measure of the probability of availability of periodical articles (p. 35).  The tendency toward bias
inherent in these measures is probably best illustrated by the measure of satisfaction reported by
patrons of these libraries.  In general, users of
smaller libraries where a smaller proportion of
books and periodicals are available, reported a
higher satisfaction rate than users of larger public libraries (72 percent versus 66 percent).

Similarly, a title-availability measure purport-
ing to measure the probability that a user will successfully find a book owned by the library (but actually measuring the probability that any book is
available) contains an inherent bias.  It is generally
known that the majority of demands are for a small
proportion of a library's collection.  Thus, the
probability that an actual demand will be satisfied
(considering that a greater proportion of these high-
demand books will be out on loan) will be much
less than the probability that any book selected at
random will be available.

Bommer's terse critique merits fuller exploration.
Using a BPR sample (or a sample from any other extensive
bibliography, such as Books for College Libraries, NUC, the
Standard Catalog for Public Libraries) clearly tells you nothing whatever about an actual patron's probability of finding
the book he wants in your catalog, unless the range of total
patron interest extends evenly throughout the entire contents
of BPR, or any other listing used as a criterion.  The probability of that being the case is approximately zero, except
perhaps among the patrons in a city as large as New York.

Using the BPR sample only tells you, by an indirect
and cumbersome route, about how many dollars you are
spending each year on the purchase of current American imprints.  Looking at your current budget allocation will tell
you the same thing, more easily and more precisely.

## Lake Wobegon's holdings

Consider now the case of the public library in Lake Wobegon,
Minnesota, "the little town that time forgot."  The reading
interests of its citizens are almost wholly confined to hunting,

fishing, baseball, auto repairing, country music, the making of Powdermilk Biscuits, and, curiously enough, to the work of a New Yorker staff writer, Garrison Keillor.  Measuring that library's catalog against the BPR random sample would probably yield a Holdings Rate of less than one percent. Yet Raoul (driver for the Warm Car Service), the redoubtable Jack himself (owner of Jack's Auto Repair), and most other citizens of Lake Wobegon all attest that the library owns virtually everything they wish to see.  Even Barbara Anne Bunson, now an undergraduate at the University of Minnesota, states the little library of Lake Wobegon always had the books she wanted when she was growing up there--although of course now that she is a university student, she does have to depend on the university library for advanced sociology texts and the like that her professors require her to read.

The true Holdings Rate of the Lake Wobegon Library, as confirmed by its patrons, is around 95 percent, rather than the scandalously low one percent rate indicated by the BPR sample.  For Lake Wobegon to achieve a 95 percent showing from the BPR sample, the town would have to buy some 25,000 new American imprints each year, at a cost of about $375,000 per year, a sum that exceeds the entire municipal budget for the last ten years.  Even if Lake Wobegon contrived to do such a foolish thing, the real Holdings Rate of its library--as measured against its own patrons' reading interests--would not rise more than a percent or two, and the town would be in hock for library materials from now to kingdom come.

For most towns and cities in the U. S., the BPR method will clearly yield a wild and erroneously low Holdings Rate.  For all 20 libraries (ranging from "small" to "large") measured in DeProspo's pilot survey, the indicated Holdings Rate ranged from a low of eight-tenths of one percent (possibly Lake Wobegon) to a high of 58 percent.  Indeed one of the large libraries surveyed showed a Holdings Rate of only 13. 6 percent.

Is there anyone prepared to believe that the true Holdings Rates (as measured against actual patron demand) are thus shockingly low in all sizes of American public libraries?  If city managers are foolish enough to believe that, and to act upon their belief, then they will order extravagant increases in the library's acquisition of new titles, and accomplish little or nothing by way of increasing actual patron satisfaction.

Artificial availability

It would be well for the DeProspo group to validate their
BPR measure by taking real Holdings Rate measures against
actual patron demand (much as Lipitz did at Yale) and comparing their results.   To date no such cross-validation has
been attempted (personal communication from Dr. Ellen Altman), nor is any contemplated.   Having nothing to guide me
but my knowledge of the great competence generally found
among book selectors in public libraries, I am willing to
predict that if the true Holdings Rates were measured, they
would fall generally in the 75 to 90 percent range in most
American public libraries.

As noted (implicitly) by Bommer in his review article,
the DeProspo method of measuring Availability Rates will
very likely yield artificially high results.   That is because
of the classic inventory phenomenon where one commonly
finds that only 20 percent of the items in a given inventory
(books or anything else) will receive 80 percent of total demand, while the other 80 percent of inventory items satisfies
only 20 percent of the demand.   Thus 80 percent of the BPR
sample is likely to be in very low demand, and the majority
of those books will be on the shelves when wanted.   Of the
remaining 20 percent of high-demand titles, half or more of
them are likely to be off the shelves.   But the overall Availability Rate, so heavily biased by the 80 percent portion of
low-demand titles, will probably work out to around 70 percent even if no systematic duplication program exists.

Availability Rates in the DeProspo pilot study of 20
libraries ranged from a low of 56 percent to a high of 81
percent.   These figures are almost certain to be artificially
high.   The true range of Availability Rates, if measured
against actual patron demands, would probably be significantly
lower, say from a low of 45 percent to a high of 70 percent.

To recapitulate:  in practically all public libraries,
the DeProspo methods of measurement will yield artifically
low Holdings Rates, and artificially high Availability Rates.
The net effect of multiplying these two rates in order to obtain the net Performance Rate is impossible to predict accurately, since the two errors in opposite directions will in
some degree cancel each other out.   But in most instances
it might be expected to yield an artificially low Performance
Rate (which is the equivalent of DeProspo's "Probability of
Availability").

The median range of Performance Rates in the large,
medium, and small libraries included in DeProspo's pilot
survey worked out to an astonishingly low figure of 27 percent for large libraries, and eight-tenths of one percent for
small libraries.   Does anyone believe the American public
would tolerate such gross inefficiency in the performance of
their public libraries?

## Upside down thermometer

Let us assume now that a public library manager does indeed have great confidence in the results obtained by applying the DeProspo measurements to his own library.   He discovers a Performance Rate of only 21 percent, resulting
from the product of a measured Holdings Rate of 30 percent
and a measured Availability Rate of 69 percent.   Looking at
these data he naturally concludes that the best remedy for
his intolerably low Performance Rate is to bring the Holdings Rate up by vast infusions of new titles.   But the real
source of difficulty is more likely to be the Availability Rate,
which looks so comparatively satisfactory that he decides to
do little or nothing by way of improving it.   Actually the
derived Availability Rate is artificially high, while the derived Holdings Rate is artificially quite low.

So instead of laying out a modest amount of funds on
duplicate copies necessary to improve an Availability Rate
that in reality may be only 50 percent, he spends a huge
amount of money to improve a Holdings Rate that may in
reality already be at a very satisfactory level of 90 percent.
The misleading properties inherent in the DeProspo measurement methodology cause him to spend a great deal of money
to accomplish minuscule improvements in the true Performance Rate, when by spending a little money instead on high-
demand duplicates he would have achieved very substantial
increases.   The DeProspo measuring information may be
likened to a thermometer with its fluid bulb placed at the
wrong end.

It is my conviction that the only trustworthy measure
of Holdings and Availability Rates are those which are applied directly to the actual users of any given library, whether it be public, academic, or special.   A particular type of
such measures that were applied in the Macalester College
Library, were described above.   I indicated their shortcomings and my moderate dissatisfaction with them.   I am not

willing to advocate their use in any other library, although I
am quite satisfied with the useful results they produced for
us.

Better methods than those I employed can be designed
by better minds: methods that will yield more reliable results, and at a cost that can readily be borne by any library.
If such improved methods can indeed be devised, they would
yield inestimable benefits to all kinds of libraries.

## $1000 prize

To promote the creation of such methods, and because I am
so convinced that young, creative minds are more likely to
hit upon them than are older and wearier heads, I am personally offering a prize of $1000 to the one library school
student who develops, in my judgment, the best new methods
for inexpensively measuring Holdings and Availability Rates,
in both public and academic libraries.

The deadline for submitting methods to me is September 1, 1978. If in my judgment none of the submissions
substantially improves on existing methods, no prize will be
awarded. It is my optimisitc forecast at this writing that a
winning method will be created, because the need for it is
so urgent and there are so many fine young minds capable
of rising to the challenge if properly stimulated.

## References

1.  Trueswell, Richard W. "Growing Libraries: Who
        Needs Them? a Statistical Basis for the No-Growth
        Collection," in Farewell to Alexandria, ed. D. Gore.
        Greenwood, 1976, p. 72-104. Trueswell's various
        investigations of library performance measurements
        began about two decades ago. The paper cited here
        is a compendium of his mature views on the subject.
2.  Buckland, Michael. Book Availability and the Library
        User. Pergamon, 1975.
3.  Morse, Philip M. Library Effectiveness. M. I. T. Pr. ,
        1968.
4.  Lipitz, Ben-Ami. "Catalog Use in a Large Research
        Library," in Operations Research: Implications for
        Libraries, ed. Swanson & Bookstein, "University of
        Chicago Studies in Library Science"; Univ. of Chicago
        Pr. , 1972, p. 129-39.

5.  DeProspo, Ernest R. et al.  Performance Measures
    for Public Libraries.  Public Library Assn./Ameri-
    can Library Assn. , 1973.
6.  Gore, Daniel.  "Zero Growth for the College Library,"
    College Management, August/September 1974 p. 12-14.
7.  _____.  "Let Them Eat Cake While Reading Catalog
    Cards: an Essay on the Availability Problem," LJ,
    January 15, 1975, p. 93-98.
8.  _____.  "The View from the Tower of Babel," LJ,
    September 15, 1975, p. 1599-1605.
9.  Altman, Ellen et al.  A Data Gathering and Instruction-
    al Manual for Performance Measures in Public Li-
    braries.  Chicago:  Celadon Pr. , 1976.
10. Urban Institute and the International City Management
    Association.  Measuring the Effectiveness of Basic
    Municipal Services:  Initial Report.  Washington, 1974.
    The relevant chapter is "Library Services," p. 33-37.
11. Bommer, Michael R. W.  Review article in Library
    Quarterly, July 1974, p. 273-275.

# BRITISH MAY USE TELEPHONES, TV's,

## TO TAP DATA BANK*

Nigel Hawkes

On 1 June a new information service with some revolutionary implications went into operation in Britain. Through the regular telephone network it provides access to a computer-based information system, using an ordinary TV set as the display terminal. It may be the biggest thing to happen to communications since the invention of radio, or it may be about to rival the Ford Edsel as a marketing disaster. The silence you hear is the sound of breath being held.

The service is called Prestel and has been devised and brought to market by the British Post Office, in collaboration with the electronics industry, the TV manufacturers, and the British Broadcasting Corporation (BBC). While it might be unfair to imply that the Post Office has been responsible for no innovations since the penny post way back in the 19th century, it does not have the image of a go-getting organization. Yet there seems no doubt that with Prestel it has come up with an idea which, if it catches on, could bring enormous changes in the office, the home, education, newspapers, and in the way information is exchanged and used.

The concept is simple. Using an ordinary telephone, a Prestel user dials a central computer packed with information on a wide range of topics, from financial data to consumer reports and mail-order catalogs. When the connection

*Reprinted by permission of the author and publisher from the July 7, 1978 issue of Science, vol. 201, pp. 33-34. Copyright © 1978 by the American Association for the Advancement of Science.

is made an index page appears on his TV screen, and by pressing buttons on a hand-held keyboard, the user can find his way into the data bank, which can hold up to 250,000 "pages" of information. (Each page holds about 150 words.) It costs him 3 pence (just over 5 cents) for the basic call, plus another 1 to 2 pence for every page he consults. The charges appear automatically on his quarterly telephone bill.

In this transaction the Post Office merely acts as the carrier, giving the user access to information supplied by more than 100 "information providers." These include the Stock Exchange, Reuters, the Consumer Association, local newspapers, chains of shops, the Meteorological Office, travel agents, the Sports Council, the motoring associations, as well as totally new "electronic publishing" companies which have been set up to exploit the new medium. The information providers can put their own price on each page of information they supply; some pages, like weather reports, or advertisements, would be free, while others, like financial information, would cost whatever their providers think they are worth. How many pages, and which ones, each subscriber has consulted is automatically recorded by the Post Office, and is billed accordingly. From the revenue received the Post Office subtracts the cost of running the service, takes its own profit, and sends the rest to the information providers. A provider whose information proves useless--and is therefore seldom consulted--will earn nothing from the system. A provider whose information is widely consulted will do very nicely; the system thus puts a premium on the success of each provider in attracting users.

On 1 June the system went live for the first time, although only in a limited way to the first few hundred users who are acting as a test market. The system should be nationwide by the beginning of 1979, although it now looks as if it will slip a few months and likely come on stream some time in the spring of 1979.

Prestel is, in fact, just one of a range of information systems which have been in development in Britain for the past decade, and are known by the generic title of "teletext." The simplest are systems for broadcasting short news items or simple information, using two spare lines from the 625-line TV signal. These two lines fall outside the area of the TV screen, so play no part in carrying the normal TV picture. Instead, they are used for carrying up

to 800 pages of written information in a format similar to
Prestel.    The information transmitted includes such things
as news reports, sports results, and gardening tips.    The
user selects the page he wants with a hand-held keyboard.

This system was developed by the BBC and the Independent Broadcasting Authority (the organization responsible
for the control of commercial TV and radio in Britain).    It
is now available, under the name Ceefax for the BBC version and Oracle for the commercial channel.    The information it supplies is free once the user has bought a specially
adapted TV set.    Unlike Prestel, the Ceefax and Oracle systems broadcast their information and are not, therefore,
interactive systems.    They are also limited in capacity by
the fact that they have only two lines in the TV signal to use
as carriers.    But they are ideally suited for the provision
of news and seem likely to dominate that end of the market.
So far, there are not very many users; those there are find
the system particularly useful when they get home at night
and want to be brought quickly up to date with the news.

Prestel is a system with wider possibilities.    There
are no limitations on the amount of information it can store,
and since it is an interactive system it can do things Ceefax
and Oracle cannot.

For example, Mills and Allen Communications Ltd. ,
one of the new electronic publishing companies which act as
information providers for Prestel, has designed a page for
the Save the Children Fund, a British charity.    The page is
an advertisement urging the Prestel user to "Press a key to
give 10 p. "    The user who does will find himself debited 10
pence on his next quarterly telephone bill, and the money
will go directly to the Save the Children Fund.    They say
that the system will simplify logistics of giving to charity
and thus encourage more people to give.    "It's charity at the
press of a button, " says Richard Hooper of Mills and Allen.

Another information provider is Currys, a chain of
480 shops specializing in consumer durables such as TV
sets, washing machines, and refrigerators.    Their pages
will consist of a catalog of products much like a mail-order
catalog.    By use of the Prestel keyboard, the user will be
able to select and purchase items from the catalog and
specify how he wants to pay.    The recording equipment notes
the order, passes it on to Currys, and the item is delivered
direct to the customer.    He need never leave his armchair.

Extending the system a little further, it could be used for working out travel itineraries and booking tickets. The user could consult the airline timetables through Prestel and then, through a link between the Prestel computer and the airline reservation computers, find out if there are any empty seats and book the tickets.

It could also, in the longer term, begin to take the place of mail. By providing each user with a keyboard equipped with the necessary electronic logic--in the form of microprocessors--it will be possible to key in a message and route it through the telephone network to a specified recipient. This could bring Telex or Teletype services to many more users. If the intended recipient of the message is out, a simple audio cassette recorder can be used to store the message, with a flashing light to indicate that a message is waiting. A copy printer can be added to the system if a hard copy is needed.

These last refinements have all been developed by the General Electric Company (no connection with American GE) and, although they will not be available immediately, could quite easily be added to the system later. They use perfectly conventional technology. Robert Clayton, technical director of the company, believes that at first these systems will be used principally in offices, but foresees their extension to the home by the end of the century.

The unanswered question is just how many people will want to use the range of services Prestel can supply. At present, a TV set equipped with the necessary extras to act as a Teletext receiver costs about twice as much as a regular TV set--around £600. But marketing has hardly begun and prices are expected to fall rapidly; by 1980, the extra cost over an ordinary TV set could be down to £60 or so, according to one firm of electronic consultants. At that price, it seems likely that most buyers will prefer the Teletext TV.

In the shorter term, companies rather than individuals may be able to justify paying more for the service. Stockbrokers can have immediate access to market prices, bookmakers to race results, travel agents to timetables, journalists to reference books and directories. Compared with a conventional computer information service, Prestel is inexpensive; Alex Reid, the Post Office's director for Prestel, says it will cost in use only one-tenth as much as existing

computer information services. "We see it as a form of
very simple and open electronic publishing where everybody
who has some information they want to disseminate can do
so quickly and cheaply," Reid says.

From the Post Office point of view, Prestel offers
another advantage. The telephone network is, they say, a
"vastly under-used asset," with the average home telephone
in Britain being used less than twice a day. By combining
Britain's 13 million telephones with its 18 million TV sets,
the Post Office hopes to get a better return from its huge
investment in telephone equipment. The TV industry also
sees it as an opportunity both to sell more sets and to recover some of the market lost to cheaper Japanese imports.

Why Britain, with its ailing TV manufacturers and its
nationalized Post Office, should have turned out to be an in-
novator in this field seems to boil down to one individual,
credited by the Post Office as the inventor of Prestel. He
is Sam Fedida, an engineer at the Post Office's research
center near Norwich. In the 1960's, Fedida was working
on the videophone, an idea which failed because the telephone network does not have sufficient capacity to carry video
signals.

Once that idea was dropped, he turned his attention to
other ways of using the telephone network and came up with
Prestel. The Post Office then devised the system and wrote
the computer software, while the TV manufacturers designed
and built the Teletext TV sets. Foreign interest in the system has been considerable, and the Post Office has already
sold the technology to West Germany. Last October the system was shown at a telecommunications conference in Atlanta
and, according to Roy Bright of the Post Office, who is responsible for selling the technology abroad, caused astonish-
ment and delight.

Not everything, however, has gone smoothly. For
years, the Post Office called the system by another name--
Viewdata--but when they came to register the name found it
was already registered by somebody else, so had to settle
for Prestel. There have also been snags in getting the data
from the information providers on to the central computer,
and in the interface between the TV sets and the telephone
network. Reid admits there have been problems, partly
caused by the fact that the system has grown in scope since
it was first thought of. But he says that the problem of ac-

cess to the computer, which had prevented the information providers from getting their data in, is now almost solved. Magnetic tape facilities have been provided, so that information providers can, if they wish, simply deliver their data on tape.

The implications of the Teletext revolution for other communications media could be considerable. It seems likely, for example, to erode the profitability of newspapers by siphoning off classified advertising revenue, and of the postal service by creating "electronic mail." This may be one reason why a number of newspapers have become involved as information providers, including the Financial Times and the Westminster Press group.

But most people believe it will be a totally new product that will not directly attack the existing media. Reid says he sees it as "a complement to the printed work, rather than a competitor," and Jack Beverley, group managing editor for Westminster Press, believes that newspapers will remain the best and cheapest medium for classified advertising. Compared with newspapers, Prestel is an expensive way of buying information; compared with computerized information systems, it is cheap. It may therefore create a totally new market which has little in common with existing media.

Alternatively, it may turn out to have no market at all. The Post Office, which has invested £28 million in the system, will be anxiously watching the results of the test market, as will the information providers, who have also invested heavily. "My position now is that we're either on the brink of a new communications medium, or we're on the brink of disaster," says Hooper. He himself is optimistic; people introduced to the system for the first time are, he says, "totally gripped by it--they're actually amazed by the technology." Whether amazement equals profits remains to be seen.

# GRANTING AMNESTY AND OTHER FASCINATING

## ASPECTS OF AUTOMATED CIRCULATION*

Barbara Evans Markuson

Two major groups watch the ever-changing scene in automated circulation. One group watches just to keep abreast
as interested professionals. The other watches because its
members plan to upgrade or implement automated circulation. The first group wants to know, "What's going on?"
"What's new?" and "What are the major issues?" The second group is absolutely merciless and wants only to know,
"What's the best, most reliable system available at the lowest cost?"

The journal article is hard put to satisfy the former,
and shouldn't even attempt to satisfy the latter. This brief
review will cover some general developments in circulation
technology, vendor and network approaches to circulation,
problem areas, and some hints on system procurement. It
will not cover all the details of specific systems, which may
be had in abundance from the vendors, and eventually are examined in the literature of technical services.

It should be remembered that some developments are
tentative, some appear to be copywriter's fancy, rumors
abound, and local systems are rarely reported while under
development, so that an author can hardly hope to deliver a
perfect state of the art. And the best system for a given
library depends on so many local factors that only detailed
analysis can support the ultimate decision.

*Reprinted by permission of the author and the American
Library Association from the April 1978 issue of American
Libraries, pp. 205-211. Copyright © 1978 by the American
Library Association.

222

With these necessary caveats, let us proceed.

## From Chain to CRT

Little did librarians realize the troubles they were making when they gave up the chained book. Chaining books provided integrity of inventory control, guaranteed on-premises accessibility, eliminated overdues, and, in general, contributed to the well-being of the public service staff. Once the chain was severed, we began ever so imperceptibly to meet more and more user demands. We added to our repertoire variable loan periods, charge-out to carrels, reserve collections on one-hour loan, interlibrary loan, and even taking holds on books out on loan. Our generosity has expanded to the occasional violation of our own rules; for example, overlooking a fine, which the computer types have termed "granting amnesty" (a coinage suggesting that the alternative is death before a firing squad).

Librarians have almost never been satisfied with circulation operations; users are perhaps even less happy. The reason is readily apparent. As more and more flexibility was allowed, as collections and systems grew, management almost inevitably failed to allocate commensurate resources. Thus our goals of security, accuracy, and reliability of inventory control and speed of service were not achievable by available resources. I mention this because there is hardly a service offered by an automated circulation system that could not be had in a manual system, if we were willing to expend the necessary resources.

In a real sense, then, automated circulation systems are the first circulation systems that begin to meet the unrealized goals we aspired to at a price we can begin to afford.

This article starts, therefore, with the unquestioned assumption that a well-designed automated system, installed with proper planning and preparation, not only will result in an operation better than the manual system it replaces, but one that will finally allow the library to deliver good service from its collections.

Although relatively few libraries have automated circulation, new developments in packaged systems, faster collection-conversion techniques, and network initiatives will combine to make it the major automation growth area during the next five years.


## Technological Underpinnings

The minicomputer is the technical development most basic to satisfactory, wide-scale automation of circulation. The price, flexibility, and sophistication of the mini made it the first computer satisfactory for library processing that could be purchased at a reasonable cost, operated in a library environment, and run by library staff. Not only has the mini had an impact on locally developed systems by freeing the library from the real or imagined evils of the parent organization's central computer, but it has been the basis for the packaged, vendor-developed system and is now becoming the basis for distributed (i. e., with decentralized computers) circulation networks tied into a large bibliographic data base.

It seems almost as if minicomputer manufacturers take their clues from Detroit, for just as Detroit annually announces that its compacts have increased head-and-leg room and larger wheel bases, the minis are also growing. Early minis could hardly support an online circulation system for a medium-sized library without tight programming and partitioning files into active/inactive status, i. e., online and offline. Recent minis are large enough so that, for many libraries, not only circulation but such additional functions as online patron inquiry or online catalog functions can also be supported.

Following the mini in technical impact was the development of small, coded, adhesive identification labels which could be machine read or scanned. This eliminated the host of problems associated with the error-prone keying of each transaction or the use of the punched card for item identification and punched reader badges, which, in addition to getting folded, spindled, or mutilated could get lost or misplaced. Librarians benefited as manufacturers and retail stores switched to use of bar-coded and OCR (optical character recognition) inventory control systems. The bar-coded identification appears on such common grocery items as the Swanson Clear Chicken Broth in my pantry, bar-code label number 5 1000 02431. The wealthier among you may examine the bottom of your bank checks for an example of a code similar to OCR codes (though using a different technology).

For various technical reasons, these codes do not lend

themselves to call-number recording; hence, the use of a random identification number for item control is a feature of new circulation systems. Both types of codes can be rapidly read with a lightweight, hand-held reader. Portable readers are also available with some systems. OCR characters can be produced by special printers, by computer line printers equipped with special OCR print trains, or by typewriters equipped with OCR fonts. As a result, the OCR user generally has more flexibility in obtaining machine-readable data than does the user of bar-code labels. Also, due to the more stringent technical requirements for printing bar codes, the OCR user has a cost advantage as well.

Among other technical developments supporting automated circulation are CRT (video or TV-like) display terminals, various printing devices suitable for producing date-due slips and fine receipts, and the interface equipment that allows terminals in remote locations to be connected via telephone lines.

## Recent Advances

Some interesting equipment has been developed for special purposes. The University of British Columbia Library and Epic Data jointly developed a terminal to solve the problem of transition from an older, punched-card system to a machine-readable label system. The terminal, which they developed to read both punched-card and bar-code label input, is marketed by Epic Data, Richmond, B. C.

CLSI, Inc. is showing a "touch" CRT Terminal. Touch terminals, which have been used in business management applications, are activated by touching the screen rather than by operating a keyboard. The system displays the choices available to the user and the user actually touches the appropriate response. This terminal, currently more expensive than CLSI's keyboard CRT, may be just the thing for users and staff whose touch is more accurate than their type.

It should be noted in passing that a laser label-reading device has been in use for some time at the University of Texas/Dallas Library. The device appears to have worked very well, but Innovated Systems, which developed it, has not pursued the library market aggressively. Since it appears that one of the firm's principal markets is oil companies, we might all concur with this marketing decision.

Small, self-contained, integrated computer systems, called small business computers (SBC), have been developed to meet the needs of small business and office automation. In one integrated desk-size unit, a single system might include the computer's central processing unit, the operator console (terminal), a small CRT display, a printer, and disc storage. Removable disc files are on floppy discs which look rather like a limp, flexible phonograph record. These systems can be purchased from about $20,000 to $30,000.

The first use of SBC technology I am aware of for circulation is a locally developed system, using an IBM 32, operating in the University of the West Indies, St. Augustine (Trinidad), Library. At least one American vendor is believed to be pursuing a similar development.

These small systems could provide an answer to automation of circulation in small libraries of any type where transaction rates are low but where automated control is desirable.

Systems are not comprised of hardware alone, and software (computer program) developments have also had an impact on circulation. Some vendors and libraries tend to write specialized programs for the entire system, but the trend seems to be toward use of commercially available generated data management and operating systems. This approach should mean more rapid system development and more favorable development costs. It may also improve long-range system maintenance, since these data management systems are common to nonlibrary systems as well.

Although hardware and software technology has allowed development of systems more attuned to circulation functions, the downward trend in price has also played a part. The report Automation and the Library of Congress published in 1963 describes a proposed circulation control system with a cost for hardware alone of nearly a million dollars. At least two vendors could deliver a comparable system today, including both hardware and software, for about a third of the cost. The proposed system did not make use of CRT terminals, which were reserved for the cataloging subsystem. These devices, then largely laboratory models, were costed at about $50,000 each. I think we can all agree that at the 1963 prices there would be few CRT-terminal circulation systems in use today. Programmers in 1963 were costed at $8,000 per annum. The downward trend in hardware and the

upward trend in labor costs have provided one of the major
reasons why automation of circulation makes economic sense
for many libraries.

## Are the New Systems Obsolete?

Despite these good reasons to automate, many will wonder
whether there might be a technological breakthrough just
around the corner that would make a currently available system obsolete. It is true that if one had completed a punched-
card system just as computers came along, or had invested
in a computer-based, batch-processing system using punched-
card readers just as minicomputers and coded labels arrived,
the resulting system would have been based on outmoded
technology.

Because vendors face this problem, too, one way to
try to gauge the state of the art is to observe what the new-
est vendors on the scene are selling. However, the real
question ought to be, "Will I get my money's worth out of a
system, based on the current state of the art, despite potential new developments? If a system is at the current state
of the art, is readily expandable in terms of added storage
and terminals, and is cost-effective over a five-to-seven-
year period, that is about all the certainty one can expect
in this uncertain world.

Generally speaking, the data-processing world is more
conservative than one might think. Not all technological
breakthroughs make it in the marketplace because of the
enormous current investment in equipment which must be
reasonably compatible with new devices. Work is underway
on voice-recognition systems, and one could envision a future
circulation system in which clerks read out call numbers and
patron IDs. If high-density videodisc recording takes hold
and lives up to some of its advanced publicity, patrons may
well be checking out whole sections of the library rather than
just individual items.

Overall, for automated circulation the more important
developments are less likely to be technical breakthroughs
than marketing approaches and network initiatives that will
greatly expand the number of libraries to be served from a
central system.

Circulation, like automation of cataloging, is a library

function which has always attracted the attention of vendors,
library cooperatives, and individual libraries.  Each of these
groups is playing a vital role in providing better answers to
circulation control.  A brief review of the developers of systems follows.

## The System Developers

There are four basic ways to acquire an automated circulation system.  Buy one, share one, build your own, or trans-
plant one someone else built.  All approaches require careful planning and all approaches have their success stories
and some tragedies as well.

Vendor-developed systems have had a reasonable success, for although the purchased system may still be a pig
in a poke, at least it will be some sort of pig.  Purchasing
a system frequently increases the possibility that a system
of known capability will be delivered within the target date
plus a few months for a given sum of money.  Since librarians understandably like to minimize risk, purchased systems have become popular.

Purchased systems are generalized systems designed
to meet the needs of the majority but providing flexibility,
within limits, to handle local variation.  The attempt to turn
a purchased system into a custom-made system can be a
pitfall for library and vendor alike; both can lose their shirts,
the latter perhaps actually, the former probably only figura-
tively.

Asking a vendor to program custom features puts the
library in the same risk situation as does local development:
it is difficult to know what will be delivered, when it will
work, and what it will cost.  The best way to start may be
to identify the generalized system that meets the majority of
your most important needs.  If you still feel that the unmet
needs make the system undesirable, you may want to build
your system locally.

Vendor circulation systems are increasingly being
described in global terms.  Literature on packaged circulation systems was available at ALA Midwinter 1978.  One
piece described a system in which "information on inventory,
acquisitions and cataloging, networking, full file inquiry, and
many other library activities are at your fingertips. "  An-

other was said to support "modules for circulation control, book acquisitions, materials booking, and payroll handling." The latest trend is to treat circulation as a special aspect of catalog inquiry or else to treat cataloging as a subsystem of circulation--I'm not certain which.

At any rate, circulation systems are described as providing subject access, authority control, public access, and various other catalog functions.  The library will perhaps want to clarify whether it is in the market for a circulation system or an online catalog system, or, if both, whether the proposed systems can handle so many functions.

Restricting our inquiry to typical circulation functions allows us to state that most packaged systems can handle most circulation functions, although the successful handling of academic reserve-book collections still remains an area the library must investigate very carefully.  Whether these systems can be extrapolated successfully to online catalogs remains to be seen and almost certainly deserves scrutiny. But the major vendors all offer systems which can handle overdues, place holds, compute fines, print overdues, and perform such circulation functions.  Where vendor offerings differ is in the method by which these functions are handled-- and by the overall marketing approach, system expandability, and cost.

The vendors also differ in the degree of continuing system support they provide.  Since it is obvious that the vendor must charge for each service to continue as a viable profit-making organization, these support services are reflected in system costs, and the library must evaluate their importance.

## Some Vendors

Space does not permit a full review of the operational characteristics of vendor systems and equipment.  Also, several vendors are not mentioned here.  Citation of or failure to mention a vendor implies neither a positive or negative opinion.  Each vendor approach and product has merits and benefits depending upon the particular library situation.

The technical design of systems is increasingly complex; therefore, it is recommended that librarians seek expert technical consultants to check out any questions about

competing technical designs offered by vendors. The library
should know whether the technical design supports the vendor's claims of response time, growth, file size, terminals
supported, and so on, and it is unlikely that this expertise
will be available on the staff.

The Gaylord circulation system is designed as a ven-
dor-operated circulation network. The local library has cir-
culation-inquiry terminals and a minicomputer which together
handle all local transactions; each evening the local minicomputer is updated from the central computer system at Gaylord
headquarters. The central computer prints out fine notices,
statistical reports, etc. The library cannot access the central computer but has online access to its own mini, which
provides item control only and does not support author and
title inquiries. These inquiries are handled by searching
frequently updated microform listings.

A unique aspect of the Gaylord system is the use of
a common central data base for all libraries and a common
item identifier for each title regardless of the holding library; this minimizes central storage requirements and, according to Gaylord, facilitates local conversion, since many
records will already be in the central file. Although the library still has a minicomputer to maintain locally, the purchaser of a Gaylord system will be relieved of many tasks
that are performed centrally. The library pays a transaction fee for each item processed in the central system. The
Gaylord system is currently the most centralized of any vendor offering.

CLSI, Inc., provides an independent, stand-alone minicomputer system coupled with a highly centralized system-
support service. CLSI programs are written in a proprietary
(vendor-owned) language, its equipment and software are sold
as a "bundled" package, and it provides a complete range of
support services for an annual maintenance fee. Among
these services are continuing program and system enhance-
ments, trouble shooting, equipment maintenance, and training. CLSI customers meet in various user groups throughout
the country, and CLSI publishes a newsletter.

Two major new entires into the field, Systems Control
and DataPhase, take a different approach. These vendors
use nonproprietary program languages and standard equipment, and they provide the customer with detailed system
documentation so that local system maintenance and enhance-

ment are possible.  Hardware maintenance is provided by
the equipment manufacturer's regular maintenance crews.
The vendors do provide support for system and software aspects.  DataPhase describes itself as a staff "on call 24
hours a day, seven days a week.  Through use of portable
terminals, we can have immediate access to your programs
to quickly correct any problems."

The 3M marketing approach falls somewhere between
those of DataPhase and CLSI.  Both 3M and Systems Control
have terminals that can only be acquired through them, but
other equipment may be purchased either from them or from
the manufacturer.  3M also uses the manufacturer's service
bureau, but this service is contracted through 3M rather
than directly with the manufacturer--as is the procedure
with DataPhase and System Control. *

Universal Library Systems, Ltd. (ULISYS), a Canadian firm, specializes in system design and software for automated circulation systems.  This recent entry into the field,
with installations at the Phoenix Public Library and the
Cariboo Thompson Nicolsa Library System (Kamloops, B.C.),
sells a packaged software system which can operate on a
Digital Equipment Corporation PDP 11/34 or 11/70 computer.
If the user already has access to these computers, ULISYS
will provide software and other necessary services to implement the system, or will assist in total system procurement.

Cincinnati Electronics markets components for automated circulation systems.  These components include the
JRL 1000 Library Circulation Terminal developed by the University of Chicago Library, a portable data terminal, and a
dual-code label printer which imprints labels with both bar-
code and OCR-A data.  This printer can also be driven by a
computer.  The device prints one line of bar code plus a
separate line of OCR-A encoded information.

---

*After this article went to press, the 3M Company announced
(on Feb. 28) that it is withdrawing its library Inventory Control System from the market, but will continue to offer its
special library terminals to circulation system builders.  Library Systems Manager Graham Gurr said, "The advanced
features of ICS make it higher priced than competitive systems, and the limited market for such an advanced system
does not warrant 3M continuing in the business."  3M is discussing alternative systems with the pilot Princeton University
and Arlington County Public Libraries.

## Network Developers

Library cooperatives and networks have long shown an interest in automation of circulation. A control circulation system provides a mechanism for resource sharing, particularly when cooperating libraries are in geographic proximity. Sharing of a minicomputer circulation system among members of a local cooperative has already proved feasible, and with the advent of minicomputer systems capable of supporting 50 or more terminals, such sharing is bound to increase.

Network developments are of interest because of their potential for integration of circulation with other shared network functions; for the possibility of member participation in development of system specifications; and for cost-sharing of system development and operation. Two networks have already announced plans to develop a network-supported circulation system.

From its early days, OCLC, Inc., has included circulation as a planned future service. Although no schedule of implementation has appeared, OCLC still plans to implement a circulation system. Systems design work is underway for maintaining member holdings records online, an obvious prerequisite for circulation.

The University of Toronto Library Automation System (UTLAS) network now serves 46 libraries and has expanded across Canada to British Columbia. Recently UTLAS announced its CIRC (Collection, Inquiry, Reporting, and Communication) system, which it describes as "an online catalog and circulation control system in a network environment." The system, said to be operating for preliminary functions, is expected to be installed at UT's undergraduate library in April 1978 and expanded outside UT by fall 1978, so that other UTLAS members can participate.

The CIRC system is a distributed minicomputer system. In Phase I, circulation minicomputers will be updated by batch processing of weekly tapes produced from the online cataloging and file maintenance system. In 12 to 18 months an online link is planned so that the bibliographic files in the minicomputer can be automatically updated as new cataloging and catalog-record updates occur on the central system. The first release calls for minicomputer access by author, title, call number, and item numbers; a future release will add subject access.

The Washington Library Network plans to integrate
its central cataloging system with automated circulation by
use of a vendor-developed system capable of interfacing with
output from the catalog data base.  The DataPhase system
has been selected for the first installation of what may become a state-wide system.  Tacoma Public Library is the
test site.


## Local Development

Local development remains an important component of automated circulation systems.  Such systems can provide helpful information--often unavailable from commercial vendors--
to others doing local systems work.  They are potential
candidate systems from which transplants can be sought; they
serve as benchmarks to compare vendor systems and costs;
and they test unique local solutions to problems.

Development of online circulation systems of increasing sophistication at Northwestern University, Ohio State University, and University of Chicago, to name but a few, have
contributed advances such as user self-charging, expansion
of user services, and, at Chicago, integration of circulation
into a total systems development.  On a smaller scale, the
recent development of an online circulation system using a
small municipally-owned computer and advanced OCR technology at the New Brunswick (N.J.) Public Library illustrates what can be done with good systems work even when
resources are limited.

The Ohio State University system, which has already
been transplanted once, is being replicated a third time at
the University of Illinois.  Plans call for the system at
Urbana to be linked to the UI Chicago Circle Campus and to
the Medical School Library in Chicago.  Statewide access to
UI resources will be facilitated through an online terminal
located at the Illinois State Library.

Circulation has also been given a boost by the use of
LSCA funds to develop local systems or help buy vendor
systems.  Some state libraries select a particular system to
provide maximum compatibility and allow use of LSCA funds
to help defray costs of local installations.

Because the stakes are so high, the competition has
been fierce among vendors bidding for state and other large

contracts. Consultant reports have prompted emotional
charges and countercharges, some of the most vituperative
of which have found their way into a few library newsletters
and journals. None of these charges should be considered
outside the context of a full and authoritative comparative
study.

## On Pros, Cons, and Conversions

This brief review of developments illustrates the complexity
and activity underway in automation of circulation. There
are good arguments pro and con on almost any point that
can be raised. For example, is circulation a purely local
function or a function best handled through a centralized
network? Many observers argue strongly that circulation is
local--why send local data over transmission lines to a central point?--and that networks couldn't cope with the loads.
I believe that the case has yet to be made on either side,
but predict that economies of scale will make network circulation services attractive for many libraries within the next
decade.

Conversion continues to be traumatic, but, clearly,
some help is now available. Tacoma Public Library reports
that it is converting by use of a "model conversion process
which is unique." TPL has loaded the Blackwell North
America data base of 1.9 million titles into its minicomputer
and is accessing the file via terminals at a charge of two
cents per hit. Statistical sampling predicted a hit rate of
about 80 percent for the 250,000 titles to be converted. Use
of CETA personnel has also reduced costs significantly. A
number of other libraries have managed to facilitate conversion by such vendor support services as offline search of
printed listings or vendor search of online files.

## Users Speak

Speakers at a recent ALA circulation institute agreed that
automation of circulation did not necessarily save money, but
clearly improved the library capability to handle greater
workloads without increased staffing. Users of vendor-
developed systems were generally, but not totally, happy.
Some problem areas were failure of vendor to deliver system refinements on schedule, inadequate system capacity,
inability to expand to larger number of terminals needed for

system-wide use, and failure to provide reserve-book circulation support.  One speaker noted that libraries generally fail to appreciate the properties of online files and have not planned adequately for conversion, data-base control, maintenance, and file integrity and security.  Many speakers emphasized the need for the library to understand thoroughly what the vendor was offering.  As one speaker put it, never let a vendor or consultant use the future tense; keep them to what can be delivered now.

Despite these problems, whether the speakers had developed or purchased a system, whether they were from a large or small library, none indicated a desire to return to a manual system.

Roger L. Funk, assistant director of ALA's Office for Intellectual Freedom, provided a philosophical and legal background on invasion of privacy.  It boiled down to the library user's right to say, "It's my business what I read, if I want you to know I'll tell you."  He argued for design of systems that protected this individual right to privacy, purged records identifying users as soon as feasible, and retained only essential information in historical files.  He noted the worthlessness of a library information policy protecting users from invasion of privacy if there is no follow-up program to ensure that every staff member is aware of the policy, understands it, and implements it.

Hugh Atkinson, director of the University of Illinois Libraries, strongly supported this view, stating that system design should not allow search-by-patron, e.g., to discover all the titles in use by a given user, and calling this type of inquiry "information too dangerous to know."  These strong views notwithstanding, some attendees considered such access essential, although they believed discretion should be used.

The potential of automated systems to infringe on individual rights needs study, along with why and for what purposes patron file searches are made.


Finding the Best System

Vendor competition results in a fair amount of pressure on any library in the market for a circulation system.  Care should be taken to treat all vendors fairly, to provide them with identical specifications, and to try to eliminate as much as possible the comparison of "apples and oranges." On the other hand, if you plan to develop a local system, evaluate your chances of success as carefully as you would review an outside vendor: what is your track record for project administration, how good is the systems staff, how secure is the financial support, how firm is the schedule?

It is not fair to compare vendor performance to a hypothetical, ideal staff. Neither should you cave in to vendor pressure and the bandwagon dash to vendor systems if you cannot accept that the offerings are satisfactory. Plenty of evidence shows that local systems design can be good-- and cost-effective.

Acquisition of a circulation system requires attention to many details. The rigor of selection may depend on such local requirements as mandatory competitive bidding. There is no excuse for the library staff involved in the selection not to understand clearly how all parts of the system work, what the cost will be, and, perhaps most important, the capability for growth. Frequently the low-bid vendor becomes the high-bid vendor when system-growth bids are included in the request, since the methods and ease with which systems can be expanded varies significantly.

Requiring vendors to bid against specific system requirements is a more satisfactory approach than ad hoc, off-the-cuff talks with sales and marketing staff, even when these are knowledgeable librarians or technical people. In recent competition for a public library system requiring 14 terminals, the bids from five major vendors varied almost $270,000 in initial acquisition costs, and by almost $300,000 when acquisition costs, annual maintenance, and hardware operating costs were calculated for the estimated seven years of system life. This illustrates the value of bids and the cost range in the market.

Good Background

The constantly changing circulation scene was noted earlier. Most surveys of circulation are technically outdated by publication date, but remain valuable for basic, unchanging guidelines. Readers interested in pursuing the subject in more detail should read four surveys: Markuson's "Automated Circulation Systems," Library Technology Reports

(July-September 1975); William Scholz' "Computer Based Circulation Systems," Library Technology Reports (May, 1977); Paula Dranov's Automated Library Circulation Systems, 1977-78, Knowledge Industry Publications, 1977; and Liz Gibson's "Evaluation of Automated Circulation Systems," California Librarian, vol. 71, no. 3, 1976. Those interested in following an automated system procurement from system specification, bidders' conferences, and conversion routines to evaluation of bidder responses should write to the Tacoma Public Library, Tacoma, Washington, for a copy of its January 8, 1978, press release. This release lists seven system documents available to other libraries interested in automation of circulation. Readers can use this material as a case history in system acquisition; but they can't project from the TPL decision the best system for their own library. It is the methodology that is of interest.

## Cough It Up

If you plan to buy or develop a circulation system, plan also to spend some money on the decision-making process. A system on which the library may spend $150,000 to $300,000 is certainly worth some front-end funding. Don't begrudge money spent to learn. Build a collection of circulation reports, vendor literature, and data-processing management reports. Read. Travel. Attend conferences. Spend money to gather accurate facts about your local situation. Hire a lawyer. Develop good, clear system specifications. Be fair to all vendors--it costs them to submit a good bid and they deserve careful consideration. Hire a consultant, or, better still, a consulting team with a range of expertise.

In your quest for a totally integrated, functional, flexible, online, interactive, compatible, incremental, operational, user-oriented, and cost-effective automated circulation system--have fun, and good luck!

# AN OBSERVATION ON SHELVING PRACTICE*

Norman D. Stevens

A common practice, especially among academic libraries, in occupying a new library building with ample shelving for future growth of the collections is to leave the top and bottom shelf of each stack section empty. This is done to provide an easy means for expansion and presumably also because those shelves are the most inconvenient to access for most users. That practice deserves careful examination at a time when increasing costs require libraries to be concerned as much with the economics of operation as the convenience of users.

Practical experience, verified by a recent series of experiments carried out by the Molesworth Institute, indicates that most browsing or other casual use of library collections involves material on those shelves that are at or near eye level of most users (four percent, top shelf; ten percent, second shelf; 45 percent, third shelf; 35 percent, fourth shelf; five percent, sixth shelf; and one percent, bottom shelf). Further investigation indicates that dirt tends to accumulate at a greater rate on empty shelves than on the tops of books or on the empty portions of shelves with some books on them. This appears to be due to the fact that removing books from the shelves and replacing them tends to dislodge accumulated dirt. Furthermore, on empty shelves dirt accumulates more rapidly on the top and bottom shelves than on the middle shelves (2 mm per year, top shelf; 1.5 mm per year, second shelf; .05 mm per year,

third shelf; . 009 mm per year, fourth shelf; 1. 3 mm per
year, fifth shelf; 3 mm per year, sixth shelf; and 4 mm per
year, bottom shelf).

In an effort to pursue the consequences of those observations, the Molesworth Institute conducted a year-long
controlled experiment in two new academic library buildings
of comparable size and complexity, with similar user populations.  In Library A the traditional practice of shelving the
collection with the top and bottom shelf of each section left
empty for future expansion was followed.  In Library B the
third and fourth shelf (counting from the top down) of each
section were left empty for future expansion.  Over the
period of that year Library A reported that 15 percent of
its users were unable to locate the item they were looking
for, whereas in Library B only four percent of the users
were unable to do so.  This was despite the fact that Library A spent a total of 933 person hours on shelf reading
and Library B only 311 person hours.  At the end of that
year Library A reported a greater accumulation of dirt (an
average of 3. 2 mm per empty shelf) than did Library B (an
average of only . 061 mm per empty shelf), and neither had
devoted any time to the removal of dirt.  The only adverse
effect was that Library B did report a greater accumulation
of miscellaneous trash (candy wrappers, old newspapers,
coffee cups, crumpled note paper, etc. ) being left on its
empty shelves than did Library A, and this required some
greater time (150 person hours per year as against 25 person hours per year) to clean up.

Some additional unanticipated observations were also
made.  While previously the circulation of the two libraries
had been comparable, in the year of the experiment Library
A showed over 100 percent increase in circulation, which
brought its circulation system and staff to a point of near
collapse; Library B, on the other hand, registered a more
manageable increase in its circulation of only 25 percent.

Unfortunately, like many other innovative experiments,
this one foundered on an unexpected development.  Initially,
Library B found that the greater visibility which resulted
from having open shelves in the middle of each stack section offered a better opportunity for the supervision of users.
The limited staff available, it soon turned out, was unable
to effectively undertake that supervision.  Instead, the incidence of exhibitionism and other unnatural acts that disturbed
users rose to an unacceptable level (1. 73 incidents a day as

against . 13 incidents per day in Library A) and the experiment had to be abandoned. The practice of leaving the middle two shelves in each stack section empty for future expansion cannot be recommended.

# Part III

# COMMUNICATION AND EDUCATION

# THE LIBRARY, TELEVISION, AND

# THE UNCONSCIOUS MIND*

Deirdre Boyle

Television--the mass medium you love to hate--has been the subject of a number of recent trend-setting books. Four Arguments for the Elimination of Television by Jerry Mander, Remote Control by Frank Mankiewicz and Joel Swerdlow, The Plug-In Drug by Marie Winn--all indicate growing popular interest in the nature of television and concern about its impact upon American culture and society. Copies of these books will undoubtedly be available in most libraries. But in how many of the same libraries will you find as well such audio-visual materials as Media Burn by Ant Farm or Report by Bruce Conner? Why aren't videotapes and films also available in libraries?

One reason seems to be the erroneous assumption that video is the same as television, everybody's candidate for extinction. In a recent interview in American Libraries, Don Roberts commented that "video dominates the environment. But if you walk into a library, you'll find video is not on the floor." In answer John Lolley wrote, expressing a view commonly held by librarians:

> Among the issues besetting libraryland, I find it very, very difficult to get upset over the fact that there are no TV sets in public libraries. In fact, you may not believe this, but I actually send my children to the public library to escape television. ... Isn't it a pleasure to visit a public library with an unpolluted environment?

*Reprinted by permission of the author and publisher from the May issue of the Wilson Library Bulletin, pp. 696-702. Copyright © 1978 by The H. W. Wilson Co.

242

Why push the panic button?

Television, as we know it in the United States, is owned and
operated by commercial interests that reflect in program
content and format the ideology of consumption.   Video is
merely the electronic encoding of audio and visual information; it can be used for ends different from those of commercial TV.   Microwave television transmission, cable, and
closed-circuit installations are only a few video alternates
to commercial TV.

What is it about the medium, though, that sends so
many into a panic?   How does it "pollute" the library?   The
rising dominance of television (and likewise all visual media)
has upset a universe in which language, linear structure, and
objectivity were accorded greater value and importance than
visual "language," associative structure, and subjectivity.
Many people, sensing a loss of control over information,
feel powerless and manipulated by a vast, alien information
environment.   The anxiety produced by the visual media's
challenge to the former order would send anyone into a
panic.   It is no wonder there is rejection of the outstanding
perpetrator of this chaos, television.

The world most librarians still function in is the
familiar world of print and the conscious mind.   This world
ignores the other reality--the unconscious, subjective domain, which is reached not through language but through
dreams.   According to Gregory Bateson in Steps to an Ecol-
ogy of Mind,

> A dream contains no label to tell one what it is
> 'about.' ... It's as if the dream had no title page.
> It's like an old manuscript or a letter that has
> lost its beginning and end, and the historian has
> to guess what it's all about and who wrote it and
> when--from what's inside it.

To accomplish this, one must be objective, but also careful
not to "force the concepts of the creature that deals in language and tools upon the dream material."

Television recreates in everyday life the associative
structure and logic of dreams.   Like dreams, television has
no tenses and seems suspended in time.   As you switch
from station to station or program to program, you may
move from a film made in the thirties to a live news broad-

cast.  Time and space collapse.  The dead live.  Distinctions between real and unreal, fact and fiction, program and
commercial, blur.  We tune in and out of programs playing
six hours a day in the backgrounds of our homes as we tune
in and out of the perpetual, background murmurings of our
unconscious minds.

The objective mind perceives only chaos.  But if one
approaches television--and other visual media--as something
without a "title page," something that requires discovery of
what it's all about "from what's inside it," this apparent
chaos can be understood as something else.  One must be
careful not to impose the concepts of language upon the
dream-like media, but instead discover the inner logic, language, and structure of the visual form.

Stocking library shelves with written studies on television simply is not enough.  For critical understanding of
the medium, visual as well as verbal analysis must be available.  The insights (and aesthetic experiences) provided by
those who "speak" the dream-language of visual media are
things you won't find in a book.

Ideally, at this point we should snap a video-cassette
into a playback deck or switch on a film projector.  Then
we would be able to judge the importance of including visual
analysis in libraries.  Since we cannot cross such media
boundaries, we will attempt a descriptive analysis of a film
and videotape that offer unique critical visual analysis of
television.

## "The President is dead"

Report, a 13-minute film by Bruce Conner, begins with radio
coverage of John F. Kennedy's fatal trip to Dallas heard over
the television image of the motorcade.  The President and
First Lady drive past, she smiling, he waving to the crowd.
The car drives past once, twice, three times, then the image flops over and the car alternately progresses from left
to right and then right to left.  There is a flash, and the
screen goes blank as an announcer reports, "Something has
happened. "

The white screen begins to flicker and pulsate strob-
oscopically, as a succession of reporters narrate the events
at the Trade Mart.  After what seems an unendurable length

of time, the flickering screen gradually fades from white to black.  Finally an image appears, a rifle being carried over the heads of the crowd, as the announcer describes the shots that rang out.

Jackie is at the airport, reaching to open the limousine door.  Each time she reaches out, the film loops back to the beginning.  She tries, perhaps five times, to open the door.  John and Jackie are waving to the crowd in the open limousine, as an eyewitness describes how he and his son heard the three shots and saw Kennedy slump forward in his seat as the car sped on.  The motorcade is shown, this time in "fits," as the movement of the car from right to left is constantly halted and backed up.  An eyewitness discloses how he's sorry he saw the look on Kennedy's face when the shot rang out.

On the screen is the countdown film leader, which rhythmically counts from 10 to 3, again and again, never going past 3.  The announcer says, "Just a moment ... Just a moment ... We'll now switch you back to Parkland Hospital."  Another voice solemnly intones, "President Kennedy has been assassinated.  It's official now.  The President is dead."  There is no sound as the leader counts down to 3 over and over again.  A picador on horseback appears, then the film cuts to the Lincoln Memorial, to Kennedy with Pope Paul, to the bow of the bullfighter in the ring, to a Catholic Mass.

News of the arrival of Air Force One is cut with a TV commercial for Jet cereal.  An announcer says, "The doors fly open on the jet," as the doors of a refrigerator open magically for a TV commercial housewife.  A waste-disposal unit looms ominously.  "The weather couldn't be better" is heard over an aerial view of an atomic explosion.  "Everyone is in their proper location" describes Lee Harvey Oswald's fatal walk and shooting by Jack Ruby.  The detailed route of the motorcade is announced as a bullet in slow motion pierces a light bulb.  "When the President stops moving, that's when there's trouble" is followed by Jane Meadows, holding a box of S.O.S. soap pads.

An announcer describes the children in Dallas trying to climb over fences, while scenes of soldiers in battle climbing over barbed wire are seen.  As the narrator describes the limousine swinging downtown to the Trade Mart, the funeral caisson heads down Pennsylvania Avenue.  Once

more the Kennedy limousine is shown with a cut to a tiger,
then a growling lion.   Throughout the film a sinister-looking
woman reappears, sitting at an IBM console, punching buttons.   She is cut with the parade route of the Kennedy inau-
guration, and the final shot shows this anonymous technician
pushing the button SELL.


## Evocation and an endless countdown

Obviously this linear description cannot convey the simultan-
eous interplay of sound and image.   Meaning stems from the
combination and juxtaposition of two or more, often opposing,
verbal and visual images.   Description, too, cannot elicit the
visceral response the viewer has to the now-frenzied, now-
calm voices; to the images evoked from memory; to the
stroboscopic light that mesmerizes and recalls the flickering
rhythm of a dying heartbeat.   Conner's images bring back
stored memories--of the tragic Kennedy assassination and of
years of shared TV experiences.   The filmmaker repeats
images in loop-like patterns:   It's as if the needle on the
record of memory is stuck.

The repetition of visual moments like Jackie Kennedy's
reaching to open the car door reiterates the repetition of
radio and TV coverage.   Such repetitions deny the finality
of any action and keep time suspended, as though the reality
of death were being held at bay.

Many of the images--verbal and visual--have multiple
meanings attached to them.   For example, the film leader
is an allusion to the "leader" in question, the head of state.
The circle with the cross inside it, typical of film leader,
suggests both a cross of martyrdom and the hairline target
of a rifle sight.   The countdown that never goes past 3 (a
convention of film leader), endlessly repeated and interrupted,
suggests the refusal to acknowledge 0--death.

Repetitions like those in Report are standard visual
patterning on TV--from instant replays in sports, to the
6 p.m. news story rebroadcast at 11 p.m., to the series
reruns year after year.   Conner exploits the TV conventions
to show how media exploited Kennedy's death.   Commercials
for cereals, soap pads, and appliances are slipped in and
interrelate ominously with the actual tragedy.   The film ends
with the antiseptically cool computer operator pushing the
button marked SELL.   One wonders, did the assassination

receive Nielsen's highest rating? Who is selling? Who is buying? What is being sold?

Few people were aware then of how the televised assassination was being shaped by media conventions (the nonstop narration, the commercials sandwiched in). Few could judge what effect viewing a real murder instead of a fictional one might have on the psyche of the nation. Seeing and hearing these familiar images, restructured by an artist/ critic, provokes reappraisal of how TV mediated our exper- ience of the event. Viewing Report also expands understand- ing of the associative relationship of television and dreams.

## A hot time in the old TV

Media Burn is a videotape of an event sponsored by Ant Farm. Interestingly, the tape owes its existence, in part, to library support: Some of the video equipment used was loaned to Ant Farm by the San Francisco PL.

The program for the "Media Burn" event notes that

> Americans are addicted to television. Television addiction has grown across America faster than heroin addiction. Of course, it has an advantage-- it's legal. Addiction to television is psychological, not physical like drug addiction, but it produces a narrowing view of reality and creates artifical needs. The mind police of 1984.
> Television news presents all the information one needs to know about the world in a tidy 30-minute package. Eight of the 30 minutes is devoted to ads, currently oil company 'image ads,' because tele- vision exists to sell advertising space. This superficial information transferral is presented as 'all the news of the day.' Zombie-like Americans reach out to change channels as Walter Cronkite says, 'And that's the way it is....'

The tape opens with a variety of TV news coverage for the Fourth of July, 1975. Traffic fatalities ... fire- works ... Bob Hope awarded the freedom medal at Inde- pendence Hall. Then the anchorperson for "Action News" reports:

> A media event is something that happens only be-

cause somebody made it happen ... only because
somebody figured the TV news cameras would show
up to watch it happen.  (It used to be called a
publicity stunt. )  Today some people decided to
stage what they call the <u>ultimate</u> media event....

The scene shifts to reporter David Louie.

It had nothing to do with the Fourth of July....
[It was] an art and culture happening called 'Media
Burn,' by members of an art group driving a
modified 1959 Cadillac through a pyramid of burning TV sets--their way of alleviating the frustration of watching TV....  Even though the artists
were knocking TV, they were using it to make
their point.  No media event is complete without
a central figure, a VIP to give credibility to the
event.  The media-conscious sponsors resurrected
John F. Kennedy for the keynote speech....  The
formalities over, they poured kerosene over and
under the TV sets and set them ablaze.  That set
the stage for the media burn.  Two daredevil
drivers in the tradition of Evel Knievel settled
into the crash car and took off....  The car, or
what's left of it, is now up for sale.  The organization which sponsored this event was Ant Farm.
What other organization would make a mountain out
of a mole hill?  It may not be good art in some
people's minds, but at least it was good entertainment.

During Louie's report fast cuts of the crowd, the
cameras, the actor-president, and finally, the burning TV
sets are shown.  Next is a clip from KPIX-TV: "If smash-
ing a 1959 Cadillac into a wall of TV sets is art, then the
world may rest tonight with a new masterpiece.  If it is
culture, then perhaps we're all in a degree of difficulty not
previously experienced in this society."  A sidekick remarks:
"Now, that is weird.  I think it's over our heads."

A WTUV-TV reporter concludes his coverage with
this: "What's it all mean?  Well, presumably, the message
is for the media, get it?"  Back in the studio, the anchorperson replies, "I don't think I want to get it."

## Unforgettable, that's what you are

The mood switches as the tape becomes Ant Farm's own coverage of "Media Burn. " A woman interviewed at the souvenir stand says, "I see this event as highlighting the themes of violence on TV. " The camera pans around the crowd and takes in the arrival of a limousine guarded by several "secret service" men. The "president" steps up to the podium, an enormous TV set. Mimicking Kennedy's vocal and rhetorical style, he addresses the crowd.

> Members of the press, my fellow Americans. ...
> Television, because of its technology and the way
> it is used, can only produce autocratic political
> forms and hopeless alienation. Who can deny we
> are a nation addicted to TV and the constant flow
> of mass media? ... The world may never under-
> stand what is done here today but the image will
> never be forgotten.

The president leaves, accompanied by the secret service. The "media matadors" arrive in a van, dressed in white suits and helmets that vividly recall astronauts at a space launch. They climb on top of the Phantom Dream Car and stand at attention as the national anthem is played. As they enter the vehicle through the roof, a camera inside shows them attaching the protective shields that are designed to seal out all light.

The rebuilt car is equipped with Video-Vision--a closed-circuit video camera mounted on top of the car, which will serve as the driver's "image-seeking guidance system. " When all systems check out, the car takes off and crashes through the bank of 50 burning TV sets. This historic scene is re-viewed from different angles and in slow motion. The drivers emerge unscathed, having "kicked the TV habit. " They are paraded around the parking lot of the San Francisco Cow Palace in hero-fashion. The tape closes with a speeded-up replay of the crash, showing people scurrying around, like ants, as television statistics appear superimposed over the scene.

## Television turned upside down

Media Burn brilliantly contrasts the conventions of TV news with an alternate version of a "media event. " The snide,

silly, and defensive remarks of the TV newspeople protect
them and their audience from the message of media burning.
It is interesting to note that none of the stations broadcasted
the "Kennedy" speech and that much of their reporting was
editorial interpretation.

The language and content of the Ant Farm coverage is
a parody of television and American culture.   Kennedy, the
first President to be made and unmade via television, is the
fitting spokesperson for the event.   By beginning with familiar television news coverage and then showing an alternate
reality through its video coverage, Ant Farm turns TV conventions and expectations upside down.   The space launches
of the sixties are satirized, as is the macho American fas-
cination with destruction, domination, power, and information control.

Not surprisingly, Media Burn has never been broadcast on television.   Plans are afoot for a somewhat edited
version to appear on public television.   If the networks are
unwilling to show criticism like this, where else is the public to have access to such information but in libraries,
schools, and museums?


Should librarians be unconscious?

Ironically, the preceeding discussion is subject to the problem of imposing the concepts of language on visual experience.   To the degree that it fails to convey the complexity
of the visual message, it supports the argument for the equal
status of visual analysis along with verbal.   It must be obvious that this analysis cannot substitute for the actual viewing of these works.

It should also be apparent that one can abhor the evils
of commercial television without rejecting video along with
it.   Report and Media Burn are only two of a number of fine
films and videotapes that offer critical insight into TV.   Also
worth considering are John Schott and E. J. Vaughn's film
Deal--a behind-the-scenes investigation of television's long-
est-running game show, Let's Make a Deal--and Tony Ramos's
videotape About Media, which shows what it is like to be the
subject of a TV news interview.

If television represents a serious problem for our
culture--which is the consensus of critics like Mander,

Mankiewicz, Swerdlow, Winn, and others--then further analysis and understanding is called for.  The analysis provided
by film and videomakers--who understand the medium and
can use it to expose how commercial TV manipulates mass
audiences--is crucial for any critical examination.

Visual media, so closely related to dreams, function
as the library professions' unconscious mind.  Just as an
individual must struggle to integrate the problematic unconscious with the everyday conscious mind, so must librarians
wrestle with the integration of the problematic visual media.

For those who are still dubious about including video
in libraries, perhaps you should sleep on it.  The answer to
your resistance may lie in your dreams.


Sources of films and videotapes mentioned

Report, 16 mm film.  b&w.  13 min.  1963-67.  Dist.:
Film-makers' Cooperative, 175 Lexington Ave., NY  10016;
Canyon Cinema Cooperative, Industrial Center Bldg., Rm
220, Sausalito, CA  94965; Serious Business Co., 1145
Mandana Blvd., Oakland, CA  94610

Media Burn.  3/4" videocassette.  color.  25 min.  1975.
Dist.:  Electronic Arts Intermix, 84 Fifth Ave., NY  10011

Deal.  16 mm film.  color.  95 min.  1977.  Dist.:  Document Studio, 489 Broome St., NY  10013

About Media.  3/4" videocassette.  color.  28 min.  1977.
Dist.:  Electronic Arts Intermix, 84 Fifth Ave., NY  10011

# THE LIBRARIAN AS YOUTH COUNSELOR*

Sara Fine

## The Issue

"Would you have any books on nerves? I mean, how can
you tell if someone is having a nervous breakdown?" Does
this scene take place in a counselor's office or in the young
adult room of a public library? To the counselor, a client's
problem has been introduced and the therapeutic process has
begun; for the librarian, a complex professional issue has
been activated. The librarian must determine how much
self-revelation to allow the patron and then set the interpersonal level on which the transaction will take place. In
the instant of reply, that decision will be clearly communicated to the patron and the scope of professional service
will be defined. The librarian will have taken a position on
whether there is a counseling function inherent in the delivery
of library service.

The issue of the librarian-as-counselor comes into
sharp focus with the quality and direction of the response
made to the cry of pain behind the patron's words. The librarian says, "Here are several books on nervous disorders.
Perhaps you can find the information you need. If not, let
me know and I'll help you find some others." The librarian-
as-counselor replies: "Sounds like something we should talk
about."

If the scripts were played out, different kinds of interactive processes would come into play and different outcomes

---

*Reprinted by permission of the author and publisher from
the Drexel Library Quarterly (1978) pp. 29-44. Copyright
© 1978 by the Graduate School of Library Science, Drexel
University.

would be likely to occur. In the first instance, the librarian and the patron stumble around in reserved, stylistic verbal games, each trying to read the meaning in the other's words. The young patron probably leaves the library with several books that contain answers to her stated request.

In the second instance, the patron has been given permission to explore and articulate the true nature of her need: her mother is behaving strangely and she is very frightened. She leaves the library with no books but 1) a sense of relief that her problem has at last found words and that someone has heard and understood, 2) a sense that she is a valuable person worthy of attentive listening, 3) the name and address of the local mental health agency. The librarian has not "performed" any therapy but yet has effectively assumed a counseling function. The difference between counseling as therapy and counseling as an interpersonal function is significant to the issue.

Therapeutic counseling is a highly complex enterprise in which professional performance requires extensive training and supervised practice. The counseling process has form and structure, theory and research behind it. In many states the practice of counseling requires licensing by credential, experience and examination. The concept of the librarian-as-counselor seems to bear little relationship to the professional practice of counseling-as-therapy.

But it does bear some relationship. Out of the practice and theory of counseling has come an understanding of human interactions that is relevant to all of us, all of the time, whenever we engage in a relationship. From the intensity of the therapy session have evolved strategies for training in organizational settings, educational institutions, professional/client relations and family groups. Paraprofessionals have been taught counseling skills, college students to offer peer counseling; even fifth graders have been taught these skills as relationship-enhancing experiences.[1] The function of "counseling," that is, helping another to explore and resolve a problem, is not the sole prerogative of the professional counselor.

There are times when each of us is counselor to another; there are times when each of us turns to another in distress. The function of counseling is an element in all relationships, whether it is done well or poorly, even if the function is unwillingly and unwittingly assumed. If the function is refused or misused, the lack of it is a dynamic in a relationship, sometimes becoming a most destructive element. The concept of the librarian-as-counselor refers to this interpersonal function, not to the undertaking of a therapeutic encounter.

There is a mystique that surrounds the counseling process that seems to arouse both anxiety and attraction. It is not the purpose of this article to argue and remonstrate that the librarian should assume a counseling function, although the bias of the writer is in strong evidence throughout. The purpose is rather to dispel some of the cloudiness, to describe what counseling is, how it operates, what it looks like, and how it can interrelate with professional library enterprises.

## A Theory of Counseling:  What It Is

Counseling is above all else a philosophic stance.  In the context of this article it derives its posture from the humanists and from the belief that in each human being there lives the potential for self-determination and self-fulfillment. Counseling, then, is a belief system about human nature. It proposes that the first, basic and irrefutable principle upon which mutual and mature relationships based--either personal or professional, intimate or casual--is a belief in the uniqueness, complexity, primitive intelligence and capacity for growth that resides in one's self and in others.  The theory avers that antisocial emotions exist, but not as basic to an individual's nature.  Rather they are reactions to the frustration of one's natural strivings for love, belonging and security. [2]

The productive capacities within an individual--for example, to reverse a failure cycle, to reassess a self-destructive belief, or to break out of a psychic paralysis-- can be released within a relationship that is accepting and nonjudgmental.  When an individual is provided with these conditions for growth, he will develop constructively, as a seed grows and becomes its potential.

The counseling stance is to provide such a climate wherever people live and work.  If it is viewed as a condition of the psychological environment, then the moment of counseling can take place anywhere, under any circumstances. It is not confined to a special room at an appointed hour.

The "placeness" of counseling is independent of place, for the aura, this ambience of being free to pound one's chest with pride or beat it in despair, goes beyond the pragmatic. It is an essence that transcends other people in a room and other business waiting to be transacted.

Counseling is a set of behaviors that are intentioned toward closeness rather than distance, self-revelation rather than withholding, harmony with another in space and time rather than disjointedness. Responses are authentic, reflecting an internal condition of receptivity within the counselor. The humanness of the other is confirmed by the acceptance of all feelings, even rage and outrage. Counseling behavior supports self-awareness, it speaks truth, it waits patiently, it follows rather than leads. It sometimes confronts, cajoles, urges, and interprets, but it never advises, pries, denies or degrades. It is a set of behaviors that presumes both innocence and wisdom, ambiguity and ambivalence, self-control and self-direction. It says, "I respect your humanness even when you feel weak and I esteem your capability to find your own strength. Now we begin from there."

Counseling is a relationship with many sizes and shapes--long-term and ongoing, or a single moment of encounter; most often it is a brief moment within the flow of a relationship. But there are two elements operating within the moment that make it distinctive: first, that the one who is in the counseling role is trying to move into the life focus of the other and to see the world through the eyes of the other; secondly, that the counselor is not acting out his or her personal needs, problems, goals or values at the expense of the other. What makes the counseling dimension of a relationship a unique interpersonal experience is that the growth of one becomes the mutual concern of both.

Belief determines behavior. Sometimes we are aware of our beliefs and feel compatible with our behavior. But often our behavior seems to belie our beliefs and our philosophy seems to stand in contradiction to our actions. A basic premise in counseling theory is that the way we behave is a manifestation of the things we consciously or unconsciously believe. Our behavior may be disguised but it does not lie. It is consistent even in its apparent inconsistency. We can feign liking, acceptance or compliance. But our facade-wearing and maneuvering is then our behavior, a manifestation of our real beliefs. We bluster and bombast when we are insecure, but our pomposity is an operational device to

cover that insecurity.    On the most profound level, we are
what we believe.

It would seem, then, that if we are to look at behavior we must first look at beliefs.   If those beliefs confirm the inherent value and potential in other people,  then
whatever one's role, profession, situation or relationship,
one would be reflecting the philosophic stance of counseling.
It must be emphasized that intention is not the same as behavior.   We may intend to nurture another's self-development
with empathy and encouragement, but behind our words are
contradicting meta-messages.   It must also be emphasized
that sometimes our responses are accidentally facilitative,
but random behavior does not have the impact of consistency.
Finally, it must be emphasized that warmth and attentiveness
communicated nonverbally often have more meaning for the
client than do verbal responses that are unhelpful.   But it is
the congruity between intention and behavior and the consistency of beliefs with responses that defines the posture of
the counselor.

## Responses and Implications:   Non-Counseling

It is very difficult to describe an interpersonal process and
to capture the nuances, subtleties, levels of meaning, history, circumstances, external contingencies, internal bom-
bardments that operate in even the most brief and simple
interaction.   But many times one's belief system begins to
reveal itself, laying itself out little by little for the other
to see.   A look at little slices of interaction, while they
cannot tell us everything, can begin to indicate a whole pattern, just as looking at a specimen under a microscope can
give some clues from a little scrap to a whole whale.   The
following are a few specimens for examination:

If one were asked to respond quickly and spontaneously
to the following kinds of statements, made by a young person
who is expressing great agitation or intense pain, the probable responses could be anticipated:

Client Statement:   "I don't know where to begin. "
Response:   "Begin at the beginning. "

Client Statement:   "Life doesn't seem worth living.
Sometimes I'd like to end it all. "
Response:   "That wouldn't solve anything. "

Client Statement: "Do you have any books on death?"
Response: "Yes, we have a collection of books on the subject."

Client Statement: "I think I'm pregnant."
Response: "Have you seen a doctor?"

Client Statement: "I'm going to quit school. I'm not getting anything out of it."
Response: "If you don't finish school there are many opportunities that will be closed to you."

Client Statement: "Now that I'm crippled I'll never get married."
Response: "Many crippled people have lived rich and full lives. I'm sure you have a good chance of marrying. If you think positively you'll realize that you have much to offer."

Client Statement: "I hate my father. I wish he were dead."
Response: "You don't really mean that. If he were dead you'd realize how much you really love him."

Client Statement: "I wasn't asked to go to the party. I'm ashamed to face my friends."
Response: "Another chance will come along. Next time you'll probably be invited."

Client Statement: "I'm just not attractive to boys."
Response: "Physical beauty isn't everything. Develop some other aspects of your personality."

Client Statement: "I don't know what I want to do when I graduate from high school."
Response: "Have you talked to your counselor?"

Client Statement: "Can I talk to you? I think I'm gay."
Response: "Sometimes young people think they are homosexual, but it's just a stage they're going through."

This exercise in responding has been used numerous times with professional librarians as well as with graduate library school students. The results are almost always the same. With few exceptions the responses are either identical with the one given or some variation with the same im-

plications.  Occasionally there is an intuitive response that
accurately reflects the belief of the responder and the intent
to facilitate a helping relationship.  Usually such a response
is random, an accident--not the result of awareness and not
consistent in subsequent interaction.  It is hard to fault these
responses.  Yet there are some issues at stake that need to
be identified, clarified and evaluated.

First of all, is the chilling fact that the responses
are predictable, as though a person and a problem have no
uniqueness and responses come in packages.  To the receiver of the message a belief becomes evident--that he or she
is a problem to be solved, not a person to be encountered.

Many of the responses attempt to offer encouragement
and the intent of the responder is to reassure.  But the effect is often just the reverse.  Does the youngster who has
not been invited to the party really believe that she will be
invited next time because someone says so?  And if she does
believe it, does that assure that it will happen?  Is she not,
in the last analysis, being patronized, dismissed?  Does she
not know that she is being patted on the shoulder rather than
being helped to cope with something that really exists for
her?  The reassuring responses, to the crippled person, the
boy who is gay, the unattractive young woman, do they not
destroy trust because the "encouragement" they offer is false?
Doesn't the client inwardly mutter, "You just don't understand," or "Just because all those great people made it
doesn't mean that I will"?  Most importantly, false encouragement discourages.  It discourages the client from facing not
only externally imposed realities, but the internal processes
that have been mobilized to cope with those realities.  It
shuts off talk.  It diminishes trust.  It forces the client to
repeat and repeat: "No, I'm sure I won't be invited," or
"But I really do think I'm gay," or "But most cripples don't
get married."  Round it goes, until maybe the listener finally
hears.  Only then can it go forward toward some understanding and insight.

Notice that each response gives a little sermon, either
directly or indirectly.  The counselor as moralist judges the
client as the misguided suppliant.  The homily is based on
the same theme--if you would only change your attitude, you
wouldn't have a problem.  Each response represents a belief
in the most traditional, conventional, socially acceptable value
system--that suicide is immoral, that parents should be loved,
that unmarried pregnancy is a misfortune, that education leads

to success, that homosexuality is a fate to be avoided, etc.,
etc. The belief of the responder, that "clean" living and
"moral" thinking will set everything right, rings loudly and
nobly to the misguided one.

In each example there is beneath the words an undercurrent of intense affect. Yet each response says clearly,
"I don't recognize the feeling. I don't want to talk about
feelings. I can't deal with strong emotions." The belief is
again in evidence. People should not exhibit intensity in public. Negative feelings are not acceptable. Notice how consistently there is a hidden message that says, "You shouldn't
feel that way." You shouldn't hate, feel rejected or experience futility.

Each response implies that the professional knows and
the client should be directed. The responder takes the lead
and the client's feeling of incompetence is reinforced. The
confounded person has come to the right place, to a stronger,
wiser, more responsible human being!

A platitude, a sermon, a question with a hidden mean-
ing--do they really carry such strong implications? Perhaps
if one followed the interaction to just the next step in the
sequence the implications would become clearer.

> Client Statement: "I hate my father. I wish he were
> dead."
> Conventional Response: "You don't really mean that."
> Client Reaction: "Yes, I do. He's a drunk. He
> beats me when he's drunk and he won't let me out of
> the house when he's sober. We'd all be better off if
> he were dead."

Consider the course the interaction might take if the response
were as follows:

> Client Statement: "I hate my father. I wish he were
> dead."
> Counseling Response: "You sound very angry."
> Client Reaction: "Yes, I'm angry. I don't know if I
> can stand it any more. When he gets drunk I'm
> afraid of him and when he's sober I'm afraid of him.
> I'm always afraid of him."

Notice the difference. The first response was defensive, trying to convince the other person of the intensity of

the feeling and the justification for it.   The feeling is still
identified as "hate."   The problem is identified as the
father's, not the client's, and therefore cannot be resolved
by the client.   The interaction is spiraling, not progressing.

In the second instance, the feeling has been accurately identified as anger, and further understood as fear.   The
counselor has communicated some beliefs:  1) your feelings
are valuable even if they are negative; 2) I can handle your
emotions even if they are intense; 3) I see you as rational
even if I don't yet see your rationale; 4) I'm willing to listen
without judging, denying or running away; 5) you can take the
lead and I will follow you.

The client has been given permission to explore his
feelings; he has been encouraged to talk about himself as
"owning" the problem rather than forcing him to focus on a
problem that belongs to someone else.   A major leap has
taken place in one interaction:  from saying, "My problem
is that my father drinks," the client has moved to saying,
"My problem is my own anger and fear.   How can I handle
and direct them?"   The client has by that verbal act gained
some understanding that you and I cannot solve someone
else's problem or manipulate someone else into changing.
We can only together try to understand ourselves.


## Counseling Behaviors:   What Counseling Looks Like

The most intensely helpful overall behaviors and attitudes
that have been identified by those who have studied and
practiced in the helping professions involve the following
elements:

1.   Total attentiveness and involvement that is active-
     ly communicated through body posture, eyes,
     fingertips, shoulders, the whole body.   The body
     does not lie; it will betray our resistances and
     our judgments and contradict our well-intentioned
     words.

2.   The ability to quiet our own "internal noise," the
     voices that remind us of work to be done or
     "appropriate" responses to make, that nag about
     an appointment to keep or a pain in the left arm;
     the ability to shut out the worry:  What shall I
     say next?   How shall I solve this person's prob-

lem? What if he stops talking? If one is truly
listening, the voices inside are quiet and the voice
of the other can get through.

3.  The acceptance of the other person as a rational
    person whose feelings and behavior, as seen
    through his or her own perspective, are logical;
    the belief that the other person has the innate
    capacity for insight, self-understanding, self-
    direction and responsibility for his own destiny.

4.  The belief that that which is denied and avoided
    produces a negative, enervating force that para-
    lyzes and renders helpless; that feelings expressed
    and pain described provide a release of energy
    and potency to act in one's own behalf. Anger
    denied festers. When it is expressed, accepted
    and understood, it dissipates, leaving one's ration-
    al self free once more.

5.  A belief in the power of the "talking cure," even
    though it involves a mystical element that cannot
    be explained. No advice has been given, no solu-
    tions offered, and often an unchangeable situation
    remains unchanged. Yet the client suddenly sighs
    or smiles and says, "I feel much better. Thank
    you for helping me." It is a magic moment that
    never fails to touch both people with a sense of
    closeness and progress.

6.  An understanding of some of the universal themes
    in human existence, a recognition of the existen-
    tial loneliness of the human condition and the need
    to find some meaning in life. Counseling responds
    not only to the intellectual and the emotional, but
    the spiritual existence of the client.

7.  The ability to laugh at one's self and with another.

The most effective verbal behaviors that have been
identified as helping responses involve: 1) a minimal encouragement to the client to continue, the assurance that
the counselor is involved and attentive (i.e., "Please go on,"
"Tell me more," "I see," "Can you tell me about it?" "Can
you describe it?" Nodding and moving toward the client are
highly effective minimal encouragements as is reflecting the
feelings that the client is expressing in one's gestures and

movements; 2) the accurate and courageous naming of the
feeling that the client is communicating.  The naming of a
feeling or a problem does not bring that feeling or problem
into existence; it already exists.  On the contrary, it dif-
fuses intensity and provides relief.  Only when the intensity
has been relieved[3] can the client begin to be rational and to
problem-solve.

If the examples of "client statements" above were
viewed from a counseling focus, a different kind of response
would emerge.  "Counseling responses" have counseling beliefs embedded in them.  In each of the statements a strong
affective element is present, one that speaks louder and with
more insistence than the literal meaning of the words.
Rather than avoiding the intensity, the counselor identifies it
and puts it out on the table, for otherwise it will remain a
frightening, large, unnameable quantity, irreducible in size,
threatening to overwhelm and engulf.  Fear, pain, anger,
and confusion, when expressed, are reduced to manageable
size.

Following are the same client-statements with the
simple, classical, "reflection-of-feeling" responses, the
basic level of empathy that is the most effective element in
the counseling-helping relationship:

Client Statement:  "I don't know where to begin."
Counseling Response:  "There are lots of things going
through your mind at once."

Client Statement:  "Life doesn't seem worth living.
Sometimes I'd like to end it all."
Counseling Response:  "Nothing seems worthwhile right
now."

Client Statement:  "Do you have any books on death?"
Counseling Response:  "Death can be a frightening
subject."

Client Statement:  "I think I'm pregnant."
Counseling Response:  "And you're very shaken up
about it."

Client Statement:  "I'm going to quit school.  I'm not
getting anything out of it."
Counseling Response:  "Being in school isn't doing
much for you."

And so with all the client-statements, the counselor responds to that which is being expressed, the cripple's sense of futility, the anger, humiliation, inadequacy, confusion, panic being expressed in the rest of the examples.

Notice that the client's reaction to these responses, that is, the third move in the interaction, will tend to be a spoken "Yes" rather than a spoken "Yes, but ..." and an unspoken "You really get it" rather than an unverbalized "You just don't seem to understand."

Notice that the responses do not deny but rather clarify the meaning of the statements, do not judge the worth of the statement, do not direct the client into the next statement. They do not offer false encouragement or criticize failure, nor do they advise, admonish or even admire. They reflect. They summarize. They accept.

Sometimes lists of examples seem simplistic and inauthentic, even gimmicky. Of course one must respond in one's own words and style and with one's own intuition to the words and style and undercurrent meanings of the client. The examples can only serve to make a point as strongly and explicitly as possible. Counseling is a unique enterprise for each of us and involves the unique exercising of our own personalities, values, beliefs and styles. It is not a technique or a tool but a way of being more authentic with ourselves and with others.

## Signalling Behaviors

There is another kind of client, one who does not directly confront a problem, but who acts it out through signalling behavior. Here the tendency of the responding person is to tighten and tense and to react not as a counselor, but as another client!

Signalling behaviors are manifested as anger, disruptiveness, righteous indignation, defensiveness, or prejudicial verbalizations. Conventional responses are counteranger or submission, active counterattack or passive sabotage, counterdefensiveness or intellectualization. We react aggressively or helplessly, and both kinds of behavior represent a client-state rather than a counselor-state. Principles of counseling, whether one is dealing with a client whose pain or problem is acted out through tears or through tan-

trums, still speak of acceptance, non-judgment, active
listening, reflective responding, and above all, the presumption that intense feeling can be diffused and handled constructively if heard and accepted.  Hostile feelings represent
a reality for the speaker.  Sometimes they are directed
against the listener, even when they originated outside of the
relationship.  Whether they are the result of the immediate
situation or are feelings misdirected, they leave rationality
immobilized until the intensity is diffused.

Again here are some examples and their conventional
responses:

> Patron Statement:  "I've been waiting for this book to
> come in for two weeks and now that I have it the
> pages that I need have been torn out.  That's what
> happens when blacks take over a place.  They de-
> stroy everything in sight. "
> Librarian Response:  "I'm sure we can find another
> book with the material you need. "

Notice that the response is submissive and placating,
but not problem-solving.  The librarian has probably resisted
saying something like:  "Surely you don't believe that," or
"That's not true.  Surely there are some blacks you know...."
The librarian has learned not to make a scene, not to get
involved in an encounter, not to confront, but rather to behave "professionally" and avoid emotional issues.

But the problem remains and the anger has not abated.
The counseling response to the anger is to name it:  "You
are very angry. "  The next statement that the patron makes
will probably narrow the issue and relate it to a personal
experience.  The process will likely be to move from a
global statement to a personal one.  Again a leap will have
taken place, and a small step toward "owning" the problem
by the patron.

> Patron Statement:  "I'd like to speak to the director.
> My fifteen-year-old brought this book home and I am
> appalled that the public library would allow such trash
> to fall into the hands of innocent children.  Why, this
> book has descriptions of different kinds of birth con-
> trol and how to use them.  How dare you allow such
> things. "
> Librarian Response:  "Would you like to fill out this
> complaint form?"

Is this appropriate professional behavior?  Perhaps.
Problem-solving?  No.  If the librarian's response were:
"It really upset you when your daughter showed you this
book," an underlying message of respect and active listening
would have been communicated.  Respect for another does
not automatically imply agreement, but it is the necessary
first step towards values modification. [4]

> Patron Statement:  A young patron has been told that
> a book cannot be taken from the library.  His response
> is an obscenity reinforced by an explicit gesture.
> Librarian Response:  "Don't you speak to me like that,
> young man.  When you can learn to speak civilly you
> will be welcome in this library."

What are the librarian's goals in this interaction?  To
force or convince the youngster to mend his ways?  To open
up a relationship between them so that he or she might have
some impact on the young patron?  In no way will this interaction accomplish either one.  Certainly dropping this kind of
barrier will accomplish nothing more than leaving a self-
righteous adult face-to-face with a self-righteous youngster,
neither listening to, caring about or having any impact on the
other.

A counseling posture opens up communication, even if
the opinions expressed are unacceptable.  An exploration of
the anger with the first patron, a validation of the parent's
concern for her child in the second, a response to the frustration felt by the third, not condoning, not reinforcing antisocial values or behaviors, but a demonstrated attempt to
listen and understand, makes it possible for the real nature
of the need or the distress to be spoken.  It is only through
interaction that values are reevaluated, beliefs challenged,
behavior restructured and feelings directed appropriately.

Perhaps the most significant effect of the counseling
posture does not lie in its impact on the other, but in its
impact on the counselor and on the quality of relationships.
The ability to listen attentively and to respond empathically
enhance every relationship and the people who live in them.


## The Librarian As Counselor:  Synergism

The concerns of young adult librarians to provide information that realistically meets the needs of young patrons, to

establish a trusting relationship, to create an environment of
accessibility and satisfaction have been voiced again and
again, from the words and works of people like Margaret
Edwards to a vocal and involved community of young adult
librarians who are beginning to define their professional role
in the new and expanded ways.   The voices describe the essence of the counseling relationship.   While librarianship may
not have a clinical counseling function, it does view itself as
a helping profession, a "client-centered" profession.   When
a reference question is a coded cry for help, an information
need buried beneath embarrassment, self-delusion, or social
constraints, of what use is it to deliver the correct information to the wrong question?   Of what use is it to give an
intellectual response to an emotional need or an emotional
response to an intellectual need?   To what purpose does one
feed the angry or frustrated client with more anger or with
a moral lesson?   It is these kinds of concerns that bring librarianship and counseling into interaction with each other.

Clients who seek professional service, whether as library patrons or medical patients, can be either enhanced or
diminished by the experience.   Professional people are often
unknowingly involved with people in crisis, sometimes a consuming, life-altering crisis, more often one of life's mild
but recurring traumas.   Crisis, regardless of its magnitude,
makes an individual more vulnerable to rejection and more
inclined to self-doubt.   It can cause one to see rejection in
a detached professional demeanor or to experience the self-
doubt that results when a professional is discreetly inatten-
tive to intense feelings, thereby inducing the added stress of
justifying those feelings to one's self and defending them to
others.

Adolescents are particularly vulnerable to feelings of
self-negation.   Those who live or work with teenagers often
find themselves in the counselor role, like it or not.   They
become "counselors" neither from inclination nor training,
but from the inescapable weight and intensity of the encounter.
The only real question is often not whether the young adult
librarian should act as counselor, but whether the counseling
is effective or ineffective.

Adolescence is a volatile time when feelings are not
only high but very near the surface.   It is a time of testing
and trying and learning about self through interaction with
others.   It is a stage of ambivalence when the "child" and
the "adult" vie for supremacy.   It is a time of painful growth

and joyful discovery.    A young person needs nourishment and validation, self-acceptance and the acceptance of others.    A sagging self-concept grows taller with attention and respect than with books and programs.    Above all, the young people with whom we interact need adults who value what they say and think and feel.

Notes

1.    Paraprofessional training projects have been developed and tested in a variety of educational and institutional settings by Wayne D. Dyer, Jeanne G. Gilbert and Catherine M. Sullivan, Bernard Guerney, M. M. Leventhal, R. L. Mosher and Norman Sprinthall, and others.

2.    The counseling theory described reflects the writing and works of the humanistic and existential psychologists: Carl R. Rogers, Erich Fromm, Abraham Maslow, Rollo May, Victor Frankl, Elizabeth Kubler-Ross, S. M. Jourard, and others.

3.    Helping behaviors have been identified and researched by Robert Carkhuff and C. B. Traux, B. L. Means, Allen Ivey, Elaine Jennerich, and others.

4.    The training designs of Thomas Gordon's P. E. T. :  Parent Effectiveness Training (New York:  Peter H. Wyden, 1974); Allen E. Ivey's Microcounseling:  Innovations in Interview Training (Springfield, Ill. : C. C. Thomas, 1976); and Thomas Harris's I'm Okay You're Okay (New York:  Harper & Row, 1969) are elaborations of the reflective mode of response.    An excellent description of the applications of this theory can be found in Alfred Benjamin's The Helping Interview (Boston:  Houghton Mifflin, 1974).

# ANY WRITER WHO FOLLOWS

# ANYONE ELSE'S GUIDELINES

# OUGHT TO BE IN ADVERTISING*

Nat Hentoff

In the early 1960s, Ursula Nordstrom asked if I'd be interested in writing a book for children. The notion had never occurred to me, but what proved tempting was Ursula's statement that, of course, I would have total freedom to write what I imagined. The result was Jazz Country, a novel about black music and the dues white boys have to pay to get inside that perilous land of marvels. The book has been read by black, white, Danish, Japanese--all kinds of kids. And for a time, I am delighted to say, it was stolen from a number of libraries more often than almost any other book.

That experience, for which I remain grateful to Ursula, was so much fun and so satisfying (because of all the letters I received from kids) that I have been writing novels for children ever since.

On the other hand, let us suppose that in the early 60s, I had been told by Ursula--or by a librarians' group--that as I wrote, I would have to remember that my book was going to be judged by the following guidelines:

> anti-racist/non-racist/racist (by omission/comission)
> anti-sexist/non-sexist/sexist
> anti-elitist/non-elitist/elitist

---

*Reprinted by permission of the author and publisher from the November 1977 issue of School Library Journal, pp. 27-29. Published by the R. R. Bowker Co. (a Xerox company); copyright © 1977 by Xerox Corporation.

> anti-materialist/non-materialist/materialist
> anti-individualist/non-individualist/individualist
> anti-ageist/non-ageist/ageist
> anti-conformist/non-conformist/conformist
> anti-escapist/non-escapist/escapist
> builds positive images of females/minorities
> builds negative images of females/minorities
> inspires action vs. oppression/culturally authentic ...

And then down in the corner, almost as an afterthought:

> literary quality/art quality.

Had anyone actually shown me such a set of guidelines, my first reaction would have been that I had suddenly
been transported to Czechoslovakia or some such utterly
stifling state. My second reaction would have been to ignore
these externally dictated "standards" entirely because any
writer who follows anyone else's guidelines ought to be in
advertising.

Yet I did not invent that list. Those are the criteria
by which children's books are judged by the Council on Interracial Books for Children, Inc. (CIBC) in their 1976 volume,
Human (and Anti-Human) Values in Children's Books: a Content Rating Instrument for Educators and Concerned Parents.

Furthermore, these and similar criteria permeate the
council's Bulletin and their public statements. To what end?
Not only to sensitize parents, educators, and librarians to
books that are "harmful" to children, but also to mount
campaigns to censor those books.

Like certain Orwellian characters, the sepulchral
representatives of the council deny that they are censors.
For instance, in a letter to School Library Journal (January
1977, p. 4), Bradford Chambers, director of CIBC--that
Watch and Ward Society--declares that he is encouraged at
the realization "by many librarians that enlightened weeding
and selection policies aimed at reducing racism and sexism
do not constitute 'censoring.'"

One librarian's act of weeding can be a writer's shock
of recognition that his or her books are being censored off the
shelves. That is, if the weeding is not part of the normal
process of making room for new books by removing those
that kids no longer read but is rather a yielding to such
slippery "guidelines" as those of the Council on Interracial

Books for Children.   The latter is censorship, as even a
child can tell you.

Let me stipulate my agreement with the political goals
of the council as they are stated on page 4 of Human (and
Anti-Human) Values....   "We are advocates of a society
which will be free of racism, sexism, ageism, classism,
materialism, elitism, and other negative values." (Such
other negative values as censorship, I would add.) I can
make this stipulation not out of piety but on the basis of
some thirty years of rather dogged if unspectacular work
toward these ends as a democratic socialist involved in all
kinds of movements to redistribute power in this land.

Politics, however, is not literature.   And children
ought to have access to the freest literature we can write
for them.   And literature must be freely conceived or it
stiffens into propaganda (no matter how nobly intended) or into
some other form of narrowing didacticism.

The council, however, is quite openly working toward
the end of having "children's literature become a tool for the
conscious promotion of human values that will help lead to
greater human liberation (Human (and Anti-Human) Values ...
p. 4)." I apologize for being obvious, but literature cannot
breathe if it is forced to be utilitarian in this or any other
sense.   The council fundamentally misunderstands the act of
imagination.

Recently, an internationally renowned writer for
children commented about the council to me: "Of course,
we should all be more tender and understanding toward the
aged and we should work to shrive ourselves of racism and
sexism, but when you impose guidelines like theirs on writing, you're strangling the imagination.   And that means that
you're limiting the ability of children to imagine.   If all
books for them were 'cleansed' according to these criteria,
it would be the equivalent of giving them nothing to eat but
white bread.

"To write according to such guidelines," this story-
teller continued, "is to take the life out of what you do.
Also the complexity, the ambivalence.   And thereby the
young reader gets no real sense of the wonders and terrors
and unpredictabilities of living.   Paradoxically, censors like
the council clamor for 'truth' but are actually working to
flatten children's reading experiences into the most misleading, simplistic kinds of untruth."

The writer quoted has never been attacked by the Council on Interracial Books for Children but nonetheless asked me not to disclose his or her identity. "Otherwise," the writer said, "they'll go after me. And that, of course, is another chilling effect of their work." In fact, no writer of books for children whom I spoke to in connection with this piece was willing to be identified, for all were fearful of the council.

I also talked--for nonattribution--to several former members of the council who supported CIBC in its early days but who left when the organization began to move toward its current function of righteous vigilantism. "At the beginning," one of them, a black librarian, said, "the idea was to really open up opportunities for black writers, illustrators, publishers, and minority-owned bookstores. God knows, that needed to be done then, as it needs to be done now. But then the council changed course and turned into censors. That's when I left. I know damn well that if everybody doesn't have the freedom to express himself or herself, I'm going to be one of the first to lose mine."

Yet the council has a ready, if rather devious, rejoinder to such talk of indivisible freedoms. Their contention is that the publishing industry has long practiced "covert censorship." By that, Bradford Chambers says he means the kinds of venerable publishing criteria that result in an "underexposure of the views of women and Third World people." And he's right. For all the belated eagerness of many houses to publish books expressing just such views, the book industry as a whole is certainly still white-dominated. (By the way, that eagerness has so far led to an excess of virtuous pap and scarcely any literature. In the rush to repent, publishers have not sufficiently searched out truly creative tellers of tales who cannot be fitted into neat, sanitized, newly "proper" molds.)

However, the answer to what the council calls "covert censorship" is hardly the council's kind of book "elimination." At base, whatever the reasons of the expungers, all censorship is the same. It is suppression of speech and creates a climate in which creative imagination, the writer's and the child's, must hide to survive.

That the council does not understand the necessarily free ambience for children's literature is regularly evident in its Bulletin as well as in its procrustean rating systems for

"worthy" books. For instance, in a recent issue of the
Bulletin (vol. 8, no. 3) there is an article about the books
that East German children are reading in grades one to six
("What Children Are Reading in GDR Schools" by Donna
Garund-Sletack). The author focuses mainly on the "messages" these books convey about sex roles. For the most
part, the books get high grades. Women are shown in a
wider range of careers than in comparable American readers; children of both sexes exercise real responsibility; individualism is downplayed (no kidding!); all sorts of positive
values are inculcated (such as helpfulness); respect for older
people is "promoted"; there are plentiful tales of racial discrimination (the East Germans are against it); and by God,
"an analysis of poverty and inequality is offered as early as
in the first grade reader. "

Nowhere in the article is there a hint that East German writers (whether their audiences are adults or children)
who offend the state do not get published any more. Some
are even given a chance to reflect on their "anti-human
values" in prison.

Freedom of expression, however, is clearly not a
focal passion of the Council on Interracial Books for Children. Correctness of perspective and attitude are its driving priorities as is stated in the council's pamphlet 10 Quick
Ways to Analyze Children's Books for Racism and Sexism:

> No. 7: 'Consider the Author's or Illustrator's
> Background.' Look at the biographical material
> on the jacket. 'A book that deals with the feelings
> and insights of women should be more carefully
> examined if it is written by a man.' If it's writ-
> ten by Phyllis Schlafly, it also ought to be care-
> fully examined. Obviously, blacks are likely to
> bring more to black themes, as Jews are to Jew-
> ish themes. But why not judge each book for it-
> self, rather than order a line up before you read?
> No. 9: 'Watch for Loaded Words.' Like what?
> 'Chairman' instead of 'chairperson.' I would take
> twenty lashes rather than be forced to use so utter-
> ly graceless a word as 'chairperson.' And what
> does that make me, according to the council? A
> stone sexist, that's what.

And so it goes--"Check the Story Line," "Look at the
Lifestyles," "Weigh the Relationships Between People," and

so on.  Fine for East Germany, if that's where you want to
write, but no different here from the John Birch Society trying to hammer its values into books for children.  Such
groups are the enemies of any writer with self-respect.

Another dulling, constricting effect of the council's
ardent work is that when successful, it produces its own
stereotypes.  During an appearance by representatives of the
council at a February 1977 meeting in New York of the National Coalition Against Censorship, Mary K. Chelton, consultant on young adult services for the Westchester County
Library System, made a good point about the council's addiction to labeling groups.  She said that the council's view
of racial minorities and women makes the groups emerge as
monolithic, with each member of these groups in total accord on any matter that affects them.  Describing herself
as a feminist, she pointed out that she knows from personal
experience that there is no unified perspective among feminists about what is most important to women now, or how
best to achieve feminist ends, or even what the term "feminist" means.

The same is true of blacks, Chicanos, and all other
so-called "Third World" people.  It is no wonder the council
considers "individualism" highly suspicious.

Yet there can be no literature without individualism--
uncategorizable individualism--sometimes flaky, sometimes
complexly rebellious, sometimes so stubbornly unassimilable
as to make the child shout in recognition of himself.  (Or
herself.  Or the chair he/she is personing. )

Collectivism is for politics.  And if the council were
to marshall its energies and foundation-financed resources
for honestly political ends, I'd join it.  Organize, bring
pressure to greatly increase the numbers of "Third World"
editors who will then find more non-white writers than white
editors are likely to.  (If only because they know a lot more. )
Organize support for "Third World" publishing firms and bookstores.  And by all means, hold sessions for librarians and
editors on ways in which the children's booklists ought to be
expanded (without censoring other books).  There is still so
little of value for children on the jazz life.  Or on the tur-
bulent, desperately complicated history of Puerto Rican independence movements.  The list is huge.

But then leave the authors alone.  Always leave authors alone. I'm not talking about editing for grammar and grace. But stay out of authors' quirkily individualistic heads in terms of what they write.

I am currently making notes for a novel, a successor to This School Is Driving Me Crazy. I am trying to imagine Sam, the maddeningly unregimentable hero, two years older. And there is a cohero, who is black. There are always blacks in my novels, and not once have I checked any of them out with the Council on Interracial Books for Children. I am trying to imagine the many intersecting reasons this black youngster, while witty, is also angry. Is he angry at the council because he is torn between collective and individual imperatives? That's a possibility. Maybe I'll by able to incorporate Bradford Chambers into the book. That's a real possibility.

And I am thinking of how the weather will be in certain scenes and trying to remember what it was like, in my teens, to be paralyzed at meeting a certain girl unexpectedly on the street. There will also be music in the book, and I am listening for those sounds. And there are voices I am after, rhythms, timbres. How do you put those into words? The council's guidelines do not tell me.

During this preliminary process and then as I write, I will have one of the council's precepts in mind: "It is the final product that counts--not the intent. We must be concerned above all with the effects of a book on the children who read it."

Exactly. Except that the council's concern with children is expressed through guarding them against any thoughts, characters, plot lines, words, and art work that might "harm" them. The council, of course, considers itself the arbiter of all of that, having discovered, by innate virtue, the sole and correct party line.

My concern with children, on the other hand, is that they find in a book what they had never quite expected to see in print--elements of themselves, dreams they're not sure but what they too may have dreamed. And a chance, as many chances as I can give them, to play with their imagination. To stretch it and bend it and peer through and around it and make whatever connections are natural between the book and themselves, the life in the book and the life outside. And I want to make them care about the people in the book,

and dig their foolishness, and maybe cry a little (I loved to
cry over books when I was a kid).    And I hope to get letters
from readers.    I will start a correspondence, as has happened after all the books before.    And my correspondents
will ask me all kinds of things, as I will them--none of
which can be fitted into those grimly symmetrical checklist
boxes so beloved by the Council on Interracial Books for
Children.

Later, probably in a library, I will meet some of the
readers of this new book, and will be astonished again at
how marvelously, though sometimes hesitantly, different each
one is.    Whether they're all black, as in Brooklyn's Ocean
Hill-Brownsville, or a motley, as in Tulsa.    And I will look
at them and think how truly stupid and destructive it is for
anyone to stand guard over the ideas that may be offered to
their lively minds.

What it comes down to is that the Council on Interracial Books for Children not only distrusts individualism
("should be discouraged as a highly negative force"), but it
also greatly distrusts children.

And that is reason enough why the council should not
be messing with children's literature.

# THE LESSER GREAT TRADITION:

## CARRY ON, CHILDREN*

Fred Inglis

It's all very well to say, with so many well-intentioned pro-
gressivists among teachers, librarians, and parents, that
children's novels are for children, but there's a touch of
bad faith about saying so.    For children's books are written
by adults, inescapably chosen by adults--that is, published
in certain numbers, paid for by pocket money and book
tokens earned by adults, put on library shelves by adults,
chosen by Puffins, by the bookseller, by the Times Literary
Supplement, by the prize-givers.    For children, there is no
getting away from grown-ups, and it's not simply natural,
it's necessary that this should be so.

These facts of life are becoming more and more contradictory as the future becomes less and less reasonably
continuous with present and past.    Without my at all wanting
to go into the gallery with the minstrels of apocalypse, and
cry doom for every year until the end of the millennium, it
surely makes sense to speak of great changes stirring and
swirling under our feet.    The reconstruction of Europe after
1945 quite rightly held and defined our imaginations for a
generation.    But new and hungry generations are marching
across the plains to tread that picture down.    Nobody can
draw a cartoon of this rough beast slouching across the
eighties in just a sentence, although Ted Hughes's marvellous monster in The Iron Man, the space-bat-angel-dragon

*Reprinted by permission of the author and publisher from
Children's Literature in Education, vol. 9, no. 2 (1978)
pp. 73-77.    Published by APS Publications Inc. , An Affiliate
of Agathon Press.

probably comes nearest to it, able as it is to devour the
world, to bump it wobblingly out of its galactic rotations, or
so to fill it with the sweet, ineffable music of the spheres
that wars are stopped and turmoil stilled.  The beast of the
future may bring hell or heaven; what on earth can we imagine of it in our children's stories?

       Answering that question brings the teacher-critic
running over the fields in his long coat.  For it asks, what
books should children read? or more particularly, what
books do I want my child--this actual eleven-year-old daugh-
ter--to have read by the time she moves on to Jane Eyre
and Wuthering Heights and Great Expectations?  And with the
best, most radical will in the world, who would not want her
to read those books, great books as they are?  It is the
merest madness to say, as some Ranters do, that the greatest English novels are merely the refuge of the petit-
bourgeoisie before the onward march of history.  These
novels are great novels because they can mean so much.
The case is closed in none of them; each contains the criticisms of the values it most cherishes.  The totality of a
great novel is such that it can never give up its life for its
ideas.  That is indeed, in Leavis's great phrase, its living
principle.  And there seems to me a great sanity in the
likelihood that when this daughter comes to Dickens and the
Brontës, she'll read them alongside the big girls' bestsellers--
alongside Rebecca and Jamaica Inn, Poldark, Whiteoaks,
alongside Jean Plaidy, Elizabeth Goudge, and Mary Renault,
in and out of Hobbiton and even Atlanta, Georgia.  For all
the awfulness and chintziness and vulgarity of these books,
they have their big, two-hearted sentimentality, their own
living principle to carry them along.  Whatever the future
holds, there is a propriety that these thick, chocolate-
covered books are among the writings of the passage to
adulthood.  In the immortal words of Benjamin Spock, "Your
child is tougher than you think," and pussyfooting round the
library for books which will bring no blush to a modern
maiden's cheek is an expense of spirit in a waste of shame.
To stick to the gastronomic metaphor, the countercultural
and homeopathic diet of chick peas, huskwheat bread, nuts
and sultanas, and raw fennel has a deadly earnest reek about
it.  Faced with its fierce, glassy intentness I would press
curry and chips, gobstoppers, cherryade, HP sauce, SMASH,
and shreddies, on the fourth year of the junior school.
Imaginations, especially when they are growing, need some
strain and risk to become strong; they seek out the chance
to sample technicolour and saccharine and fatty platefuls.
There's no saying who might thrive on it.

This is not to argue against all prohibitions.  Daphne
du Maurier will probably be good for a child--or as we
might more accurately put it, she is well worth reading.
Mickey Spillane or Skinhead couldn't possibly be.  The evidence is not in what the books do to children (or adults, for
that matter) but in what they are in themselves.  And if this
sounds truistic, I can only say that in the confusion abroad at
the moment about censorship, pornography, permissiveness,
and the rest, it is worth talking in truisms.  It would have
to be a specially horrible sort of adult who took an eleven-
year-old to see The Omen or Carrie, and horrible too to
give the child a Hammerhead novel or Selby's The Room.

The moral questions are inextricably psychological as
well, and it is a useful polemical point to make if I say that
psychology and ethics entail one another.  One can't, that
is, have morality without a corresponding account of both
psyche and soma.  But it is more useful to speak with the
Continentals and with the mad prophet of the airways, the
courageous and pioneering David Holbrook, of "philosophical
anthropology."  If one is selecting from a tradition "a great
tradition," then one needs to know what are the questions
one is putting to the tradition in order that certain images
of reality and pictures of the world will look like answers.
A tradition is, after all, one of the forms of life within
which we move and have our being; we enter it much as a
swimmer enters water, and its conventions are what keep us
afloat.  The house of fiction prefigures one such tradition.
But within that house are many mansions, and when we come
to choose our residences, we choose them with an eye on
how they suit our demands on life.  We have to choose even
more carefully when we are looking for books to suit the
children.

For we are, as I said, caught in the contradiction
between the necessary dominance of adults over children and
a cosmology that in its strong preference for what Mary
Douglas calls zero-structure affirms the battlecries of individualism as the master symbols of morality.  In the heavy
perspiration of the top rating scented-soap operas on TV,
Fathers and Children, Another Bouquet, and so forth, the
only moral bond which is allowed to check the hectic, irres-
sistible call of radical personalization is the bond of parent
to child (once it has been born, of course--heaven help the
foetus).  These are the sterile politics of rights, and they
are called upon to mobilize the whole of public values, insofar as that means the criteria of rationality by which people

justify what they do. The appeal to sincerity and authenticity and to self-fulfillment presupposes the porousness of
institutions; the substitution of integrity for dignity, of truth
to self for loyalty, of courageous independence for duty, are
conditions of a world whose richest members have so organized the mammoth divisions of their labour that the individual is left to do everything that matters for himself. You
may lament or you may celebrate the changes, but the fact
is that once the oath has been replaced by negotiation, the
promise by the (breakable) contract, membership by competitive autonomy, then you are no longer at home in any place
and have nowhere to lay your head.

These are tendencies that have made it possible for
Richard Gregory to propose the fiction-making creativeness
of every individual as the model for a new experimental
psychology. Such a proposal could hardly have made sense
to a society of more fixed and stable institutions. But the
divisions of labour and of value, the huge tendency of industrial societies, have forced father out to work and mother
to become the curator of the Romantic reality which is the
experience of our inner subjectivity. The great nineteenth-
century novelists were either women or strongly feminine in
part of their disposition (and the more complete as a result).
The best novelists for children are, I suggest, biased in the
same way. They turn to writing novels (or the mass analogy of a novel, the TV film) because the moral history I
have potted here makes the novel the natural instrument of
moral exploration. (The latter word echoes a great modern
ideal: the hero is an explorer, not a pilgrim.) For novels,
to adapt a fine phrase of John Berger's, walk like children.
They do not touch the ground at every point. They walk,
run, bound, stop to inspect something closely, hurry on
again, according to the pace of reader and narrator. The
homely metaphors of "keeping up," "making strides," "getting lost," "feeling out of one's depth," "feeling at home
with" fit the moral-psychological experience of novel-reading
perfectly.

And if all this is so, what kind of books compose a
tradition adequate to the puzzles, the joys, and terrors of
modern rulelessness, the lone and level sands of the free
spirit, what sorts of books can this child take to her desert
island?

The moral and cultural point of Gregory's idea is that
fictions stand to life as metaphor to reality. They are an

image of alternatives and possibility.  So if we speak of the
best children's books in a famous formulation, as bringing
to an intense focus "an unusually developed interest in life,"
"a vital capacity for experience," "a marked moral intensity,"
then these noble phrases in no way suggest closure or rigid-
ity or, worst of all portentousness.  The reason why The
Mouse and His Child, The Iron Man, Alice, Swallows and
Amazons, Winnie-the-Pooh, Carrie's War, Midnight Is a
Place, The Wind in the Willows, Tom's Midnight Garden,
are all as marvellous as they are,  is that their energy of
characterization, their vitality and comedy, are of a piece
with their moral seriousness.  And these generalities take
their force, as these days they must, from the moral effort
to make experience mean something at a time when--as I
argued--zero-structure and radical personalization (Bernstein's phrase) leave the individual with everything to do for
himself.  "Meaning" is then particular:  the mouse and his
child make their funny little commune out of the wasteland
of the garbage tip which still lies on the road to West Egg.
The mole leaves his stuffy, comfy respectability to find a
more venturesome self and a friendship that passes understanding.  Alice faces out the intolerable adults by virtue of
her selfless (but self-confident) zest for their vast and comic
awfulness.  Tom discovers the honours of age and its loveli-
ness.  And Carrie, carefully and timidly, finds the comfort
in the strength of love.

These are lessons which children can learn, as they
say, by discovery.  No one would be so crass as to mark
out the necessary values which a modern child should, in the
mouthfilling jargon of the curriculum developers, conceptual-
ise and assimilate.  Thus, moral autonomy from Dawn Wind;
mutual interdependence from Watership Down; physical courage from The Hobbit; domestic patience from The Long Winter; unquenchable resilience from The Wolves of Willoughby
Chase; racial understanding from The Cay; class tolerance
from Gumble's Yard.  The prating solemnity of some critic-
advocates would lead you to suppose that a children's novel
is simply a moral exercise somewhere between The Guardian
features page and a Schools Council project in educating for
personal relationships.  It has, however, been the great
strength of English literature--of which children's fiction is
a part--since Blake, Wordsworth, the Brontës, and Dickens,
that its sense of responsibility goes far beyond the individual
and his personal relationships.  The test to have in mind is
that children's novels be characterized by their responsibility
to the demands of immediate life.  It is a human not a polit-

ical point to say that a children's novel, written as it is both for present and future, should seek out lives and forms of lives which may return a credible meaning to such great names as "honour, love, obedience, troops of friends."

## References

Bernstein, Basil (1977) "Aspects of the relation between education and production" in Class, Codes and Control, Vol. 3 (rev. ed), London & Boston: Routledge & Kegan Paul

Gregory, Richard (1974) "Psychology: towards a science of fiction," New Society 16 November 1974, reprinted in The Cool Web, Margaret Meek et al (eds), Oxford: the Bodley Head, 1977

# THE MEDIA AGE:  SOME BRUTAL TRUTHS*

Estelle Jussim

The Alumni Day Program Committee selected an overall
rubric of Technology in Libraries:  Media and Computers.
I am seriously dissatisfied with such a title.

If there is any primary, fundamental brutal truth
about this media age, it is that technology is not something
which we can isolate, wrap up, stamp and slap into some
convenient shelf in a library, but that all of the communications technologies--and these include computers--have so
transformed the potential of libraries that they constitute a
total environment, not in libraries, but all around and in between.  If we acquiesce in the title generously offered us for
this meeting, we are unconsciously separating ourselves,
isolating ourselves in buildings.  And if there is anything
about which I am absolutely certain in our profession, it is
that a library is not a building, but a process, a process
involving the interchange of information by as many means
as possible.

If there is any primary brutal truth about this media
age, it is precisely that communications technologies have
begun to alter the ways in which we live, think, and do
business.  Communications technologies have begun to make
it possible for us to bring information to people instead of
bringing people to information.  They have, therefore, called
into perplexity the basic characteristic of libraries, and, in
that dastardly way in which communications technologies have
always performed, have begun to alter professional roles,
functions, preparation, goals, and capabilities.

---

*Reprinted by permission of the author and publisher from
the Fall 1977 issue of NEEMA Views (New England Educational Media Association), pp.  5-9.

While we have mistakenly allowed ourselves to be
terrorized by gadgets, and while we have become bedazzled
by playthings, the scientific and artistic communities have
seized upon the camera, the motion picture, the videotape,
and the interplanetary scanner to pursue types of research
which only these technologies have made possible.   The behavioral scientist, the biophysicist, the anthropologist, the
sociologist, the cultural historian, the architect and the de-
signer, rely upon the visual information supplied to them
through the recording mechanisms of communications technologies.   While some of us have been fighting that most
futile and anachronistic battle about the superior values of
words over pictures, or pictures over words, there has
come about a complete revolution in the way that information has been generated, used, and transformed.

Just as the computer has altered certain research
strategies, so the generic camera has created tremendous
potential for exploring the characteristics of complex realities.   There is not a moment to lose, my friends, for providing intellectual access to visual information will require
an almost completely new orientation.   More importantly, to
understand the ways in which communications technologies
alter social, political, and economic relationships will require a new orientation.   If there is any fundamental, brutal
truth about this media age, then it is that we cannot view
only our own little corners, where we hope safely to enclose
technology within our safe brick buildings.   We need to look
at the whole spectrum of communications media and see, as
objectively as we can, the continuum of media from the
smallest instructional unit all the way to the implications of
national mass media.   For a commitment to one--that is, to
one type of instructional medium--is inevitably and crucially
linked to the impact of the mass media.

It would be patently absurd, for example, to continue
to regard schools as self-enclosed territories where we
preach the classics and honor the most essential skill of
reading when outside the world is watching television for 6. 5
hours each day per family, including such marvels of intellectual and ethical stimulation as the Gong Show and the
Bionic Woman.

If there is another brutal truth to the media age, it
is that the library profession has been exceedingly laggard
about providing access through any form except print.   Yet
Mr. Justice White, in delivering the opinion of the Supreme

Court on the Red Lion Broadcasting case, remarked, "It is
the right of the public to receive suitable access to social,
political, esthetic, moral and other ideas and experiences
which is crucial." As I indicated earlier, much new and
important research is generated by, not simply reported by,
the new media, especially forms involving photography. If
the public has a right to receive suitable access to social,
political, esthetic, moral and other ideas and experiences,
then our profession has a mandate to provide that access.
Any hesitation about facilitating this access through all forms
of communications technologies constitutes a serious breach
of professional ethics. We need the tricks of diplomacy and
the art of persuasion to convey this message to boards of
trustees, library directors, school supervisors.

One of the most brutal truths of our media age is
that the library professional schools have been exceedingly
laggard about providing appropriate exposure not just to the
gadgets of educational technology but to the research which
instructs us about the characteristics of communications
media, especially on interdisciplinary levels.

A medium is merely a physical channel which permits
the transmission of ideas from the head of one human being
to the head of another human being. But to understand the
nature of the physical channel and its special limitations and
capacities is only the beginning of our task. For we must
concern ourselves with what is being communicated and how
it will be deciphered. We need to understand the process of
communication, the encoding and decoding of messages. And
to do this we have to stop thinking about gadgets and start
thinking about people.

In education, for example, Marshall McLuhan observed
some years ago that we attempt to bolster outdated curricula
by the use of the new media. We apply the new media like
quack doctors applying poultices of chicken blood and spiders'
legs: without knowing or even pretending to know how human
beings respond in a total environment of psychic suggestion
and social pressure. We rush to association seances in which
the new media are displayed like cereal boxes, and we judge
them burdened by heaps of untested and very sugar-coated
assumptions. It is no wonder that we stumble. We study
mechanistic charts of the channels of communication as if
they could ever possibly reveal anything about the complexi-
ties of motivation, cognitive dissonance, cultural significance,
intuitive grasp, and creative ingenuity.

The textbooks continue to reproduce Claude Shannon's little flow chart which, in reassuring little boxes, starts with an information source for a message which is then encoded into a transmission channel, decoded by a receiver, and the chart ends with the same arrow (pretending to be a message) arriving straight and true at its destination. The assumption that communication takes place along directionally reliable lines should by now have been rejected as one of the most palpably misleading of all paradigms.

One of the most brutal truths we need to learn is that communication is not only not neutral, as the chart pretends, and that its outcomes are not predictable, as the chart implies, but that it occurs in a context which consists of everything from sociocultural backgrounds, the physical states which include hunger and fatigue, the physical environment which may be somehow inimical to understanding or too threatening to permit attention to the message, the emotional readiness to receive a concept, isomorphism of thesaurus and vocabulary from sender to receiver, the amount of previous exposure to a concept or similar concepts, the intellectual genetic ability to acquire--that is, to understand and retain--the meaning of the message, and the ability to transform a concept into future behaviors.

[Note: a number of short films were shown and discussed at this point.]

A communications message was presented through film: it seemed straightforward enough; yet the message turns out to be different for each of us because we bring our own individual context to the experience of it.

We need to learn about communications processes, that is obvious. We need to learn how language functions to structure visual experience. We need to learn how to interpret the potential of a mediated experience for a variety of different cultural contexts. Perhaps the time is ripe for me to suggest a series of "needs to learn" and then we can draw our own conclusions.

I suggest that this Media Age demands of us that we acknowledge the following tasks, for these tasks are the "brutal truths" about communications media which we need to learn.

We need to understand the characteristics of communi-

cations media as technologies, as systems for delivering
messages, and we need to discover how the nature of those
systems structures the messages which are delivered.

We need to learn the syntax and semantics of new
visual media in the same way we learned the syntax and
semantics of verbal language. Sometimes we can only learn
these by learning to use the camera.

We need to understand the influence of communications
media as social instruments and their relationship to social
control, political exploitation, economic monopoly, and how
the social uses of media reveal deeply established cultural
biases.

We need to learn the truths about ourselves as individual and institutional agents of change, as communicators and
as participants in networks of communication, as links in the
immensely profitable business of the production of broadcast
media as well as prepackaged messages in all forms from
print to videotape.

We need to acknowledge the truths about our limited
education in communications processes, in social psychology,
in sociology, in linguistics, in the psychology of perception,
in the nature of visual messages.

We need to learn the truth that as a profession we
are unfortunately prone--as David Engler observed--to put
"the cart of the machine before the horse of purpose." We
need to learn the truth that the profession has yet to come
to a concensus about a hierarchy of human and humanitarian
values, that we tend to be elitist, and that we need to be
more and more broadly educated.

We need to learn the truth that people operate out of
the principle of least effort, and that thinking about anything
but purely technical issues requires considerable and often
painful effort.

And lastly, perhaps, most importantly, we need to
learn the most painful, the most brutal truth of all: that,
in the words of Antoine de St. Exupery--"We do not discover
truth; we create it. "

There are no media truths standing like marble gods
for us to worship. "Truths" must be tested and retested,

for again and again we have seen seemingly rock-hewn
truths crumble into despised dust.   We need, therefore, to
learn how to judge the reliability of research into the nature
and effects of media, so that a healthy scepticism will replace a dangerous gullibility.

We create the truth:   one brutal truth which emerges
from any study of the media profession is that it is only
recently that women have been allowed to enter it.   The
Media Age seems to be an age of machines, and women have
not been encouraged to feel competent with machines.   The
Media Age, as it affects libraries and media centers, has
seemed to become an age of men and machines, with women
hauntingly in the background because they have once more
been conditioned to accept second best, the passive roles,
the clean jobs, the less well-paid jobs.

The situation is slowly changing, but it needs great
attention to make sure that change survives.   There has been
seared into women's souls that to tinker with machines is
essentially and inherently "masculine"--therefore, to become
involved with communications media is somehow fatal to
"femininity."   There has also been seared into women's
souls that to be vigorous in any dimension is not acceptable.
Women have a poor self-image, thanks to years of condition-
ing starting with the cradle.   The profession therefore needs
to address itself to some brutal truths indeed.   These are
brutal truths in any age, not only in an age of Media.   But
it is the Media Age which has clarified the situation to an
extraordinary degree.

I would like now to summarize some observations
from the Bulletin of the Simmons College Graduate Program
in Management, with a note of thanks to the developers of
that program, Professors Margaret Hennig and Anne Jardim.
In sum:   Less than 5% of today's middle managers are wom-
en.   Why?   The answer lies partly in career pathing.   The
typical management career path moves individuals from an
initial experience in a technical or specialist's role to the
more general role of a middle manager.   From that point,
career paths tend to lead upwards to new levels of specialization demanding a more conceptual approach to decision
making.

In terms of progressive job functions, the specialist's
job is essentially one of applying particular kinds of technical knowledge to the solution of primarily routine problems.

Supervisory responsibilities at this level are closely related
to task completion and to the proper use of techniques and
skills.   In contrast, the middle manager's job is much more
one of coordination with counterparts in other functional
areas, relating work of a specific group to larger purposes
and objectives.   Higher level management is closely involved
in setting long-term directions and developing policies for
entire functional areas in order to give coherence to the operation of the enterprise as a whole.

Looked at in this way, career paths leading ultimately to the most senior levels of management inevitably depend
on that first important transition from technical or specialist
supervision to the broader and much less precise role of a
middle manager.

This kind of career path is extremely difficult for a
woman to follow.   She tends to enter an organization with
aspirations which differ significantly from a man's.   She
tends to concentrate on the acquisition of competence in whatever may be her current job and to let career advancement
take care of itself.   The informal system of relationships
and mutual assumptions and expectations, a critical source
of learning and support along the path to middle management,
does not work for her as it does for men.   In contrast, the
great majority of men in management take it for granted that
their first job will lead step by step upward through the management ranks.   A culture of shared beliefs, assumptions,
expectations, supports them; they are taught, tested, and
promoted within formal and informal systems overwhelmingly
made up of men.

In the past, many competent women sought to overcome the difficulties they faced by becoming specialists and
remaining specialists within narrow hierarchies of other
specialists.   Their management responsibilities were essentially limited to the supervision of other specialists.   Little
in personal or work experience has prepared women to make
risk decisions.

[End of summary.]

I find this long statement so perfectly applicable to
the present state of media management in libraries and
media centers that I believed it was vital to share it with
you.   If the many women in this audience want to become
Directors of Learning Resource Centers (and you can count

on the fingers of one hand the female directors of really
large and complex centers of this kind) you will not only
have to overcome all the usual stereotypes about the inability of women to manage, but you will have to confound all
of the stereotypes about women and machines.   To do that,
you will first of all have to examine your own misconcep-
tions about what women can and cannot do.

The men in this audience also need to be encouraged,
for they, too, require courage and strength to face the com-
plexities of the Media Age.   Abraham Maslow, in his Toward
a Psychology of Being, talks eloquently of "The Need to Know
and the Fear of Knowing." I quote: "We tend to be afraid
of any knowledge that could cause us to despise ourselves or
to make us feel inferior, weak, worthless...." "We tend to
avoid personal growth because this, too, can bring another
kind of fear, of awe, of feelings of weakness and inadequacy.
And so we find another kind of resistance, a denying of our
best side, of our talents, of our finest impulses, of our
highest potentialities, of our creativeness. "

In attempting to enter the Media Age, we are all
pushed and pulled by ambivalences.   We fear testing ourselves with the new; we fear discovering some new talent
within ourselves which would alter the status quo.   We fear
the unknown; yet to be human is to seek the unknown and to
conquer it.   We fear to probe too far lest somehow we be
punished for our hubris.

I quote from Maslow again: "The unfamiliar, the
vaguely perceived, the mysterious, the hidden, the unexpected,
are all apt to be threatening.   One way of rendering them
familiar, predictable, manageable, controllable, i. e. un-
frightening and harmless, is to know them and understand
them. "

Many of us need to come to terms with the fact that
our "education" ceased some time ago; we have not re-
examined our assumptions, our foundations in research.
Many of us may need to re-evaluate our career goals, to
reaffirm the excitement which once drew us into the media
field.   To do this, we may need--literally--to go back to
"school," to make a new beginning.   Beginnings need not
terrorize us:   they open up new avenues not only to professional advancement but to that most satisfying and important
of all endeavors, the encouragement of personal growth.

Anyone who comes to terms with his or her need for

continuing education becomes eligible for the Simmons Four-E
award: the four e's stand for Exercising the Grey Matter,
Escalating the Input, Energizing the Inertia, and Emancipat-
ing Oneself from Ignorance.

If there is any other meaning to the Media Age than
the bombardment of our senses by a superfluity of images,
noises, and computer printouts, it is that the Media Age is
the age you yourself are when you discover that something
new is going on out there, and you recognize your need to
find out about it.

# CHILDREN'S LIBRARIANS:

## Managing in the Midst of Myths*

Caroline M. Coughlin

When was the last time a library director called children's services "the glory of the public library movement"? Why are children's librarians having difficulties with library administrations after years of seemingly blissful existence?

In recent years many children's librarians have expressed concern over the deterioration of children's library services in many large urban public libraries. They believe that the future of library service to children is threatened by the elimination of children's services coordinators; the integration of youth and adult collections; and the stress on family programs, as opposed to child-oriented programming. There are still a few unconverted print-oriented librarians who believe that films and records create undesirable barriers between librarians and children.

Less outspoken but equally concerned about children's services are the rural and suburban-based children's librarians. These librarians are often struggling with problems of adequate funding and book distribution rather than questions of service ideology and status. But in a way, the drive of children's librarians to maintain a children's room of their own is indicative of the present-day plight of all librarians serving youth.

*Reprinted by permission of the author and publisher from the January 1978 issue of School Library Journal, pp. 15-18. Published by R. R. Bowker Co. (a Xerox company); copyright © 1978 by Xerox Corporation.

There is some evidence that youth librarians have
stunted their own career development and in doing so, have
harmed the very service they wish to promote.   Many of the
younger children's librarians have rejected upward or lateral
mobility in their institutions and have remained sequestered
under the supervision of a mature children's coordinator.
Often coordinators have chosen specialist roles rather than
the more general middle and upper management roles.   The
entrance of a few males into children's work has not altered
the fact that this service area remains an overwhelmingly
female enclave.   Some children's librarians seem to have
unresolved internal conflicts about their professional roles.
They are drawn toward the role of a traditional woman who,
as wife and mother, is given permission to express her
nurturing tendencies.

As a group, children's librarians have perpetuated
beliefs and behavior patterns that may lead to the elimination, downgrading, or ostracism of children's services.
Other library professionals, as well as other child-oriented
professionals may lose patience with these outmoded youth
librarians.   In doing so, they will abandon their support for
the concept of public library service to children, or refuse
to listen to the cries of school media personnel and young
adult librarians searching for status and recognition.

## The Tender Technicians

If one is to accept the idea that children's librarians support
archaic beliefs and behavior patterns that are handicaping
them as they pursue their current jobs, it is vital to explore
the history and present reality of this controversial premise.
Dee Garrison, a social historian, has researched the role of
women in 19th-Century America and explored roles chosen by
different groups of women as they became active in society.
One such group were female librarians, who Garrison af-
fectionately calls "the tender technicians."[1]   In her work,
certain subgroups of female librarians stand out and early
children's librarians are the subject of much careful analysis.   Proof for the generalizations made about the character
of early children's librarians' work and philosophy of service
comes from the record of their own statements and actions.
Garrison develops certain propositions central to our understanding of the similarities between 19th- and 20th-Century
children's librarians.

> In common with the founders of other service pro-
> fessions for women, the early women librarians
> are best understood as proponents of that sexual
> ideology with strong anti-feminist implications
> which dominated the thought of the great majority
> of middle-class Americans at the turn of the cen-
> tury.   This ideal gave woman a separate nurturing
> temperament which was complementary to that of
> the male and defined women as biologically superi-
> or in their capacity for spirituality and fine emo-
> tions. [2]

Given this antifeminist belief in a distinct nurturing
function, it is easy to see how different functions could be
rationalized and delineated for male and female librarians.
Since the care of children had been a woman's task in the
general society, it was logical to build upon the nurturing
talents of female librarians by permitting them to develop
library service to children.   At the time it was expected
that women librarians would <u>want</u> to concern themselves primarily with the task of nurturing children's minds.   The
victim should not be blamed for doing the only thing the
mores of the time permitted; rather it must be stressed that
a continued adherence to outmoded, unscientific beliefs about
women (and therefore about female librarians, and in particular, children's librarians) as superior nurturers can, and
is, resulting in an impasse or losing situation for all in-
volved--administrators, children's librarians, and youth.

The emphasis on the nurturing role of the female librarian directly affected the development of children's service.

> Throughout the 1880's women slowly evolved the
> essentials of library work with children--careful
> censorship of books, separate rooms with small-
> scale tables and chairs, and a kindly maternal
> guidance designed to lead the child, unsuspecting,
> to a predetermined standard of reading. [3]

Prominent forerunners of children's services such as
Minerva Sanders, Caroline M. Hewins, and Effie Louise
Power can be quoted at length to illustrate the moral certainty that guided their creation of this new role of cultural
and spiritual nurturer of children, but the motto of the
Cleveland Public Library's 1897 Children's Library League
can be used to briefly summarize their goals--"Clean Hearts,

Clean Hands, and Clean Books!" Mass immigration further
strengthened the resolve of children's librarians to Ameri-
canize the foreign child, and storytelling, "the only means
by which we can get the children honestly to want the books
we want them to want,"[4] was added to the job description of
the skills called for in children's librarians.

The reason for this continued stress on morality is
hinted at in Florence Butler's article on children's libraries
and librarians in the Encyclopedia of Library and Information
Science. According to Butler, "the basic goals of children's
service have changed little [emphasis added] since the publication of Effie Louise Power's Library Service for Children
in 1929."[5] The goals are to "provide children with good
books supplemented by an inviting library environment and
intelligent and sympathetic service and by these means to
inspire and cultivate in children love of reading, discriminating taste in literature, and judgment and skill in the use of
books as tools."[6] To have goals and programs that remain
essentially unchanged from 1880 to the present day is a feat
almost legendary in our changing society. We are not a
Victorian society but it appears that children's librarians are
still obligating themselves to nurture their charges into a
mode of behavior that places primary value on general goodness and beauty as found in literature.

If the rest of the library profession also subscribed
to these Victorian goals for children's services (or any library service) and Victorian beliefs about the role of female
and children's librarians, there would be no discontinuity;
work with children in libraries could continue as an unchallenged and beloved aspect of library service. Garrison suggests that in the earlier period:

> In the children's section of the library created and
> staffed by women, female librarians were free, as
> in no other area, to express unchallenged, their
> self image. Because their activities blended so
> thoroughly into the Victorian stereotype of the fe-
> male, their endeavors remained substantially unex-
> amined by male library leaders.[7]

However, it appears that there has been a primary
shift in emphasis from dispensing goodness to dispensing
ideas on the part of all other groups in librarianship. Many
children's librarians do not see the difference this makes to
the development of their goals and programs. It means no

less than the abandonment of their nurturing role in favor of
a role most women have avoided for years--intellectual excellence.

        If children's librarians were to abandon their old role,
they would cease having to justify their work in terms of the
good they can do, which is conditional in nature, and could
develop goals based on the human right to equality and intellectual activity.


## Change and Growth

It is the 100 years of children's librarians promising goodness and, by implication, good children, that have brought
them to today's impasse with library administrators who no
longer share the moral mind set of children's librarians and
are now questioning the "sacred truths" they promote.   The
recent past certainly is a warning that differences in philosophy abound.   One has only to observe the demise of the
children's coordinator, the struggle with the ALA Intellectual
Freedom Committee over the Children's Services Division's
(now the Association for Library Service to Children) Re-
evaluation Statement, and the difficulty of youth librarians in
achieving positions of influence on bodies such as the National Commission on Libraries and Information Science and ALA
Council to see that times have changed ... that children's
librarians and children's library service are no longer automatically allowed a room of their own.

        The real question to face is whether the beliefs and
actions that guided children's librarians in the past are im-
mutable or if the specialty is capable of growth and change.
If change and growth is impossible, children's librarianship
deserves to die; however, there is no real basis for arbitrar-
ily deciding that growth is unattainable.   Rather, children's
librarians in planning for their own career development must
examine the principles that foster professional growth and
apply them to the future of library service to children.

        In 1912 Herbert Putman addressed a class of women
library students at Simmons College and admonished them
for lacking a sense of proportion, for peevishness, and for
being absorbed in small details.   These criticisms have also
been leveled against children's librarians by present-day library directors.   As with any image, there is a grain of
truth in it.   Promulgating a program with an outdated and

unexamined philosophy, resisting involvement in total library
programming (actively or passively), and concentrating on
minute details, such as coloring name tags for story hours,
are actions that are seen by most library directors as ir-
responsible, lacking in innovation, and undeserving of managerial recognition.   It is no longer sufficient to blindly accept Anne Carroll Moore's unsophisticated goal of "bringing
children and books happily together"[8] as the total career
goal for a children's librarian.

While the early circumscribed roles may have led to
petty or peevish behavior, the present situation is infinitely
freer and children's librarians, along with other women with
jobs, are now finding society relatively receptive to their
entrance into the ranks of career professionals on a nonsexist basis.   In order to enter this arena, youth librarians now
need to free themselves from the remnants of their antifeminist attitudes and prepare to deal as adults and equals with
the group that has both power and slightly different mores--
the males who are the majority of library directors.

Anne Jardim and Margaret Hennig in their book The
Managerial Woman offer an analogy that compares women in
organizations with strangers in a distant country. [9]  Thoughtful guests learn the language, customs, and adapt to the
rules of the land they are visiting.   The authors make no
value judgment about which group's (visitor or host; woman
with job or career businessman) belief structure is better,
they merely report the observed differences and suggest
techniques for achieving congruence.   We may not want to
recognize it, but at present library administration is overwhelmingly a man's world and thus, to use the Hennig and
Jardim concept, it is a foreign country.

By basing their discussion on extensive consultation
with male-dominated business organizations, doctoral research
on successful women executives, and interviews with female
business students and executives, Hennig and Jardim have
developed a precise and insightful data base on the role of
women in business today.   The influence of the nurturing demands of the 19th Century are still evident in the work patterns of most men and women.   Men develop careers; women,
jobs.   It is the rare woman who stops waiting for something
other than a job and consciously turns her job into a career.
However, it does occur (typically about ten years into a
field) and at that point, some women--who call themselves
lucky--begin a delayed commitment to a career.   They often

remain divided about family and career responsibilities and frequently develop a very internalized reward system, enjoying a career because it gives them personal growth or it helps others. Men choose careers early, develop a win or lose strategy about the stages in their careers, and are more conscious of both their efforts and the elements in their environment that foster career growth.

Reading the chapters in The Managerial Woman that discuss the above findings in detail is akin to listening to the life stories of female librarians and library school students as they hover between taking a job and building a career. We have no research comparable to Hennig and Jardim's for children's librarians, but pieces of the pattern emerge in Marilyn Gell's personalized account of five successful women librarians. [10] The Gell article can be examined for clues relative to career development among women librarians. Of the five women featured, only one began her career in a school library; for two others, there was some brief involvement with young adult work; none came from the public library children's services field. Four of the five women served long periods of their careers as supervisors before moving to management responsibilities; and the fifth, a younger person, stressed the need for demonstrating all-around technical competence to prove herself.

Statements similar to those of the women discussed in The Managerial Woman appear throughout: "The harder I work, the luckier I get. I enjoy being the only woman. I have personal peace with my private life. You have to go after jobs." According to Hennig and Jardim these comments are typical of women who may still not fully understand the difference between their tentative acceptance of a career and a man's conscious career development. The first two statements are seen as typical feminine responses that reject the skills of planning and strategy in favor of luck, or permit the woman to view herself as a unique phenomenon. By contrast, the second two statements are illustrative of areas where ambivalent feelings have been resolved and increased career growth has followed.

The Managerial Way

Observations of children's librarians over a period of years have led me to hypothesize that those children's librarians with 19th-Century nurturing mores and views of childhood

experience many of the dilemmas highlighted in The Managerial Woman.  While research to document or refute these
observations would be ideal, the fact is that there is little
research money directed toward children's services and it
seems unlikely that in the near future there will be funds for
such study.

If my speculations are correct--that an adherence to
outmoded concepts of femininity, childhood, and the role of
working women have caused a disparity in beliefs between
male library administrators and female children's librarians--
the solutions may be to adopt some of the Hennig and Jardim
insights.

Children's librarians should note the distinction these
authors make between women as supervisors and men as
managers.  Many of the women studied overinvested in technical skills development and remained supervisors of a de-
partment--responsible for routine, predictable, and specific
jobs in a familiar subject.  This type of woman is more concerned with how one plays a game or in the quality of particular relationships.  Contrast this with men who, as boys
playing team sports, learned the dual personal skills of
adaptability and playing to win, and use these skills as managers directing change.

There are a great number of children's librarians who
do not have the male "win some, lose some" attitude developed in team sports and have therefore chosen not to interact in a managerial way with the larger library community.
They seem to prefer to remain in children's rooms--idealiz-
ing children and acquiring the technical skills to influence
them.  If all a children's librarian desires is a routine, risk-
free job, there is no need to move from the room until it
closes.  If, however, there is some desire for achieving
positions of status and influence within the library structure
in order to affect children's services, it is vital that children's librarians move from their cozy rooms through the
ranks of supervisors to the arena of management.  Children's
librarians must learn how to deal with male and female
superiors, how to accept greater and greater risks and responsibilities, and how to manage their own career development by learning entirely new skills in mid-career instead
of continually polishing the same set.

Technical skills enabled women to enter the work
force, but these never guaranteed promotion or recognition.

Avoiding this particular kind of trap may mean moving out
of the children's area with its limited promotional opportunities.  The first step is not abandonment of children or children's services, but an analysis of other related functions
and a decision to broaden one's experience, skills, and visibility.  By using techniques such as participation in problem-solving groups, developing support groups, and empha-
sizing competencies delivered rather than the personality of
the deliverer or recipient, it is possible to begin the personal transition from supervision to management as charted
by Hennig and Jardim.

Self-analysis and situational analysis can revolution-
alize library service to children.  If children's librarians
can free their own intellects from the sentimental dogmas
about themselves and children carried over from the 19th
Century, they may be able to liberate library service to
children.  They will see children as growing people with
minds that need information and knowledge.  They can begin
to view themselves as leaders and participants in the full
exchange of ideas in, around, and about librarianship.

For some children's librarians, a new conceptualiza-
tion of their role will free them from unconscious self-
images as keepers of the store of goodness.  They will then
seek decision-making power in librarianship--a greater as-
piration than the right to maintain a room of their own.
There is a sentence in The Managerial Woman which is telling enough to deserve poster status in many children's librarians' offices:  "Hard work in the absence of goals and
workable plans to achieve them remains just that--hard
work. "

It is now nearly 100 years since children's librarianship developed as a specialty.  New goals and workable plans
are needed for the next century if we are to manage children's services wisely and avoid being trapped by myths.
As a start, it would be helpful, if in the next year or two--

- children's librarians learned one new skill not
  directly related to children's services;
- each state, regional, and national library associations' children's section invited one less children's
  book author to their programs and one more speaker
  on planning, managing, or evaluating services;
- instructors of children's library services invited a
  resident campus expert in the related areas of

sociology, management, or research methods to
speak to students;
● a few children's librarians, library educators, and
   library association types who have done all of the
   above met to brainstorm further strategies for
   promoting children's services and share the results
   with the rest of us.

## References

1.  Garrison, Dee.  "The Tender Technicians," Journal of
    Social History, Winter 1972-73, p. 131-59.
2.  _____.  "Women in Librarianship."  A Century of
    Service (American Library Association, 1976), p. 147.
3.  Ibid. , p. 152.
4.  Ibid. , p. 153.
5.  Butler, Florence.  "Children's Libraries and Librarian-
    ship," Encyclopedia of Library and Information Sci-
    ence (Marcel Dekker, 1970), vol. 4, p. 560.
6.  Ibid.
7.  Garrison, "Women in Librarianship," p. 151.
8.  Butler, p. 561.
9.  Hennig, Margaret & Anne Jardim.  The Managerial
    Woman (Anchor, 1977), p. 185.
10. Gell, Marilyn.  "Five Women," Library Journal, Nov.
    1, 1975, p. 177-83.

GUTENBERG OR DIDEROT?

Printing as a Factor in World History*

H. D. L. Vervliet

## I. The Modern Age:  The Classical Concept

Huizinga's Waning of the Middle Ages ends somewhere in the
fifteenth century.   The title of this famous work implies the
idea of an approaching end and hence of a subsequent new
beginning.   In works of reference, in general history books,
in manuals and school-books this new beginning is called the
"Modern" Age.   From the sixth century[1] onwards until the
end of the Middle Ages the equivalents of this rather subjective term were used antithetically not, of course, to the
Middle Ages, but to antiquity; modern historical writing uses
it in what is possibly a useful and commonly accepted but
undoubtedly a purely theoretical fashion to compartmentalize
the ordered account of the long path which humanity has
travelled since its beginnings.   Generally a number of events
or occurrences are considered causatively or symptomatically
important to the new period.   The following three have practically become classics:

> a.   the voyages of discovery by the Portuguese (first
> half of the fifteenth century) and Christopher Colum-
> bus, culminating in the discovery of Central and South
> America (1492);
> b.   the collapse of the Byzantine Empire and the fall
> of Constantinople (1453);
> c.   the "great" inventions:  the compass (1269), gun-

---

*Reprinted by permission of the author and publisher from
the Winter 1978 issue of Quaerendo, pp. 3-28.

powder (thirteenth/fourteenth century), [2] and printing
(1455).


2.  The Distinguishing Marks of the Modern Age

All this--we are taught--gave rise to the partition of the old
(the Middle Ages) and the new (the Modern Age), to the creation of a new sort of society.  Historians describe the "new"
with terms like "the end of the chivalrous feudal system,"
"the inception of the modern centralized state," and "the
dawn of capitalism as an economic system"; cultural historians refer to "the entrance of individualism, the awakening
of the passion for beauty, the victory of worldliness and
joie-de-vivre, the conquest of earthly reality by the spirit,
the revival of the heathen lust for life, the new awareness
of personality."[3]  The art historian points to the reduced
importance attached to the symbolic meaning of the subject
to be depicted--this has been called the "allegorese" of
medieval thought[4]--, the beginning of the reproduction of
nature as an object, no longer as a symbol, the cult of the
humane, of the natural, the visual.  The philologist draws
attention to the revival of a purer and more general knowledge of the classical languages:  not only Latin, but also
Greek and Hebrew.  The religious historian stresses the rise
and the taking root of the Reformation.

     The more cautious writers take care to relativize the
importance of the partition:  the ways of history do not suddenly swerve; the first impulse towards the Modern Age is
to be found in the Middle Ages themselves--Petrarch, for
example, though a true representative of the fourteenth century, can hardly be called a true representative of the Middle Ages; to connect the influx of Greek scholars resulting
from the fall of the Byzantine empire with the rise of the
Renaissance and Hellenism is, in absolute terms, incorrect.
On the other hand the "modern" factors enumerated above
did not have an immediate influence from the middle of the
fifteenth century onwards.  Before the middle of the sixteenth
century the economic importance of the geographical discoveries was relatively slight; the practical military significance
of gunpowder was not really exploited until much later still, [5]
and as regards the invention of printing it has been pointed
out that in many countries the products of the early presses
tended to prolong rather than abbreviate the Middle Ages.
And if we consider interest in the natural sciences and technology to be an essential feature of modern Europe, its be-

ginning must nonetheless be clearly placed somewhere in the
seventeenth century, with people like Galileo, Francis Bacon,
Descartes, Huygens and Newton.

## 3.  The Historiography of the Modern Age

Despite these restrictions, from about the middle of the
nineteenth century there has been a growing consensus about
the essential character of any difference between the Medium
Aevum and the period which followed it.

Certain great historians may be considered to be the
standard-bearers of this historical awareness.  In general
history one thinks first and foremost of Jules Michelet (1855),
who in romantic lyrical fashion stressed the difference between the dark Middle Ages and the shining Renaissance. [6]
The historical school of Göttingen, and Ranke in particular,
confirmed Michelet's intuitions by detailing the typical structure of the newly emerging great national states and its fundamental difference from the political organization of the early
Middle Ages.

In the field of cultural history Jacob Burckhardt and
his Cultur der Renaissance in Italien (1860) are regarded as
definitive. [7]  Georg Voigt, in his famous Die Wiederbelebung
des classischen Alterthums oder das erste Jahrhundert des
Humanismus (1859), provided the scholarly substructure for
long-standing views of such as Erasmus about the renascentes
bonae litterae, [8] or of people like Rabelais on the restitution
des bonnes lettres. [9]  They thus consecrate the scholarly use
of the French word "Renaissance," a term which was unknown
to the Renaissance itself and which does not occur until 1718
in the Dictionnaire de l'Académie. [10]

## 4.  The Counter-Renaissance

The historiographical approach to the fundamental importance
of the Renaissance as the beginning of something essentially
different was not on the whole disputed, except, recently, by
the adepts of the "Counter-Renaissance." [11]  Those who doubt
whether the Renaissance can be attributed epochal significance
seem to me to occur chiefly in three fields of scholarship:
medieval history, the history of science and technology, and
economic history.

## 5.   The Medievalists

The first of these three groups is the oldest.  What Ferguson[12] called, not without justification, the "revolt of the
medievalists" began between the two World Wars.   In 1927
Charles Haskins wrote his Renaissance of the Twelfth Cen-
tury--since then it has been fashionable to place the origins
of the typical distinguishing marks of the Modern Age--its
individualism, its capitalism, and its political ideas--far
earlier than the fifteenth or sixteenth century, and indeed to
unearth them, as germs or seeds, from the thirteenth century onwards.[13]   Or as Herbert Butterfield put it in a paradox: "The Renaissance?  One of the most typically medieval things the Middle Ages ever produced."[14]

Since then it has also been possible to use the word
"Renaissance" as a generic term,[15] and to talk of a Carolingian, an Ottonian and a Byzantine renaissance.   Here
modern medievalists take a completely different line from
the nineteenth-century romanticists in their judgement of the
Middle Ages.   The romanticists admire the Middle Ages
precisely because of their differentness:  because they were
pious, irrational, idyllic, chivalrous, grotesque.   The medievalists, by contrast, stress that the Middle Ages are the
same as, related to, or the predecessor of, the Renaissance.
Huizinga called this group the "evolutionists" of the Renaissance,[16] a nice metaphor reflecting the trend to increasingly
early dating of the beginning of the Renaissance.


## 6.   The Historiography of Science

Our second group of sceptics is formed by the historians of
the natural sciences.[17]   Perhaps it was Lynn Thorndike in
his eight-volume History of Magic and Experimental Science
(1923-58) who involved himself most deeply in its criticism:
writing of the "so-called Renaissance," he decided that in
comparison with thirteenth-century scholars the followers of
Petrarch had scientifically regressed rather than progressed.
To Thorndike the Renaissance is a legend, a cultural myth.
The individualistic Renaissance tended rather to drive mankind away from a collaborative and cumulative activity which
he regards as characteristic of a scientific attitude.   For
such historians, printing, in its mechanical and technological
aspects, is scarcely an invention of importance.   The spinning-wheel, the loom, the cross-bow, spectacles, the button, the clock, the magnet and the compass are all equally

claimants to their attention.  Like printing, they are all considered very small steps in the direction of the great technological revolution of the nineteenth century.


## 7.  Economic Historiography

After the Second World War, finally, in the matter of de-
limiting the Middle Ages the Counter-Renaissance found support among the economic historians. [18]  Perhaps their findings are important enough for us to pause for a moment to
consider them.  On the strength of ever more numerous and
thorough detailed studies of the evolution of population,
prices, and manufactured goods, there is at present a tendency to suppose that history, taken as a whole--l'histoire
massive--remained virtually unchanged from about 1300 until
some time between 1700 and 1800.  This new branch of historical writing cultivates "cliometry," the use of numbers in
history.  Rather than on factual history--l'histoire évênemen-
tielle--which is concerned with facts, people, dynasties and
structures, it concentrates on "serial" history, which sub-
ordinates the individual and the unique fact to long-term
trends, long sequences within the general flow of events in
time, themselves approached and expressed chiefly in terms
of figures.  As opposed to an intuitive, "soft" approach to
history, such as that taken, shall we say, from Herodotus
to Ranke, we now have a "hard," mathematical approach
which makes use of all the latest methods culled from the
fields of statistics, sociology and probability theory.


## 8.  "L'Histoire Immobile"

"Serial" historiography is practiced first and foremost by
industrial and economic historians.  Their general thesis
was recently advanced in provocative fashion by the French
historian Emmanuel Le Roy Ladurie.  His inaugural lecture
to the Collège de France in 1974 bears the title "L'histoire
immobile."[19]  From about 1300, he suggests, thus summar-
izing several earlier studies,[20] until about 1700 the findings
of "serial" history point to a fundamental stability in demographic and economic trends--he calls this l'histoire im-
mobile--so that all dynastic, cultural and scientific facts
must be regarded as no more than insignificant ripples in an
otherwise totally flat progression.  For convenience' sake
Le Roy Ladurie confines himself to l'hexagone français, but
he asserts that his conclusions are valid for the European
macro-region.

His argumentation is based on two sets of figures:
the first is a series of population counts, the second is of
agrarian production.  Thanks to Vauban we know that the
population of France in 1700 was somewhere between nine-
teen and twenty million.  Four centuries earlier, in about
1330, the comparable figure was seventeen million--a figure
arrived at through a cumulation of many detailed regional
studies which for the most part rely on a count of house-
holds.  For four centuries, in other words, the population
growth index was more or less zero.  How did France (and
by implication the whole of western Europe) succeed in
achieving a zero growth-rate, when we ourselves know how
difficult it is to do so now?  Essentially, the answer is that
the equilibrium was the result of ecological and biological
factors which, though highly effective, were not necessarily
attractive.

One of the prime reasons, says Le Roy Ladurie, lies
in the stagnation of agricultural production.  There have been
two agricultural revolutions in Europe:  during the first, in
the eleventh and twelfth centuries, the feudal labourers of
the Middle Ages slowly but surely brought large areas of
virgin soil under cultivation; the second, which took place
during the nineteenth and twentieth centuries, was chiefly
chemical and technological in character.  From the thirteenth
to the eighteenth century grain yields, except for temporary
fluctuations, remained the same.  Consequent upon the formation of large states from the fourteenth century onwards and
the wars which in turn followed from it, the real growth
which feudalism had brought to western Europe collapsed.
From the fourteenth century onwards, Europe developed
mechanisms which checked any appreciable growth in the
population.  These mechanisms were twofold:  in the first
place there was the unification microbienne; in the second
place there was war.

Microbial equilibrium was brought about by the plague
epidemics.  A bacillary community came into being on a
world-wide scale:  the crusades, invasions by Mongols and
Turks, and trading caravans combined to spread the pandem-
ics throughout Eurasia.  The discovery of the American continent was just as important to the demographic stability of
Europe (which imported syphilis from the New World) as it
was to that of America itself (which imported smallpox from
Europe).  Syphilis destroyed the French army at the gates of
Naples; smallpox decimated the Aztec forced labourers working on the rebuilding of Tenochtitlan, the future Mexico.

This microbial equilibrium received powerful support from a second factor: war. The so-called modern state no longer wages local, feudal wars, but wars on a national or international scale. During the Middle Ages the damage inflicted by warfare remained limited: from the fourteenth century it became wholesale. Many national states were ruled by people with big teeth and small ideas. Modern war inflicts deep wounds not only in space, but also in time: wars lasted thirty, eighty, a hundred years. This is not to say that the fighting itself was necessarily particularly murderous: it was principally the indirect consequences of the hostilities, in the form of epidemics, the impoverishment of populations subjected to physical mutilation (remember Bosch and Brueghel), pillaging, and the dislocation of agrarian life, which had Malthusian effects.

The relatively small army--some eight thousand men-- which Richelieu sent through France from La Rochelle to Montferrat caused the death from the plague of something like a million Frenchmen after 1627. Few of the victims can have been aware that this was the price that had to be paid for the policies of a cardinal intent on the suppression of Protestantism. Thus to condemn war as a prime factor of destruction is to condemn the standing army and the modern state whose necessary tool it is.

This interpretation of developments in history as a whole is in direct contrast to the panegyrics to the modern state which have become a familiar note in the writings of political and "institutional" historiographers. It is admitted, to be sure, that we owe certain economic, social and cultural attainments to the modern state: nevertheless, it remains a fact that the modern state is still a military affair (more than half of government spending is on the armed forces) and that it is precisely this element which has a fundamentally destructive influence on growth. This stability on the edge of the abyss continued from the fourteenth to the eighteenth century: the discoveries of the fifteenth and sixteenth centuries, in themselves important, did not and could not do anything to change it. They did not, in fact, impinge at all on the existence of the mass of the common people. For Le Roy Ladurie the religious wars of the sixteenth century are yet further proof: a natural fate which breaks the grandly self-proclaiming growth of the Renaissance. War is the ultima ratio of the system. In the intermittent periods of peace or truce, epidemics take care of the maintenance of the ecological balance. Any upsurge in the population almost immediately corrects itself by means of infectious diseases, the necessary concomitants of an overpopulation incapable of being absorbed by the environment.

Le Roy demonstrates that it is this combination of war and disease which is responsible for the stagnation of the population and the general socio-economic situation during the long "stationary" period between 1300 and 1700--not the oft-cited famines (which are a consequence, not a cause), nor planned birth control (a technique which failed to penetrate to the mass of the people).

## 9.   Traditional Support for the Importance of Printing

From three different angles--the history of the Middle Ages, l'histoire sérielle and the history of the natural sciences and technology--the thesis has thus been undermined that the Modern Age brought with it anything that was fundamentally new.   The immediate inference, of course, is that the invention of printing, too, played no important or essential role in the course of history.   It is an unavoidable question: is the vital importance of printing in history not something which has been overrated, [21] like the Renaissance:   a legend, a myth?

Pausing for a moment before answering this question,[22] we may ask ourselves how and when printing's claims to importance first arose.   It soon emerges that an interpretation in favour of printing is far from being a relatively recent invention by romantic historians.   On the contrary, it is an opinion whose foundations lie practically as far back in time as those of printing itself.

## 10.   The Views of Printers and Publishers

It is common knowledge among those who take an interest in these matters that Gutenberg was a remarkably modest man:[23] no colophon, no printer's address, no publicity of any kind is associated with the editions ascribed to him.   His immediate successors, first his partners and later his competitors, Johannes Fust and Peter Schoeffer, are already more explicit:   from about 1465--some ten years after the presumed date of the Gutenberg Bible--we find them announcing in their colophons that printing is an ars perpulchra[24] or an ars nova imprimendi seu caracterizandi.[25]

The Italian testimonies are more extrovert: for the
publisher of the <u>Epistolae</u> of Jerome[26] in 1468, the humanist
Johannes Andreas de Bussi, secretary to Nicolaus de Cusa[27]
and later librarian to the Vatican, printing is of divine origin: "In our time gave Christendom a gift which enables
even the pauper to acquire books."[28]  In his edition of Pliny
in 1471 Lodovico Carbo chants the praises of the invention of
printing and proclaims its importance for the new flourishing
of scholarship and science; to Nicolao Gupalatino (in his edition of Mesue, Venice, c. 1471) printing was the means of
receiving and preserving knowledge.[29]  During this same
early period, around 1470, the Parisian prototypographer
Guillaume Fichet repeatedly expressed his opinions about the
importance of the new art.  In a poem in <u>fine</u> of Barzizza's
<u>Epistolae</u>[30] he refers to an <u>ars prope divina.</u>  In the intro-
duction printing is associated with the great work of redis-
covering the Latin authors[31]--one of the first occasions on
which humanism and textual criticism are associated with
the new art.  In the following year, 1471, he published the
<u>Orthographia,</u> by the same Barzizza.[32]  In his dedication to
Robert Gaguin, Fichet acknowledges the importance of printing for the spread of knowledge: "Gutenberg gave us letters
with which all sayings and all thoughts can be written, re-
written and handed down to posterity."[33]


11.  <u>Men of Letters as Advocates</u>

Such praise may have a somewhat suspicious sound, coming
as it does from convinced and materially interested practitioners of the new art.  But outside the relatively narrow
circles of printers and publishers, too, there was a conviction that printing was something not of the ordinary.  In
1498 Sebastian Brant, the creator of the famous <u>Narrenschiff,</u>
wrote the following verse:

> Was sonst nur der Reiche von einst und der König
>     zu eigen besessen,
> Findet sich jetzt überall auch in der Hütte, ein
>     Buch.
> Dank d'rum den Göttern zunächst, doch billigen
>     Dank auch den Druckern,
> Den ihrem Geist zuerst hat diese Bahn sich gezeigt,
> Was den weisen Griechen und den findigen Römern,
> Diese Erfindung von jetzt stammt aus germanischen
>     Geist.[34]

In the sixteenth century, printing--as a historical

phenomenon--aroused interest in three quarters:   first,
among authors, especially humanists; second, among the
supporters of Protestantism; and third, among the "Moderns," in their Querelle des Anciens et des Modernes--this
last discussion eventually turning into a call for a western
European scholarship.

Erasmus's praise of Aldus Manutius[35] is well known:
"Should one desire to compare the services done to scholarship by the princes," he writes in the Adagia (II, 1. 1), "the
highest praise must be accorded to Ptolemy.   Yet his library
was limited by the narrow walls of his palace:  but Aldus
builds a library limited only by the frontiers of the world
itself."   And he continues:  "If Aldus is permitted to work
for a further few years, every scholar will have scientifically perfect editions of all good authors, and that in four languages:   Latin, Greek, Hebrew and Aramaic."

For the sake of utter veracity it should be pointed
out that this passage is accompanied by an attack on the bad
printers who, for paltry gain, put texts on the market which
are full of mistakes.   Nevertheless, Erasmus has here
sensed the essential difference between a scriptural, restricted form of communication and a typographical communication
which could make world-wide distribution possible.

For Erasmus's contemporary and friend Thomas More
printing and paper were so important that he found them
worthy not only of acceptance by the Utopians but also of
virtual re-invention by them:

> Thus, trained in all learning, the minds of the
> Utopians are exceedingly apt in the invention of the
> arts which promote the advantage and convenience
> of life.   Two, however, they owe to us, the art of
> printing and the manufacture of paper--though not
> entirely to us but to a great extent also to them-
> selves.   When we showed them the Aldine printing
> in paper books, we talked about the material of
> which paper is made and the art of printing with-
> out giving a detailed explanation, for none of us
> was expert in either art.   With the greatest acute-
> ness they promptly guessed how it was done.
> Though previously they wrote only on parchment,
> bark, and papyrus, from this time they tried to
> manufacture paper and print letters.   Their first
> attempts were not very successful, but by frequent

experiment they soon mastered both.   So great was
their success that if they had copies of Greek authors, they would have no lack of books.   But at
present they have no more than I have mentioned,
but by printing books they have increased their
stock by many thousands of copies. [36]

Writing to his son Pantagruel from Utopia, Gargantua expresses the analogous opinion of Rabelais:

> Maintenant toutes disciplines sont restituées, les
> langues instaurées:  grecque, sans laquelle c'est
> honte que une personne se die sçavant, hébraïcque,
> caldaïcque, latine; les impressions tant élégantes
> et correctes en usance, qui ont esté inventées de
> mon eage par inspiration divine, comme à contrefil
> l'artillerie par suggestion diabolicque.   Tout le
> monde est plein de gens savans, de précepteurs
> très doctes, de librairies très amples, et m'est
> advis que, ny au temps de Platon, ny de Cicéron,
> ny de Papinian, n'estoit telle commodité d'estude
> qu'on y veoit maintenant, et ne se fauldra plus
> doresnavant trouver en place ny en compaignie,
> qui ne sera bien expoly en l'officine de Minerve.
> Je voy les brigans, les boureaulx, les avanturiers,
> les palefreniers de maintenant, plus doctes que les
> docteurs et prescheurs de mon temps.   Que diray-
> je?   Les femmes et les filles ont aspiré à ceste
> louange et manne céleste de bonne doctrine. [37]

## 12.   The Reformers' View

The role which printing played in the spread of the Reformation is well known.   Not without justification, Luther has been
described as the first journalist. [38]   In his hands printing
developed from a peaceable love of art or money into an
instrument of aggression for the eradication of the papacy,
granted by God himself as the "highest and extremest act of
grace, whereby the business of the Gospel is driven forward;
it is the last flame before the extinction of the world. "[39]
The great appreciation which printing found among Protestants
was spread further in the middle of the sixteenth century by
the English historian and martyrologist John Foxe.   To him
it was "a divine and miraculous invention. "   There is an
equation between knowledge and printing:

> The Lord began to work for his church ... with

> printing, writing, reading.... How many presses
> there be in the world, so many blockhouses there
> be against the high castle of S. Angelo, so that
> either the pope must abolish knowledge and print-
> ing, or printing must at length root him out. [40]

Since then the great part played by printing has become a
locus communis in the historiography of the Reformation and
the religious wars. As regards the Netherlands, attention
was drawn to this by as early a writer as Hooft,[41] and
Schiller was eloquent in following his example: "Durch
dieses Organ sprach ein einziger unruhiger Kopf zu
Millionen."[42] Some decades later Victor Hugo has the hero
of Notre Dame de Paris pointing to an incunabulum and then
to the cathedral and declaring to Louis XI: "Ceci tuera
cela."[43]

## 13. The Moderns

The last school of thought which attached great importance
to the value of printing comprises the "Moderns" in the
famous "Querelle des Anciens et des Modernes." This had
its origins in the Questione della lingua whereby the new
Italy, aroused by Dante's De vulgari eloquentia, searched for
a new language between Latin and the numerous Italian dialects.[44] Its French counterpart, the Querelle des Anciens
et des Modernes, laid a constant emphasis on the originality
of new inventions:[45] it was the "Modernes" who kept alive
the story of the importance of printing. To them, inventions
were important as witnesses to the value, or rather the
equality, and later the superiority of modern man compared
to the ancients. This argument was used very early, in
1499, in De rerum inventoribus by Polydore Vergil, an
Italian contemporary of Erasmus who was in effect the first
historian of science and who later went into exile at the
court of Henry VIII.[46] The excellence of the great libraries
of Hellas and Rome cannot be compared, he asserts, with an
invention of his own times, viz. a new manner of writing
whereby in one day by one man more can be produced than
formerly by many scribes in a whole year. Joachim du
Bellay, in 1549, endorses this view completely: "l'imprimerie ...," he writes in his Deffence et illustration de
la langue francoyse,[47] "avec tant d'autres non antiques
inventions ... montrent que ... les esprits des hommes ne
sont point si abatardiz qu'on voudroit bien dire." A year
later, in 1550, Girolamo Cardano, the Italian physician and

humanist, was of the opinion that "antiquitas nihil par habet."[48]

Possibly the most pronounced expression of praise came from the sixteenth-century historian Louis Le Roy, or Ludovicus Regius, who was in fact one of our first historians of civilization (c. 1510-77). A pupil of Guillaume Budé, he was lector regius or professor of Greek at the Collège de France. The main title of his work is De la vicissitude ou variété des choses en l'univers; it appeared in 1575. Regius reveals himself as a resolute opponent of the old wisdom of Solomon, "Nil novi sub sole," and of the static view of history; he also rejected the regressive theory, that of the Golden Age, expressed in verse by Ovid and later by D'Urfé, by the pastoral poets, and by Rousseau. To be sure, he is full of sympathy and admiration for the achievements of the ancients, of Islam; but there is no period which arouses his enthusiastic admiration more than his own period, the Renaissance. To him, the progress which has been made during his own time is manifest:

> Dauantage la Theologie plus digne de toutes qui sembloit aneantie par Les Sophistes, a esté grandement illustrée par la cognoissance de l'Hebrieu & du Grec, & les anciens docteurs de l'Eglise qui perissoient és librairies, mis en evidence. En laquelle oeuvre l'imprimerie a porté grand ayde, & rendu l'accroissement plus facile ... [49]

Elsewhere he confirms:

> Car depuis cent ans, non seulement les choses qui étoient auparavant couvertes par les ténèbres de l'ignorance sont venues en évidence, mais aussi plusieurs autres choses ont été connues, qui avoient été entièrement ignorées des anciens: nouvelles mers, nouvelles terres, nouvelles façons d'hommes, moeurs, lois, coutumes, nouvelles herbes ... arbres ... minéraux ... nouvelles inventions trouvées, comme celles de l'imprimerie, l'artillerie et l'usage de l'aiguille et de l'aimant pour les navigations ... des anciennes langues restituées ... [50]

He also gives a detailed description of printing, including punch-cutting and type-founding, which appears to have escaped the notice of the majority of book historians. [51]

These views of the Moderns are not exceptional.
Jerome Cardan, Petrus Ramus and Guillaume Postel formed
in their turn the "theory of progress" and described the role
which discoveries and inventions, especially that of printing,
play in it. [52]   As regards their attitude to the old and the
new, their ideas were directly opposed, for example, to those
of the fourteenth-century bibliophile Richard de Bury, viz.
"that their [i. e. the ancients'] successors scarce suffice to
discuss the attainments of those that went before them or to
receive even through a compend of their doctrine what the
ancients produced by prolonged investigation."[53]

Early in the seventh century Francis Bacon summarized these judgements (prejudices?) in favour of printing
most forcefully in the 129th aphorism of his Novum organon
(1620):

> Again, it is well to observe the force and virtue
> and consequences of discoveries, and these are to
> be seen nowhere more conspicuously than in those
> three which were unknown to the ancients, and of
> which the origin, though recent, is obscure and
> inglorious; namely, printing, gunpowder, and the
> magnet.   For these have changed the whole face
> and state of things throughout the world; the first
> in literature, the second in warfare, the third in
> navigation; whence have followed innumerable
> changes, insomuch that no empire, no sect, no
> star seems to have exerted greater power and in-
> fluence in human affairs than these mechanical
> discoveries. [54]

## 14.   Scribal and Typographic Communication

Is there any benefit to be had from wondering, in a sort of
inverted science fiction, what our society would look like
without printing?   Is such a question just as pointless as
that which Trevelyan asked himself in his essay "If Napoleon had won the Battle of Waterloo"?[55]   I shall not embark
upon such an exercise; but I will pause a while to look at
what seems to me to be the essence of the historical significance of printing.

From a global point of view the history of printing is
part of the history of human communication.   There is no
doubt that it is not written but spoken language that is both

the oldest and the most used means of communication of
_Homo_ _sapiens_.   The two other important forms of communi-
cation--gestures and writing--certainly play a clearly sub-
ordinate role in terms of quantity.   Equally, however, it
would. seem to be incontestable that the rapid development
which mankind has experienced during the post-oral era--
roughly during the past five thousand years--has been fundamentally influenced by the novel techniques with which man
has equipped himself:  means whereby individual memory and
personal experience could be expanded into collective memory and communal experience which would cross the frontiers
first of groups, tribes, nations, and later of generations.
In the unfolding history of civilization major roles have been
played by techniques first of conservation, later of distribution, of human communication.   The post-oral history of
communication is distinguished by three great moments:
first, the invention of writing in the third millennium B. C.
in Sumer and Egypt, and a millennium later in China; second, the invention of letters, i. e. the alphabet, in Phoenicia,
somewhere in the second millennium B. C.; finally, the invention of printing, now half a millennium ago.   Each of
these moments meant a great leap forward in mankind's
memory capacity and hence in man's capacity for taking
decisions.

     Seen in this perspective the traditional western divi-
sion of history into four periods of equal importance, antiquity, the Middle Ages, the Modern Age, and the present,
is scarcely a tenable proposition.   But to see the Modern
Age as a new beginning does appear to be justifiable.   In
the fifteenth century a fault-line develops between the post-
oral, i. e. the scribal, and the post-scribal, i. e. the typographic, eras--in fact, between two periods with, as regards
intellect and scholarship, two completely different systems
of communication.

     To simplify matters and look only at the general out-
line, we may describe oral communication as a one-dimen-
sional, linear phenomenon of the simple development and
conclusion of a communication.   It is of secondary importance
whether that communication takes place between two people
or between a larger number.   The scribal stage adds a second dimension, viz. fixation of the communication.   The
typographic stage, finally, amplifies the system with a third
dimension, viz. diffusion.   Regarded in this light, the Middle Ages are seen to be the end of ancient civilization rather
than the hesitant beginning of the modern.

Our own traditional methods of diffusion (we might
equally well use the term publication, if we bear in mind
that this must include not only the functions of the publisher
himself but also the entire process of distribution from publisher through printer to bookshop and library) are labour-
intensive in the extreme.   In recent times they have come
under pressure from new and more cost-effective techniques,
such as the "publication on demand" system.   At the same
time, more and more data, statistics and reports are being
stored, unpublished, in computers to which only those fortunate enough to possess the knowledge necessary for the operation of a highly expensive and sophisticated technology
have access.   Now that we can see all this happening, perhaps it will be useful to pay some attention to the essential
difference between a scribal civilization--one characterized
by a total or almost total lack of diffusion--and a typographical, and hence widely diffused, communicative society.

## 15.   The Role of Printing in Post-Scribal Communication

Printing brought with it the end of what might be termed the
feudality of knowledge.   A scribal society preserves the
products of its minds and simultaneously locks them away in
the limitations of the manuscript, which frequently acquires
all the features of a unicum even if, in objective terms, it
is no such thing; it is kept carefully, because of its preciousness, in an ambry, scriptorium, or library.   In contrast,
printing emphasizes the triviality of the written word.   The
aspect of preciousness is pushed aside.   During the manuscript Middle Ages the value of a well produced book was
the equivalent of half the annual stipend paid to a skilled
craftsman; in the sixteenth century it represented no more
than a day and a half or two days' work.   In the Middle
Ages, communication by manuscript was unable to become
one of the major tools of scholarship--at least, not if one
considers scholarship to be something built up stone by stone
from the discoveries and attainments of successive generations. [56]   It was printing that made a permanent Renaissance
possible:   without it, the western Renaissance would have
been doomed to disappear after a few generations, just as
the renaissances of the Ptolemaic, the Carolingian and the
Macedonian-Byzantine empires all faded away without any
permanent form of transmission. [57]   It was printing that developed Petrarch's brain-child into a progression which
transcended the centuries; just as the lack of a printing tradition consigned most of Leonardo da Vinci's inventions to
oblivion until the nineteenth century.

Printing gave <u>Homo</u> <u>sapiens</u> the means whereby he could raise himself to the level of a <u>Homo</u> <u>conscius</u> (literally, man who knows with others) who could compare and appreciate critically, who could look around him, even backwards, and who could build on a collection of data which exceeded a hundred or a thousand times the richest medieval library (some tens or hundreds of volumes). In Erasmus's time it made possible a "university without walls," just as now it helps to create the "invisible college," the fine wiring of unofficial information-transference between those at the top of every branch of scholarship. In fact, the worldwide diffusion of a message guarantees not only the permanence of knowledge and culture but also their continued cooperative or antagonistic development.

<u>Homo</u> <u>conscius</u> was aware that his time was different. Vision in perspective was not only an attainment of the artistic, geometric and geographic Renaissance, it was also present in the existential insight possessed by fifteenth-century and sixteenth-century man. Joannes Trithemius, the father of modern bibliography, points to this element; so does Ludovicus Regius, the humanist referred to earlier. [58] It is also present in the work of Petrus Ramus, the French philologist and philosopher and distant forerunner of McLuhan who was possibly the first to observe the transition from the old dialogizing, oral type of transmission of ideas to the new visual model inherent in printing. [59]

## 16. Economic Aspects of Diffusion

The diffusing character of printing has had far-reaching effects in uncoupling written communication from religion, in standardizing it and in enhancing men's critical faculties; these elements were either lacking or present in a different form in antiquity and the Middle Ages.

The diffusion itself is inherent in the technology of early-chemical-mechanical printing:[60] after the costs incurred in printing the first copy, the costs accruing for subsequent copies diminish progressively. As the average impression rose from a hundred or two hundred copies in the middle of the fifteenth century to ten times that number at the beginning of the sixteenth, so the price of each copy fell rapidly. A familiar example will serve as an illustration: in 1466 a German bible cost twelve guilders, in 1470 nine, in 1483 six, and in 1510 less than one guilder. [61]

Certainly, there are objections to attempting to compare
these prices with those charged for manuscripts: they could
vary so much in the lavishness of their decoration and so
on. The story told by Giovanni Andrea de Bussi, the proof-
reader at the first press in Rome, mentions, however, that
in 1470 a book which normally cost a hundred guilders could
now be had for twenty. The fall in prices gave an unfore-
seen impulse to the commercialization and laicization of the
largely sacred object which the book had been hitherto.

It is undoubtedly true that the rise in literacy among
non-clerics was not a phenomenon which was caused by
printing. Perhaps, indeed, the converse was the case. Attention has rightly been drawn to the formation and multiplication of medieval universities and chancelleries, the upsurge
in trade and commerce, the need for book-keeping, and the
spread of popular devotion, all of which led to literacy
spreading outside the circles of the clergy. [62] The oral era,
the age of the minnesingers and troubadours, of preaching,
of reading aloud, was clearly on the wane from the fourteenth
century onwards. [63]

## 17. The Secularization of the Scriptorium

Frequently, and with good reason, attention has been drawn
to the role played in the Netherlands and Germany by the
Brethren of the Common Life. Their objective was by teaching and providing reading-matter--the pulpit was often denied
them because of their status as laymen--to maintain religious
and moral traditions. Here there is a paradox, for at one
and the same time they both smoothed the way for printing,
by promoting private, individual reading, and laid obstacles
in its path, by reintroducing a form of scriptorium which had
effectively died out more than a century previously, i.e. the
monastic scriptorium. Certainly, the Brethren did their
writing "pro domo et pro pretio," for their own use and to
order: but they also did it quite in the spirit of the scholas-
tic view of the acceptability of reward and the impropriety
of profit; they worked, without explicitly seeking monetary
gain, sub specie aeternitatis. In the light of economic history their high-minded penmanship had been completely superseded when the new orders of the thirteenth century--the
Dominicans and Franciscans--abandoned the old Benedictine
ideal of work and writing and concentrated their efforts on
preaching and teaching. In the scriptoria of the new universities non-clerics took the place of monks and friars, who

went off to seek salvation in other ways than writing. [64]
Over half a century before Gutenberg the university scriptoria and the bibliophile and, a little later, the humanist scriptoria, all of which operated on a commercial basis, were in
full swing. [65] It was they, and not the followers of Geert
Groote, who provided the immediate stimulus for the invention of printing.

Publishing, as we know it from the middle of the
fifteenth century, was at this time undoubtedly still completely in statu nascentis[66]--one only has to think of the Burgundi-
an and Florentine scriptoria, for example, or a manuscript
publishing-house such as that of Dietbold Lauber in the
Alsace[67]--but at any rate the production, reproduction and
sale of books was taken out of the church's sphere of influence and passed into that of commerce and later of industry.


## 18.   Johannes Gutenberg von Gensfleisch

Technological inventions frequently come about when an individual (or a group of individuals) assumes that the expected
gains are greater than the costs of realizing a change. [68]
An essential element in the invention of printing was the fact
that since the fourteenth century the book in France, the
Rhineland, and Italy, had been secularized and absorbed into
commercial life, into a context of money, investment, and
profit.   With hindsight it is easy to say that this condition
had already been created in the Strasburg of 1440 and the
Mainz of 1450:  history will not deny it.   But if we pay
some attention to the archival documents and records per-
taining to the invention of printing, it soon becomes clear
that Gutenberg was far from being the only possible inventor, inspired by a divine genius.   The cult of personality,
and the cult of the unique fact, with which Clio sometimes
blinds her admirers, has long concealed the fact that Gutenberg was first and foremost an inventor, not a printer:
certainly, he was obsessed, but not by the idea of printing.
His concern was with more general problems to do with
mechanical and metallurgical mass-production.   Proof of
this is found in the experiments which he conducted, before
the invention of printing, designed to start up industrial
production of mirrors cast in lead and intended for mass
sales on pilgrimages such as that to Aix-la-Chapelle in
1439. [69] The plan failed:  and it may have been partly because of that, and in the same context, that the idea was
formed to do something about the laborious manual copying

of the indulgences which were sold at such places in such
vast numbers.  This being so, it is clear that in its turn
printing helped to bring about the further secularization of
books on a scale which could hardly remain without consequence for European civilization.  The ecumenism of the
Latin Church, fundamentally unbroken by Lollards, Albi-
genses and Hussites, now shattered in its own Great Schism
under the pressure of printed Lutheran and Calvinist writings whose success could not be prevented even by the newly
emerging censorship.

The secularization of the book was a Greek and Roman phenomenon which had failed to survive beyond antiquity.  The Middle Ages and Islam turned back to the oriental
view of the holy status of the Book. [70]  The late Middle
Ages, and in particular the Renaissance with its printing,
turned back again to the laicizing cultural phenomenon of
antiquity.  As with all social processes, the new was slow
to oust the old, and the old sacred character seems still to
survive in what sociology calls the "cultural stigma" of the
world of books. [71]  At the same time this "cultural stigma"
explains the high opinion which many insiders have of themselves (publishing and bookselling is "an occupation for
gentlemen") and the reputation for conservatism which publishers, booksellers, and librarians often seem to have
among outsiders.

It was not entirely fortuitous that this secularization--
in chronological terms--occurred at a time when in the first
place medieval craftsmen were beginning to master a number
of metallurgical skills, [72] and when in the second place the
more or less unlimited availability of paper made possible
the breakthrough of printing in economic terms. [73]  But it
would be a mistake to exaggerate this mechanistic approach:
to trace the invention of printing back to the introduction of
the spinning-wheel into Europe sometime in the eleventh century or to the subsequent increase in the production of linen,
the raw material for paper, [74] or to see it as a further development of the invention of oil paint in the twelfth or thirteenth century, and of oil-based ink, [75] may not, in certain
contexts, be inaccurate; but it would be to miss the essential
quality of the true innovation that printing was.


19.   Printing and Standardization

Another consequence of the secularization of books was the

fixing of the national languages and the end of Latin as the common language of scholarship and science. Linguistically, printing has played a paradoxical role in that it first led to a clear advancement of the vernacular at the cost of Latin as the means of scholarly communication, and then brought about the regeneration of the internationality of the language of science--this time by promoting more modern languages: first French, later English.

The French, English and German orthographies all owe their standardization to printing. [76] The English noorse, servaunt finally become nurse, servant; French excripture, jeusne become écriture, jeune. As regards French, both Plantin and the Elzevirs played their part in this evolution. In 1663 Corneille demanded the use of the "lettres hollandaises" (v and j instead of u and i). Diffusion on the micro-plane of the national language was brought about partly by the Reformation's standpoint on the use of the vernacular, and partly, viz. in the Romance languages, by the self-confidence of fifteenth-century Florence and following on from that, the italianizing Pleiade in sixteenth-century France. All languages owe the standardization of their punctuation to printing and to the fact that reading aloud was superseded by silent reading.

On the plane of the universal language of communication, Latin remained the undisputed world leader during the sixteenth century. Copernicus, Vesalius and Kepler all published in Latin. Simon Stevin, however, used the vernacular in his military manuals for Prince Maurice and the Military Academy of the Netherlands. During the next century there was rivalry between various languages in the world of scholarship and science: Grotius, Harvey, Van Helmont, Comenius, Spinoza, Huygens, Leibniz, Newton and Van Leeuwenhoek still published all or most of their work in Latin, but Galileo, Boyle, Descartes and Locke were already beginning to proclaim the supremacy of the national languages, even in science. [77]

In the course of its first century, printing also standardized its outward appearance. In the case of types, the sixteenth century brought the end of the use of the widely varying gothics, at least as far as the world languages, Latin, French and English, were concerned. Gothics continued to be used, however, in chapbooks and in locally bound religious literature. During the second half of the sixteenth century it was superseded by roman and italic, the

two sorts of type still favoured today.   By way of Italy and
its book-keeping system, Arabic numerals spread throughout
Europe, though the basic arithmetical notation (the simple
and unambiguous convention of $+ - \times \div =$ ) did not find final
acceptance until the seventeenth century. [78]  Here too, diffusion brought standardization, and standardization intellectual
progress.

## 20.   Printing as an Instrument of the Critical Faculty

Another, final, aspect of printing is the broadening of the
critical faculty, [79] or, as Baron put it, the rise of "a new
type of thinking. "[80]   The omnipresence and the very economics of printing put an end to a dual evil:   first, that of
epitomization--the abstraction of texts which often led by
way of abridgement to the suppression of the original, an
understandable but pernicious habit of the copyists of the
manuscript era. [81]  Without printing, the enthusiastic humanistic "ad fontes" would soon have succumbed through the
copyist's fatigue.   Second, that of the usurpation and blurring
of authorship.   It is the lack of controls, of an opportunity
for checking, rather than vulgar plagiarism, that is the chief
cause of so many erroneous or incomplete ascriptions. [82]
The constant accessibility of many--often contradictory--au-
thors and authorities teaches the modern reader a sense of
perspective:   he becomes sensitive to the contradictions in
the vast volume of written work to which he is now multi-
fariously, en masse, and visually exposed. [83]  The magic of
the scriptural begins to collapse.   Faith, the philosophy par
excellence of the Middle Ages, fades. [84]

   The sixteenth-century conflict of strict Ciceronianism
and the eclecticism of Erasmus was merely a preliminary
exercise of the constant sharpening of the critical faculty
which was to follow:   later generations fell to attacking
other authorities than the merely literary.   Can we even
guess at the revolution caused by the twenty or thirty million printed copies which the presses distributed during the
first half-century of the existence of typography, to the
limited numbers of inhabitants and readers of western Europe? [85]  In the following century this number was to increase
tenfold.   An example may help to illustrate this.   Two hundred and twenty-eight manuscript copies of Alexander de
Villa Dei's famous rhymed Latin grammar are known to
exist.   Possibly there were at one time ten times that num-
ber--say two thousand copies--for a period of some two and

a half centuries.  At the same time there are two hundred
and seventy-nine incunabular editions of this work, representing some three hundred thousand copies for the requirements of half a century. [86]  For his development into <u>Homo
conscius</u>, <u>Homo typographicus</u> has invented aids unknown to
his predecessor of the scribal age:  the title-page, which
establishes author and edition, and pagination. [87]  Taken
together, these two devices make possible exact references
to particular parts of any given author's work.  The exact
reference--quite different from the mere name of the author
or the even vaguer "ille auctor," or "ut aiunt," or "quidam
tradunt"--is a direct consequence of the general availability
of books and has at the same time brought about the necessary conditions for the critical study and use of the work of
others. [88]

## 21.  Printing and Progress

There is absolutely no doubt but that the beginnings of printing were founded on medieval conditions, that the new art
flourished initially on techniques and customs which were
already present in the scriptoria, that in the beginning it
produced texts which were not materially different from those
of the previous generation.  Nevertheless it is a fact that
printing and perhaps printing alone made literacy, i.e. reading and self-education, such a stable and widespread element
of people's lives and such a social power in western society
that from the eighteenth century onwards a general improvement in the material and cultural living conditions of the
common man became possible. [89]  Its vital influence may be
judged from a comparison with those civilizations which in
the fourteenth and fifteenth centuries had reached an unmistakably higher plane than those in the west--the Chinese,
for example, or Islam--but which then, for linguistic or
religious reasons, failed to accept printing.  In Europe, by
contrast, the pressure of the printed word led during the
seventeenth and eighteenth centuries to the gradual rise of
the technological, political and cultural preconditions whereby it became possible for the West to break through the historical strait-jacket of zero population growth. [90]

Historians, who themselves say that they can find no
economic or technological explanation for European supremacy
from the sixteenth to the nineteenth century, are possibly
wrong to pass by the abstract yet real significance of information technology, i.e. the importance of communication be-

tween scholars and scientists and the role which printing
played in it. [91]   Its working to the advantage of an improved
and more intense communication ought, indeed, to be recognized as more important than the effects of the wholesale
emigrations of craftsmen and scholars, however far-reaching
and significant they may have been, in this period of religious
persecution. [92]

We stand here before a virtually unexplored and un-
exploited field of study:  the evolution of the distribution of
information; the "information gap" between the "information-
rich" and the "information-poor"; the balance between centralized, controlled information (censorship, legal deposit,
etc.) and information generated at the local, decentralized
level (pamphlets, the freedom of the press, etc.)--subjects
which in the present context of the technological changes in
information distribution are not without their importance. [93]

As a symbol of this maturation of western critical
and technological thought, founded on the secularizing technology of printing, the title of my lecture refers to Diderot.
It might equally have referred to "Encyclopédie," or "Enlightenment," or "Royal Society," or "Journal des sçavans,"
or "Philosophical Transactions"; or simply to the first newspapers, which, three and a half centuries ago now, helped to
play a part, in Amsterdam as elsewhere, in the progress of
human knowledge.

## References

1.   The term was first used by Priscian and Cassiodorus;
     cf. Forcellini, Lexicon totius Latinitatis, s. v.

2.   G. Sarton, Introduction to the History of Science,
     vol. ii, pt. 2 (Baltimore 1931), pp. 1030-1 and 1036-7.

3.   J. Huizinga, "Het probleem der Renaissance," in:
     Verzamelde werken, vol. iv (Haarlem 1949), p. 231.

4.   S. Dresden, "De betekenis van het boek in het
     humanisme," in:  Forum der letteren, 7 (1966), p. 219.

5.   T. Esper, "The Replacement of the Longbow by Fire-
     arms in the English Army," in:  Technology and Culture,
     6 (1965), p. 393; for a long time the cannon remained
     less effective than the perfected medieval "trébuchet";

Lipsius (d. 1606) calls the cannon a bird-scarer (De militia romana, lib. v, 20), a judgement applauded by Benjamin Franklin as late as 1776. Cf. G. Sarton, Introduction to the History of Science, vol. iii, pt. 2 (Baltimore 1948), pp. 1548-50.

6.  H. Butterfield, Man on his Past: the Study of the History of Historical Scholarship (Cambridge 1955), pp. 130-4; Huizinga, op. cit., pp. 242-3; H. Spangenberg, "Die Perioden der Weltgeschichte," in: Historische Zeitschrift, 127 (1922-3), pp. 1-49.

7.  J. Huizinga, op. cit., pp. 244-9.

8.  J. Huizinga, Erasmus (Haarlem 1947), p. 111.

9.  J. Huizinga, "Probleem der Renaissance," p. 233; W. K. Ferguson, The Renaissance in Historical Thought: Five Centuries of Interpretation (Cambridge, Mass. 1948), pp. 30-1; H. Hornik, "Three Interpretations of the French Renaissance," in: Studies in the Renaissance, 7 (1960), pp. 43-66; H. Weisinger, "Renaissance Accounts of the Revival of Learning," in: Studies in Philology, 45 (1948), pp. 105-18; D. Hay (ed.), The Renaissance Debate (Huntington 1976).

10.  J. Plattard, "Restitution des bonnes lettres et Renaissance," in: Mélanges offertes par ses amis et élèves à M. Gustave Lanson (Paris 1922), pp. 128-31; J. Trier, "Zur Vorgeschichte des Renaissance-Begriffes," in: Archiv für Kulturgeschichte, 32 (1950), pp. 45-63.

11.  A term borrowed from the history of art (e. g. H. Haydn, The Counter-Renaissance (New York 1950)), but here used in a purely historiographical sense.

12.  The Renaissance in Historical Thought, pp. 330-85.

13.  C. Neumann, "Ende des Mittelalters? Legende der Ablösung des Mittelalters durch die Renaissance," in: Deutsche Vierteljahrschrift für Literaturwissenschaft und Geistesgeschichte, 12 (1934), pp. 124-71.

14.  H. Brown, "The Renaissance and the Historians of Science," in: Studies in the Renaissance, 7 (1960), pp. 27-42 (quotation on p. 29).

15. E. Panofsky, Renaissance and Renascences in Western Art (Stockholm 1950).

16. "Het probleem der Renaissance," p. 249.

17. H. Brown, "The Renaissance and the Historians of Science," in: Studies in the Renaissance, 7 (1960), pp. 27-42.

18. W. K. Ferguson, "Recent Trends in the Economic Historiography of the Renaissance," in: Studies in the Renaissance, 7 (1960), pp. 7-26.

19. E. Le Roy Ladurie, "L'histoire immobile," in: Annales: économies, sociétés, civilisations, 29 (1974), pp. 673-92.

20. W. K. Ferguson, op. cit. (see n. 18 above).

21. The New Cambridge Modern History, vol. i (Cambridge 1971), p. 4.

22. E. Eisenstein has written widely and with penetration on this subject, e. g. "Some Conjectures about the Impact of Printing on Western Society and Thought: a Preliminary Report," in: Journal of Modern History, 40 (1968), pp. 1-56; "The Advent of Printing and the Problem of the Renaissance," in: Past and Present, 45 (1969), pp. 19-89; "The Advent of Printing in Current Historical Literature: Notes and Comments on an Elusive Transformation," in: American Historical Review, 75 (1970), pp. 727-43; "L'avènement de l'imprimerie et la Réforme," in: Annales: économies, sociétés, civilisations, 26 (1971), pp. 1355-82 (published in English under the title: "The Advent of Printing and the Protestant Revolt: a New Approach to the Disruption of Western Christendom," in: Transition and Revolution, ed. R. M. Kingdom (Minneapolis 1974), p. 235-72).

23. H. Widmann, "Gutenberg in Urteil der Nachwelt," in: Der gegenwärtige Stand der Gutenberg-Forschung (Stuttgart 1972), pp. 250-72.

24. Cicero, De officiis, 1465 (GW 6921); id., 1466 (GW 6922).

25. Donatus, Ars minor, 1468-9 (GW 8718).

26.  BMC, pt. iv, p. 5.

27.  E. J. Kenney, The Classical Text:  Aspects of Editing
     in the Age of the Printed Book (Berkeley 1974),
     pp. 12-15.

28.  R. Hirsch, Printing, Selling and Reading, 1450-1550
     (Wiesbaden 1974), p. 1.

29.  K. Schottenloher, Bücher bewegten die Welt:  eine
     Kulturgeschichte des Buches, vol. i (Stuttgart 1951),
     pp. 114-15.

30.  GW 3675.

31.  Redintegrandis etiam latinis scriptoribus insignem
     operam navas.

32.  GW 3691.

33.  F. Pfaff, "Guillaume Fichets Brief über die Erfindung
     der Buchdruckerkunst," in:  Centralblatt für
     Bibliothekswesen, 5 (1888), pp. 201-6.

34.  K. Schottenloher, op. cit., p. 115.

35.  D. J. Geneakoplos, "Erasmus and the Aldine Academy
     of Venice:  a neglected chapter in the transmission of
     Graeco-Byzantine learning to the West," in:  Greek,
     Roman, and Byzantine Studies, 3 (1960), pp. 107-34.

36.  Thomas More, Utopia (Yale edn., 1965), pp. 182-4.

37.  F. Rabelais, Pantagruel, vol. ii, pt. 8 (Pléiade edn.,
     1970), pp. 204-5.

38.  L. W. Holborn, "Printing and the Growth of a Protes-
     tant Movement in Germany from 1517 to 1524," in:
     Church History, 11 (1942), pp. 123-37; M. H. Black,
     "The Printed Bible," in:  The Cambridge History of
     the Bible, ed. S. L. Greenslade (Cambridge 1963),
     pp. 408-75; E. L. Eisenstein, "Protestant Revolt" (see
     n. 22 above), pp. 235-72.

39.  Black, art. cit., p. 432.

40.  Ferguson, Renaissance, pp. 54-5; Eisenstein, Protes-
     tant Revolt, p. 237.

41.  P. C. Hooft, Alle de gedrukte werken (ed. W. Hellinga and P. Tuynman, 1972), pp. 211-12.

42.  Fr. von Schiller, Geschichte des Abfalls der Vereinigten Niederlanden von der spanischen Regierung (edn. München 1922), pp. 100-1.

43.  V. Hugo, Notre Dame de Paris (edn. Garnier, 1959), p. 208.

44.  C. Grayson, A Renaissance Controversy: Latin or Italian? (Oxford 1960); Geschichte der Textürberlieferung der antiken und mittelalterlichen Literatur; vol. ii (Zürich 1964), p. 441.

45.  R. S. Wolper, "The Rhetoric of Gunpowder and the Idea of Progress," in: Journal of the History of Ideas, 31 (1970), pp. 589-98.

46.  Hain 16008; cf. Lib. ii, 7.  The work was extremely popular: before Vergil's death (1555) it was republished more than thirty times.  Because of its Erasmian tenor and attacks on the Roman church, it was placed on the Index in 1555.  Cf. D. Hay, Polydore Vergil: Renaissance Historian and Man of Letters (Oxford 1952), pp. 52-78.

47.  Paris 1549, pp. 53-4.

48.  Quoted by R. S. Wolper, op. cit., p. 590.

49.  De la vicissitude ..., lib. x (Paris 1583), p. 208.

50.  L. Le Roy, Considerations sur l'histoire universelle (Paris 1567), pp. 7-9; quoted from G. Atkinson, Les nouveaux horizons de la Renaissance française (Paris 1935), pp. 404-5.

51.  De la vicissitude ..., lib. ii (Paris 1583), pp. 41-3. Cf. also A. H. Becker, Loys le Roy (Ludovicus Regius) de Coutances (Paris 1896), pp. 249-51.

52.  H. Weisinger, "Ideas of History during the Renaissance," in: Journal of the History of Ideas, 6 (1945), pp. 415-35; H. Weisinger, "The Renaissance Theory of the Reaction against the Middle Ages as a Cause of the Renaissance," in: Speculum, 20 (1945), pp. 461-7.

53.   Philobiblon, trans. A. Taylor (Berkeley 1948), p. 57.

54.   Ed. F. H. Anderson, 1975, p. 118.

55.   G. M. Trevelyan, "If Napoleon Had Won the Battle of
      Waterloo," in: Clio, a Muse (London 1930), pp. 124-
      35.

56.   E. Zilsel, "The Genesis of the Concept of Scientific
      Progress," in: Journal of the History of Ideas, 6
      (1945), pp. 325-49.

57.   Petrarch's emendations of Livy, for example, were
      already lost after only half a century of purely manu-
      script transmission. Cf. E. J. Kenney, "The Charac-
      ter of Humanist Philology," in: Classical Influences on
      European Culture, ed. R. R. Bolgar (Cambridge 1971),
      pp. 122-3.

58.   H. Weissinger, "Renaissance Accounts of the Revival
      of Learning," in: Studies in Philology, 45 (1948),
      pp. 111, 116.

59.   W. J. Ong, Ramus, Method, and the Decay of Dialogue
      (Cambridge, Mass., 1958), p. 79; idem, "System,
      Space, and Intellect in Renaissance Symbolism," in:
      Bibliothèque d'humanisme et renaissance, 18 (1956),
      pp. 221-39, esp. p. 228.

60.   Diffusion is not necessarily present in what I call the
      "new" (optico-magnetic) printing.

61.   C. C. de Bruin, De Statenbijbel en zijn voorgangers
      (Leiden 1937), p. 89; K. Haebler, Handbuch der
      Inkunabelkunde (Leipzig 1925), pp. 150-7; R. Hirsch,
      op. cit. (see n. 28 above), pp. 68-70.

62.   J. W. Adamson, "The Extent of Literacy in England
      in the 15th and 16th centuries," in: The Library, 10
      (1929-30), pp. 163-93; H. S. Bennett, English Books &
      Readers, 1475 to 1557 (Cambridge 1970), pp. 19-29.

63.   H. J. Chaytor, From Script to Print (Cambridge
      1950), pp. 135-7; R. Irwin, The Heritage of the Eng-
      lish Library (London 1964), pp. 197-221.

64.   C. H. Talbot, "The Universities and the Medieval Li-

brary," in: The English Library Before 1700, ed. F.
Wormald and C. E. Wright (London 1958), pp. 66-84;
D. Hay, "Literature: the Printed Book," in: The New
Cambridge Modern History, vol. ii (Cambridge 1958),
p. 360.

65. Of the extensive literature, the most recent is Talbot,
op. cit., and P. Saenger, "Colard Mansion and the
Evolution of the Printed Book," in: The Library
Quarterly, 45 (1975), pp. 405-18.

66. R. K. Root, "Publication Before Printing," in: Proceedings of the Modern Language Association, 28 (1913),
pp. 417-31.

67. C. F. Bühler, The Fifteenth-Century Book: the
Scribes, the Printers, the Decorators (Philadelphia
1960), pp. 60-1.

68. D. C. North & R. P. Thomas, "An Economic Theory
of Growth of the Western World," in: The Economic
History Review, 23 (1970), pp. 1-17.

69. K. Köster, "Gutenbergs Aachener Heiltumsspiegel,"
in Das Werck der Bücher (Festschrift Horst Kliemann)
(Freiburg 1956), pp. 96-123; idem, Gutenberg in Strassburg (Mainz 1973); C. W. Gerhardt, "Was erfand
Gutenberg in Strassburg?" in: Gutenberg-Jahrbuch
1970, pp. 56-72.

70. The Koran calls the Jews (and Christians) "The People
of the Book"; cf. H. I. Marrou, Histoire de l'éducation
dans l'antiquité (Paris 1948), pp. 418-19.

71. L. Heinsman, W. van Teeffelen, Concernvorming in de
Nederlandse boekenwereld (Amsterdam 1975), pp. 15-16.

72. F. A. Schmidt-Künsemüller, Die Erfindung Gutenbergs
als technisches Problem (Mainz 1951).

73. G. S. Ivy, "The Bibliography of the Manuscript Book,"
in: The English Library Before 1700, ed. F. Wormald
and C. E. Wright (London 1958), pp. 32-65, esp. pp.
36-7.

74. L. White, "Technology Assessment from the Stance of
a Medieval Historian," in: American Historical Review, 79 (1974), pp. 12-13.

75. G. Sarton, op. cit., vol. iii, 2, p. 1564.

76. A. Schirokauer, "Der Anteil des Buchdrucks an der Bildung des Gemeindeutschen," in: Deutsche Vierteljahrschrift für Literaturwissenschaft und Geistesgeschichte, 25 (1951), pp. 317-50; M. L. Huffines, "Sixteenth-Century Printers and Standardization of New High German," in: Journal of English and Germanic Philology, 73 (1974), pp. 60-72.

77. E. J. Dijksterhuis, De mechanisering van het wereldbeeld (Amsterdam 1950), pp. 268-71.

78. L. Febvre, Le problème de l'incroyance au XVIe siècle (Paris 1962), pp. 424-6.

79. W. D. P. Weightman, Science and the Renaissance (Edinburgh 1962), p. 13.

80. H. Baron, "Towards a More Positive Evaluation of the Fifteenth-Century Renaissance," in: Journal of the History of Ideas, 4 (1943), pp. 21-49, esp. p. 40.

81. C. H. Talbot, op. cit., p. 77.

82. E. P. Goldschmidt, Medieval Texts and their First Appearance in Print (London 1943), p. 98.

83. A. R. Hall, "Science," in: The New Cambridge Modern History (Cambridge 1958), vol. ii, pp. 389-91.

84. M. M. Postan, "Why Was Science Backward in the Middle Ages?" in: M. M. Postan, Essays on Medieval Agriculture and General Problems of the Medieval Economy (Cambridge 1973), p. 83.

85. K. Dacks & W. Schmidt, "Wieviel Inkunabelausgaben gibt es wirklich?" in: Bibliotheksforum Bayern, 2 (1974), pp. 83-95.

86. K. Schottenloher, Bücher bewegten die Welt, p. 119.

87. Cf. also the introduction of chapters and verses, which render a frequently reprinted book like the Bible "referable": cf. M. H. Black, "The Printed Bible," in: The Cambridge History of the Bible, ed. S. L. Greenslade (Cambridge 1963), pp. 419, 442-3; E. J.

Kenney, The Classical Text:  Aspects of Editing in the
Age of the Printed Book (Berkeley 1974), pp. 152-7;
F. J. Wittly, "Early Indexing Techniques:  a Study of
Several Book Indexes of the 14th, 15th and Early 16th
Centuries," in:  The Library Quarterly, 35 (1965),
pp. 141-8; R. Hirsch, op. cit. (see n. 23 above),
p. 48.

88.  W. J. Bouwsma regards the existence of printed uniform codes of law as one of the positive influences on
modern jurisprudence.  Cf. "Lawyers and Early Modern Culture," in:  American Historical Review, 78
(1973), pp. 303-27, esp. p. 317.

89.  R. Rürup, "Die Geschichtswissenschaft und die
moderne Technik," in:  Aus Theorie der Geschichtswissenschaft (Festschrift H. Herzfeld) (1972), pp. 49-
85, esp. p. 79; W. F. Ogburn, "Inventions, Population, and History," in:  W. F. Ogburn, On Culture and
Social Change (Chicago 1968), p. 66; K. J. McGarry,
Communication, Knowledge and the Librarian (London
1975), pp. 127-45.

90.  A. R. Hall, "Scientific Method and the Progress of
Techniques," in:  The Cambridge Economic History of
Europe, ed. E. E. Rich and C. H. Wilson (Cambridge
1971), vol. iv, pp. 100-1.

91.  R. L. Heilbroner, "Do Machines Make History?" in:
Technology and Culture, 8 (1967), pp. 335-45.

92.  Technology in Western Civilization, ed. M. Kranzberg
& C. W. Pursell, Jr. (New York 1967), vol. i,
pp. 85-6.

93.  E. B. Parker, "Implications of New Information
Technology," in:  Public Opinion Quarterly, 37 (1973-
4), pp. 590-600.

# CANADIAN LITERATURE:

The Making of a Magazine*

George Woodcock

Canadian Literature was founded in 1959. Eighteen years later, in 1977, it is the center of a whole constellation of journals dealing critically with the great upsurge of Canadian writing that has taken place during the intervening period, such as Essays in Canadian Writing, the Journal of Canadian Fiction, Canadian Children's Literature, the Canadian Reader, the Canadian Fiction Magazine, Books in Canada, and CV II (specializing in Canadian poetry), all of which have come into existence since Canadian Literature and mostly during the last decade. Canadian Literature, when it appeared, was the first journal in its field, and it was one of the very few magazines operating in the rather bleak landscape of Canadian writing almost two decades ago.

Literary magazines in Canada up to that time had come and gone with a high degree of ephemerality. When I arrived in the country in 1949, there were exactly three English-speaking literary journals in the country: Contemporary Verse, Northern Review, and the Fiddlehead, published, respectively, in Victoria (British Columbia), Montreal (Quebec), and Fredericton (New Brunswick). (Decentralization has always been a strong feature of Canadian literary journalism.) There was also the Canadian Forum, a durable monthly Toronto journal of affairs and the arts with a mildly pinkish tinge, and there were three university quarterlies that published some literary criticism: Queen's Quarterly

*Reprinted by permission of the author and publisher from the Fall 1977 issue of Serials Librarian, pp. 13-20. Copyright © 1977 by The Haworth Press.

(the best of them and published in Kingston), University of
Toronto Quarterly, and Dalhousie Review (published in Hali-
fax). This thin cross-country line of magazines (none of
which published much criticism of Canadian writing) was
supplemented in those days by a weekly radio program of
quite high standards, "Critically Speaking," produced by the
Canadian Broadcasting Corporation from Toronto but using
critics from all over the country. This was all we had:
nothing like the New York Times Book Review or the Times
Literary Supplement; nothing even like the regular reviewing
of the New Republic, Nation, or New Statesman, all of
which, together with Edmund Wilson's reviews in the New
Yorker, we read with envy and frustration because we had
nothing resembling them of our own. Even the dwarfdom of
our publishing industry was partly due to the lack of the
flow of criticism and reviewing, which acts like a mediating
film between writer and reader.

        Since the early 1960s Canadian literary journals have
been given an unprecedented durability by the subsidies that
the Canada Council, and in some provinces the local arts
councils, now gives to magazines that have proved their
worth. But before council support began there was usually
nothing but the editor's pocketbook and the moral and financial help of his friends to keep alive a magazine that was
most unlikely to make enough out of sales to meet its printing bills. And so, early in the 1950s, two of the literary
journals I had found in existence on my arrival expired;
these were Contemporary Verse and Northern Review. In
1956 Tamarack Review was founded in Toronto, with Robert
Weaver as editor, to take up the vacant space, and in its
twenty-one years of publishing, Tamarack has become the
mandarin of Canadian literary magazines, publishing the
poetry and fiction, and sometimes the autobiographical and
travel essays, of almost every living Canadian writer of any
importance.

        But Canadian Literature was the first magazine devoted
to the study and criticism of Canadian writers and writing,
and indeed I believe I am correct in saying that it was the
first journal devoted entirely to literary criticism ever published in the country. Here I have to shift gears into the
autobiographical, for I have been the editor of the journal
from its foundation to the point of my retirement, which
will take place this year, and I have made no pretense of
editing it in anything but a personal and doubtless idiosyncratic way, since it is my view that editing is as much a

matter of flair; of creative intuition, as any other art (which is, of course, why journals edited in committee are always so dull and indefinite).

But if the critical point of view that has guided this journal through its career has been--faults and all--my own, the impulse that set the journal into motion was a group one. I started to teach at the University of British Columbia in 1956. I already had considerable experience in reviewing and criticism, and I had edited a literary journal, Now, in London from 1940 to 1947. I was also one of the group that founded the New York magazine Dissent, and in Britain I had worked on the anarchist journal Freedom, which was where I learned my distrust of editing by committee.

When I reached the University of British Columbia there was vague talk about starting a literary journal and about the possibility of my being asked to edit it, but nothing materialized at that time, and in 1957 I went away for a year to France on a Royal Society Fellowship and returned in the summer of 1958 to find that the magazine project had begun to crystallize. At first the idea of a magazine devoted to Canadian studies on a rather broad scale (like Trent University's Journal of Canadian Studies which was founded some years afterwards) was floated, and I was drawn into discussions relating to it, but the idea was not sharply defined and it lapsed. Then an ad hoc committee was formed that consisted mainly of librarians and members of the English Department. The most active members of the group were: Neal Harlow, the university librarian, who later went on to Rutgers; Inglis F. Bell, one of the assistant librarians; the poet Roy Daniells and S. E. Read of the English Department; and Geoff Andrew, who combined English teaching with the vice-presidency of the university. Between them they narrowed the original proposal to a journal devoted to the study and criticism of Canadian writers and writing. They then delegated Inglis Bell to approach me with the invitation to become editor.

My own reactions were at first ambivalent. I was at that time far from a specialist in Canadian writing. I had written some essays on Canadian or near-Canadian novelists like Hugh MacLennan and Malcolm Lowry, I had been reviewing Canadian poets in England even before I returned to Canada in 1949, and since that time I had been reading widely in Canadian fiction and verse, but that did not make me yet an echt Canlit man. However, I had already become

concerned over the question of criticism in Canada.  I had
long held a theory, emerging out of my reading of seventeenth-
century English and nineteenth-century American writers, that
one of the signs of a literature's coming of age is the emergence of criticism as a shaping element--the emergence, to
quote Wilde's definition, of "The Critic as Artist," the essentially creative critic whose work mediates between the
literary genres and between writer and public, and who himself forms a part of the continuum that is a living literature.
Until such a criticism exists, I had come to believe, no literature can be said to be really mature or to be reaching
out toward all its limits of expression.

In an essay in the Dalhousie Review (Woodcock 1955),
I had applied this theory to the situation of literature in
Canada, which I felt had individual critics but not yet the
kind of movement of criticism that was needed.  After examining the field of academic studies and newspaper reviewing I had reached the conclusion that

> there is at present, to all intents and purposes,
> no creative school of Canadian criticism.  At the
> same time, it seems evident that Canadian writing
> has reached that stage in its movement towards
> self-conscious identity when the creative function
> of the critic as a unifying and defining element in
> the emergent tradition becomes necessary.  Many
> Canadian writers have attained a sophistication in
> which they are conscious of working in isolation,
> and that isolation is not merely a question of
> geography, of men working in small towns strung
> across the CPR or in cities which are too small
> or too culturally undeveloped to provide the re-
> wards in money and prestige or the organised lit-
> erary life they might find in capitals like London
> and New York.  It is an isolation that springs
> from a feeling that they are no longer the colonial
> dependents of English or American traditions, but
> that at the same time there is no community of
> Canadian writing, no evident unity in all the ap-
> parently scattered paths which they and their fel-
> low-writers are taking.  The sense of unity which
> they are conscious of lacking can only be provided
> by a developed criticism which is able to evaluate
> Canadian literature in terms of native experience
> and also of the wider currents of thought and life
> that represent the universal in world literature.

And I ended by pointing out that for the present such an
emergent criticism would probably have to express itself
through periodicals, since publishers would not immediately
be willing to take the risk of publishing books of criticism
even if these were written, and that existing periodicals in
Canada were not organized to fill the gap.    Therefore, I
said in my terminating sentences, "it seems to me that a
Canadian journal devoted specifically to the critical consideration of native and world literature is a goal to be aimed
at, a minimum beginning.    For now, more than ever before,
we should foster that critical spirit which can bring Canadian
writing out of the hesitations of adolescence and into the self-
consciousness of maturity. "

Offering me, as the University of British Columbia
group did in 1958, the editorship of a magazine that I myself had proposed three years before was in fact a notable
challenge, and when I accepted, it was as much because I
had been put on my editorial mettle as because of my interest in the field I would be covering.    I still felt the journal
to be necessary, and I felt that my combination of editorial
experience and a fresh inside-outside approach conditioned
by my experience of the English literary world would be
enough to start the journal.    The gaps in my knowledge I
would have to fill as I went, which I have done assiduously
ever since.

So, somewhere about Christmas 1958, the genesis of
Canadian Literature was planned.    Since it was to emerge
under the aegis of a university, and since academics are
chronically addicted to collective decision making, a committee was formed, but fortunately it was chaired by that
urbane man Roy Daniells, who shared my own views about
the necessary independence of editors, so there was no difficulty about gaining immediately my first point, that all
strictly editorial decisions should be my own, and the committee should be mainly an advisory body, to lay down vague
general rules of policy and to assist in solving the material
problems of launching the journal.    The committee turned
out to be as willing as any Cheshire cat to dissolve with a
smile, and the real work of starting the journal was that of
a few practical people.    The librarians were great supports
on the business side:  Inglis Bell was the first business
manager, spending many hours on promotion; Basil Stuart-
Stubbs, now university librarian at the University of British
Columbia, organized the mailing out of the journal from the
library basement; and Dorothy Shields looked after advertis-

ing.  Later on, as the journal became more self-supporting
(it has never reached complete independence from Canada
Council and university subsidies), we were able to relieve
these voluntary pioneers with a paid staff (one part-time
worker), but a great deal of the cottage industry feeling
still lingers, even after eighteen years, and working bees
are still sometimes organized to meet emergencies.

One essential preliminary that caused few difficulties
was the design of the journal.  We commissioned Robert
Read, one of the best of Canadian typographers, and he
created the spacious classical format which in eighteen years
we have never found any reason to change, except that with
rising costs we have had to tighten it up a little to get more
words on the page.  Bob Read introduced us to our printer,
Charles Morriss of Victoria, one of the finest craftsman
printers in western North America, and again there was no
reason to change; the association has continued to this day,
and in eighteen years the standard of workmanship has never
slipped.

As for the editorial philosophy of Canadian Literature,
it began and has continued as a critical magazine in the
broadest sense rather than as a scholarly journal; Horizon,
Partisan Review, La nouvelle revue française define its
affinities of approach rather than PMLA.  A narrowly academic journal, devoted to the kind of close textual analysis
that was still fashionable in the late 1950s, would have been
irrelevant in the Canadian context of the time, and, again,
I had already established my task in the Dalhousie Review
article (Woodcock 1955) which in hindsight I realize was much
more an originating manifesto for Canadian Literature than I
perceived at the time.  There I said:

> The Canadian critic, when he emerges, will have
> a wider task to embrace; he will have to be some-
> thing of a psychologist, something of a sociologist,
> something of a philosopher, something of a mythol-
> ogist, besides having a developed consciousness of
> formal values and an imagination that is both cre-
> ative and receptive.  He will be concerned with the
> peculiar nature of Canadian experience, what makes
> the temper of our life--despite so many superficial
> resemblances--essentially different from the Amer-
> ican or the British, and how this regional pattern
> of living and thinking and reacting affects the work
> of Canadian writers.  But he will also be aware of

trends in other countries, and will have to consider
in what relation life and literature in Canada stand
to the world continuum. He will have to delve into
the past for the unifying threads and probe into the
future for the sense of direction. But he will also
not lose sight of the fact that, within the culture,
each writer is inalienably an individual, with his
own psychology, his own reaction to experience.
This experience, which includes language and the
whole complex of natural and social and cultural
influences to which he is subjected, will mark the
writer off as a Canadian--or an Englishman or a
Russian--but the spark that gives its life to his
work will be that of the unique intelligence dealing
with those problems of thought and morality which
are universal.

Perhaps I was asking a great deal, and perhaps no
single critic who has written in Canadian Literature has
brought together quite all the qualities I demanded; nevertheless, I think anyone reading all the issues that have appeared--
seventy-two of them up to this writing--will find all the elements of that approach combined and recombined in various
permutations.

The formal plan of Canadian Literature was simple.
There would be an editorial, reminding the reader of matters of topical concern in the world of Canadian writers.
A group of long essays would follow, combining the historical perspective with imaginative analysis so that books and
writers would be seen in relation to each other and to their
world. Special issues would be and were devoted to such
general concerns of the literary world as publishing and the
interconnections of the various arts; there would be chroni-
cles of current developments, and space for controversy. I
hoped that in this way a kind of continuing history-cum-sur-
vey of Canadian writing and the world of letters in this
country would be established, and I think that if one reads
over all the issues of Canadian Literature, this, among other
things, does emerge. A large section of the journal would
be devoted to review articles (long enough to probe into the
depths of a work), and in the early days we seriously set
out to notice in some way every publication of a literary
nature that appeared in Canada, at least in the English language. In both the essay and the review sections I hoped to
give broad attention to Canadian writing in French as well
as in English, and the annual bibliography that we published
for more than a decade covered works in both languages.

The immediate question was how to find the critics
to write in a journal that was in fact breaking new critical
ground.  There were already some distinguished Canadian
critics, like A. J. M. Smith and Northrop Frye, and literary historians like Desmond Pacey, but they were somewhat
isolated, and there were comparatively few younger critics;
newspaper reviewing in Canada was execrable at that time
and--except for one or two papers like the Globe and Mail--
it has not greatly improved.  Smith and Pacey rallied immediately to Canadian Literature; they appeared in the first
issue.  Frye never quite approved of my approach to criticism and has always stood aloof.  The real task was to establish a body of critics who would write fairly regularly but
not so often as to give the impression of a clique journal.
Prophets of gloom were numerous; it was often said that
after a year I would run out of both critics and subjects.

And I might have done so if I had not been fortunate
enough to start Canadian Literature just before the beginning
of the sixties, when Canadian cultural nationalism emerged
as a force in the country and literature took on an unanticipated vitality that expressed itself through a host of new
writers and of new little magazines and small publishing
houses to produce their works.  From the beginning there
was never any lack of interesting subjects or of new books
worth discussing, and very soon I had to abandon my plan
to review every new literary work, for even in English
alone, from 1964 onwards, the number of new books appearing was far more than any quarterly could hope to notice.

To find writers was initially more difficult, and there
were several early issues that I had difficulty in filling.
The problem was solved in two ways.  First, I began to encourage practicing writers--poets, novelists, and dramatists,
many of them quite outside the academies--to write for me,
either about their own work or, more often, about the work
of other writers.  This approach was so successful that in
1974, when I collected for Oxford University Press a little
anthology (Poets and Critics) of seventeen of the best critical essays in Canadian Literature, ten of them were actually
written by practicing poets.  Some idea of the extent to
which Canada's leading creative writers have contributed to
the success of Canadian Literature can be seen from a quick
list of some of the better-known among our hundreds of con-
tributors:  Margaret Laurence, Roderick Haig-Brown, Hugh
MacLennan, Margaret Atwood, Frank Davey, John Glassco,
Earle Birney, Louis Dudek, Irving Layton, R. G. Everson,

Al Purdy, John Newlove, Dave Godfrey, D. G. Jones,
Dorothy Livesay, Tom Marshall, Miriam Waddington, Eli
Mandel, P. K. Page, Mordecai Richler, Jack Ludwig, A. J.
M. Smith, Audrey Thomas, Ethel Wilson.

At the same time, the rise in cultural nationalism was
accompanied by a growing interest in Canadian writing.  Canadian literature courses began to proliferate, and every
year more criticism that was well written and imaginative
began to reach me from the universities.  Two of these
younger critics, D. G. Stephens and W. H. New, became
associate editors of Canadian Literature, and I have valued
their advice and help and the friendship that came from
working together.  It would be presumptuous to suggest that
the presence of Canadian Literature caused this wave of new
criticism and new critics; my thesis would suggest that the
time for such a development had come through the maturing
of the literature, but the fact that Canadian Literature was
there, ready to consider interesting new work, was perhaps
the kind of guarantee that kept younger critics working, so
that very soon we had moved out of the position of sometimes wondering whether there would be enough material to
fill an issue to the other extreme of wondering how we could
make use of all the good potential contributions that arrived.
With Canada Council's help the magazine was lengthened, but
a limit to such expansion has been imposed, particularly
during the last three or four years, by sharply rising costs,
which have also prevented us from making the shift our resources in material might justify, from quarterly to monthly
publication.  So now we reject many interesting pieces, and
still have managed a backlog of essays that will take two
years to print.

There is no space here to dilate at length on the
changes that have taken place in Canadian writing since I
began publishing Canadian Literature eighteen years ago, but
I can at least say that I have found the sixties and the seventies in Canada exciting and fruitful decades in which literature in this country has become diversified and deepened in
ways none of us foresaw in the fifties; one has had the sense
of being in the flow of history and in some degree of even
making it.  I believe that Canadian poets in the present age
are as good as their counterparts in any other English-
writing culture, and I believe that many of the world's best
fiction writers in French are to be found in Quebec.  And
if, as I think, the magazine Canadian Literature became
steadily more interesting to read (as it certainly did to edit)

through the sixties, this was because of the entirely new
relationship that developed between criticism and the other
fields of writing, so that only a few old-fashioned romantics
like Morley Callaghan and Earle Birney kept up the traditional poet-critic feud; most of the poets and many of the
novelists were themselves turning their talents to criticism.

      Inevitably, I have regrets.   There are pieces in the
early issues of the journal that now embarrass me because
their acceptance shows that I was still fumbling for the first
two years toward a clear definition of where Canadian writing was going.   And then there is what I can only describe
as the fiasco of our attempt to make Canadian Literature a
bilingual journal that would see Canadian writing--in French
and in English--as a symbiotic unity.   I tried hard to interest Quebec writers, but I soon learned that their compass
was set toward Paris and there was no deflecting it so far
out of its course as to make Vancouver a desirable direction.   I do not think this had a great deal to do with sepa-
ratist sentiment; I think it sprang from a wider indifference
toward the English culture in Canada on the part of the
Francophones.   Only a few of the better-known Quebec writ-
ers--three at most of the writers I really respect--responded
to my approaches, and at no time did publishable contributions in French run to much more than a tenth of the length
of any issue.   In the end I sadly resigned myself to seeing
Quebec writers through the eyes of Anglophone scholars.
That was our major failure, but hardly our fault, since there
never has been a successful bilingual journal of any kind in
Canada.

      For the idiosyncratic, and at times perhaps even ec-
centric, character of Canadian Literature, as compared with
most other journals that come out of academies, I make no
apology.   I have edited it in the only way I know, which is
to make a magazine as much a work of creative design,
even if on a different level, as a poem.   A literary journal
really succeeds only insofar as it assumes a character that
is more than the sum of its contents, and in developing its
own direction and impetus it takes its place among the
oeuvres of its age.   And that, remembering the sense of
creative fulfillment I have gained from editing it, I hope
will be the case with Canadian Literature.   I suppose every
writer develops a hierarchy of favorites among his works,
and looking at the long shelf of Canadian Literatures, I suddenly see them collectively as one of my books, written

with larger verbal elements than words, but still indubitably
a work with its own form and direction, and not one of my
worst.


Reference

Woodcock, George.   "A View of Canadian Criticism."
        Dalhousie Review, 36 (1955):   226-233.

# Part IV

# THE SOCIAL PREROGATIVE

# INTELLECTUAL FREEDOM AND YOUNG ADULTS*

Dorothy M. Broderick

## Who Are the Censors?

When one reads library literature it is easy to come away with the impression that it is always outsiders who are the censors, the people who would limit young adults' right to free access to information. The impression is given since librarians rarely (if ever) write about their own censorious actions, although reading letters-to-the-editor columns in various periodicals will offer some insight into many librarians' lack of commitment to the principles of intellectual freedom.

Attempts to limit the rights of young people come from many sources. In the school setting, attacks come from boards of education, superintendents, principals, teachers, librarians, the clerical staff, and probably even from an occasional student. Attacks come from the community in the form of complaints by individuals or from organized groups. In the public library setting complaints may originate with the board of trustees, the directors, and the professional or clerical staff. The public library also receives complaints from individual members of the public as well as from organized groups.

There are no reliable statistics as to the number of censorship attempts made in any given year since most attempts appear to be handled behind the scenes; only as incidents are debated in public or become court cases do they

---

*Reprinted by permission of the author and publisher from the Drexel Library Quarterly (1978) pp. 65-77. Copyright © 1978 by the Graduate School of Library Science, Drexel University.

come to our attention.  Excluding the outcomes of these public cases, we have no way of knowing how often the censorship attempt is successful and how often it fails.  However,
it is possible to assume that the disposition of complaints
nationwide follows a pattern similar to that found by Woodworth in her excellent study, Intellectual Freedom, the Young
Adults, and Schools; A Wisconsin Study:

> In examining the resolution of the case and com-
> paring it with the initiator of the complaint we see
> a general picture of the schools' tendency to resist
> censorship attempts from outside the system, and,
> often, to acquiesce in similar efforts from inside
> the system.  Within the school, censorship tries
> by principals or superintendents or school board
> members are quite generally fatal to the material,
> and result in its removal or restricted access.
> Sometimes these tries are resisted by librarians
> and teachers.  Less effective are the attempts by
> teachers where administrators, librarians and other
> teachers combine to resist (except for the control
> of their classes).  However, if a librarian objects
> to a library book chances are he/she will not
> select it for purchase, will restrict access to it,
> or will remove it after a problem has surfaced.
> These matters are rarely reported directly, but
> surface through comments on selecting for the
> conservative nature of the community, and the like.
> We also note, parenthetically, that equally rare is
> the librarian or teacher who entertains the possi-
> bility of having made a selection error.
>    Some of the most interesting cases are those
> involving an organized group of citizens, parents
> or not.  The ranks of the education [establishment]
> close, often supported by the school board.  When
> the membership of the school board splits, the
> battle begins in earnest, often with forays into
> adjoining communities--all avidly covered by news-
> papers and television who sometimes see little re-
> lationship between freedom of the press and com-
> batting censorship.  For that matter, such rela-
> tionships are not always clear to students, librar-
> ians, teachers, administrators, and the general
> public. [1]

There are three points in Woodworth's observations
that I want to discuss.  The first is that it is very clear

that the status of the person or group objecting is a major determinant of whether the attack results in censorship or a
defense of freedom.   It is a sad, but true, commentary on
our society that high status people's opinions carry more
weight than low status people's.   For the school librarian
or the public library young adult services librarian this fact
translates into the necessity of assuring that the high status
people in their institutions (library directors, principals, for
example) understand the need to stand firm and defend youth's
right to information.   Too often youth librarians ignore discussing a commitment to the Library Bill of Rights with
their superiors, hoping the occasion will not arise when they
will need to know where these superiors stand.   In the middle of a fight is a bad time to discover you lack support
from above.

The second point in Woodworth's commentary that
deserves highlighting is when she says that few librarians
and teachers are willing to admit to having made a selection mistake.   This comment reflects the classic dilemma
of youth services librarians:   does one respond to a complaint by defending the particular book being attacked, or
does one focus on the right to read without reference to the
book?

That question leads me to my third and most important point:   Woodworth is absolutely right in stating that few
people involved in these controversies connect the attacks
with such concepts as freedom of speech and freedom of the
press.   Few of them have any understanding of what legal
rights young people have, and few understand that it is impossible to build a defense around the First Amendment and
at the same time concern oneself with the content of the
material being attacked.   Neither schools nor public libraries are apt to buy materials that courts are likely to rule
obscene, libelous, or inciting to riot (the three categories
most likely to be censored with court approval), so cases
involving schools are adjudicated in relation to the rights of
the young people, the rights of school board members, or
the rights of teachers, and not on the basis of the quality of
the material attacked.   Since so few adults, including newspaper editors and members of the electronic media, have an
understanding of the First Amendment, it is very difficult to
hold a public debate on "the right to read," without finding
oneself also forced to defend the particular material under
attack.

The preceding discussion has been limited to situations

where adults are making the complaints against materials
selected by other adults.   But there is another type of censorship found in the schools, namely attacks by adults upon
the writings and expressions of opinions by young people.
These attacks almost always originate from the high status
people within the system:   members of the board of education, principals, or teachers, and all too rarely do the young
people find adults willing to side with them as they fight for
their rights.   For that reason, the remainder of this paper
is devoted to the legal rights young people have and how
those rights are ignored or violated by adults who ought to
be assuring them.

## First Amendment Rights of Youth

In the past decade major strides have been taken in assuring
youth protection under the First Amendment.   One of the
strongest statements spelling out youth's rights is found in
the Supreme Court decision on Tinker v. Des Moines:

> In our system, state-operated schools may not be
> enclaves of totalitarianism.   School officials do not
> possess absolute authority over their students.
> Students in schools as well as out of school are
> 'persons' under our Constitution.   They are pos-
> sessed of fundamental rights which the State must
> respect, just as they themselves must respect their
> obligations to the State.   In our system, students
> may not be regarded as closed-circuit recipients
> of only that which the State chooses to communi-
> cate.   They may not be confined to the expression
> of those sentiments that are officially approved.
> In the absence of a specific showing of constitu-
> tionally valid reasons to regulate their speech,
> students are entitled to freedom of expression of
> their views. [2]

It must be noted, however, that the Supreme Court is much
more willing to grant First Amendment protection to expressions that do not cause trouble.   In this, the treatment of
minors and adults is no different:   the closer the expression
of free speech comes to being effective, the more likely the
Court is to approve its being suppressed. [3]

With that reservation, it is still possible to say that
students now have a legal right to free expression that was

not imaginable twenty years ago. The Tinker case involved
the right of students to wear black arm bands protesting the
war in Vietnam, but the long range effect of the ruling has
been to accord to the high school press the rights held by
professional journalists. Librarians working with young people should make sure that high school journalists are familiar with Manual for Student Expression: The First Amendment Rights of the High School Press. [4] Rights that are not
exercised might just as well not exist, and one responsibility
librarians have is to make sure young people know what
rights they have. [5]

Informing young people of their rights can cause a
librarian trouble since many school administrators are very
unhappy with the idea of students having basic rights. The
National Association of Secondary School Principals is the
leading opponent of a free high school press. The NASSP
can often be found filing amicus briefs in support of school
officials seeking to censor school newspapers. It has also
issued a memorandum to its members in which it attacks
court decisions, saying, "It will be a tragic day for American education if first amendment rights are stretched and
distorted to guarantee a total freedom of editorship to the
students. "[6]

As one reads through the literature of censorship attempts by school officials, it becomes clear that they do not
like, respect, or trust the judgment of students. The language is that of the most traditional views of educators: the
students are vessels into which wisdom is poured by all-
knowing adults; the emotional content of statements by school
officials is that of fear of and dislike for young people.
Since it is these attitudes that create the conflicts between
school administrators and young people, it is necessary to
take the time to demonstrate their existence, bearing in
mind that the attitudes are not peculiar to school officials
but permeate our society.

Adult Attitudes Toward Youth

People who write about the relationship between adults and
youth, whether writing for the popular press or scholarly
journals, like to go back in history and quote the ancient
Greeks, Romans, and Egyptians to show that adults have always disparaged young people. This technique has been described by The Group for the Advancement of Psychiatry in
Normal Adolescence:

> From the beginning of recorded history there are
> references to youth which suggest that adults char-
> acteristically view adolescents with considerable
> ambivalence.... More often than not, and certain-
> ly this is currently true, the expressed attitudes of
> adults about adolescents tend to be negative and
> take the form of severe criticisms, dire predic-
> tions, and sweeping generalizations leveled at them
> not so much as individuals but as a generation that
> poses a threat to the existing social order. [7]

No group in society is more inclined to view adolescents as threats than school personnel. What is criticism,
however severe, for most adults becomes outright hostility
on the part of teachers and administrators. In The Vanishing Adolescent, Friedenberg commented on this hostility:

> Adults who do not basically like and respect
> adolescents--and this includes a large proportion of
> those who make a career of working with them--
> are badly frightened by the increasingly democratic
> relationships between adolescents and adults that
> are coming to prevail in our society. [8]

Long before Jerry Farber wrote The Student as Nigger, [9]
Friedenberg had drawn a similar analogy concerning the relationship between adults and adolescents:

> The tolerant, reasonable, democratic approach to
> 'teenagers'--like the comparable approach to
> formerly discriminated racial groups--is based on
> a premise of greater respect for them than the
> earlier attitude of coercive, if paternalistic, domi-
> nance. This much is valuable. But the same dif-
> ficulty arises as in the improvement of interracial
> relations. In order for this to occur smoothly,
> the members of the dominant group must like and
> respect the subordinate group a good deal in the
> first place [emphasis added]. If adults dislike or
> fear adolescents, the change will make those
> adults more frightened and more hostile, because
> it is a very real threat to their continued domina-
> tion. [10]

It is doubtful that even Friedenberg was prepared for
the level of hostility adults were to express toward young
people in the late 1960s and early 1970s. It would be pos-

sible to fill a large book with quotations verifying that hostility, but for me none has the same impact as that recorded
by James Michener in Kent State. As Michener says, "The
conversation was so startling that more than usual care was
taken to get it exactly as delivered." For the same reason,
I am quoting it in its entirety.

Mother: Anyone who appears on the streets of a
city like Kent with long hair, dirty clothes or barefooted deserves to be shot.

Researcher: Have I your permission to quote that?

Mother: You sure do. It would have been better
if the Guard had shot the whole lot of them that
morning.

Researcher: But you had three sons there.

Mother: If they didn't do what the Guards told
them, they should have been mowed down.

Professor of psychology (listening in): Is long hair
a justification for shooting someone?

Mother: Yes. We have to clean up this nation.
And we'll start with the long-hairs.

Professor: Would you permit one of your sons to
be shot simply because he went barefooted?

Mother: Yes.

Professor: Where do you get such ideas?

Mother: I teach at the local high school.

Professor: You mean you are teaching your students such things?

Mother: Yes, I teach them the truth. That the
lazy, the dirty, the ones you see walking the
streets and doing nothing ought all to be shot. [11]

Now, that mother and teacher may be the extreme example
of adult hostility toward young people, but if most teachers
would not condone shooting barefooted, long-haired youth, 80

percent of them do believe that corporal punishment is necessary to maintain discipline in the schools. [12] Moreover,
the Supreme Court agrees with those teachers even though it
does not allow correctional institutional officials to use corporal punishment on incarcerated young people. [13]

Hostility toward a group leads inevitably to attempts
at suppression of both freedom of expression and freedom of
behavior. Uniformity of thought and uniformity of action are
the goals of suppressors and any deviators are perceived as
threats to the power group (which they are).

Thomas I. Emerson, the outstanding legal scholar on
the First Amendment, writing about the balance between freedom of expression and social control, might well have been
writing about schools in relation to students when he observed:

> Suppression promotes inflexibility and stultification,
> preventing the society from adjusting to changing
> circumstances or developing new ideas. Any so-
> ciety, and any institution in society, naturally tends
> toward rigidity. Attitudes and ideas become
> stereotyped; institutions lose their vitality. The
> result is mechanical or arbitrary application of
> outworn principles, mounting grievances unac-
> knowledged, inability to conceive of new approaches,
> and general stagnation. Opposition serves a vital
> social function in offsetting or ameliorating this
> normal process of bureaucratic decay. [14]

Librarians working with young people in schools and
public libraries need to be aware of the hostility they and
their colleagues may have for young people. If our personal
inclination and professional commitment is to the young people rather than to the institution employing us, we should
understand the trouble that can descend upon our heads.

## Adult Power Struggles

Before returning to a discussion of the rights of young people, I would like to remind readers that not all censorship
attacks are within the institutions concerned, whether school
or public libraries. Of all the external battles, the one that
is most difficult to deal with is a split between members of
the school board or the library board of trustees. When
such a split occurs, the book or film or periodical being

fought over is rarely the major issue.  Rather, the two
groups are fighting to determine which will control the board.
Essentially this is what the infamous Down These Mean
Streets case in Flushing (NY) was all about. 15  When the
governing board is fighting among itself, any discussion of
the "right to read" is unlikely to have any affect on the argument, even if the complaint ends up as a court case.  In
the Down These Mean Streets case, the school board won
its day in court primarily because it did not completely remove the book from the school system, but rather imposed
restrictions on its use.

On the other hand, when the Strongsville (Ohio) board
of education ordered the removal of books and ordered they
not be taught, the U. S. District Court not only refused to
condone such action but ordered the board to replace the
books. 16  In doing so, the Court observed in a footnote:

> On the other hand, it would be consistent with the
> First Amendment (although not required by it) for
> every library in America to contain enough books
> so that every citizen in the community could find
> at least some which he or she regarded as objec-
> tionable in either subject matter, expression or
> idea. 17

At the moment, the Supreme Court has not been
presented with a clear-cut case of censorship by a school
board (the Strongsville decision was not appealed, so it remains applicable only to Strongsville).  Given the present
climate of conservatism and the large number of attacks on
school materials, the chances are that the Supreme Court
will be called upon to lay down some ground rules to provide
a balance between the school board's responsibilities to make
decisions and its obligations to provide for diversity.  Librarians should follow court cases carefully, and try to understand the legal bases for decisions.


Behavior Rights with Library Implications

In recent years both the Supreme Court and numerous state
courts have extended some very interesting rights to young
people in relation to their control over their own bodies.
This trend should be of particular interest to librarians since
one of the pressing problems for librarians working with adolescents is the extent to which young people are entitled to

the full range of information and referral services (I&R) in
sensitive subject areas.  "Sensitive" is the euphemism for
I&R on abortion, birth control, drug addiction, and venereal
disease.  Both public and school librarians share the fear
that by referring a young person to a Planned Parenthood
clinic or an abortion counseling service they will be putting
their jobs on the line, or worse, many librarians do not admit such problems exist among "their" young adults.

The problems do exist in every community on the
North American continent, and pretending they do not is no
way to demonstrate professionalism.  Admittedly it is not
easy to incur the opprobrium that can come when a community standard is perceived to have been violated by an adult
entrusted with the welfare of young people.  We all realize
that just one person in a community can cause a crisis if he
or she is willing to make a few telephone calls and write a
letter or two to the editor of the local newspaper.

School librarians are off the hook on this dilemma
because they can always refer the student to the school psy-
chologist or counselor and ever after ignore the young person's problem.  For public librarians, the situation is quite
different and since there are no court rulings on the question
of a librarian's right to provide needed information, we must
deal with the question of I&R services by analogy.

Clearly of the four issues mentioned, abortion is the
most explosive, arousing the most emotions and lending itself to the least unanimous public expression of views.  Yet,
abortion is the one issue for which there is a national standard.  In 1976, in Planned Parenthood of Central Missouri v.
Danforth, the Supreme Court ruled that states may not grant
to parents the right to deny an abortion to minor children. 18

Treatment for venereal diseases is also the right of
young people without parental consent in all states, although
a few states do set lower age limits of 12 or 14, with Iowa
the only state setting the minimum age at 16.  A similar
situation occurs in relation to treatment for drug addiction.
Only in relation to the right to obtain contraceptives does the
law vary widely from state to state, and even in this category, no doctor has ever been found liable for prescribing a
contraceptive to a minor.

A characteristic shared by the rights outlined above
is that they all apply to behavior.  This fact strengthens the

argument that librarians should provide information freely on
all the topics to all young people regardless of their age.
It is important to understand the difference in law between
expression and behavior:  generally speaking, both laws and
court decisions are more willing to limit action than to limit
freedom of expression.   This being the case, it follows that
in areas where freedom of action is guaranteed, there can
be no basis for limiting access to information that would
form the basis for making an informed decision about a contemplated action.   In plain English, doesn't it strike you as
silly to deny information about abortion to a female adolescent who is legally entitled to have one?


## Implementation Steps

To help us justify providing I&R in these critical areas of
human decision-making, we need to develop a body of writings and position papers that place the weight of the library
profession behind such actions.   At the moment, the American Library Association supports the right of parents to
limit access to information for their children as long as they
do not attempt to limit access for other people's children. [19]

Given the court rulings and state laws mentioned
above, it strikes me as anachronistic for ALA to hold that
parents have the right to restrict their children's access to
information.   We do not need to go to the opposite extreme
and write a document that says parents have no rights.
More appropriately, the document would focus on the ways
in which librarians will not side with parents in their attempts to limit their children's access to library materials.

The new policy statement I would like to see developed
would state:  1) the library will not serve as an arbiter between parent and child; 2) all young people, regardless of
age, will be given library cards on their own recognizance;
3) parents who prefer their children not use the library
should so advise their children of that fact; and 4) no administrative procedures will be developed that directly or
subtly impose restrictions upon minors that are not imposed
on all library clientele.

Accompanying the policy statement should be examples of positive steps libraries can take to bring to the attention of both adults and young people the rights youth has
in our society.   Such steps might include, but not be limited

to, collecting and publicizing court cases that involve youth rights; purchase and prominent display of publications that spell out youth rights; and programs that provoke public discussion about the legal rights and responsibilities of youth. The library should do joint programming with other youth service agencies. For example, at least once each year the library should provide the forum for the Planned Parenthood clinic personnel to explain the services available from the clinic. It would not be inappropriate in my mind for the library to have as part of its nonbook materials, the complete kit of birth control methods that Planned Parenthood advisers use when discussing various methods with clients.

Our goal in all of this is not to take sides; not to tell people they must use birth control methods, or once pregnant have an abortion. Rather, the role of the library as an information agency is to buy and publicize the materials that will allow young people to make informed decisions about their own lives. Informed decision-making is what intellectual freedom is all about.

Notes

1. Mary L. Woodworth, Intellectual Freedom, the Young Adult, and Schools; A Wisconsin Study, rev. ed. (Madison: University of Wisconsin-Extension, 1976), p. 59.

2. Tinker v. Des Moines Independent Community School District, 393 U.S. 503 (1969). Reprinted in The Rights of Students (New York: Avon, 1977), pp. 123-131.

3. Thomas I. Emerson, Toward a General Theory of the First Amendment (New York: Random House, 1966), pp. 51-53.

4. Manual for Student Expression: The First Amendment Rights of the High School Press (Washington, D.C.: The Student Press Law Center, 1976). The address of the Student Press Law Center is Room 1112, 1750 Pennsylvania Ave, N.W., Washington, D.C. 20006.

5. The Rights of Students; An ACLU Handbook, compiled by Alan H. Levine and Eve Cary (New York: Discus/Avon, 1977).

6. National Association of Secondary School Principals, memo, quoted in Student Press Law Center Report 4, Spring 1977, p. 7.

7. Normal Adolescence: Its Dynamics and Impact, formu-

lated by the Committee on Adolescence, Group for
the Advancement of Psychiatry (New York:   Scribner's,
1968), p.  7.

8.   Edgar Z.  Friedenberg, The Vanishing Adolescent (New
York:   Dell Publishing Co. , 1962), p.  27.

9.   Jerry Farber, The Student as Nigger (New York:
Pocket Books, 1970).

10.   Friedenberg, p.  25.

11.   James A.  Michener, Kent State:  What Happened and
Why (New York:   Random House, 1971), pp.  454-455.

12.   Nat Hentoff, Does Anybody Out There Give a Damn?
(New York:   Knopf, 1977), pp.  13-51.

13.   Ingraham v. Wright, quoted in Children's Rights Report,
Volume 1,  no.  8,  May 1977.

14.   Emerson, pp.  11-12.

15.   For an analysis of the case as seen by the attorney for
the plaintiffs, see Alan H.  Levine, "School Libraries:
Shelving East Harlem," Civil Liberties, January 1973.

16.   "The Strongsville Decision," School Library Journal,
November 1976, pp.  23-28.

17.   Ibid. , p.  25.

18.   Planned Parenthood of Central Missouri v. Danforth,
2 Family Law Reporter, 3039 (June 29,  1976).

19.   "Free Access to Libraries for Minors; An Interpretation of the 'Library Bill of Rights,'" in Intellectual
Freedom Manual (Chicago:   American Library Association, 1974), pp.  16-17.

ETHICAL AND LEGAL QUESTIONS

IN PROVIDING HEALTH INFORMATION*

Norman Charney

When I received the invitation to speak at this Conference,
I looked at the topic that I was to lecture on and I was very
happy to see that it was titled "The Ethical and Legal Questions in Providing Health Information" because I know all the
questions.   I'm not sure I know all the answers.

As a personal introduction, I am in the general practice of medicine in La Mirada, California.   I am board certified in Family Practice.   I was one of the first Diplomates
of the Board, and also one of the first Diplomates to be re-
certified--in February of this year.   I graduated from Western State University College of Law in 1971 and was admitted
to the bar at that time.   I have a law office in Fullerton,
California.

In the discussion earlier this afternoon, I heard that
people are still in awe of their physicians and that the doctor is the so-called "big man."   Doctors are human beings
and they make mistakes--hopefully not careless mistakes.
They are approachable, and I think the public has to be made
aware of the fact that doctors are approachable.   The more
a doctor is approached, the more civilized you make him and
the better the practice of medicine within this country will
become.   The same type of approachability should apply to
practitioners in dentistry, nursing, podiatry, and all the
allied health professions.

*Reprinted by permission of the author and publisher from
the January 1978 issue of the California Librarian,   pp. 25-
33.

I would like to address my topic from two different viewpoints: legal and medical.  Let's talk about the legal aspects first.  As health information providers there are several areas of the law with which you should be concerned. The first is Statutory Law as it applies to the State.  The Business and Professions Code, for example, and the Health and Safety Code, which regulates and controls the practice and the licensing of doctors, dentists, nurses, etc.  Then there is the Penal Code.  I really can't think of any good examples of how you might, through providing health information, violate the Penal Code, so I won't even discuss it.

But in relation to the Business and Professions Code, there is some concern among health information providers about being accused of practicing medicine without a license. It's my opinion that if you provide information and information only--not opinion, not diagnosis, not treatment--you'll never be accused of practicing medicine without a license. I think the liability in that area is not even worth discussing. But the issue was raised at another meeting of librarians that I attended, and so I would like to put it to rest.  If you practice your profession as you have been trained and as your experience dictates, then you won't have any problems of that nature.

There is another area about which you should be concerned, and that is Civil Law.  Civil Law can be divided into two areas.  One area is known as Tort Law.  That involves one man's relation to another.  When you get "rear-ended" on the freeway, the person who did it has committed a tort upon you.  Tort Law is divided into intentional torts and negligence.  Intentional torts are acts which are done with purpose and cause damage (e. g. , assault, battery, fraud, false imprisonment, etc. ).

Fraud and misrepresentation is one type of tort in which librarians might get involved.  Before I go any further, I want to state that I do not think there have been any cases involving librarians or health information providers. You can rest assured that this is strictly theoretical.  (However, with the number of lawyers that are being produced these days, some enterprising young attorney is going to find a case somewhere. )  Thus, you should know that, if you are hesitant about disseminating the truth and you, with all good intentions, say something misleading in an attempt to make a person happy, you may be misrepresenting and committing a fraud.  If this person relies upon the representation that you made and he does injure himself because of it--for example, he doesn't make out his will correctly or he plans a long trip when he only has three months to live, and he or his family is injured as a result of your misrepresenting the truth--theoretically there could be a cause of action.

I think defamation is an area in which problems might arise much more easily than in the area of fraud and misrepresentation. Take the example of a patient who calls and says, "I want to know this information." You provide the information. The patient then says, "My doctor said something else." If you say, "Well, your doctor is a quack" or "Your doctor doesn't know what he's talking about" or "I'd go get another doctor," you could be in serious trouble.

As far as negligence is concerned, I don't think librarians could get into any trouble because it would have to be proved that the librarian had a duty and failed to act in a proper manner based on his or her knowledge, experience and training, and as a result of that damage resulted which proximately flowed from the negligence.

Constitutional Law--The Constitution of the United States--is relevant to this discussion also. If you refuse to provide information that has been requested of you, or if you attempt to restrict it, I think someone could suggest that there is a violation of the constitutional right to know. I don't think anybody has brought such a case to court, but you should be aware of these potential constitutional issues.

Contract Law will enter into a librarian's deliberations at times because many municipalities, universities and agencies have contractual relationships with libraries and there can be contractual legal implications.

That's as much as I want to say about the legal aspects. The second area we need to understand is the medical aspect. What is medicine? I like to think of it as a dichotomy. The first is the science. The science, of course, is constantly changing. That which is decreed today as "holy truth," tomorrow is no longer true and there's a new "truth" replacing it. The second part of it is the art: how the practitioner uses scientific "facts" in the practice of the profession. Of course, the art is as varied as the number of practitioners. Thus, there are variations in art, in addition to a constantly changing scientific field and there can be any number of combinations and permutations. I

think as health information providers we need to consider
this when we find conflicting opinions or contradictory information on methods of treatment.

Unless one is qualified to make a judgment on someone else's opinion or someone else's work, I think one should
simply realize that there are a variety of possibilities which
can boggle the mind, even sometimes the mind of a medical
professional. I can easily understand how conflicting opinions could confuse a layman who is untrained in medicine.
If you remember what I just said about the science and the
art and the combination thereof, you will not be overly concerned about apparently contradictory opinions that you may
discover.

Next I would like to review the nature of the publications that are available to you. First, there are treatises
that are written for the health professional. They are not
meant for the layman to read or interpret. They are meant
to teach and to reaffirm or to disseminate new information
to the professional: the physician, the dentist, the nurse,
etc. Within the category of professional treatises there is
the standard, well-recognized text which almost every physician has heard about, studied in medical school and continues
to rely on. Then there is the new work, the work that's
controversial, or the older work that's still in controversy.

Secondly, there is material that is written for laymen.
Again there are well-recognized, well-authored works. On
the other hand, there are controversial works that are theoretical and the motivation for which we don't always sell
books or to sell vitamin pills or to sell diet preparations.
I know that you are well aware of some of these books, and
to avoid myself getting into a position of defaming somebody
I won't mention any titles.

When evaluating works from either category, we have
to consider the following four points:

1.  Is the work and the writing reliable?
2.  Is the writing dated?
3.  Does the writing require interpretation?
4.  Is the writing mostly of historical interest?

I think it is essential that a person receiving information understand the nature of the publication from which
the information comes. For example, when presenting some-

one with information from a standard medical text used to
train doctors, one might say: "This book was written for
doctors, to be interpreted by doctors, and everything in here
is not the 'holy truth.' Next week there may be a book out
that will say that some of these items are no longer true.
As a matter of fact, there may be some literature in the
doctor's office now that says some of these things are not
true, so when I read this to you, understand that it takes a
professional to interpret it." If it's a lay article that you
are quoting, say something such as: "This information has
been put into simple language and all of the author's implications may not be clear. The author wants you to understand it, but it may either be too simplified for you, or still
too sophisticated for you, and, therefore, the ultimate answer
will come from someone who can put this information into
perspective so that you will understand it."

    Why is the demand for medical information increas-
ing? I believe that media coverage of medical topics has
been an important contributing factor. For example, television carries many programs about doctors, and newscasts
often report on controversial or new medical events. Also,
some newspapers do not treat medical topics in a careful,
balanced manner. Many times newspapers will print an
article because the medical information it contains sounds
exciting. For instance, the newspaper may print that drug
"x" cured cancer in a rat. However, the reporter did not
find out or did not include the fact that an hour after the
cancer was cured the rat died. The cancer was cured, but
the patient didn't survive. Also, popular magazines now
constantly carry articles on health topics. I don't think you
can go past a newstand without seeing a Redbook, McCall's
or Cosmopolitan that has some type of medically related
article splashed across the cover: "How to Lose Weight by
Eating Raisins" or "How to Avoid a Heart Attack by Walking
Up Three Flights of Stairs Every Day."

    The current malpractice situation--which may itself
be stimulated by the news media or by the sophistication of
our population--has also contributed to the demand for medical data. Patients may not trust what the doctor has done,
and therefore they initiate their own research on the matter.
(They may avoid consulting a lawyer because they fear it
will cost too much. However, there are ways of getting
legal information that are not prohibitively expensive.)

    One issue emanating from the current malpractice

crisis is the "informed consent" requirement which has made
it mandatory that physicians get from patients a consent that
is based on a real understanding of the situation.   The physician cannot say simply, "Well, it's going to be okay Mrs.
Smith.   I tell you it's okay; therefore it is okay." Rather,
that physician must say, "These are your risks.   These are
your reasonable alternatives.   Do you understand it?   Do
you still want to go  through with it?"   A doctor will often
present this information in a manner intelligible to another
practitioner, but in terms the patient does not understand.
The patient may not understand what a fibroma is, or what
metastasis means.   She may not understand the nature of
chemotherapy or x-ray therapy.   Yet, for whatever reason,
the patient may not say, "I don't understand.   Could you explain it?"   Even if the patient did ask for an explanation, in
all probability the doctor would pull his hair and say, "I
don't have time to give you a full course in medicine."
Maybe he would be justified in saying this.   The doctor
probably shouldn't be required to explain every illness or
treatment in depth.   I think it is the responsibility of the
patient to find some of this information for himself if he
doesn't understand it all.   That's why we have health information providers, and that's why you have so much work to
do.   Another reason for the increased demand for medical
information is the growing educational level of the population.
As people become more sophisticated they want to know more
about diseases and treatment.   Finally, the mysticism of
medicine is slowly dissipating.

        Now, what are the effects of this increased demand
for information?   Is this a bad thing?   It's my personal
opinion that the increased interest has been good for American medicine and the health situation in the United States.
Partially as a result of this quest for information by the
public, we now have continuing medical education as a requirement for State licensure of physicians and some other
health professionals.   At one time the doctor hung up his
shingle and could read Mad magazine thereafter.   Now he at
least has to expose himself to medical information after being
licensed.

        I think most doctors have always done that.   In my
experience, my colleagues kept themselves pretty well informed.   Nevertheless, now doctors are definitely required
to stay well-informed.   There is now recertification for
specialists.   Again, up until recently, once one became
board certified, one was considered the "holy see" as far as

that specialty was concerned--nobody was going to question a
certified doctor's credentials.   Now questioning is occurring.

We now have Boards of Medical Quality Assurance.
Before there were Boards of Medical Examiners, and "examine" is just what they did.   A doctor was examined and,
if passed, received a license.   Thereafter, he could thumb
his nose at the Board of Medical Examiners because they
weren't going to examine him anymore.   Now we want quality assurance.   We have laymen on the Boards of Medical
Quality Assurance as well as on other boards.   We have utilization reviews at hospitals and at various clinics; the work
done by health professionals is reviewed to see if they are
utilizing the facilities appropriately.   We now have the advent of PSRO Professional Standards Review Organization,
where the physician will review other physicians' work to
determine whether the standard of practice is being maintained.

I think what I have said gives you a good summary of
both legal and medical considerations that should be understood.   I would now like to comment on some of the questions that were asked in the previous session.

The first question was, "The doctor found cancer of
the uterus; the patient wants to know more about uterine
cancer, and she has some financial problems."   My comment on that question is that the patient certainly has a
right to know more because she has to give an informed
consent for either surgery or radiation therapy or chemotherapy, and the only way that she's going to be able to give
that informed consent is to know about uterine cancer.   One
might ask, "Why doesn't she get this information from her
doctor?"   I think that's a good point.   However, some people are more curious than others and would like to read
about their condition at their own leisure; then they can also
read definitions of terms they don't understand.   A physician
cannot always explain diseases and treatment in a clear and
concise manner because he's just not trained to do that.   If
he did do it, then he'd be spending all of his time explaining
medical conditions to patients and he wouldn't have time to
treat all the patients.   There is still a shortage of medical
personnel in this country, and I think that you as health information providers are of great assistance to the medical
profession and will become more so in the future.

Some of the comments from the audience on that question indicated there was a frustration that you couldn't do enough for such a person: "This woman had a medical problem, a financial problem, and various other problems, and what could we do?" Remember you're not social workers and you're not psychologists. You're supposed to provide information. I think if you provide the information the other workers who can help this particular person will manifest themselves, either through the information that you provide, or by reason of the patient being informed and realizing what she needs.

The second question was, "Are foods with artificial colors dangerous to my health?" By way of an answer, I can only think of another question: "Is living dangerous to your health?" I think in your position as health information providers, all you can do to answer a question on food additives is say, "Well there is a book or a pamphlet or literature submitted or presented by the FDA which says this particular additive is considered safe or this particular additive is not considered safe, but I as an individual can't tell you whether it's safe or not because you may have some particular medical condition about which only your doctor or some other health professional can advise you. For example, plain salt--nobody considers that dangerous--yet for a lot of people salt can be fatal." So it's not a question that you can give a flat answer to. You should be sure to instruct a patron that you can only tell him what it says in the printed article, but you can't make an interpretation because you're not qualified: you don't know their particular problems--and even if you did know their problems you couldn't analyze it adequately. Then they can take the information you give them and go to their doctor and say, "Hey, the FDA says this about this and I seem to be eating it, taking it, sleeping with it, or doing whatever. What do you think?" At that point, most physicians would be happy to discuss the matter with the patient.

There's been some discussion here of the fact that doctors are annoyed by the information you're disseminating. I think that those doctors who are annoyed should stay annoyed, because I don't think there's any harm in the truth and I don't think there's any harm in disseminating good information. However, if they're getting the feedback, "Well the librarian said that you're wrong about this," then I could see where they might get upset and I think they would have a right to be upset.

There were some questions about disseminating infor-

mation concerning fatal diseases.   It has always been my
feeling that, "If you don't want to know the answer, don't
ask the question." Most people who have been diagnosed as
having a fatal disease already know that it's fatal and they
just want some information to reconfirm that because they
don't want to plan to die in six months and find that they're
going to live for twenty years.   I can understand that telling
someone he suffers from a fatal disease might be shocking
to you, because you get some transference.   You say to
yourself, "If that were me, I wouldn't want anybody telling
me I was going to die in six months." But I don't think we
should prejudge a person's reactions to learning about a
disease he has.   I think we should tell it as it is.   If you
feel that perhaps you have an unstable individual on the other
end of the telephone and it is your policy to read things over
the phone, then you might say, "I think that the information
might best be gotten from this particular book, and if you'll
come into the library we'll provide you with the book and
you can read it." In my opinion that would be the best way
to handle such a situation.

        At this point, there must be many people anxious to
throw questions at me, so let's open it up.

        Question:   In an earlier discussion, you were talking
about patients who did not quite understand a particular disease and wanted to know more about it.   Could you clarify
what you feel the physician's responsibility is in explaining a
disease to his patients?

        Answer:   A physician should explain adequately what
the problem is, what the treatment is, and what his individual patient must do in order to get the problem under control.   However, in his discussion, he may inadvertently use
the words that the patient does not understand fully.   Then
the patient might ask the doctor, for example, "What does
'purulent discharge' mean?" The patient could do that, but
if the patient had ten different items that needed clarification,
it could get to be burdensome for both the doctor and for the
patient.   So after the patient gets some basic information I
think he should be able to go to the library and look up some
of the things he doesn't understand.   Then he could more
adequately go back to the doctor and say, "I read this about
my disease, and you didn't mention anything about this, or
if you did I didn't really understand it.   Could you explain
it?" Then the physician is getting an informed patient and
there can be an intelligent interchange between the doctor
and the patient.

Question: As a family physician, do you recommend specific books for your patients if they ask for more information on a particular problem?

Answer: If they ask, yes. Sometimes I'll volunteer it. There are many physicians' aids, pamphlets and booklets provided by a myriad of organizations to help a doctor disseminate information without using valuable time that is needed to care for other patients. There are doctors who have video cassettes; they will sit a patient down and the cassette will discuss topics such as diabetes and diet, or menopause, or a hysterectomy and what to expect afterwards.

Question: Do you see the possibility of health services being structured in such a way that there could be a person working with the physician who would take responsibility for providing information? I think patients would prefer to discuss a medical condition with a real live person rather than to read about the condition or watch a video cassette.

Answer: That's why I said there is a growing need for health information professionals; such professionals exist now at many hospitals. For example, at some hospitals a dietician is available for not only inpatient service but the outpatient community service as well. Some hospitals also have liaison nurses--nurses that link the patient and the doctor and provide the patient with information from a nursing point of view.

Question: In private practice, what is there?

Answer: In private practice, as far as I know, there isn't anybody who can say, "Look, you have diabetes. It's a complicated disease and I want you to know all about it, and rather than just tell you a few words about it, I'd like you to go and see so-and-so who will give you a course covering what you need to know about your condition." I know what you mean. It would be nice if the doctor had a health information professional in his office.

Question: For instance, in a group practice could a health educator be hired by the physicians?

Answer: That would probably be practical at Kaiser Permanente Medical Center or Ross-Loos, but I think in an individual doctor's office, there would not be enough work to keep an information specialist. A regional information office would be more practical.

Question: I'm worried about the problem of medical books becoming dated. Should we possibly not recommend a book that's over five years old, or two or three years old? I don't have enough knowledge to know how current the information should be.

Answer: It depends on your library. My own personal opinion is that the age of a book is not important as long as the patron is told, "This book is ten years old. I don't know how good it is." It's up to the requestor to decide whether to use it or not--whether to waste his time reading it. It depends on his motivation. He may even be interested in the historical aspects of the subject.

Question: I had the following experience: I was away, my mother-in-law was here alone, and she broke her foot. The doctor provided her with a cast clear to her knee and said, "Go home and take care of yourself." She couldn't even get over the curb. He knew nothing about the agencies which might help her. Perhaps there should be a program such as this one today presented for physicians so that they could learn about the agencies available to help their patients.

Answer: I agree, because most doctors don't know about these agencies. In my experience, one of the major areas in which agencies could help is with emotional crises. The only thing I know about is the crisis unit at the county hospital. There may be other resources, but I don't know of them, and I know that most of my fellow physicians don't know of them.

Question: [from Dr. Ruth Heifetz] This is a question that is close to my heart, because I teach in a Department of Community Medicine, which is usually the lowest department in terms of power and status in the medical school. I think what we're seeing as medical science expands and becomes more technical, is more and more attention being given to the "scientific" part of medicine. Medicine isn't viewed as a social science, which it also is. I think that education in the social science aspects of medicine does not take place in medical schools. It's unfair to generalize from Dr. Charney's experience because he is that very rare breed of animal called the "general practitioner." What he does with his patients is very different from what the 80 percent of the doctors who are specialists are able or interested in doing for their patients. I felt that you, Dr. Charney, touched somewhat lightly on the controversies in

medicine and the fact that it is an art, and that there often
are not absolute answers.  That's the reason for many of
the problems we have discussed today.  Imagine the dilemma
of a woman who goes to two different surgeons and one says,
"A radical mastectomy is what you need," and the other
says, "That's all right.  We'll just do some minor surgery
and you'll be fine."  Or the woman to whom one surgeon
says, "Out with your uterus," while another physician suggests conservative, non-operative treatment.  I think there
has to be a place that people can turn for the available, current information and opinion on a subject.  With our incredible
technology, we should have some way that people can be
plugged into the most current information, in lay terms, so
that people can understand the options.  People here today
are saying doctors should not be left off the hook.  I think
doctors should continue to try to provide information--should
be pressed by their patients to do so, but I think there are
other levels that have to be provided as well.  So few health
problems have clear cut causes or solutions, we must provide public access to the controversial issues and treatments.
Hopefully many of you here today will play a role in improving this public access to health information.

Answer:  In my opinion, for many medical questions
it is impossible to find a single "best" answer because the
doctor that says the uterus comes out and the doctor that
says the uterus stays in can both be correct.  The doctor
that says surgery is needed gets the best results with surgery and the other doctor gets the best results the other way.
So, there are no definitive answers of any kind.

Question:  Yes, but the information you just gave us
should be available to people so they know that different options in the right hands could be equally effective.  I suspect
very few women would choose the radical mastectomy if they
knew there was an equally effective alternative treatment.

Answer:  Then we have to go back to grade school
and to health education courses and make sure these courses
teach and that everybody grows up with knowing medicine is
not an exact science--at least the practice of medicine isn't.
Therefore, in cases of controversy the patient has to make
the ultimate decision.  All the medical profession can do is
say, "There are five treatment alternatives available now.
Maybe a better one will develop later but you can't wait.
You have to take one of those five alternatives.  There can
be complications with any of the five.  These are the prob-

lems that can develop.   You choose the alternative and we'll try to do our best. "

Question:   You said earlier that physicians are not necessarily aware of all the services that they can utilize. Would you go to your medical library, either in your hospital or at a university, as a central resource for information on services?   Would you or your staff use a medical library as a place to find out what resources were available?

Answer:   I think that would be nice.   I would certainly like to know that that service is available.

Question:   It is.

Answer:   I don't think that the practitioner in the field knows that it is.

Question:   We were just discussing back here that representatives from health information agencies should go to medical meetings.

Answer:   Right.   They should have a booth and say, "We have this information for you doctor.   Why aren't you calling on us?"

Question:   How about a panel of information providers giving a presentation at medical meetings?

Answer:   Sure, I think a booth or a panel would be a terrific idea.   I've never seen it.   The only thing I see in medical meetings is a booth set up to sell you an oil well or to get you to invest in raising cattle; that is outside of the legitimate booths.

Question:   The problem is that we in the audience today represent many diverse information agencies.   We are not one group.   There isn't one representative who can say to you, "Dr. Charney, you've got a great idea.   We will present a panel at the next annual meeting of this or that medical group. " Although maybe it could be done on a local level.

Answer:   I think if you started on a local level, it would possibly filter up to the regional and national levels. Also, remember that I have no influence with the medical association, and that all the things I have said today are based on my education and experience and training, and are strictly my own personal opinion.

# THE PROBLEM OF PORNOGRAPHY*

Murray Hausknecht

For a walker through Times Square or the downtown areas
of many American cities a stop for a newspaper means a
confrontation with the tastelessness of Screw and Hustler; a
glance at a record shop window discloses an album-cover
photograph, reproduced on a rooftop billboard, of a bound
woman, while a nearby movie marquee promotes the dubious
delights of an X-rated movie featuring children.   One is
overcome by a sense that the texture of public life has become coarsened and that some natural boundary between public and private worlds is being wantonly violated by a barrage of pornography.   It is hard to resist crying out,
Enough!

 The cry, though, is or can be a prelude to a call for
censorship, and the uneasiness that thought produces is reinforced by the reality of prosecutions against porno-film
actors and the publisher of Hustler.   One's discomfort is
increased by the recognition that such prosecutions gain
legitimacy from our disgust with the daily encounter with
pornography.   All of which prompts the questions, What can
be done?   What ought to be done?

 By pornography I mean any written or visual representation of sexual behavior--explicitly and vividly presented--
whose sole intent is sexual arousal.   By "erotic writing" or
"erotica" I mean an explicit representation of sex within a
context in which it is treated as part of the human experience
and in which the sexual material is not used solely to stim-

*Reprinted by permission of the publisher from the Spring
1978 issue of Dissent, pp. 193-208.   Copyright © 1978 by
the Dissent Publishing Corp.

ulate arousal. (Throughout, it is to be understood that what
is said about "writing" applies also to movies.) In short,
erotic writing is work that tries to achieve the traditional
end of art. However, erotica can be converted by the reader into pornography; that is, it can be used simply for the
purposes of arousal.

Pornography is usually condemned because it is equated with obscenity, that which is dirty, shameful, and degrad-
ing. If, however, we do not accept such traditional beliefs
about sex, then the mere fact that pornography stimulates
sexual excitement cannot, by itself, be grounds for condem-
nation. Pornography is also accused of other evils, as in
Irving Kristol's pronouncement that "pornography ... is inherently and purposefully subversive of civilization and its
institutions."[1] On a less Spenglerian level this translates
into accusations that pornography causes a breakdown in
sexual morals and the family, and encourages juvenile de-
linquency, sex crimes, and other perversions. Whether
pornography does have these far-reaching consequences is
an empirical question, a difficult enough problem even without the assumption that an end to civilization is "inherently
and purposefully" intended. This evokes a picture analogous
to the old stereotype of the bearded anarchist gleefully working on the bombs that will destroy the regime. But all one
really need assume about the poor hack scribbling away is
that he hopes someone will become excited.

* * *

The National Commission on Obscenity and Pornography,
which completed its work in 1970, sponsored a number of
research studies ranging from the quasi-experimental to
opinion surveys, and consequently we are in a better position than previously to deal with the empirical question. The
results must be accepted with more than the usual reservations, since the methodological difficulties of social-psycho-
logical research are compounded by the nature of the problem. Even when the effect may be observed by direct
measurement of physiological changes, the Heisenberg Uncertainty Principle complicates matters: the instrumentation
measuring sexual arousal tends to inhibit response. In addition, none of the "experimental" studies assessed the long-
range effects of pornography, and, for obvious reasons, no
studies involved children. Still, with all their limitations,
the findings seem to justify the following propositions:

(1) Exposure to pornographic materials produces sexual

arousal "in substantial proportions of males and females." Heterosexual materials rather than homosexual or sadomaso- chistic materials are more significant in producing arousal.

(2) Continued exposure to pornography results in satiation of arousal and interest.

(3) Established patterns of sexual behavior are not signifi- cantly altered by exposure to pornography. After exposure there is an increase in coital activity by those with an available sexual partner, but the effect disappears within 48 hours. Those without available partners or those who mas- turbate regularly show increases in masturbatory activity, but this too disappears within two days.

(4) Exposures to pornographic stimuli have little or no effect on "established attitudinal commitments regarding either sexuality or sexual morality."

(5) There is no relation between criminal sex offenses, other forms of crime, and juvenile deliquency and the use of por- nography. [2]

Obviously, these findings can have only an indirect impact on popular beliefs about pornography. Research re- sults by themselves no more inhibit attempts at censorships or legal prosecutions than scientific findings on race can by themselves eradicate prejudice and discrimination. It is possible to argue, though, that in the current cultural situa- tion it is difficult to conceive of the antipornography forces mustering strength to bring back "the bad old days" when D. H. Lawrence and Henry Miller were under-the-counter items.

On the other hand, notwithstanding the recent and rapid changes in attitudes toward sex, these very changes contribute to the strength of the antiabortion movement and the opposition to the Equal Rights Amendment. These anti- feminist forces are reinforced by the zealous foes of pornog- raphy. The recent defeats of ERA, while not wholly a re- sult of the fears and anxieties generated by "the sexual rev- olution," show how strong this opposition can be. The Hustler prosecution and that of the actors by district attorneys on the political make also indicate that traditional civil liberties problems have by no means been completely settled. Such legal actions have a "chilling effect" on free speech; they encourage self-censorship and caution among publishers and producers who are not a notably courageous lot.

Restrictions on anything resembling freedom of speech
and thought obviously touch the most deep-seated sentiments
of liberals and radicals.    But more is at work here than
mere political opinion, for the radical also tends to be attracted to a position on pornography and erotica like that of
Paul Goodman.    In one of his "utopian essays" Goodman
starts from the premise that the need for pornography is a
result of "a general repressive antisexuality" to which censorship contributes.    But, he continues, we are living in a
period of transition, a time when ideas about sex are breaking through the barriers of repression.    We now require
laws and attitudes that permit the once repressed drives "to
reappear as themselves and come into their own equilibrium,
according to organic self-regulation."    It is necessary to
allow art and artists to perform their traditional function of
"dreaming forbidden thoughts, assuming the forbidden stances,
and struggling to make sense."    In the long run a free and
uninhibited flow of erotica would help demolish sexual repression and, ultimately, the need for pornography. [3]

Utopian essays, by definition, deal with the long
range, but life is always lived in the short run.    Today we
experience an almost uninhibited flow of explicit material
that is more pornographic than erotic, and it is more likely
to raise our hackles than our hopes for the future.    We long
for Goodman's prophecy of an end to repression to come
true, but we worry about the consequences, between now and
then, of the uncontrolled availability of pornography.    Feminists, for example, worry about the image of women that
pornography encourages, and sometimes find themselves un-
sympathetic to traditional civil liberties arguments and utopian visions.    And so, in spite of political prejudices, one
begins to pay closer attention to the arguments that can be
made for restrictions on pornography.

* * *

One argument, just a step or two removed from a knee-jerk
puritanism, is the reiteration of the traditional stereotypes
of a direct relationship between pornography and unacceptable
behavior--e.g., a viewing of Deep Throat encourages prom-
iscuity.    This simplistic view is modified by a second argument:    findings like those of the Commission on Obscenity
and Pornography overlook the long-range consequences; it is
inconceivable that the widespread availability and use of pornography can have no effect on social institutions, the culture, and attitudes and behavior of people.    So Kristol is

convinced that it undermines civilization, while a novelist
and critic like George P. Elliott believes that pornography
is an attack on "society as such" because it subverts the
institution of the family. [4]  Such propositions often rest on a
philosophical justification of censorship.   The legitimacy of
censorship, says Walter Berns, rests on "the positive role
of law.   This role finds law as the promoter of virtue, as
a means to habituate to virtue...."[5]   Or, as he put it in a
later article, there is a "necessity for the law to make a
modest effort to promote good character."[6]   The virtuous
man, the person of good character, is one whose morality
and conduct conform to the requirements of nature.   In the
deep background, then, are natural law theories that hold,
in David Spitz's words (describing a position he does not
himself accept), that freedom does not "involve a choice to
act 'wrongly.'"[7]

One of the difficulties of assessing the argument about
the long-run effects is that frequently the necessary distinction between pornography and erotica is not made.   Elliott,
for example, sees the danger to society as emanating from
"erotic nihilists" like Henry Miller whose work has "literary
value ... enough to redeem its pornography but not enough
to make one ignore its destructive intent."[8]   Since it is work
like Miller's that has such dire consequences, his novels
must have some qualities not found in books filling the racks
of "adult bookstores."   Obviously, if Elliott is correct, it
is erotic writing rather than pornography that subverts "society as such."   But against this mere assertion of fact,
there is the plausible argument that neither pornography nor
erotic writing can have the effects claimed for them.

                              *  *  *

Pornography is concerned only with sexual arousal; it raises
no questions about the significance of sex in the life of individuals or society.   The pornographer concentrates on sex
alone; he takes the everyday world in which sexual behavior
occurs as given and unproblematic.   An acceptance of the
givenness of the world is a necessary condition for successful pornography, since the presumed pleasures to be derived
from the representations of intercourse are hard to come by
if one is distracted by discourse on the meaning and significance of human sexuality.   Because sex is treated in isolation from all other aspects of life, its representation is ap-
prehended as having no pertinence to the totality of a person's experience.   Whatever values and attitudes toward sex

a person brings to reading or viewing of pornography remains
unchallenged by that experience. This accounts for the common and seemingly paradoxical reaction to porno movies--
that they are sexually arousing and boring.

Changes in behavior that are stable and not simply the
result of external coercions involve changes in beliefs and
attitudes to which we must be persuaded. Persuasion trans-
forms the ways of understanding oneself, the world about
one, and the relationship between self and the world. In
phenomenological terms, behavioral change requires a new
construction of reality. It is precisely at this point that
pornography fails: the construction of a new social reality
is founded on social discourse while pornography is solely
concerned with sexual intercourse.

Unlike pornography, art is concerned with exploring
the relationships among people and their worlds with the
aim of involving and moving the reader. When we identify
with characters or adopt attitudes toward them we enter their
world, and the more we are captured by the created world
the greater the possibility that it can affect ideas and beliefs
in the real world. In effect, being moved by a work of art
means entering into discourse with "another" social reality,
and such discourse can make our reality problematic. Whatever power "erotic nihilists" can exercise rests on that function of art. But the power is easily exaggerated.

Anthony Burgess, himself a novelist, noted in an essay on pornography that "didactic works" like Mein Kampf
and Das Kapital have had more influence than books "which
merely represent life, no matter how onesidedly."9   Art
does not mean to instruct or persuade, which is not to say
that art cannot affect ideas and beliefs or that "books make
no difference." But very few works of art in any era have
had significant historical effects (as opposed to idiosyncratic
effects on individuals). Uncle Tom's Cabin, for example,
is said to have influenced feelings about slavery, but one
must take into account that the novel built on already existing abolitionist sentiment. To put the matter baldly: art
has an effect only when people are prepared to be affected.
The effect art can have in these circumstances is to support
and perhaps accelerate changes already underway in the society and culture.

How limited is the independent power of art alone can
be appreciated in our present situation. If we ask what kind

of writing has had the most effect on "the sexual revolution,"
it is clear that "didactic works" like those of Masters and
Johnson, The Joy of Sex, and the mountains of print produced by ardent feminists fiercely dedicated to changing the
hearts and minds of women and men have exercised the
critical influence.  Or, to put the same point differently,
books like Uncle Tom's Cabin owe their influence less to
their quality as works of art than their intent to instruct and
persuade.

* * *

In the absence, then, of empirical evidence and plausible
arguments one must remain skeptical of the presumed long-
run consequences of pornography and erotica.  But even if
one were to grant that they undermine civilization and social
institutions, the justification for censorship rests on grounds
unacceptable to liberals and radicals.

        To say that pornography and erotic writing endanger
institutions is to say that they affect beliefs and opinion about
the proper way to organize social relationships, about the
appropriate means for accomplishing the tasks necessary to
maintain society.  These are political questions, and censorship would prohibit exposure to a full range of politically
relevant perspectives.  To defend censorship is to assume
that existing social arrangements represent the best of all
possible worlds, or, since we already know what the proper
relationships among people ought to be, citizens need not be
distracted by wrong and incorrect views.  Even if one only
believes that the present arrangements are more bearable
than what would result from the unrestricted availability of
pornography, our historical experience suggests that censorship more often than not kills what it is ostensibly designed
to protect.  Those prejudiced in favor of freedom must reject anything that interferes with people's right to free political choice.

        Can nothing be done, then, to secure ourselves
against the daily offense of pornography?

        The arguments about pornography and its effects ap-
ply only to adults and not to children.  Our lack of knowledge
about its effects on children combined with the plausibility of
arguments that they are at greater risk from pornography
than adults favor retaining the present restrictions on children's access to it.  Similarly, the use of children in por-

nographic movies can and ought to be prosecuted under child abuse laws.   Beyond this we shall have to be satisfied with more limited goals.

All cities have zoning laws that separate, for example, industrial from residential land use.   For most people pornography is like the noxious stink of a glue factory, and just as we locate the factory away from homes so we can zone to restrict our public encounters with pornography.   We can limit the location and number of establishments dealing solely with pornography.

A zoning ordinance designed to protect residential areas from "adult bookstores" and porno movie houses would restrict them to business and entertainment districts where anonymity has always cloaked the pursuit of anomalous pleasures.   In cities that have escaped the blight of urban renewal there are residential neighborhoods overlapping these districts; some are traditional "slums" while others are "respectable" middle-class areas.   Residents of these neighborhoods, as well as those whose occupations bring them to the center of the city, will be more exposed to the offensiveness of pornography than others.   But this location has always had similar disadvantages.   Neighborhoods are "slums," in part, because their inhabitants already have to contend with such social pollutants as prostitution and drugs, and some of the most exclusive and expensive neighborhoods of Manhattan overlook the smoke and brutal ugliness of Consolidated Edison's generating plants.   Similarly, in some cities pornography will defile public places to a greater extent than in others.   When a city like New York tries to attract tourists as a great place to visit it encourages the trade in pornography.   After all, the attraction of the metropolis always has been the promise of pleasures unavailable at home.

This modest proposal implies that here as elsewhere in the life of the society, we must bear the consequences of the beliefs that define us as political beings.   Just as the commitment to freedom of speech or due process of law means that we put up with a flow of ethnic and racial scurrilities and the occasional freeing of an obvious criminal, so too we must continue to contend with the burden of pornography.   Our consolation is the austere one that the alternative to freedom would prove rather more burdensome.

References

1.  On the Democratic Idea in America. (New York: Har-
       per & Row, 1972), p. 40.
2.  U. S. Commission on Obscenity and Pornography. The
       Report of the ... (Washington, D. C.: U. S. G. P. O.,
       1970), pp. 163-243. Further analyses of the research
       done for the commission are reported in a special
       issue of the Journal of Social Issues, vol. 29, no. 3,
       1973.
3.  Utopian Essays and Practical Proposals. (New York:
       Random House, 1962), pp. 55, 57.
4.  Conversions. (New York, Dutton, 1971), pp. 164-65.
5.  Freedom, Virtue and the First Amendment. (Chicago:
       Henry Regnery Co. --Gateway Edition, 1965), p. 240.
6.  "Pornography and Democracy: The Case for Censor-
       ship," Public Interest, Winter 1971, p. 14.
7.  "Freedom, Virtue and the New Scholasticism," Commen-
       tary, October 1959, p. 314.
8.  Elliott, op. cit., p. 164.
9.  "What is Pornography," in Douglas A. Hughes, Perspec-
       tives on Pornography. (New York: St. Martin's
       Press, 1970), p. 5. This anthology also contains
       versions of the Goodman and Elliott articles.

Lionel Abel


Malinowski, writing some years back on the sexual life of
savages, told us that when nothing else could stimulate them,
the natives of the Trobriand Islands often told sexual jokes.
Apparently, this was their last--as it was their best--recourse
against continuing ennui. The anthropologist did not make it
quite clear whether, when bored, they turned directly to
stories and jokes about sex, or only after other efforts to
raise their spirits had failed. But if it can be said that
under certain circumstances they turned to pornography--the
word "pornography" is perhaps not quite applicable here--in
any case it must be noted that they did not contribute to the
advancement of any specialists in pornography. Certainly
they did not aid forces destructive of their society every
time they felt tired of life and looked to stories or jokes
about sex to help them back into it.

        From which we may learn two things: (1) There are
life-enhancing as well as life-destroying ways of referring to

sex, and the sexual act. (The life-enhancing quality of references to sex in Shakespeare and, most especially, in
Rabelais can hardly be covered by the terms "pornography"
and "obscenity," which properly describe the kind of literacy
and photographic material regularly published in Hustler and
Playboy magazines.) And (2), in the Trobriand Island cul-
tures, references to sex were allowable under particular
conditions subject to social opinion. There were no quarrels
among the people of the islands, I take it, as to the exact
definition of pornography; the tribesmen knew intuitively when
and under what circumstances it was proper and even right
to talk amusingly of sex.

Now the kind of pornography we encounter while walking through Times Square, and in the downtown areas of most
American cities--quite well described, by the way, though
with insufficient indignation, by Murray Hausknecht--has no
relation whatever to any positive life value to which I, or
Mr. Hausknecht, for that matter, could point. These sexual
displays seem exclusively directed to making life seem worthless to anyone who still feels any kind of awe or reverence
for it. What the pornographic literature and spectacles in
these areas indicate is not at all that certain practices are
now socially acceptable, but that society has withdrawn from
certain parts of our cities and relinquished these to forces
that are either purely commercial or purely criminal.

Murray Hausknecht fears that protests against pornographic literature and shows might lead to a censorship that
would also be directed against more genuine kinds of communication. No doubt censorship is a dangerous instrument,
and one that has often been misused. It is required, though,
if social opinion lacks force, as it certainly does right now,
to control pornography. Years ago people would have been
ashamed to be found reading Hustler, which now awaits you
every time you visit the barber shop. If society is nonexistent in some areas, then, of course, there has to be legal
action against pornography, unless we can be reconciled to
the horrors of downtown America.

Mr. Hausknecht has referred to "knee-jerk" Puritan
reactions. I don't have the faintest notion of what he can
have in mind. I doubt very much if there is any kind of
Puritanism now extant that can be properly so characterized.
And I would accuse Mr. Hausknecht of knee-jerk reactions
to anything said by Irving Kristol, even when what Mr.
Kristol has said is perfectly sound. Apparently Mr. Kristol

has expressed the opinion that pornography is destructive of civilized life.   Objecting, Mr. Hausknecht asks, Where is the empirical evidence?   Now the question is naive.   We can hardly subject civilizations to controlled experiment so as to determine their tolerance or intolerance of pornographic displays and obscene literature.   Mr. Kristol can of course speak for himself, but when he says pornography is destructive of civilization he may have meant merely precisely what Mr. Hausknecht means when he inveighs against the sexual displays on Times Square:   such displays are not consistent with civilized life as we know it.   And I would give one more argument.   The idea expressed by Paul Goodman (he is cited on this very point by Murray Hausknecht) that our civilization is sexually repressive conveys, to me at least, the implication that the maintenance of our civilization requires the censorship of pornography.   Now it was against such censorship that Goodman initiated his "dirty speech" campaign.   So the very idea with which Goodman justified his promotion of "dirty speech" was that communications of this type were needed to undermine our "civilization" as Mr. Kristol has inferred.

A contemporary Spanish radical, Tierno Gaván, has written movingly on the trivialization of life in modern times, noting especially the trivializing of the erotic.   This last he lays up to the current trend to antiasceticism.   He is not an ascetic himself, and he is not in favor of asceticism--he wants us to accept our destiny, which, as he sees the matter, must necessarily take the form of antiasceticism and trivialization.   But we do not have to be concerned here with what Tierno recommends.   What is interesting about the writer is that he has not joined the chorus of those who find modern Western civilization too "repressive" for their taste--Tierno rightly finds it antiascetic and, as a consequence, trivializing.

* * *

Now one of the most important effects of pornography is to trivialize the erotic.   Is that to be our destiny?   Certainly it is one that is in line with most psychoanalytic thinking, with the outcry against any kind of inhibition, and with the high regard for everything low now favored in intellectual circles.   I think that Murray Hausknecht is speaking for all these trends when he tells us that radicals naturally tend to protest against inhibitions of any kind.   In fact, the assertion is quite false.   Radicals, if we are to include among

them revolutionaries also, have in most instances been
rather ascetic, and represented asceticism ideologically.    It
was not the aristocrats of England who closed down the
theaters in the 17th century.    It was not the courtiers of
Versailles, but Robespierre, the social radical, who thought
the pursuit of sexual pleasures contrary to the good of the
Republic.    And coming closer to the present time, didn't we
hear it said that Castro prohibited sex among the men and
women fighting with him in the Sierra Maestra?

I do not accept the view that the trivialization of sex
is something for which we are inescapably destined.    Here,
I think, one has to be certain of one's values rather than of
any particular set of facts.    The trend is certainly toward
trivialization, but this trend, too, can pass.    And here we
touch on what may be one of the deepest antinomies of the
present order of things.    There are many like Mr. Hausknecht,
who would rather not censor literature or displays because they
think censorship itself uncivilized.    But on the other hand, the
trivialization of the erotic is also barbarous, for the barbar-
ian may be described as the diminished man, the one whose
experience of life (and sex) has been attenuated.    Civilization
and trivialization may, in fact, be incompatible.

Joyce's Ulysses is often mentioned by defenders of
pornography because Ulysses, too, was at one time prohibited.    Now when I first read the novel--it was in the early
30s--I did admire Molly Bloom's "dirty speech" and unconscious soliloquizing at the book's close.    In fact I admired
her whole soliloquy for its uninhibited expressiveness.    Today I think less of it.    Certainly it is not equal to the
speeches of Cleopatra in Shakespeare, or of Phaedra in
Racine's great play.    All the same it remains an extraordinary outpouring of thoughts and feelings.    We know, of course,
that Molly Bloom had not seen Times Square or the downtown
of any contemporary American city.    Given her common sense
and feeling for life, had she seen Times Square as Mr.
Hausknecht and I have seen it, she would, I believe, have
expressed herself quite differently at the end of Ulysses.
Instead of her forthright "yes," she would as forcefully have
repeated "no."    Molly, go ahead now.    You've seen the city:

> And I thought not them but someone else and I
> could never ask any of them with my eyes to ask
> again No and if anyone asked me I would say No
> to just say No and I would not put my arms around
> anyone or draw anyone down let no one feel my

breasts No and let their hearts be fucking like mad
and No I said No I will not No


George P. Elliott


On the basic issues, I pretty much agree with Hausknecht.

(1) Pornography is offensive.   However, the Goodmanesque
benefits supposed to accrue from removing all restrictions
on it seem to me not just dubious, as they seem to
Hausknecht, but foolish, since I can't imagine that dirty sex
can be freed without also releasing those other things, some of
them very dangerous, with which it is involved; but let that pass.

(2) Censorship is even more offensive.   However, as an
artist I note that nearly all artists, in nearly all ages and
countries, have worked under social restrictions of varying
intensity, some of these in the form of overt censorship
laws, and that occasionally these very prohibitions inform
the work of art, sometimes to its advantage.   Don Quixote,
one of the supreme stories, would not be as it is unless
Cervantes had worked under a Most Catholic censorship, and
to imagine that he would have told that story better had he
been unrestrained is mere liberal fantasy--other, yes, but
not better.   But the whole question of the relationship between artist and censorship is too intricate to go into here;
besides, it is only one of many free-speech issues and not
the determining one.

(3) Therefore, let us protect society at large, not by forbidding public pornography outright, but by sequestering it.
Agreed.

My disagreements with Hausknecht have to do with
the complexity of the issues.   It seems to me that he finds
the whole matter so distasteful that he simplifies it unreal-
istically.

For one thing, he does not deal with the difficulty of
sequestering mass-distributed pornography--books, magazines,
movies, television.   It can be done, but doing so involves
much more governmental machinery than he (or I) would like
or than the ACLU thinks the First Amendment allows; by
comparison, maintaining a red-light district is simple.

Additionally, he makes much too neat a division be-

tween pornography and "erotic" art. In reality, some valid
works of art contain parts that are simple pornography, and
there are many--very many--borderline instances where the
categories are most unclear. No rules can be formulated
that will guide law-enforcement officers. The distinctions
must be made case-by-case, and this calls for magistrates
of some sort, whether bureaucrats or, as I prefer, boards
of censors. A nasty business all around; but, if you are
going to sequester, you must have someone to say "this is
to be sequestered, that not," and under this necessity I think
citizens' committees less likely to abuse their power than
minor bureaucrats. But, whatever the best answer,
Hausknecht evades the whole question.

He also proposes the opinion that true art does not
instruct or persuade. No doubt in esthetic discussions true
art does not. But actual art in the real world often does.
Dostoevsky, Dickens, Shaw, Brecht, Pound--they are never
didactic in intent and effect? Come off it. But even if an
artist has no didactic intention, I believe--though I cannot
demonstrate with sociological surveys, I believe, as most
societies believe, hence the restrictions they erect--I believe
that the effect of art may be not purely and tidily esthetic
but also moral, obscurely, remotely, unprovably moral,
modifying attitudes and thereby behavior. Furthermore,
pornography has sometimes been used as an instrument of
didactic purpose: Sade. The Marquis announced himself
an enemy of society; his own society (first under the Mon-
archy, then under the Revolution except for a brief period
during the Terror, then under the first Empire) saw him as
an enemy and so treated him and his writings; his works,
of which pornography is an essential ingredient, are powerful antisocial, immoral weapons. He is the extreme case,
and though, as Burgess says, no novelist is as efficacious
as Hitler or Marx, Sade is efficacious enough to be worri-
some. I am in favor of sequestering his books, not because
they do no harm, but because all that is involved in totally
censoring them is likely to do more harm.

In addition to these simplifications, Hausknecht weak-
ens his case by what I conceive to be some wrong emphases.
He minimizes the power of pornography; it is a low, bad,
unclean art, but an art that is of some intrinsic power and
is sometimes put to the service of a vile persuasion. He
leaves unmentioned what I take to be a self-evident fact, that
any healthy society, including one as libertarian as ours, pro-
tects itself against such outrages against what it holds to be

decent custom as public pornography; I know that this opinion is respectable and that respectability has long been
tarnished as bourgeois, but, like a good many other things
that radicals dismiss as burgeois, to sequester pornography,
like sequestering prostitution, seems to me civilized, whether
bourgeois or not, and to let pornography run rampant, as we
now do, largely unrestrained and even condoned to the extent of allowing it to be advertised and discussed with approval in the public press, seems to be decadent, a classic
instance of that license which is liberal excess. Most important, Hausknecht exaggerates the malignant power of censorship, as though any and every censorship were as bad as
the totalitarian variety; for example, it is by no means true
on the face of it that "censorship more often than not kills
what it is ostensibly designed to protect," though a possible
argument might hold that this has been true in the parish of
history we inhabit, the Enlightened West in which censorship
as such has come to be seen by many as an abusive instrument of oppression rather than as an ordinary function of
government, subject to abuse of course but not so bad when
generally agreed upon.

All the same, in the matter of what to do about pornography now, Hausknecht's case is my case.


Cynthia Fuchs Epstein


In the small Ohio city where I used to work, it was common
knowledge that every month or so the American Legion would
show "dirty" movies. Members of the post would gather,
and after the flag had been saluted and the padre had blessed
the meeting and (ostentatiously) left the hall, all would settle
down for an evening of beer and stag films. No one in the
community, not even their wives or parents, openly objected.
The Legion practice in southern Ohio was probably not very
different from that in other areas. It was as American as
motherhood and apple pie.

No doubt, many functions were served by men gathering in this fashion; almost tribal, a prototypical ritual of collective conscience according to the gospel of Emile Durkheim.
Men and their brothers engaging in forbidden games, analogous
to the secret societies in preliterate groups whose rituals
serve to band men of maturity together, to initiate adolescent men to their ranks, and to set themselves apart from

women.   Practices that underscore men's particularity, often
to their hierarchical advantage.

One might even argue that when pornography is
legalized and publicly offered, it is no longer offered in a
form that serves the "weness" of community but rather contributes to alienation and anomie.   Pornography for the individual and not the group causes sex to become an anonymous experience.   (A colleague has even instructed me that
the best way to watch a pornographic movie is alone; to
bring a friend is to introduce an element of "relationship,"
which dilutes or confuses the total porn experience.)

But perhaps we shouldn't simplistically sentimentalize
pornography as a positive expression of group solidarity.
We know, after all, that what is functional for the in-group
may precipitate antagonisms to the out-group.   What are the
further consequences of pornography?   Whom does it serve?
Whom does it help?   Whom does it harm?

We do not know much about the answers.   Only the
crudest measures have been used and I question the way the
questions have been conceptualized and put.   Sociologist Ned
Polsky informs me that the incidence of child molestation
went down in Denmark with the ending of all restrictions on
pornography.   He has argued that pornography provides the
opportunity for persons to act out sexual needs vicariously
or through fantasy that defuses possible antisocial expression.   If this is so, the case for unlimited pornographic expression has some merit.   Yet, one may ask, how truly
related are the factors in this presumed causal relationship?
As far as I know, no social scientist has ever done community studies to see what are the consequences of porn experiences for the "normal population," outside a laboratory
setting.   No one studied what happened to those American
Legionnaires in Ohio after their monthly meetings, but I can
speculate on what investigators would have found.   Some
probably managed to supress their aroused urges and some
probably were put straight to bed, victims of the evening's
beer.   However, we can infer from findings of the 1970
Commission on Pornography that some, sexually aroused,
mated with their wives with renewed vigor.   And some, (we
are discovering this with alarming frequency) may have
drunkenly beaten the wives who wouldn't.   (The courts deny
it is rape if the husband forces sex on his wife.)   Others
may have mused through the week about that pert waitress
in the diner who is always really "asking for it anyway" and

may have tried a tickle or some remarks.  I don't think
that even regression analysis will tell us whether the porn
movies might have contributed to the events surmised above,
or the drink, or the "we" spirit of the boys getting together
without the women.

As I interview people whose opinions I value on the
perplexing problem of censorship and freedom and pornography, which led me to these series of reflections, I find that
some of my best male friends and colleagues (who are hardly Mr. Middle America in their intellect or taste) turn out
to be porn-movie regulars.  These are men of sensitivity,
of civil libertarian mind, who write and act in their private
lives as committed feminists.  For them, in varying degrees,
porn is a voyage into erotica; a way of touching base with
their elemental being; a lift from a world of words and ab-
stractions; a diversion or dream.  They are not turned mean
by exposure to pornography but are turned on or off to sexuality, depending on whether they've experienced the porn as
"good" or "bad."  They argue for license as freedom and
contend that expression of sexuality in any form (save that
which depicts and uses children) opens and expands the individual and collective opportunity structure.

If they were in fact models of most men, or if 95
percent (or 80 percent or 50 percent) of the legionnaires
were like them, I could easily subscribe to unqualified freedom.  I find fault in their reasoning although I concede they
are accurate in part.

As Murray Hausknecht points out, there is porn, and
there is porn that is erotica.  There is the not so bad old
stuff such as Fanny Hill and the work of Frank Harris,
there is "literature" such as Lady Chatterly's Lover.  There
are also the X-rated movies in sections such as New York's
42nd Street, the monthly perusal of Playboy, a skim of
Penthouse at the barber's, and glances at the covers of
Hustler and similar magazines at the news stand.

The movies seen by my academic friends turn out to
be not bad politically.  Indeed, one colleague assures me
that the movies he sees depict an equal enthusiasm by wom-
en and men for the satisfaction of erotic pleasures.  Yet
what of the pornographic literature and media that bears a
message of inequality and exploitation?  Take The Story of O
and even the high art of Henry Miller, which the feminist
community decries as debasing to women and evocative of

ugly images regarding them.   What of pornography that exploits the weak?   Most of the colleagues whose wisdom I've
sought claim not to be attracted to whips and chains and
don't come much into contact with porn based on pleasure
through brutality.

But there is a large business in pornography that depicts exploitation and brutalization of women, and men (though
to a lesser degree).   Pornography doesn't originate these
views but it does aid and abet them.   It legitimates a set of
attitudes for a public unfortunately prepared to subscribe to
the notion that pain can be pleasure, particularly on the part
of women.   This view, grounded in folk culture and a cor-
rupted Freudian psychology, has serious and dangerous political overtones.

* * *

In the absence of knowing just how much pornography is to
blame, but suspecting its impact, I would like to curtail expression of certain kinds of messages that demean and hurt
groups of people.   Because I am for nonsexist terminology
in text books and against the media presentation of black men
and women as shuffling, illiterate, lazy and inept, or of
Jews as crafty and avaricious, I am also against porn movies, television programs, and magazines that portray wom-
en--and men--as victims who love their victimization.

It is argued that censorship is dangerous because the
censors are not qualified to make judgments.   But those who
question the qualifications of the censors--and who deny that
anyone is qualified to censor--exercise standards of judgment
in their everyday lives and indeed often make their living by
making judgments.

These same persons, who deny any right to judge the
presentation of sexual matter, impose standards of excellence
in English composition, piano playing, or research techniques
in their own fields.   Outside their fields, they often express
fury about bad films, theater, art, and home decoration.
Who shall judge, they ask, and in the next moment they are
judging the worthiness of a political candidate, the system of
Justice in the U.S., or when it became decent to travel in
Spain or buy a Volkswagen.   In fact, they judge and censor
the use of poor grammar in texts, the behavior they consider
inappropriate, and the spread of ideas they consider to be
abhorrent.

Every society imposes standards of taste, of morality, and of behavior.  One may not strike another person; to do so is to commit the crime of assault.  One may not falsely accuse another person to his or her detriment; to do so is to commit the crime of libel.  It is not considered a limitation of one's personal freedom to be denied the right to freely express anger and hatred of a type that is detrimental to the health of society.  Many otherwise responsible citiziens have opposed such community measures as mandatory schooling, innoculation, fluoridation of the water, and prohibitions on dumping of raw sewage into public water.  Which side were we on?  Somehow any restriction on pornography is symbolic to some of an end to freedom of speech and an end to poetry and beauty.

Yet it is within the nature of social life to permit freedom in some areas and not others, to judge the cost of freedom and of its restrictions, and to make decisions about what social good may be served.  We are capable of deciding to teach Bellow and not Irving Wallace in a course on the modern novel and surely we can decide to retain James Joyce and not Hustler.  Many aspects of the good society entail decisions for less freedom and more restrictions.  I can think of some right off:  restrictions on cars that use large quantities of gasoline, tomatoes that are gassed to ripeness, possession of guns, littering, cigarette advertising, and the playing of transistor radios on public beaches.  I also think it would not be too great a denial of freedom of personal expression or art in America to prohibit films indicating that the highest form of sensuality is to hack up your lover as the grande finale of the sex act.  I believe we should censor pornography that insults, defames, and encourages assault on people, men or women.  I believe that words and pictures have power.  I fear the point of view that is insensitive to the implications of the pornography that is grounded in society's tolerance of brutality toward women or men.  Clever as we are, I think we can work out a way to differentiate between the pornography that is bad for our culture, ourselves and our families, and that which is a frolic into the world of sensuality or even a tolerable vulgarity.

We've all marched to ban the bomb and to prevent radioactive fall-out even though some scientists said it wasn't clear how much fall-out was injurious to the health.  Perhaps there's something to be said for an ounce of prevention in matters of the psyche.

Irving Howe

My response to pornography is not so much to be socially
alarmed as imaginatively disheartened.  I don't know what
damage, if any, it does to society or the future generations.
I don't know if it encourages rape or stimulates perversion.
I don't know if it threatens the family.  But when I walk
along 42nd Street in New York City and pass the peep-hole
joints, the hard-core movie houses, the shabby bookstores,
I find myself growing depressed.  Is this what humanity, or
even a portion of it, has come to in the late years of the
20th-century?

The association of sex with brutal violence, the
ideologizing of sadomasochism, the reduction of love to
snickering mechanics, the fixation upon bodily organs that
in their photographic enlargement can seem as disgusting as
Swift said they were--all these point to some profound de-
rangement of life that no one, to my knowledge, has fully
explained as yet.  Why should men, even the "rejects" of
our society, find pleasure in all this?  Or do they find
pleasure?

Before worrying about "what to do" with regard to
pornography, I'd like to know a good deal more about it.
The prevalent liberal assumption has been that pornography
is a by-product of repression, sexuality twisted and sickened
into pathology.  But there seems in recent decades to have
occurred a decline in social repression, yet the interest in
pornography has visibly grown.  To which, in turn, the
usual answer is that a partial release of repressive mechanisms brings, not immediate health, but an outburst of the
symptoms of the disease caused by the repression.  This is
an argument hard to check, impossible to refute.  Suppose
it isn't true?  In any case, who knows?

The conclusion from the liberal premise is that we
must go all the way toward removing social restraints upon
sexuality, even if many of the immediate consequences are
unattractive.  There can surely be no serious return to
older modes of repression, denial or even discipline--to
speak of a return of Victorianism is to indulge in a fantasy
or, at best, a metaphor.

My guess is that democratic societies probably have
no choice but to go along with this outlook, ragged as it is

and uncertain as we may be about its premises.   Still, the
thought must haunt one:  Suppose we go "all the way" (how
does one do that?) toward the release of socially enforced
repression, and what if then we still don't enter a time of
shared health and well-being but instead witness a growth of
the debasing, corrupt, inhumane values and tastes upon which
pornography feeds?

* * *

So I walk along 42nd Street and, seeing what one sees there,
I remember Trotsky's expectation, at the end of his book
Literature and Revolution, that mankind would yet rise to the
levels of Goethe, Beethoven, and Marx.   It's not a program
I find entirely attractive, nor is there much evident need to
worry about it; but still ... the sheer moral ugliness of the
porn scene, the waste and distortion it suggests of human
capacity--how can that be reconciled with social hopes?   I
find 42nd Street more destructive of my morale as a socialist than all the neoconservative polemics of the last 30 years.

Still, the argument for censorship doesn't seem persuasive.   Does anyone remember Prohibition?   At this point
in history, after all we have tasted of the age of totalitarian-
ism, how can anyone suppose that the possible benefits of
censorship could outweigh the probable dangers?

Which isn't to say that certain modes of social protection might not be considered.   If you want to go into one
of those joints for $5 and see what you see and do what you
do there, I don't propose to stop you.   But I see no reason
why I or my kids should be forced to look, when we walk
along the streets, at the stuff that delights you and disgusts
me.   Go to the porn movie but don't oblige me to look at
its stills just because I'm walking by.   Get your Hustler in
a brown paper wrapper, but don't oblige me to be hustled
by it just because there's a newstand round my corner.

Such a limited management may be feasible, I'm not
sure.   But it doesn't begin to get at the deeper problem,
the endlessly depressing question of why so many people
yield themselves to the wretched stuff.

David Spitz


Only salacious individuals are likely to deny that pornography

is a serious problem.  It offends many people, and in a
particularly objectionable way, because some pornographic
displays are often unavoidable.  But people are offended by
many things, and unless it can be shown that a distasteful
item or practice adversely affects their interests and not
merely their sentiments, or stands in a necessary (causal)
relationship to criminal conduct, or seriously impairs rather
than marginally troubles a community's quality of life--none
of which (with respect to pornography) has yet been conclu-
sively demonstrated--we should hesitate to meet that practice
by censorship and other legal sanctions rather than by moral
and social disapprobation.

It is of course a familiar stratagem, perhaps derived
from our Puritan heritage, to seek to exorcise an evil by
legislating against it.  But evil is not easily or always
eradicated by political fiat, and the use of legal instrumen-
talities may introduce still greater evils.  It may be useful
to recall some of these potential (I think highly probable)
dangers.

First, who will be the censors--an elegant word for
petty bureaucrats--who will distinguish "obscene" from acceptable literature (books, magazines, films, plays, etc.),
observing the careful distinction drawn by sober thinkers
like Murray Hausknecht between "erotica" and "pornography"
and employing standards that yield clarity of meaning and
ease of administration rather than extensive and bewildering
judicial wrangling?

If censorship is really to work--and here I urge a
rereading of Milton's Areopagitica--the censors must begin
by cataloguing and proscribing all scandalous works already
in print, prohibit the importation of all foreign writings
until they have been examined and approved, expurgate those
works that are partly useful and excellent and partly pernicious, and require all new materials to be submitted prior
to publication.  Such arduous tasks require censors of unusual quality and diligence, and very many of them to boot.
Where will we find them?

By the very nature of the task they are likely to be,
as Milton argued, second- or third-rate minds, "illiterate
and illiberal individuals" who will refuse their sanction to any
work containing views of expressions at all above the level
of "the vulgar superstition."  Men and women of worth would
obviously refuse such an assignment as tedious and unpleas-
ant, and as an immense forfeiture of time and of their own

studies. Such censors as we would be likely to get would be
a constant affront to serious (for I worry not about scurril-
ous) writers, and could only do more harm than good.

Second, does legislation in matters of morality produce significant compliance? Can we safely ignore the
American experience with laws designed to curb or eliminate
prostitution, gambling, the sale and consumption of intoxicat-
ing beverages, the use of marijuana and other drugs, and
the like? Such legislation has not only been ineffectual. It
has created classes of criminals where none existed before;
it has contributed to (if not encouraged and perhaps required)
the growth of organized crime, including smuggling, the black
market, and police corruption; it has promoted a general
contempt for, and widespread disobedience of, law; and it
has in unacceptable ways invaded the realm of privacy.

Third, is not legislation that seeks to suppress or
discourage pornography through heavy taxation intrinsically
discriminatory? Will this do more than deny it only to the
poor? Is it not enough to torture the limits of liberty?
Must we also attack the principle of equality?

A final point. Those who--like the Irving Kristols
and Herbert Marcuses of this world--would invoke the law
to repress what they do not like mistake the very nature of
the goodness they affirm. They would impose their "right"
morality on others, but--even if their morality is "right,"
which is surely contestable--they forget that law as a means
of coercion does not ensure but inhibits the truly moral act,
which is the free and responsible choice of right action. One
is not good when he acts on a choice delegated to others.
Indeed, one is then less than human. For what does it mean
to be a person, a good person, if not that one himself
chooses between good and evil, virtue and vice, truth and
falsehood? Those who would deny him that choice, who insist instead that he forsake his reason and his right to free
decision-making and place his conscience into their custody,
demand that he cease to be a mature and responsible individual. Where, then, do evil and presumption reside?

Murray Hausknecht

A Rejoinder

Lionel Abel seems to suggest that, if only I were more in-

dignant, the way he and I react to Times Square could be
taken as a standard of "civilized life as we know it." That
my tastes and behavior are a measure of civilization is a
powerfully attractive idea, but I fear that it is the road to
madness and, politically speaking, concedes too much to the
Robespierre within us all.

What distinguishes a Robespierre is not his specific
beliefs but that he knows what is "contrary to the good of the
Republic"; that he confounds "civilization" with his own
values.  The difference between a Robespierre and the rest
of us is that he can and does use the power of the state to
enforce his certainties.  Lurking within all of us, however,
is a willingness to impose, given half a chance, our certainties on others.

This Robespierre beneath the skin peeks out at us in
the comments of Abel, Cynthia Epstein, and George P.
Elliott.  Censorship, says Abel, is required, because now
"social opinion lacks force" and "society is nonexistent in
some areas."  Even if we accept these as meaningful terms
of discourse, it is clear that what is not being enforced is
only Abel's notion of what "social opinion" should be or
Elliott's idea of what "decent custom" ought to be.  To say
that "society is nonexistent" is to assume that mere anarchy
rules and then, "of course," there must be "legal action
against pornography."  Similarly, Epstein knows what is
"detrimental to the health of a society" and does not hesitate
to list "the decisions for less freedom and more restrictions"
needed for "the good society."  Even when she is less cer-
tain--"without knowing just how much pornography is to
blame, but suspecting its impact"--she is prepared to employ the full power of the state against it.

The Robespierre within is encouraged by a moral
indignation that often feeds on empty words.  A term like
"civilization" as used by Irving Kristol refers to something
more than Abel's standards of civility in human relationships.
Its connotation embraces art, science, philosophy, technology,
social institutions--that complex social and cultural entity
characteristic of a society or historical era.  Abel is correct, therefore, in saying that when it is used in this global
fashion without further specification no statement about it can
be proven or disproven.  (When confronted with such vacuity
it is useful to naively inquire about the Emperor's clothes.)
Yet the vision conjured up by the notion of "civilization" en-
gulfed by pornography further inflames the sense of outrage
that justifies a readiness to take extreme measures.

Although outrage must command due respect--it is,
after all, a sign of moral commitment--it tends to provoke
an impatience that overrules our customary good sense.
Surely it is Epstein's moral indignation that causes her to
say because we "are capable of deciding to teach Bellow and
not Irving Wallace ... we can decide to retain James Joyce
and not Hustler." Our ability to make judgments is not the
issue; humans, if nothing else, are clever, distinction-making,
categorizing beings.   But it is one thing to omit Irving Wallace from a course on the modern novel and another to bring
the full majesty of the law against Hustler.   Good sense demands that when we consider the latter possibility we first
carefully attend to the kind of questions suggested by David
Spitz rather than the demonic action of a Robespierre.

One reason we tend to overlook these questions is
our readiness to use the power of the state to deal with the
evils arising from capitalist economic institutions.   It is
historically demonstrable that the vast inequalities of capitalist society limit freedom, the ability to make choices.
Using the power of the state to mitigate the effects of capitalism is an attempt to extend the range of freedom.   Bringing state power to bear on a phenomenon like pornography is
an entirely different matter.   Not only are we uncertain
about the effects of pornography but, as Spitz suggests, the
use of the law "inhibits ... the free and responsible choice
of right action."   In this sphere the power of the state
limits human freedom rather than enhancing it.

The artist has to contend not only with Robespierre
but with the urge to teach.   Elliott incorrectly assumed that
I deny the intent is present.   Its presence is most apparent
when the writer surrenders to it and we know precisely what
it is we are being instructed in and persuaded to.   Sade and
Pound, who in the Cantos instructs us on Social Credit policies and tries to persuade us to a hatred of Jews, are
cases in point.   But who, besides those who wished to be,
have been instructed or persuaded by them?   The artist is
most likely to have an effect when the didactic intent is controlled by and subordinated to aesthetic demands.   Brecht,
no doubt, has affected individuals, but surely they were not
instructed by him in Marxist doctrine or persuaded to membership in the Communist party.   It is because the relationship between the artist's intent, his actual work, and its
effects remains mysterious that literary criticism prospers.

Elliott is correct, of course, in pointing out that I

ignored some difficulties in the proposal to zone pornography. Still, he may be overstating some of these difficulties. Categorization, no matter how clever we are, will always create "borderline instances where the categories are most unclear"--that is one foundation of the legal profession's prosperity. It is a problem not unique to the distinction between pornography and other work. Nor does the proposal to zone pornography imply that the police will make the decisions in disputed instances; the idea of zoning suggests a different body. The proposal assumes that once the X-rated movie and the material that normally appears in "adult bookshops" are limited to a few sections of the city there will be fewer complaints about pornography and significantly less demand for complete censorship. Zoning would still leave us with the "moral ugliness" or pornography, but in an imperfect world that is preferable to the certainties imposed on us by a Robespierre.

RIGHT HERE IN RIVER CITY:

A. L. A. , CENSORSHIP, AND ALTERNATIVES*

Ken Kister and Sanford Berman

ALA Reference & Subscription Books Review Committee as Censor: Experiences

The encyclopedia critic understands that threats of censorship
are part of the job.  When I agreed to edit the Encyclopedia
Buying Guide (formerly General Encyclopedias in Print), I
assumed--incorrectly, as it turned out--that any significant
attempts to influence or restrict my critical judgments would
come from the encyclopedia publishers.  After all, the industry has an enormous investment to protect.[1]  Moreover, it
costs a bundle to produce, adequately maintain, and successfully market a quality set.  A negative review can sometimes irreparably damage the prospects for a new encyclopedia or kill off one which lacks "name" appeal.[2]  Under such
circumstances, publisher pressure on the critic, either legal
or extralegal, is not unexpected.  And indeed in the case of
Encyclopedia Buying Guide 1975-1976, there were occasional
abortive efforts by a few publishers, via both threats of
legal action and extralegal maneuvers, to remove or tone
down strong criticisms.

Paradoxically, however, the most effective censorship
I have encountered since undertaking the Buying Guide project
in 1974 has come not from the encyclopedia publishers but
the Reference & Subscription Books Review Committee

*Reprinted by permission of the authors and publisher from
the January-February 1978 issue of CALL (Current Aware-
ness--Library Literature, pp. 3-5.  Copyright © 1978 by
Goldstein Associates.

(RSBRC) of the American Library Association. There have been three distinct instances when the Committee or its brass have acted to prohibit or inhibit my efforts in the area of encyclopedia criticism. Taken singly, none of the incidents is disturbing enough to provoke public comment. But when viewed together, especially as a chronological sequence, they constitute a pattern of censorious activity which brings dishonor on a once worthy reviewing service and, moreover, mocks the ALA's lofty preachments on intellectual freedom.

My introduction to the Committee as censor occurred in 1975 when I asked for permission to quote from RSBRC reviews in Encyclopedia Buying Guide. 3 The request was denied unanimously by the full Committee. 4 The reason given was that "the procedure is fraught with danger because it links the opinion of ALA with that of a commercial publisher."5 Of course ALA and the Committee have every right to refuse such a request, but the reason for the action is difficult to grasp. Not only does RSBRC welcome advertising from the very publishers whose products it reviews, but the Committee routinely grants these publishers permission to excerpt or even reprint its reviews in toto. So much for linking ALA's opinion with that of commercial publishers. The bottom line is that encyclopedia publishers can freely quote RSBRC reviews whereas an independent review source like Encyclopedia Buying Guide cannot.

My next experience with the censorious habits of RSBRC was more unsettling. I gave several telephone interviews during the course of preparing the Buying Guide to journalists writing consumer articles on purchasing a general encyclopedia. A couple of useful articles resulted, particularly a syndicated piece by Robert Dallos of the Los Angeles Times. One interview, however, was with the tabloid National Enquirer, which ran a brief article headlined "Americans Spend $500 Million A Year On Encyclopedias" (February 24, 1976, p. 60). Shortly after the Enquirer piece appeared, I received a call from an encyclopedia executive who began the conversation by saying that "All hell's broke loose" in his office because of the Enquirer item and that his phone was "ringing off the hook," or words to that effect. He went on to complain that I had mentioned specific sets in the interview, which he thought was not proper. He also objected to my opinion that encyclopedia yearbooks are "overpriced luxuries." I felt qualified to comment on the comparative quality of individual encyclopedias and the value of

encyclopedia yearbooks and said so.   I also felt a 150-word
article in a sheet like the National Enquirer was hardly
worth stewing about, and said that too.

I thought no more about the matter until a week or
so later when I received a letter from the Editor and Secretary of RSBRC, the Committee's top paid employee.   The
letter began, "... all hell broke loose about two weeks ago.
My telephones have not stopped ringing since."6   The letter
went on to accuse me of "making pronouncements on encyclopedias and encyclopedia yearbooks, which ones to buy and
which ones to avoid purchasing."   Obviously I had poached
on the private preserve of RSBRC and ought to shut up forth-
with.   But the really disturbing aspect of this incident is the
apparent collaboration between an encyclopedia executive and
the Editor and Secretary of RSBRC. 7   In view of the Committee's public posture of impartiality, this sort of activity
can only be termed scandalous.

My most recent experience with RSBRC censorship
comes as no surprise:   Encyclopedia Buying Guide 1975-1976
will not be brought to the notice of librarians and others who
use RSBRC reviews and notes for selection purposes. 8   This
despite the fact the Committee is a principal authority on
general encyclopedias and, according to its masthead, attempts to cover "reference books likely to be of general
interest."   Encyclopedia Buying Guide is of such general
interest that Gene Shalit featured the book in an omnibus
review of new reference works on The Today Show last September.   It should be noted that previous editions of Encyclopedia Buying Guide (when it was called General Encyclopedias in Print) were reviewed by The Booklist, not RSBRC.
Upon inquiry, however, I was told by Booklist's adult books
editor that, no, Booklist would not review Encyclopedia Buying Guide because her staff lacked the requisite knowledge to
review a book on encyclopedias and that the book has been
passed on to RSBRC for review.   But as already noted, the
Committee also refused to review the book.   One of the several rather unconvincing reasons the Committee (or its Editor
and Secretary) advanced for not reviewing Encyclopedia Buying Guide was that Booklist has covered previous editions.
This is called Catch-22 ALA style.   Ultimately I raised a
little hell with Booklist's editor and he was generous enough
to print a small notice under professional reading in the
"Children's Books" section!9

More than ten years ago, Jesse Shera took the Com-

mittee (then called the Subscription Books Committee) to task
for its censorious and even paranoid behavior. "All procedures are cloaked in anonymity and shrouded in secrecy,"
wrote Shera. "There is a disturbing irony in the fact that
a profession that so prides itself on intellectual freedom
should sanction near star-chamber methods."[10] Back in the
late 1960s the Committee did clean up its act a bit, publishing its criteria for membership and a procedures manual
which is available to interested parties at a nominal cost.
It is evident, however, that the fundamental mind-set has
not changed.

There is something rotten at 50 East Huron Street.
If you don't believe me, move right along to Sandy Berman's
bill of particulars. Perhaps the current president of ALA
will initiate an investigation into the recent activities of
RSBRC. What's under the reference rock might startle
some people.

--Ken Kister


References

1.  Annually U.S. publishers and distributors sell more than
    half a billion dollars worth of encyclopedias and re-
    lated products, counting sales abroad. In recent
    years domestic sales have dropped while the overseas
    market continues to expand. Compared with the $25
    billion Americans spend each year on liquor or $100
    billion on clothes, encyclopedia sales are chicken feed.
    From another perspective, encyclopedia revenues ac-
    count for roughly 15% of the total annual dollar vol-
    ume of the American book industry.

2.  A case in point is the RSBRC negative review of The
    American Peoples Encyclopedia (see Booklist, July 15,
    1974, pp. 1206-1208). In a memorandum to the Com-
    mittee protesting the review, the publisher noted:
    "The 'not recommended' review ... has brought the
    company to the virtually final conclusion that it must
    drop APE from its line. Beyond that, the 'not rec-
    ommended' makes it impossible for the company to
    dispose of this encyclopedia on any reasonable basis."

3.  In 1973, prior to my becoming editor of Encyclopedia
    Buying Guide (then General Encyclopedias in Print),
    the R. R. Bowker Company convened an ad hoc panel
    of knowledgeable people to advise on restructuring the
    publication. The panel, which included the Editor and

Secretary of RSBRC, reached consensus on several
points, including the recommendation that only RSBRC
reviews be excerpted in future editions. Yet when I
petitioned the Committee for permission to quote, the
Editor and Secretary spoke against the idea.

4.    I should note that eventually I was permitted to quote
      two sentences from the article "Purchasing a General
      Encyclopedia," published first in Booklist (March 15,
      1969) and later reprinted and widely distributed in
      pamphlet form. To deny such permission would have
      been difficult since I was the principal author of the
      article.

5.    RSBRC Minutes of Meetings, January 20 and 21, 1975,
      p. 5.

6.    Letter from the Editor and Secretary of RSBRC, dated
      March 17, 1976.

7.    Even the citation to the Enquirer article was similarly
      misdated by both parties.

8.    I was so informed in a letter from the Editor and Sec-
      retary of RSBRC, dated March 1, 1977.

9.    The Booklist, May 1, 1977, p. 1358.

10.   Jesse Shera, "Without Reserve: Caveat Venditor,"
      Wilson Library Bulletin, XL (June, 1966), 955.


ALA Publishing as Censor: A Bill of Particulars

Item:  In 1970, ALA Publishing Services invited and en-
       couraged me to write a book-length critique of LC
       subject headings. I did. The manuscript was titled
       Prejudices and Antipathies. And ALA refused to pub-
       lish it. The reason: They branded it "vituperative"
       and "intemperate." But in fact they thought it too
       critical of such a "venerable and respected institu-
       tion." (By contrast, Scarecrow Press afterwards
       published the tome with much speed and no static.)

Item:  About 3 years ago, Library Resources & Technical
       Services--organ of ALA's Resources and Technical
       Services Division--ran a lengthy, slashing review of
       Prejudices and Antipathies. I promptly submitted a
       detailed rebuttal. That rebuttal has never been
       printed, nor even formally acknowledged.

Item:  The Hennepin County Library Cataloging Bulletin has
       been steadily produced every 2 months for nearly 6
       years. Last year it won the H. W. Wilson Library
       Periodical Award.

● To date, this award-winning magazine has never
  been formally reviewed in any ALA publication (like
  LRTS, RQ, JOLA, SMQ, or Choice).  And that's
  not because nobody got review copies.

● Box score for mentions or citations in ALA publications:  2 (of an essentially trivial sort) in American
  Libraries; 1 in LRTS (and that only because of a
  direct complaint to the person who writes their
  yearly cataloging round-up).

● E. J. Josey devoted almost a full paragraph to the
  Bulletin in his 1976 ALA Yearbook article on "Social
  Responsibility."  Miraculously, no Bulletin entry
  appeared in the index.

(Parenthetically, neither Catalogue & Index nor International Cataloguing have condescended to either cite
or review the Bulletin, while the H. W. Wilson Co.
rejected it for Library Literature coverage with the
marvelous explanation that they could find nothing in
it to index!)

Item:  The Coordinator of ALA's Jewish Caucus was asked
       to write an essay for the 1976 ALA Yearbook.  She
       did, calling it "Libraries & the 'Jewish Question'."
       An ALA editor didn't like that title, wanting one that
       filed under "J" instead.  The Coordinator named me
       to negotiate.  I did.  And we compromised on "The
       'Jewish Question' and Libraries."  What finally printed
       out was "Jewish Caucus, ALA."  Which doesn't make
       quite the same impact.  The ALA editor also didn't
       like the opening paragraph, which connected the origin
       of the Caucus to growing antisemitism, and further
       linked that with Arabs and oil.  He preferred that we
       not include anything as controversial as "Arabs and
       oil."  During a telephone conversation he actually
       said something tantamount to this:  that the people
       who wrote the pieces on Asian Americans and Native
       Americans hadn't mentioned "Arabs and oil," why
       should we?  Well, the paragraph stayed in, probably
       because we insisted that the whole article be killed
       otherwise.  However, "Antisemitism"--a virtual re-
       frain throughout the essay--somehow missed getting
       indexed.  And a short sentence about a Caucus re-
       quest to LC for creating and using more Jewish-re-
       lated heads--like SHTETL and KIBBUTZ--got scrapped
       completely.  Without forewarning.

Item:   A SRRT resolution some 2 years ago criticized ALA
        publishing patterns and made a few constructive sug-
        gestions.  This is how it went:

> WHEREAS the first stated priority of ALA is social
> responsibility and
> WHEREAS the ALA Publishing Department has in-
> creasingly devoted itself and its resources to is-
> suing costly, esoteric works like the Double Ele-
> phant Portfolio, German Exile Press in America,
> and a history of strictly California libraries that
> are not relevant to contemporary professional
> needs and could more appropriately be published
> by university presses, state library associations,
> and--in the specific case of Voices from Brooklyn--
> the pertinent public library,
> ALA SRRT THEREFORE calls upon the ALA Execu-
> tive Board to direct the Publishing Board and its
> Editorial Committee to undertake the publication
> of valuable, necessary materials more responsive
> to the priority indicated by membership, e.g.,
> the HERSTORY Index, UPS Index, a Black genea-
> logical handbook, women's periodical index, and
> labor periodicals index.

As SRRT Newsletter editor at the time, I received a
nice letter from an ALA editor expressing interest
particularly in the UPS and HERSTORY projects.  Indeed, he requested contact-information, which I gladly
and quickly supplied.  Later I received another letter,
this one expressing regret that ALA--having duly in-
vestigated both projects--wouldn't be able to undertake
either of them.  Which would seem fair enough, except that ALA Publishing conducted that "investigation"
without every directly contacting the UPS and HERSTORY
people!

Item:   In 1974, an American Libraries' stringer sent an in-
        quiry to a Senator concerning the National Commission
        on Libraries and Information Science, specifically
        asking if they were allowed to conduct secret meetings.
        ALA's Washington lobbyist learned of that query and
        complained to the Executive Director.  The Executive
        Director subsequently ordered that the reporter be
        fired.  The American Libraries' editor complied with
        this order.  And then resigned in protest.  So did 3
        other staff members.  This was a clearcut act of

interference with a legitimate journalistic activity.
In its finality, it was an act of prior censorship.
Naturally, apart from SRRT, no ALA body or publication forthrightly denounced what had happened.   (Ah,
but what if a similar event had taken place in poor,
benighted Kanawha County?)

Conclusions/opinions:

1. ALA and other standard library media seldom
   print anything significant about or by flesh-and-
   blood library users, non-professional staff, and
   library school students.   Almost never do they
   run anything on the influence of publishing con-
   glomerates on reading patterns and library buying.   Rarely do they carry anything sharply critical of "venerable and respected institutions."
   And they also miss fairly obvious follow-ups:   like
   immediately interviewing ALA staff and Division
   Presidents on the likely effects of last July's
   [1976] racism/sexism resolution.

2. Vitality, candor, and real controversy thrive not
   in ALA and major commercial magazines, but
   rather in the "alternative" library press, those
   dozen or more independent publishers and magazines that the Establishment and profit-making
   "biggies" have either ignored or trivialized, in
   effect limiting their circulation, audience, and
   impact.

3. If that assessment makes sense:   a) get your libraries to subscribe to as many alternative mags
   as possible; b) buy all the personal subs you can
   afford; c) demand that Library Literature index
   more non-mainstream titles; and d) to avoid editorial tampering (if not gutless rejection), publish
   your own stuff in the "alternatives."

                                        --Sanford Berman

ALTERNATIVE LIBRARY LIT. *

Sanford Berman, Compiler

ALA/SRRT Newsletter.  SRRT Clearinghouse, 60 Remsen St.
(Apt. 10E), Brooklyn, NY 11201.  1969.  bimonthly.
$5 p. a./ALA members; $3/non-ALA; $20 institutions.
Back-issues @ $1.  ISSN 0065-9096.  Indexed in: CALL.

"Vital information concerning ALA Social Responsibilities
Round Table activities, publications, & other materials
related to social change in libraries. ...  Fold-out format
gives this carrier of good tidings a really different look."

ALA/SRRT Task Force on Gay Liberation.  Barbara Gittings,
Coordinator, P. O. Box 2383, Philadelphia, PA 19103.
Checks payable to "Barbara Gittings--TFGL."

Gay Bibliography.  5th edition (1975), with 1976 Supple-
    ment.  10 pages.  25¢/single copy, $1/5 copies.  In-
    quire re bulk rates.

"A selective list of materials that support positive
views of gay experience or that help in understanding
gay-related issues.  252 non-fiction entries: books,
pamphlets, articles, periodicals, audio-visuals (annotated), bibliographies and directories."

Also available: "Gay materials core collection list" (Re-

*Reprinted by permission of the author and publisher from
the January 1, 1978 issue of Library Journal.  Published by
R. R. Bowker Co. (a Xerox company); copyright © 1978 by
Xerox Corporation.  Updated and revised by the author for
this reprinting, January 31, 1979.

vised 1977; SASE), "Gay books in format for the blind
and physically handicapped" (SASE); "Can young gays
find happiness in YA books?" (March '76 WLB reprint;
50¢).


Alternatives in Print: Catalog of Social Change Publications,
1977/78. Compiled by the ALA/SRRT Task Force on
Alternatives in Print. 5th edition. New Glide Publications, 330 Ellis St., San Francisco, CA 94102. 1977.
198 pages. $12.95 cloth, $8.95 paper + 50¢ postage/
handling. ISBN: 0-912078-49-9 (paper), 0-912078-50-2
(cloth).

"The engagé PTLA ... a directory of 1,500 human-
hearted organizations ... involved in changing, freeing,
enabling ... and publishing books, pams, tapes, films
about it. Their mission is communication, not commerce.
For some reason, they've been locked out of the (ahem)
National Bibliography, and by extension, our library
shelves.... A wealth of resources issued in the United
States, Canada, & Europe--ideal for librarians, educators,
booksellers, & concerned citizens.... Get a copy for
acquisitions, for reference, for yourself--let the sun
shine in!" This edition, in new $8\frac{1}{2}$ x 11" format (like
Books in Print), lists over 25,000 multi-media items and
includes a geographical directory of publishers/producers.
(6th edition due Fall 1979 from Neal-Schuman Publishers,
64 University Place, New York, NY 10003.)


Booklegger Press. 555 - 29th St., San Francisco, CA 94131.

Booklegger Magazine. 1973. quarterly. Issues 1-2,
5-16 @ $2. Publication suspended after v. 3, no. 16
(Autumn 1976); resumed mid-1978 with "Bookazine"
series, to be issued "sporadically." Single copies of
v. 4, no. 17 (Summer 1978), The Passionate Perils of
Publishing, jointly authored by Celeste West and Valerie Wheat, @ $5. "Magazine will reincarnate as The
Feminist Review of Books if the weather's good."
Next "bookazine" topic: Anarcha-Feminism. Indexed
in: CALL, Library Literature.

"A positively unique piece of library lit., this anar-
chist-feminist magazine bursts its pages with hard-
packed bibliographies, stimulating articles, and lots of

fun.... Can be counted on for reviews of some of the
great mass of small press unreviewed materials, new
ideas for YA and kids' stuff, and a peep at the media.
Nothing finer. "

Women's Films in Print:  An Annotated Guide to 800
16mm Films by Women.   Compiled by Bonnie Dawson.
1975.  165 pages.  paperbound.  $4 (prepaid), $4. 50
(billed).  ISBN 0-912932-02-5.

"An astounding job of researching & documenting the
history of women filmmakers and a guarantee that these
films will not be lost. "

Positive Images:  A Guide to Non-Sexist Films for Young
People.   By Linda Artel & Susan Wengraf.   1976.    167
pages.  paperbound.   $5 (prepaid), $5. 50 (billed).
ISBN 0-912932-03-5.

"Candid, thoughtful evaluation by feminists.... Essential as a programming tool & buying guide. " Also
includes entries for video-tapes, filmstrips, slide
shows, & photographs.

Synergy.   Issues 1-42 (1967-1973).   Write for back-set
quotes.

"The Mother of The Library Free Press, cream of the
dream 60s, " edited by Celeste West and originally published by the San Francisco P. L. 's Bay Area Reference
Center.

Collectors' Network News.   James Danky, Acquisitions Section, State Historical Society of Wisconsin Library, 816
State St. , Madison, WI 53706.  1977. bimonthly.   $6
p. a. , $1/sample copy.  Indexed in:  CALL.

"Succeeding Russ Benedict's Top Secret, CNN--through
reviews, bibliographies, letters, notes, interviews, articles, and duplicates-lists--supplies practical ideas & data
for collecting, processing, and publicizing alternative/
'extremist'/offbeat periodicals & ephemera.   A highly useful acquisitions, reference, and cataloging tool. "

Council on Interracial Books for Children.   Room 300,
1841 Broadway, New York, NY 10023.

Interracial Books for Children Bulletin. 1966. 8 nos.
yearly. $10 p. a. /individuals, $15/institutions, $5/
students. Two-year rates: $18/individuals, $25/insti-
tutions. Indexed in: CALL, Education Index.

"Features incisive analyses of defamatory stereotyping
& blatant omission in textbooks & juvenile trade titles,
energetically promotes authentic minority-group publishing, & abounds with otherwise hard-to-find data on
pertinent resource groups and materials...."

Human--and Anti-Human--Values in Children's Books: A
Content Rating Instrument for Educators and Concerned
Parents. 1976. 280 pages. $14.95 cloth, $7.95
paperbound.

"238 books published in 1975 are examined for sexism,
racism, materialism, elitism, individualism, conform-
ism, escapism, and ageism--as well as for cultural
authenticity and effect on the self-image of female
and/or minority children.... Introductory essay defines the criteria...."

Racism in the English Language. By Robert B. Moore.
1976. 23 pages. paperbound. $2.

Two History Texts: A Study in Contrasts. By Robert B.
Moore. 1976. 21 pages. paperbound. $1.50.

Sexism and Racism in Popular Basal Readers, 1964-1976.
Based upon a 1973 report by the Baltimore Feminist
Project, with a 1975 postscript by Mary Jane Lupton
and an Afterword by the Racism and Sexism Resource
Center for Educators. 1976. 43 pages. paperbound.
$2.50.

Racism in Career Education Materials: How to Detect It
and How to Counteract Its Effects in the Classroom.
1975. 32 pages. paperbound. $2.50.

Fact sheets, brochures, bookmarks, lesson plans, posters:
Write for complete free catalog.

Directory of Ethnic Publishers and Resource Organizations,
1976. Compiled by Beth J. Shapiro. Distributed by
Office for Library Service to the Disadvantaged, American

Library Association, 50 East Huron St. , Chicago, IL
60611.  1977.  $1. 50.  89 pages.  spiral binding.

"An outgrowth of the Directory of Minority/Third World
Publishers and Dealers compiled for several years by
Joan Neumann for the ALA/SRRT Ethnic Materials Information Exchange Task Force," this edition covers 295--
mainly Third World--publishers and groups.  Entries include address, telephone number, a statement of "major
purpose/emphasis," and publication details.  Three indexes
identify archival and research collections, distributors, and
subject specialties.  A superb product.


Emergency Librarian.  Phyllis Yaffe, 39 Edith Drive,
Toronto, Ontario, Canada M4R 1Y9.  1973.  bimonthly.
Individuals:  $9 p. a. /American, $7/Canadian; students:
$3; institutions: $10; international: $12.  Microfiche
back-issues available from McLaren Micropublishing, Box
972, Station F, Toronto, Ontario, Canada M4Y 2N9.
ISSN 0315-8888.  Indexed in:  CALL, Library Literature,
New Periodicals Index.

"A pleasure to read, a source of much practical info, a
spirited, aggressive vehicle for alternative librarianship...
Articles ... are written with style and conviction and ...
consistently illustrated with taste....  A Canadian publication ... distinctly aware of its own national origins, EL
expresses concerns that will be familiar to many librarians in the United States.  Recommended for all library
science collections and for librarians everywhere. "


Hennepin County Library.  7009 York Avenue South, Edina,
MN 55435.  Orders and checks (payable to "Hennepin
County Library"):  Secretary, Technical Services Division.

Authority File.  1977.  quarterly.  $30 p. a. , $7. 50/
single cumulations.

A 42x microfiche service that "contains in one alphabet
over 140, 000 terms representing personal and corporate
authors, subject headings, and the names of traced individuals, groups, and producers.  Also includes cross-
references, as well as HCL-generated 'public notes,'
which supply the user with background or explanatory
data, and 'catalogers' notes,' which furnish distinguishing information for similar name or subject forms. "

Cataloging Bulletin. 1973. bimonthly. $12 p. a. /institu-
tions, $6/individuals. Back-issues @ $1. 50. Indexes:
nos. 1-10 ($3), 11-20 ($5), 21-30 ($5). ISSN 0093-528X.
Indexed in: CALL.

"Variously reports new or altered HCL cross-references,
format-rules, DDC-numbers, & subject headings, citing
authorities, precedents, & applications; relates cataloging to total library service & the 'real world'; involves
both readers & HCL staff in the cataloging process; and
provides a genuinely open forum for cataloging-related
ideas, innovations, criticism, & even muckraking. ...
A highly readable magazine ... recommended for all
librarians who catalog or use the catalog. " Winner,
1976 H. W. Wilson Library Periodical Award.

Jewish Librarians Caucus Newsletter. Sylvia Eisen, JLC
Treasurer, 690 Anderson Avenue, Franklin Square, New
York, NY 11010. 1976. quarterly. $5 p. a.

A lively amalgam of letters, reviews, editorials, reprints,
resource-notes, and news concerning Jewish issues, materials, and library services.

Librarians for Social Change. John L. Noyce, Box 450,
Brighton, Sussex, United Kingdom BN1 8GR. 1972.
3 nos. yearly. $10 p. a. /U. S. libraries, $4/individuals.
Single copies @ $3. Indexed in: CALL.

"The purpose is to cover material and viewpoints usually
not found in the existing English library press. " Letters,
book reviews, and articles have variously dealt with radical collections, censorship, workers' control in libraries,
racism, sexism in children's literature, info-politics, and
the "irrelevancy of the Library Association. " While
there's "minimal attention to format ..., the content is
gutsy and refreshing. " Editor/publisher Noyce also produces the quarterly British Alternative Press Index ($7
p. a. /individuals, $14/libraries; back-issues available from
v. 1, no. 1, Jan. -June 1976), guides to alternative bookshops and publishers, and special bibliographies (e. g. , on
Appropriate Technology), a Directory of Alternative Periodicals, the latest (1978) edition distributed by Harvester
Press, 2 Stanford Terrace, Hassocks, Sussex.

Library Insights, Promotion & Programs. Dawn Heller/

Ann Montgomery, POB 431, LaGrange, IL 60525.   1976.
monthly.   $15 p. a.

An 8-pager, "chock-full of inexpensive ideas for programs, displays, bulletin boards, and other kinds of PR
guaranteed to serve your public more effectively and ...
to generate enthusiasm and support for your library. "

REFORMA Newsletter.   Carmen Martinez, Treasurer, c/o
East L. A. Library, 4801 East Third St. , Los Angeles,
CA 90022.   $10 p. a. /members, $3/library school stu-
dents, $10/institutions, $12/commercial corporations.

Organ of REFORMA, the National Organization of Spanish
Speaking Librarians, formed by a group of bilingual librarians in July 1971 "to emphasize the best possible library service to the nation's 17 million people of Hispanic
heritage. "  Includes announcements, reports, bibliographic
data, and job listings.

Sex Is a Touchy Subject:  A Select Bibliography of Books,
Pamphlets, and Films on Sex and Sexuality for Young
Adults.   Compiled by Bay Area Young Adult Librarians.
Orders to:  Richard Russo (BAYA), 2343 San Juan Avenue,
Walnut Creek, CA 94596.   1976.   $2 (prepaid), $2. 50
(billed).   23 pages.   paperbound.

CONTENTS:  Plumbing (emphasis on physiological aspects
of sex). - Sexuality (sexual aspects of personality and
lifestyle). - Love and romance (emotional aspects of human
relationships). - 16mm films about sex/sexuality. - Useful
pamphlets.   "A critical guide to YA sex-lit. and model
selection tool. "

Sipapu; A Newsletter for Librarians, Editors, Collectors,
and Others Interested in Alternative Publications, Including
Third World, Dissent, Feminist, Self-Reliant and Underground Publications.   Noel Peattie, Route 1, Box 216,
Winters, CA 95694.   1970.   semiannual.   $4 p. a. (Cali-
fornia subscribers add 6% tax); free to exchange papers,
library school students, and prisoners.   ISSN 0037-5837.
Indexed in:  CALL.

"Publishes news of conferences, selected book and periodical reviews, and above all interviews with people in the small/alternative press scene (e. g. , Dustbooks' Len Fulton, feminist underground cartoonist Lee Marrs, & librarian/COSMEPer Jackie Eubanks).... The writing throughout is clear, informative, and entertaining. Recommended for all libraries. "

Title Varies. P. O. Box 704, Chapel Hill, NC 27514. 1973. bimonthly. $5 p. a. Calendar year basis only. Back-numbers @ $3/volume (v. 1-2), $6 (v. 3) or $1/issue. ISSN 0092-6108. Indexed in: CALL.

"This 'serial to end all serial title changes' somehow manages to combine both wit & seriousness in a perfect blend. Its aim ... is altogether admirable. And the style is, quite simply, delightful.... Because the editors feel that TV must move beyond just chronicling and protesting title changes, there have lately been some substantial articles on other aspects of serial librarianship as well as reviews of relevant books and periodicals. Recommended for any library that subscribes to anything. "

U*N*A*B*A*S*H*E*D Librarian. G. P. O. Box 2631, New York, NY 10001.

Unabashed Librarian: The "How I Run My Library Good" Letter. 1971. quarterly. $15/p. a. Back-issues @ $4. Add 10% foreign postage. ISSN 0049-514X. Indexed in: CALL, Library Literature.

"Ingenious roundup of ideas for improving service and saving time, money, & tempers.... A gold mine, it also includes very useful bibliographies as well as art & editor Marvin Scilken's sense of humor. "

GO, PEP, and POP!: 250 Tested Ideas for Lively Libraries. By Virginia Baeckler and Linda Larson. 1976. 72 pages. paperbound. $3. 50 (prepaid), $4. 50 (billed), $1 extra per copy for out-of-U. S. postage/handling.

"All libraries will benefit from these imaginative low-cost/no-cost ideas. Written by two who practice what they preach, it's a joyous combination of the possible & the improbable.... Even the already lively library

will find some new tricks.... Do not pass go without
collecting this PR gem for your shelf."


Women in Libraries: Newsletter of the ALA/SRRT Task
Force on Women. Kay Cassell, 44 Nathaniel Boulevard,
Delmar, NY 12054. 1970. 5 nos. yearly (Sept. -June).
$4 p. a. /individuals, $6/institutions. Back issues @ $6
each volume (v. 1-7). Index: v. 1-7 ($3. 50). Indexed
in: CALL.

"News of past, present, and future TFW programs, plus
lots of notes on women's literature hot off the presses....
A quick & easy way to keep up to date on new publications
and TFW progress."


Women Library Workers. P. O. Box 9052, Berkeley, CA
94709.

Newsletter. 1975. bimonthly. $3-10 p. a. /WLW mem-
bers, $5/institutions & non-members. Indexed in:
CALL.

"Lets WLW members stay in touch with what other
chapters are up to as well as providing a forum for
discussion of WLW's philosophy and organizing program.... A simpatico way to get the news."

SHARE: A Directory of Feminist Library Workers. 3d
edition. 1978. 58 pages. paperbound. $3 (prepaid),
$3. 50 (billed).

Geographic arrangement, with name, subject, & organization indexes.


Young Adult Alternative Newsletter. Carol Starr, 37167
Mission Blvd., Fremont, CA 94536. 1973. 5 nos.
yearly. $4 p. a. (prepaid), $4. 50 (billed). Indexed in:
CALL.

"YAAN has definitely got that 'special something,' a distinct personality plus a helluva lot of nitty-gritty info &
ideas. A bevy of correspondents tell what's going down,
YA-wise, in their own coast-to-coast bailiwicks. And
there's a marvelous plentitude of acquisitions-data, in-

ventive suggestions, & CSD/YASD news.... Exuberant,
hip, and practical. "


Sources/readings

Danky, James P. and Michael Fox: "Alternative library
  periodicals, " Wilson Library Bulletin, v. 51, no. 9 (May
  1977), p. 763-68.

Eubanks, Jackie: "A. I. P. adventures, " Booklegger Magazine,
  v. 1, no. 1 (Nov. /Dec. 1973), p. 4-7.

Leita, Carole: "Liberated fronts, " Booklegger Magazine,
  v. 3, no. 13 (Jan. 1976), p. 24-5.

"Libraries as a feminist resource, " New Woman's Survival
  Sourcebook (Knopf, 1975), p. 158-59.

Peattie, Noel: "Sipapu: tunnel between two worlds, " in
  Revolting Librarians (Booklegger Press, 1972), p. 133-36.

West, Celeste: "The library free press, " Booklegger Magazine, v. 1, no. 2 (Jan. /Feb. 1974), p. 24.

Wheat, Valerie: "The library free press, " Booklegger Magazine, v. 4, no. 17 (Summer 1978), p. 69-72.

Whitney, Gail: "Update on little library and library-related
  serials, " American Libraries, Nov. 1975, p. 613-14.

Yaffe, Phyllis: "A free press in our lifetime, " Emergency
  Librarian, v. 4, no. 1 (Sept. /Oct. 1976), p. 27-8.

Yaffe, Phyllis: "Small mags, " Emergency Librarian, v. 4,
  no. 2 (Nov. /Dec. 1976), p. 24-5.

# NOTES ON CONTRIBUTORS

LIONEL ABEL is a playwright, critic, and professor of English at the State University of New York at Buffalo.

SANFORD BERMAN is head cataloger at the Hennepin County Library, in Edina, Minnesota and editor of the HCL Cataloging Bulletin.

DEIRDRE BOYLE is an assistant editor of Wilson Library Bulletin and author of Expanding Media and Children's Media Market Place.

FAY M. BLAKE is a lecturer in the School of Library and Information Studies, University of California at Berkeley.

DOROTHY BRODERICK has taught at nine library schools in the United States and Canada. She has been active in the American Library Association for over twenty years. She recently started VOYA: Voice of Youth Advocates, a new magazine for young adult librarians.

CAROLINE M. CAUGHLIN is at Rose Memorial Library, Drew University, Madison, New Jersey.

RODERICK CAVE is course tutor in the MA program (archives, library and information science and education) at Loughborough University's Library and Information Studies Department. He was formerly Unesco Lecturer at the Department of Library Studies, University of the West Indies.

NORMAN CHARNEY, MD, JD, is in general medical practice in Mirada, California, and is also a practicing lawyer, with offices in Fullerton.

HENRY BATHOLOMEW COX is an attorney in Maryland. He holds a doctorate in American history.

GEORGE P. ELLIOT is a poet, novelist, essayist and short
     story writer.  He is currently professor of English
     at Syracuse University.

CYNTHIA FUCHS EPSTEIN is associate professor of sociol-
     ogy at Queens college, City University of New York,
     and a writer on the role of women and the law.

SARA FINE is assistant professor in the Graduate School of
     Library and Information Science, University of Pitts-
     burgh, where she teaches communications, counseling,
     and group dynamics.  She is also a licensed psychol-
     ogist in the Commonwealth of Pennsylvania.

MAURICE J. FREEDMAN is on the faculty of the Columbia
     University School of Library Service.

THOMAS J. GALVIN is Dean of the University of Pittsburgh's
     Graduate School of Library and Information Science.

DAVID GERARD teaches at the College of Librarianship, in
     Wales.

DANIEL GORE is director of Macalester College Library in
     Saint Paul Minnesota.

LAUREL A. GROTZINGER is professor in the School of
     Librarianship at Western Michigan University.

MURRAY HAUSKNECHT is professor of sociology at Lehman
     College, and an expert on Urban Sociology.

NIGEL HAWKES lives in England and is a contributor to
     Science.

NAT HENTOFF is a writer on jazz, civil liberties, and
     human rights, as well as fiction for children.  He is
     on the staff of the New Yorker, and is a columnist
     for the Village Voice.  His latest book for children
     is This School is Driving Me Crazy.

IRVING HOWE is an author, historian and critic, editor of
     Dissent, and author of numerous works on politics
     and writing.

FRED INGLIS is a reader in the Advanced Studies Division
     at Bristol University's School of Education.  He was

previously a school teacher.  He is the author of The Englishness of English Teaching and Ideology of the Imagination.

DAVID ISAACSON is general reference librarian and assistant professor at Western Michigan University.  He is a former college English teacher.

ESTELLE JUSSIM is an associate professor at the Simmons College School of Library Science.

DAVID KASER is a professor at Indiana University's Graduate Library School, former director of libraries at Cornell University, and for several years editor of College and Research Libraries.

JACK KING is the university librarian at Hamline University in Saint Paul, Minnesota, and teaches a course there in the history of military intelligence.

KENNETH KISTER is author of the Encyclopedia Buying Guide, and the Dictionary Buying Guide.  He was a member of the Reference and Subscription Books Review Committee, 1966-1970.

KARL LO is head of Asiatic Collections at the East Asian Library, University of Washington, Seattle.

BARBARA EVANS MARKUSON is executive director, Indiana Cooperative Library Services Authority.

ERIC MOON, immediate past president of the American Library Association, has recently retired as President of Scarecrow Press.  He is currently Editorial and Professional Relations Consultant for Grolier, Inc.

ANNE NELSON, a 1976 graduate of Yale, has been published in Harpers and the Nation.  Her first book, on Puerto Rico, will be published by Random House in 1980.

JESSE SHERA is Dean Emeritus, School of Library Science, Case Western Reserve University.

DAVID SPITZ is professor of political science at Hunter College, and is interested in political philosophy.

NORMAN STEVENS, when not engaged in directing the Molesworth Institute, is university librarian at the University of Connecticut, at Storrs.

H. D. L. VERVLIET is extraordinary professor of book and library history at the University of Amsterdam.

GEORGE WOODCOCK is former professor of English at the University of British Columbia, and founding editor of Canadian Literature.